Washington
and
Cornwallis

Washington and Cornwallis

The Battle for America, 1775–1783

Benton Rain Patterson

TAYLOR TRADE PUBLISHING
Lanham • New York • Dallas • Boulder • Toronto • Oxford

This Taylor Trade Publishing hardcover edition of *Washington and Cornwallis* is an original publication. It is published by arrangement with the author.

"Boston, 1775–1776" (chapter 2, page 13), "Charleston and Its Harbor" (chapter 3, page 31), and "The Battle of Cowpens, January 17, 1781" (chapter 22, page 265) are reprinted from George F. Scheer and Hugh F. Rankin, *Rebels and Redcoats* (New York: Da Capo Press, 1987).

"Trenton, 26 December 1776" (chapter 8, page 84), "Princeton, 3 January 1777" (chapter 9, page 92), and "Brandywine, 11 September 1777" (chapter 11, page 124) are reprinted from *Battles of the Revolutionary War 1775–1781*, by W. J. Wood. © 1990 by William J. Wood. Reprinted by permission of Algonquin Books of Chapel Hill.

"Charleston and Environs" (chapter 19, page 217) is reprinted from *Redcoats and Rebels: The American Revolution through British Eyes* by Christopher Hibbert. Copyright © 1990 by Christopher Hibbert. Used by permission of W. W. Norton & Company, Inc.

"Camden and Vicinity" (chapter 20, page 234) is reprinted from Mark M. Boatner III, *Encyclopedia of the American Revolution* (Mechanicsburg, Pa.: Stackpole Books, 1966). Reprinted by permission of Stackpole Books.

Published by Taylor Trade Publishing
An imprint of The Rowman & Littlefield Publishing Group, Inc.
4501 Forbes Boulevard, Suite 200
Lanham, Maryland 20706

Distributed by National Book Network

Library of Congress Cataloging-in-Publication Data
Patterson, Benton Rain, 1929–
   Washington and Cornwallis : the battle for America, 1775–1783 / Benton Rain Patterson.
      p. cm.
   Includes bibliographical references (p.) and index.
   ISBN 1-58979-021-9 (hardcover : alk. paper)
   1. Washington, George, 1732-1799—Military leadership. 2. Cornwallis, Charles; Cornwallis, Marquis, 1738-1805. 3. United States—History—Revolution, 1775-1783—Campaigns. I. Title.
E312.25.P38 2004
973.3'3'0922—dc22   2003021382

⊗™ The paper used in this publication meets the minimum requirements of American National Standard for Information Sciences—Permanence of Paper for Printed Library Materials, ANSI/NISO Z39.48–1992.
Manufactured in the United States of America.

Dedicated to the memory
of my dearest friend and wife,
Patricia Roberts Patterson

Contents

viii   CONTENTS

Acknowledgments

The author is immensely indebted to and hereby expresses his deep gratitude to those whose works helped make this book possible, and without which the task of writing it would have been immeasurably more difficult. The author wishes especially to acknowledge the help he drew from the *Encyclopedia of the American Revolution* by Mark M. Boatner III (Mechanicsburg, Pa.: Stackpole, 1966) and *The Spirit of 'Seventy-Six*, edited by Henry Steele Commager and Richard B. Morris (New York: Da Capo Press, 1995). Other works that helped:

Thomas E. Baker, *Another Such Victory* (Fort Washington, Pa.: Eastern National, 1999).

George Athan Billias, editor, *George Washington's Generals and Opponents* (New York: Da Capo Press, 1994).

John Buchanan, *The Road to Guilford Courthouse* (New York: John Wiley & Sons, 1997).

Harrison Clark, *All Cloudless Glory* (Washington, D.C.: Regnery, 1995).

Burke Davis, *The Campaign That Won America* (Fort Washington, Pa.: Eastern Acorn, 1982).

Wilma Dykeman, *With Fire and Sword* (Washington, D.C.: National Park Service, 1991).

Howard Fast, *The Crossing* (New York: ibooks, 1971).

Richard Ferrie, *The World Turned Upside Down* (New York: Holiday House, 1999).

Thomas J. Fleming, *Cowpens* (Washington, D.C.: National Park Service, 1988).

Douglas Southall Freeman, *Washington* (New York: Touchstone, 1968).

Christopher Hibbert, *Redcoats and Rebels* (New York: Avon, 1991).

H. L. Landers, *The Virginia Campaign and the Blockade and Siege of Yorktown 1781* (Washington, D.C.: U.S. Government Printing Office, 1931).

Robert Leckie, *George Washington's War* (New York: HarperCollins, 1992).

Charles Patrick Neimeyer, *America Goes to War* (New York: New York University Press, 1996).

George F. Scheer and Hugh F. Rankin, *Rebels and Redcoats* (New York: Da Capo Press, 1987).

Frederick William Baron von Steuben, *Baron von Steuben's Revolutionary War Drill Manual* (New York: Dover, 1985).

Alan Valentine, *The British Establishment, 1760–1784* (Norman: University of Oklahoma Press, 1970).

Franklin and Mary Wickwire, *Cornwallis and the War of Independence* (London: Faber & Faber, 1970).

W. J. Wood, *Battles of the Revolutionary War* (New York: Da Capo Press, 1995).

CHAPTER One

The Commander in Chief

B ig enough at six feet three and two hundred pounds to be impos-
ing, Colonel George Washington was a noticeable figure in the
distinguished gathering, the only man there in a uniform, the blue-
and-red uniform of the Virginia militia. Like the other delegates to this second Continental Congress, convened in the Pennsylvania Statehouse in
Philadelphia in May 1775, Washington was there as an official representative of his province to help decide what the affronted citizens of England's
thirteen American colonies should do next in their growing quarrel with
their mother country, which within the past four weeks had exploded into
armed conflict.

Not an orator, not easily moved to outspokenness, the forty-three-
year-old Washington sat and listened while others did the speechmaking,
creating in the minds of many of his fellow delegates an impression of
Washington as an appropriately reserved, serious-minded military man,
which to a large extent he was, or had been. He had entered military service in 1754 as lieutenant colonel of the Virginia militia and shortly thereafter had led two companies of militiamen to victory over a French and
Indian force in the Battle of Great Meadow, on Virginia's northwestern
frontier, at the beginning of the French and Indian War. Five weeks later,
however, he was forced to surrender to the French at Fort Necessity. He
later became aide-de-camp to British General Edward Braddock and managed to survive the Battle of the Wilderness in July 1755, during which
Braddock was mortally wounded and his army routed in its attempt to
drive the French from Fort Duquesne. In August 1755, Washington, then
twenty-three years old, was appointed commander of the Virginia militia.

In 1758 the Virginia militia under Washington was joined to a British army that finally prevailed at Fort Duquesne, and Washington returned home, resigned his commission, got married and settled down to life as a prosperous planter and businessman, widely acclaimed as a home-grown war hero. At present he was serving as the elected commander of the militia of Fairfax County, which was Virginia's most important militia regiment.

That he considered himself a soldier—and wanted others to think of him as one—was evidenced by his wearing of his uniform in Philadelphia. That others did indeed so regard him was evidenced by his having been appointed to head a committee to propose a policy for the defense of the Colony of New York, where a force of revolutionaries had days earlier, on May 10, captured Fort Ticonderoga at the northern end of Lake George. When that committee's work was completed on May 19, Washington had then been appointed chairman of a committee that was instructed "to consider ways and means to supply these Colonies with ammunition and military stores." That committee's report had been submitted to the Congress on June 1, and on June 3 Washington had been given still another committee assignment: to figure out how much money the Congress would have to raise in order to finance the military preparations being recommended.

By the time his committee work was done, some delegates were proposing that the Congress authorize a Continental Army and appoint a commander in chief to direct the colonies' military efforts. John Adams of Massachusetts was convinced that Washington was the man for the job. Washington, Adams declared, "by his great experience and abilities in military matters is of much service to us."

It wasn't only respect for Washington's experience and abilities that moved Adams. Political considerations accounted for a big part of his enthusiasm for Washington. Massachusetts, Adams's home province, was already at war, the battles of Lexington and Concord having been fought within the past month. Its militia, with other New England militias, was now besieging Boston, attempting to contain the 12,000-man British army that occupied the city. Massachusetts's representatives were pleading for Congress to send troops, arms and supplies to aid the cause.

Adams was urging that the Congress authorize an army drawn from all thirteen colonies, with the troops of the four New England provinces, already in the field, as its core. The political danger was that the nine colonies of the middle and lower Atlantic coast, from New York southward, would see such an army as a New England army, fighting in New

England for New England's interests, particularly if its commander was a New Englander.

Adams felt strongly that the person to command the American army should *not* be from New England. (He also thought the commander in chief should be someone other than a professional soldier and should be someone born in America.) In his diary he confessed the problem and proposed a solution:

> ... we were embarrassed with more than one difficulty ... a Southern party against a Northern, and a jealousy against a New England army under the command of a New England general. Whether this jealousy was sincere, or whether it was mere pride and a haughty ambition of furnishing a Southern general to command the Northern army, I cannot say, but the intention was very visible to me that Colonel Washington was their object, and so many of our staunchest men were in the plan that we could carry nothing without conceding to it. ...
>
> Full of anxieties concerning these confusions, and apprehending daily that we should hear very distressing news from Boston, I walked with Mr. Samuel Adams in the State House yard for a little exercise and fresh air, before the hour of Congress, and there represented to him the various dangers that surrounded us. He agreed to them all, but said, "What shall we do?"
>
> I answered him that he knew I had taken great pains to get our colleagues to agree upon some plan, that we might be unanimous; but he knew that they would pledge themselves to nothing; but I was determined to take a step which should compel them and all the other members of Congress to declare themselves for or against something. "I am determined this morning to make a direct motion that Congress should adopt the army before Boston and appoint Colonel Washington commander of it."[1]

That day, June 14, 1775, with his fellow delegates assembled around him following the opening of the day's session of Congress, Adams stood to his feet and began to speak, laying out the urgent need for an American army with a unified command. At the end of his short speech he moved that Congress adopt the army now in the field outside Boston and appoint a general to command it. He allowed that this was not the proper time to nominate a general, but, he said, he felt no hesitation in declaring that he had "but one gentleman in my mind for that important command, and that is a gentleman from Virginia who is among us and very well known to all of us, a gentleman whose skill and experience as an officer, whose independent fortune, great talents and excellent universal character would command the approbation of all America and unite the cordial exertions of all the colonies better than any other person in the Union."[2] Samuel Adams, his cousin, also from Massachusetts, seconded the motion.

At the first mention of his name, Washington, sitting near the door, rose from his chair and darted from the room, retiring to the library to allow his colleagues to discuss freely what was, for all practical purposes, Adams's nomination of him to be America's commander in chief.

John Hancock, president of the Congress, was in clear view as Adams spoke, and on Hancock's face Adams could see obvious pleasure when Adams was talking about the militia army outside Boston and about the enemy, but when Adams named Washington as his choice of commander in chief, Hancock's expression changed dramatically. The rich, self-assertive, young Hancock, Adams's fellow Bostonian, was keen on becoming commander in chief himself, even though he had no military experience. "I never remarked a more sudden and striking change of countenance," Adams later commented. "Mortification and resentment were expressed as forcibly as his face could exhibit them." When Samuel Adams seconded the motion, John Adams noticed, "that did not soften the President's physiognomy at all."[3]

Several delegates declared their opposition to Washington's appointment. It wasn't that they had anything against Washington personally, they said; it was just that they thought the New England army was doing all right as it was, having contained the British in Boston, which was all that was expected or desired of them for the moment. Eventually, discussion was postponed to another day.

John Adams was a lawyer who had become one of Congress's most influential members, and he promptly went to work buttonholing and lobbying his congressional colleagues. He discovered that the support for Washington was overwhelming. The majority that favored Washington's appointment was so large that Adams was able to persuade the dissenters to withdraw their objections.

When Congress reassembled the next day, June 15, the discussion of the previous day was resumed. Washington stayed away. At last the delegates passed a resolution that a general be appointed to command all troops of the united colonies. Then Thomas Johnson, a delegate from Maryland, took the floor and nominated Washington for the position. There were no other nominations, and the delegates unanimously elected Washington.

That evening at supper some of the delegates, addressing Washington as "General," told him that he had been elected commander in chief. After supper he drafted his response to the Congress, to be delivered following his official notification.

The next morning, June 16, when Congress met again, President John Hancock informed Washington of his election. "The President has the order of Congress to inform George Washington, Esquire, of the unanimous vote in choosing him to be general and commander in chief of the forces raised and to be raised in defense of American liberty," Hancock announced formally. "The Congress hopes the gentleman will accept."

Washington accepted with characteristic modesty. He pulled from his pocket a piece of paper on which he had written his acceptance speech the evening before and began reading to the members of the Congress:

> Mister President, though I am truly sensible of the high honor done me in this appointment, yet I feel great distress from a consciousness that my abilities and military experience may not be equal to the extensive and important trust. However, as the Congress desire, I will enter upon the momentous duty and exert every power I possess in their service and for the support of the glorious cause. I beg they will accept my most cordial thanks for this distinguished testimony of their approbation.
>
> But lest some unlucky event should happen unfavorable to my reputation, I beg it may be remembered by every gentleman in this room that I this day declare with the utmost sincerity I do not think myself equal to the command I am honored with.
>
> As to pay, sir, I beg leave to assure the Congress that as no pecuniary consideration could have tempted me to have accepted this arduous employment at the expense of my domestic ease and happiness, I do not wish to make any profit from it. I will keep an exact account of my expenses; those I doubt not they will discharge, and that is all I desire.[4]

At dinner his congressional colleagues congratulated and toasted him. "To the commander in chief of the American armies!" Washington was in no mood to celebrate. He was feeling too many misgivings. To his friend and fellow Virginia delegate, Patrick Henry, he pessimistically confided that "from the day I enter upon the command of the American armies I date my fall and the ruin of my reputation."[5]

In a letter to his brother John he further reflected his doubts about his ability to do all that was being asked of him. "That I may discharge the Trust to the Satisfaction of my Imployers is my first wish," he wrote. "That I shall aim to do it, there remains as little doubt of, but this I am sure of, that in the worst event I shall have the consolation of knowing (if I act to the best of my judgment) that the blame ought to lodge upon the appointers, not the appointed, as it was by no means a thing of my own seeking, or proceeding from any hint of my friends."[6]

To his closest confidante, his wife, Martha, he wrote:

> I am now set down to write you on a subject which fills me with inexpressible concern, and this concern is greatly aggravated and increased when I reflect upon the uneasiness I know it will cause you.
>
> It has been determined in Congress that the whole army raised for the defense of the American cause shall be put under my care, and that it is necessary for me to proceed immediately to Boston to take upon me the command of it.
>
> You may believe me, my dear Patsy, when I assure you in the most solemn manner that, so far from seeking this appointment, I have used every endeavor in my power to avoid it, not only from my unwillingness to part with you and my family, but from a consciousness of its being a trust too great for my capacity, and that I should enjoy more real happiness in one month with you at home than I have the most distant prospect of finding abroad, if my stay were to be seven times seven years.
>
> But as it has been a kind of destiny that has thrown me upon this service, I shall hope that my undertaking it is designed to answer some good purpose. You might, and I suppose did, perceive from the tenor of my letters that I was apprehensive I could not avoid this appointment, as I did not pretend to intimate when I should return. That was the case. It was utterly out of my power to refuse this appointment without exposing my character to such censure as would have reflected dishonor upon myself and have given much pain to my friends. . . .[7]

On June 23, 1775, in a falling rain, General George Washington, resigned to his task, mounted his horse and in the company of his newly appointed staff, rode out of Philadelphia, north toward Boston, to assume his leadership of America's army—and America's cause.

CHAPTER Two

The Army before Boston

O n Sunday, July 2, 1775, Washington arrived at Cambridge, Massachusetts, at the center of an army of American revolutionaries encamped outside Boston. He was led by an escort to the home of the president of Harvard College, Samuel Langdon, where, he was told, he should make his headquarters. In his entourage, among others, was the odd, British-born Charles Lee, a former general in the Polish army and now, by act of Congress, a major general in the American army. Lee would also be quartered at Langdon's home (one room of the house was reserved for Langdon himself).

At his new headquarters Washington met some of his chief officers, including Major General Israel Putnam of Connecticut and Major General Artemas Ward, commander of the Massachusetts militia, who was directing the siege and who, by order of Congress, was Washington's second-in-command. Putnam and Ward were both experienced soldiers and militia leaders who had received appointments to the Continental Army following Washington's election. Congress had made the appointments without benefit of consultation with the commander in chief.

That afternoon Washington took with him Generals Putnam and Lee and a group of other officers and rode out to inspect the army's fortifications. The inspection tour would give Washington his first look at the American militiamen who in a losing fight had badly mauled British regulars at the Battle of Bunker Hill on June 17.

The American lines formed a crescent extending about nine miles from end to end, from the Mystic River, north of the city of Boston, southwestward through Cambridge, then south across the Charles River, then curving southeastward through Roxbury to Dorchester. The British forces they faced were confined to the city of Boston, Boston Neck—a narrow strip of land that connected the city to the mainland, like a causeway—and the Charlestown peninsula, which the British had seized from the Americans in the aftermath of the Battle of Bunker Hill.

From horseback atop Prospect Hill, about a mile northeast of Cambridge, Washington could look across the mouth of the Charles River and see the city of Boston to the southeast. His eyes shifting to his left, he could see the rise of Bunker Hill, now defended by British redcoats, and beyond it, at the tip of the peninsula, lay the city of Charlestown, burned by the British during the Battle of Bunker Hill and now a charred ghost town, all but a handful of its 2,700 residents having fled.

Not everything he saw pleased him. Although some of the army's works were well placed in strong defensive positions in the rolling country-side, he found others that were neither well placed nor well built. One of the problems, he soon discovered, was the army's lack of engineers, needed to design and direct the construction of fortifications. Nevertheless, Washington ordered new works built and others strengthened. Over the next several days, the quirky, gawky ex-Polish general, Charles Lee, would himself lend a hand, though not without complaint. "I work like ten post horses," he remarked. "Our miserable defect of engineers imposes upon me eternal work in a department to which I am rather a stranger."

Washington's aim in strengthening his army's lines, he said, was "to secure, in the first instance, our own troops from any attempts of the enemy and, in the next, to cut off all communication between their troops and the country . . . to prevent them from penetrating into the country with fire and sword."

During his inspection of the positions near Roxbury, on July 5, Washington met for the first time young Henry Knox, proprietor of a popular Boston bookstore, the London Book Store, well known for stocking books on military subjects for the benefit of British army officers, who comprised a substantial part of his clientele. Knox, now 25 years old, was a military buff who had joined the Massachusetts militia when he was 18, had become an ardent student of military affairs, with a particular interest in artillery, and was an avid reader of the military books in his store. Though a civilian in the spring of 1775, he had volunteered his services to Artemas Ward at the Battle of Bunker Hill and recently had helped lay out the defensive works near Roxbury, where the Americans faced the British positions just south of Boston. Massively built at about six feet tall and

250 pounds, Knox was an impressive young man. He had been on his way to Cambridge when he came upon Washington and Ward and the rest of Washington's inspection party, headed in the opposite direction. Knox offered to show them the American positions intended to block Boston Neck, the British land route out of Boston, and the generals let him lead them to the works. During that contact with Knox, Washington was immensely impressed by him.

The more Washington saw of the troops besieging Boston, the clearer it became to him that what he had been given command of might be an army, but it was not an army of soldiers. "They are by no means such troops, in any respect, as you are led to believe of them from the accounts which are published . . ." he told his brother Lund. "I dare say the men would fight very well (if properly officered) although they are an exceeding dirty and nasty people."[1] Their faults included a lack of personal hygiene, resentment toward discipline, disrespect toward officers, disorderliness and general ignorance of things military.

Washington quickly set out to turn those dirty troops into disciplined soldiers. He wouldn't wait for their fortifications to be expanded and strengthened; he would start immediately, training and disciplining them. Some of the worst faults he found among the officers. The officers, he wrote to his brother Lund, "generally speaking are the most indifferent kind of people I ever saw. I have already broke one colonel and five captains for cowardice and for drawing more pay and provisions than they had men in their companies; there [are] two more colonels now under arrest, and to be tried for the same offences. . . . It was for their behavior on that occasion [the Battle of Bunker Hill] that the above officers were broke. . . ."

One of the first orders Washington issued upon assuming command was for his regimental commanders to submit returns on the strength of their units. He had been advised that the total force besieging Boston numbered between 18,000 and 20,000 men. He wanted precise numbers and a proper breakdown on his troops. He expected the commanders to have those numbers ready to be reported. They didn't, however, and they took days to get them. When their reports finally came in, on July 9, Washington learned that his army amounted to no more than 16,600 enlisted men, including noncommissioned officers, and of that number only 13,743 were present and fit for duty.

As Washington took on more of the responsibilities of his command, his problems seemed to increase. From the very first day at Cambridge, he had to deal with the explosive situation caused by Congress's having appointed general officers without regard to, or knowledge of, the existing seniorities and the abilities of the general officers of the New England militias. Israel Putnam of Connecticut had been appointed major general in the Continental Army over his senior in the Connecticut militia, Brigadier General Joseph Spencer. In anger, Spencer went AWOL and returned to his home in Connecticut without bothering to tell Washington of his grievance or his intentions. John Thomas, a lieutenant general in the Massachusetts militia, was appointed by Congress a brigadier general in the Continental Army, a flagrant demotion, and made junior to two other brigadier generals, Seth Pomeroy and William Heath, to whom he had been senior in the Massachusetts militia. A physician and a capable, experienced general, a man Washington—and the American cause—could ill afford to lose, Thomas was threatening to retire because of the slight.

More alarming was the threat of losing a large part of the army. Most of the troops were militiamen who had signed up for a fixed time, and if they could not be persuaded to extend their service time, they would have to be replaced or the revolutionary army would rapidly diminish. In addition, many of the militiamen considered their service so voluntary that they thought they should be free to come and go as they liked, even before their enlistment time was up; when they took a mind to, they simply left camp and went back home to take care of whatever business concerned them.

Shortages became a plague. The army was lacking in arms, ammunition, artillery, gunpowder, tents, material to make tents, adequate clothing, adequate provisions, and, most critical of all, money to pay the troops and buy what they needed. Washington's administrative woes were steadily mounting.

By July 17, two weeks after Washington had taken charge, some order at least had begun to come to the ragtag American army. One observer, the Rev. Mr. William Emerson, described what he had seen in the American camps:

> ... every tent is a portraiture of the temper and taste of the persons that incamp in it. Some are made of boards, some of sailcloth, and some are partly of one and partly of the other. Others are made of stone and turf, and others again of birch and other brush. Some are thrown up in a hurry and look as if they could not help it—mere necessity—others are curiously wrought with doors and windows done with wreaths and withes in the manner of a basket. Some are your proper tents and marquees, and look like the regular camp of the enemy.[2]

Emerson particularly noticed the effects of Washington's imposition of discipline on the troops:

> There is a great overturning in camp as to order and regularity. . . .
> The Generals Washington and Lee are upon the lines every day. New
> orders from his Excellency are read to the respective regiments every
> morning after prayers. The strictest government is taking place, and
> great distinction is made between officers and soldiers. Everyone is
> made to know his place and keep it, or be tied up and receive not
> 1000 but thirty or forty lashes according to his crime. Thousands are
> at work every day from four till eleven o'clock in the morning. It is
> surprising how much work has been done.[3]

Washington reorganized the besieging army into three divisions of two brigades each. He named Major General Artemas Ward commander of the division occupying the right side of the American lines, with Brigadier General John Thomas (the physician-general, who had been persuaded not to leave the army) and Brigadier General Joseph Spencer commanding the two brigades of that division. He named Major General Israel Putnam (the troops called him "Old Put") to command the division at the center of the lines. One of Putnam's brigades was still being formed; the other was placed under the command of a senior colonel. To command the division on the left, Washington named Major General Charles Lee, with Brigadier Generals John Sullivan and Nathanael Greene commanding the two brigades. He had already appointed Brigadier General Horatio Gates to be his adjutant general and now he appointed a judge advocate general to organize and oversee the military courts and he appointed a commissary general to direct the procurement of provisions. He appointed a quartermaster general to procure equipment and supplies, and he developed an existing intelligence unit.

He took time to instruct his senior officers in their responsibilities. "Be strict in your discipline," he urged. "That is, to require nothing unreasonable of your officers and men, but see that whatever is required be punctually complied with. Reward and punish every man according to his merit, without partiality or prejudice. Hear his complaints; if well founded, redress them. If otherwise, discourage them in order to prevent frivolous ones. Discourage vice in every shape, and impress upon the mind of every man, from the first to the lowest, the importance of the cause and what it is they are contending for."[4]

He also made a point of getting to know many of his officers, making a practice of having them, a few at a time, dine with him and his staff, his so-called "family." He became well known for treating his officers with respect.

Needing insignia to identify the rank of his uniform-less army's officers and men, Washington devised a color code. He ordered his general officers to wear a pink ribbon across their chests, field-grade officers (majors, lieutenant colonels, and colonels) to wear red or pink cockades, captains to wear yellow or buff cockades, subalterns to wear green cockades, sergeants to wear red cloths on their sleeves, and corporals to wear green cloths on their sleeves. Washington himself would wear a blue ribbon across his chest.

By the end of August so much improvement had been made on the American lines that Washington, though still distressed by a lack of discipline and professionalism among his troops, was able to sit down with some satisfaction and reflect favorably on the state of the siege:

> As we have now nearly compleated our lines of defence, we [have] nothing more, in my opinion, to fear from the enemy, provided we can keep our men to their duty and make them watchful and vigilant. But it is among the most difficult tasks I ever undertook in my life to induce these people to believe that there is, or can be, danger till the bayonet is pushed at their breasts. . . .[5]

Near the end of September, Washington's attitude turned dark, like an approaching storm cloud. His worries about the army, which was in increasing want of adequate clothing, equipment and supplies, grew alarmingly larger and more serious. From his headquarters in Cambridge (he had moved out of the Harvard president's home and was now quartered in the abandoned home of loyalist John Vassall, who had fled to Boston when the revolutionaries took over Cambridge), Washington wrote a desperate message to the president of the Continental Congress:

> . . . my situation is inexpressibly distressing to see the Winter fast approaching upon a naked Army, the time of their service within a few weeks of expiring, and no provision yet made for such important events. Added to this, the military chest is totally exhausted. The Paymaster has not a single dollar in hand. The Commissary General assures me he has strained his credit to the utmost for the subsistence of the Army. The Quarter Master General is precisely in the same situation, and the greater part of the Army in a state not far from

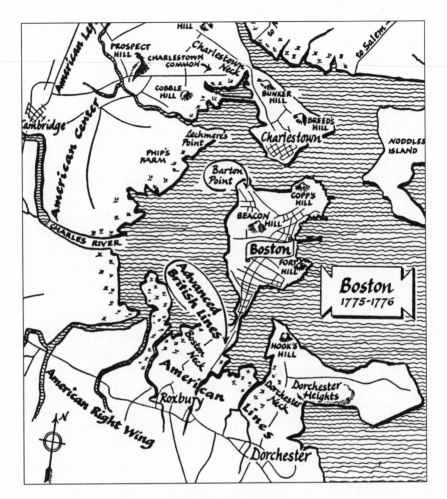

Boston 1775–1776

mutiny, upon the deduction from their stated allowance. I know not to whom to impute this failure, but I am of opinion, if the evil is not immediately remedied and more punctuality observed in the future, the Army must absolutely break up.[6]

More than a month later the situation was no better. Washington's frustration over the absence of necessary support was now nearing the boiling point. He protested:

What an astonishing thing it is that those who are employed to sign
the Continental bills should not be able, or inclined, to do it as fast
as they are wanted. They will prove the destruction of the Army if
they are not more attentive and diligent. Such a dearth of public
spirit and want of virtue, such stock-jobbing, and fertility in all the
low arts to obtain advantages of one kind or another, in this great
change of military arrangement, I never saw before and pray God I
may never be witness to again. What will be the ultimate end of these
manoeuvres is beyond my scan. I tremble at the prospect.

We have been till this time enlisting about three thousand five
hundred men. To engage these I have been obliged to allow furloughs
as far as fifty men a regiment, and the officers, I am persuaded,
indulge as many more. The Connecticut troops will not be prevailed
upon to stay longer than their term (saving those who have enlisted
for the next campaign, and mostly on furlough), and such a dirty,
mercenary spirit pervades the whole that I should not be at all surprised at any disaster that may happen.

In short, after the last of this month our lines will be so weakened that the minutemen and militia must be called in for their
defence; these, being under no kind of government themselves, will
destroy the little subordination I have been laboring to establish, and
run me into one evil whilst I am endeavoring to avoid another; but
the lesser must be chosen.

Could I have foreseen what I have and am likely to experience, no
consideration upon earth should have induced me to accept this
command. . . .[7]

Meanwhile, the war sputtered on. There were scattered exchanges of
fire from patrols of the two stalemated armies, intermittent artillery fire
from both sides, and sporadic, mostly ineffectual, sniper fire from the
American lines; two British soldiers on patrol were taken prisoner at
Charlestown Neck, a British advance post near Roxbury was taken and
burned, a lighthouse was raided by a force of 300 Americans that captured
the 32 British marines who were guarding it and several workers who were
repairing it.

Impatient with the inactivity, and wishing a resolution of the siege
before enlistments ran out at the end of the year, Washington began enter-
taining a change in the strategy of merely keeping the British bottled up
in Boston. On September 11 he called a conference, a council of war, of

eight of his top officers to ask them what they thought of the idea of an offensive that would send an American force across Boston Neck while at the same time another American force would storm Boston by boat. Major General Charles Lee liked the idea. The other generals didn't. Boston Neck was too narrow, they argued. It would bottleneck the American force. A water-borne assault would expose the Americans to too much enemy fire, they said. They didn't like the odds of success. After the meeting, Washington wrote to Congress that although his council of generals was negative toward the plan, "I can not say that I have wholly laid it aside."

Congress, acting independently of Washington, already had authorized an offensive on another front, having received a report that Canada's military governor, Sir Guy Carleton, was making preparations to invade the colonies with a force of about 800 troops and was inciting the Indian nations at the same time to make war against the American colonists. To combat the threat, and possibly with the thought of making Canada a fourteenth American colony, Congress on June 27 had directed the sickly Major General Philip Schuyler of New York, whom it had appointed commander of the "New York department" of the revolutionary army, to lead the campaign. After a series of delays, Schuyler, because of ill health, finally turned over his force of about 1,700 Connecticut and New York militiamen to his second-in-command, Brigadier General Richard Montgomery of New York, and by September 16, Montgomery was leading his army to its first objective, Fort Saint Johns, on the Richelieu River, a fortification that commanded the northern entrance to Lake Champlain, the presumed British invasion route to New York.

Washington was thinking of a way his army might assist that campaign, which, if successful, could thwart any British effort to seize the Hudson River valley and thereby separate New England from the rest of the colonies. He also devised a plan to stop supplies from reaching the beleaguered British troops in Boston, in an attempt to starve the British into submission.

In October Washington was notified that a committee from Congress was coming to Cambridge to confer with him. Congress wanted him to invite to the meeting the governors of the four New England colonies—Connecticut, Massachusetts, Rhode Island, and New Hampshire—as well as representatives of the colonies' legislatures. Congress wanted to know how many men Washington would need for the winter, when the activities of both the British and American armies presumably would be curtailed. It wanted to know if Washington thought the soldiers could take a cut in pay and what sort of provisions they needed and what additional regulations were needed. The committee was coming with a whole list of questions for which Congress wanted the commander in chief's answers.

The committee arrived in Cambridge on October 15. Its members were Benjamin Franklin of Pennsylania, Thomas Lynch of South Carolina, and Benjamin Harrison of Virginia, a friend of Washington. The meetings with Washington and his staff and the New England representatives extended over several days. From the meetings came the conclusion that Washington's army should comprise 26 regiments of eight companies each, a total of at least 20,370 men, exclusive of artillery and special rifle units. In response to Washington's question of whether, in case he decided to assault Boston, he should burn the city, the committee members told him that Congress itself would have to make that decision. The committee members reported that Congress had, however, already agreed that Washington should feel free to launch an assault on the British in Boston if he deemed an assault practicable.

In November, while barracks were being constructed and firewood was being stockpiled and blankets were being sought to see his troops through the New England winter, Washington determined to do something about his lack of sufficient artillery to bombard Boston effectively in advance of a possible American assault and, if possible, give the Americans' artillery at least parity with the artillery of the British. Washington reassigned sixty-five-year-old Colonel Richard Gridley to be the Continental Army's chief engineer; and to replace him, without waiting for congressional approval, Washington on November 17 appointed young Henry Knox colonel of the Continental Regiment of Artillery, an undermanned, underequipped outfit that Knox would be expected to turn into something worthy of its name.

One hundred sixty miles away (as the crow flies; about 300 by tortuous mountain road and trail), at Fort Ticonderoga, American revolutionaries held within their keeping upwards of 50 pieces of artillery, captured from the British when the Americans overran the fort in May. Knox proposed marching to Ticonderoga, loading the artillery onto boats, floating them down the length of Lake George, then transferring them to sledges and dragging them over and through the mountains of New York and western Massachusetts all the way to the siege lines outside Boston.

A gargantuan undertaking, but Washington thought it just might work. It certainly was worth a try. He ordered Knox to carry out the plan.

Knox and his detail reached Fort Ticonderoga on December 5. He found fifty-nine serviceable pieces of artillery—including cannon ranging from four-pounders to twenty-four-pounders, (the kind of siege gun needed for an assault on Boston), howitzers, and mortars. The guns ranged in size from a foot to eleven feet in length and from one hundred pounds in weight to nearly three tons. He also found a barrel of flints needed for firing the pieces, as well as twenty-three boxes of lead from which ammunition could be cast. He and his men wrestled and manhandled the guns onto three boats, with the aid of teams of oxen. On December 9 they cast off and, under sail and oar power, headed south down the length of Lake George. With men and ordnance having survived a few threatening mishaps, they arrived safely at Fort George, at the southern tip of the lake, on December 15. From there two days later Knox wrote a report to Washington:

> I returned to this place on the fifteenth and brought with me the cannon. . . . It is not easy to conceive the difficulties we have had in getting them over the lake, owing to the advanced season of the year and contrary winds; but this danger is now past.
>
> Three days ago it was very uncertain whether we should have gotten them until next spring, but now, please God, they must go. I have made forty-two exceeding strong sleds and have provided eighty yokes of oxen to draw them as far as Springfield, where I shall get fresh cattle to carry them to camp. . . .
>
> I have sent for sleds and teams to come here and expect to begin to move them to Saratoga on Wednesday or Thursday next, trusting that between this and then we shall have a fine fall of snow, which will enable us to proceed further and make the carriage easy. If that shall be the case, I hope in sixteen or seventeen days' time to present your Excellency a noble train of artillery.

Good news was coming from Colonel Knox, but there was more bad news from the American lines outside Boston. Washington had received word on November 29 that at least 1,500 men, about 12 percent of his army, were absent from their posts, having been given furloughs as an incentive for re-enlisting. In that same report Washington had been informed that there was little chance that Connecticut troops could be induced to stay on past the end of their service time, which would expire on December 10. They would have to be replaced temporarily by minutemen, the immediate-response militiamen who served only for short periods, until militias from the other colonies could reach Boston to take the place of the Connecticut militia. Washington doubted that militiamen from the other New England colonies, now manning his lines, would be any more willing than their Connecticut neighbors to extend their service time, which would expire at the end of December.

While those dismal thoughts occupied him, Washington learned that the British were moving troops from their Bunker Hill positions and ferrying them across the Charles River to Boston. He could think of only two reasons for the redeployment. The British commander in chief, General William Howe, recently appointed to the command, was either pulling a large segment of his troops into Boston for shelter from the winter weather or, having received information that Washington's troops were leaving, he was concentrating his forces for an assault somewhere on the weakened American lines. The imminent diminution of American troop strength suddenly had become still more dangerous. Preparing for the worst, Washington issued orders that the Connecticut militiamen were not to leave their posts, despite the expiration of their enlistments, until new militias arrived to replace them. In so doing, he realized, he risked possible mutiny.

On December 11 a happy event diverted Washington temporarily. In the company of a sizable entourage, Martha Washington arrived in Cambridge to visit her husband through Christmas. It was the first time they had seen each other in seven months. With her were Mrs. Horatio Gates, wife of Washington's adjutant general, Washington's stepson, whom he had adopted, John Parke "Jack" Custis, and his wife and George Lewis, Washington's nephew.

When the Connecticut troops were released from duty, as they left the Americans' camps, they were, Major General Charles Lee reported, "so horribly hissed, groaned at and pelted, that I believed they wished their aunts, grandmothers and even sweethearts, to whom the day before they were so much attached, at the Devil's own place." Connecticut's governor, Jonathan Trumbull, an enthusiastic supporter of the revolutionary cause, wrote to Washington that he had received reports of the behavior of the Connecticut troops with "grief, surprise and indignation" and had called the Connecticut legislature into special session to address the matter. "You may depend on their zeal and ardor," he said, "to support the common cause, to furnish our quota, and to exert their utmost strength for the defence of the rights of these colonies. Your candor and goodness will suggest to your consideration that the conduct of our troops is not a rule whereby to judge of the spirit of the colony."

As a result of the cool, if not hostile, reception the Connecticut troops received on their arrival back home, and the shaming by relatives and neighbors, many of the Connecticut militiamen changed their minds and re-enlisted.

In the report he wrote to Congress on Christmas Day, Washington said recruits for the new Continental Army totaled some 8,500 men. That would be his fighting force come January 1, 1776, a total horrifyingly short of the 20,370 Washington had told Congress he needed and which had been authorized.

After Christmas and New Year's had passed, a new count revealed that of the new army's total strength, only 5,582 men were actually present and fit for duty. In a tone of despair, Washington wrote of his continuing predicament:

> Search the vast volumes of history through, and I much question whether a case similar to ours is to be found; to wit, to maintain a post against the flower of the British troops for six months together, without powder, and at the end of them to have one army disbanded and another to raise within the same distance of a reinforced enemy. It is too much to attempt. . . . For more than two months past, I have scarcely emerged from one difficulty before I have plunged into another.[8]

To his military secretary, Joseph Reed, away on leave in Philadelphia, he wrote, "How it will end, God in his great goodness will direct. I am thankful for his protection to this time. We are told that we shall soon get the army completed, but I have been told so many things which have never come to pass that I distrust everything."[9]

By January 8, 1776, newly arrived militiamen had raised the total of men present and fit for duty to 10,209, still less than half of what Washington had asked for, but enough for the commanders along the American lines to fill in the dangerous gaps created by the troops that had departed at the end of the year. Washington's spirits lifted considerably when Colonel Henry Knox arrived back at Cambridge on January 18. On that same day Washington held another council of war. Encouraged by news of the imminent arrival of Ticonderoga's big guns (they followed Knox into the outskirts of Boston about a week later), Washington's chief generals now finally agreed to an assault on Boston, to be made as soon as practicable. Washington quickly wrote to the governors of the New

England colonies asking for more troops, pleading for thirteen additional regiments of militia needed to make an assault possible.

Unaccountably, the British had not tried to take advantage of Washington's turnover of troops at year's end. General Howe apparently had moved his troops from the Charlestown peninsula into Boston only to house them for the winter. The defensive crisis virtually past, Washington now at last would take the offensive. In response to his question about burning Boston, Congress had given him a blank check to treat Boston as he saw fit: "Resolved, that if General Washington and his council of war should be of opinion that a successful attack may be made on the troops in Boston, he do it in any manner he may think expedient, notwithstanding the town and property in it may thereby be destroyed." Like Washington, Congress realized that a decisive defeat of the British army in Boston could bring the war to a quick and welcome conclusion. Boston therefore could be sacrificed.

By now Washington and the members of Congress had learned that the American campaign in Canada had failed. The American commanding officer, Brigadier General Richard Montgomery, had been killed in an assault on Quebec in near-blizzard conditions on the night of December 31– January 1. The commander of the force sent by Washington to aid Montgomery's effort, Colonel Benedict Arnold, had been severely wounded in the assault, and the Americans had been turned back with heavy, humiliating losses. Their defeat was making victory at Boston all the more hoped for by Congress.

Still lacking sufficient gunpowder for his newly acquired artillery, Washington searched for an alternative to an infantry assault that would necessarily be preceded by a prolonged bombardment. On February 13 he scouted Lechmere Point, directly east of Cambridge, on the banks of the Charles River, opposite northwest Boston, and saw that the river had frozen over there, all the way across the channel to the Boston side of the river. He drew up a plan to send an attack force across the ice immediately, before the weather could warm enough to break up the ice, taking the British by surprise.

His generals, to a man, turned thumbs down on the plan. They agreed, however, that some sort of action must be taken soon, before expected British reinforcements would arrive from England in the spring. Together with Washington, they devised a plan to lure the British out of Boston and force a showdown at a battleground upon which the Americans would hold the advantage.

The plan called for the seizure and fortification of Dorchester Heights, a pair of steep hills, unoccupied by either British or American forces, which overlooked Boston on the southeast and gave a clear view of Boston harbor. From positions on those hills Colonel Henry Knox's artillery could rain shot and shell on the British and possibly provoke them to come out of Boston and attempt to force the Americans from the heights. The fortification of Dorchester Heights would be done with stealth, under the cover of darkness, so that the British would be suddenly surprised and unable to counter the move before the Americans could make the heights fully defensible. In so doing, the Americans would be following the model of their action at Breed's Hill, the rise on which the major part of the Battle of Bunker Hill was fought eight months earlier. There the revolutionary troops had dug a strong redoubt during the night, and the British at daybreak the next morning were alarmed at the sudden sight of Americans entrenched and looking down their throats in Boston. That maneuver by the Americans had brought a quick reaction from the British, precipitating the Battle of Bunker Hill. Washington and his generals hoped to repeat that sequence of events, though this time with a different outcome.

The American troops had dug the Breed's Hill entrenchments in June. This was February. Now the ground was frozen hard, a foot and a half below the surface, making digging extremely difficult. Some other way to fortify Dorchester Heights would have to be found.

While preparations for the seizure of the heights were under way, Washington received intelligence that set off a new tremor of anxiety. The British were reported to be loading their artillery and other equipment aboard a flotilla of transport ships—an indication that General Howe, before the Americans could implement their plan, was going to evacuate his army from Boston and sail somewhere down the long Atlantic coastline to a new point of invasion, forcing Washington to move from Boston to counter it. Washington and his army now would have to work fast, lest their quarry slip away.

On the night of Saturday, March 2, 1776, the Americans made their first move, intended to divert the enemy's attention away from Dorchester Heights. Colonel Knox's artillery batteries on Lechmere Point and Cobble Hill, northwest of Boston, opened fire on the British, who responded in kind. The American bombardment was repeated Sunday night. Then, about 7 p.m. on Monday, March 4, as darkness settled over the landscape, Brigadier General John Thomas, the physician-soldier, formed up a work party of 1,200 troops and an 800-man covering force and led them out of

Roxbury, marching toward Dorchester Heights, taking with them 360 oxcarts loaded with tools and the materials with which they would fortify that high ground above Boston.

Lieutenant Colonel Rufus Putnam of Massachusetts, an engineer and cousin of Israel Putnam, had come up with the idea of constructing above-ground fortifications that would not require digging deep into the frozen earth. Chandeliers (movable wood-frame parapets) were to be prefabricated by Colonel Putnam's engineers and would be carried by oxcart to the intended sites on Dorchester Heights and there assembled. Inside the chandeliers' framework would be placed fascines (bundles of wooden sticks, tied together), gabions (wickerwork cylinders filled with dirt) and bales of hay. Also carried in oxcarts would be wooden barrels to be filled with earth and rocks. They would be lined up together in front of the fortification, like a wall, as if to give cover to the American troops. Their real purpose, however, was to be turned on their sides and sent rolling down the steep, smooth slopes of Dorchester Heights' treeless hills, crashing into and bowling over redcoat infantrymen as they advanced up the slopes toward the American positions. The fortifications would include abatis (logs imbedded into or against the ground at one end and sharpened into a point at the other end, closely spaced and angled toward the enemy as a barrier to man and horse). Trees in nearby orchards would be felled to provide the logs.

All of that was to be accomplished overnight. Luckily, the revolutionaries had the light of a full moon to work by and mild nighttime temperatures in which to work. A ground haze helped to hide the activity from British sentries across the harbor. The noise of the work party as it assembled the prefabricated chandeliers and constructed the abatis, the sounds of the workers' picks, shovels, axes, and hammers, were concealed by the booming of the American cannonade, which began, as arranged, at 9 p.m. from artillery emplacements at Lechmere Point, Cobble Hill, and Lamb's Dam at Roxbury, and by the answering fire of the British artillery. Drivers of the ox teams, after their carts were unloaded, returned to Roxbury for additional cartloads. By 10 p.m. two small forts, one on each hill, had been erected, sufficient to protect their defenders from musket fire and grapeshot. Four more were to be built, positioned to defend the Americans' left flank and rear. Colonel Knox's hardy gunners hauled up more than twenty artillery pieces, along with ammunition, and mounted them on the fortifications, in easy range of the British. Troop reinforcements, including five companies of riflemen, arrived to defend the works.

At 3 a.m. members of the work party were finally relieved and allowed to get some sleep.

At daybreak on Tuesday, March 5, the awakening British looked up and saw what had transpired while they slept. Phase one of the revolutionaries' operation had been accomplished. Washington's army was now breathing down the necks of the British. "The entire waterfront of Boston lay open to our observation," an eyewitness, Major John Trumbull, son of the Connecticut governor, reported. As the daylight hours passed, General Thomas's men continued to work, putting finishing touches on the fortifications while the British took steps to counter the Americans. "During the day we saw distinctly the preparations which the enemy were making to dislodge us . . . ," Major Trumbull related. "We saw the embarkation of troops from the various wharves, on board of ships, which hauled off in succession and anchored in a line in our front, a little before sunset, prepared to land the troops in the morning." Washington went to see the scene for himself, riding up to inspect the fortifications and check his troops' readiness.

The Americans were lying expectantly in wait, hoping the British would attack, eager for them to come. "We were in high spirits," Major Trumbull reported, "well prepared to receive the threatened attack. Our positions . . . were strong by nature and well fortified. . . . We waited with impatience for the attack, when we meant to emulate, and hoped to eclipse, the glories of Bunker's Hill."

On the heels of a British infantry assault on the heights would come the planned next phase of the American operation. Four thousand American militiamen, aboard forty-five bateaux and under the command of Major General Israel Putnam, were poised to cross the river, storm ashore on Boston Neck, and strike the British right flank and rear, landing behind the British defenses on Boston Neck and cutting the redcoats off from the city of Boston, trapping them between the two American forces and under the fire of the artillery on Dorchester Heights.

General Howe would not order an assault that day, Tuesday, since by the time he was prepared to do so, the tide had turned against him, running out of the harbor, toward the sea. The weather, too, turned. In the late afternoon the winds of a slowly mounting storm swept in, the temperature dropped, and rain began to fall. Howe also had to give up thoughts of assailing the American emplacements on Dorchester Heights with his artillery. The barrels of his guns could not elevate to a high enough angle to fire on the heights with effect.

During the evening and throughout the night the storm, blowing in from the south, increased in fury, with heavy rain and winds. In that downpour Washington ordered his artillerymen to make certain their powder was kept sheltered and dry.

Around midnight the storm reached near-hurricane strength and it continued throughout Wednesday and into Wednesday night. From their position on Dorchester Heights the Americans could see that the British plans and ships had suffered in the storm. Major Trumbull reported that the "storm . . . deranged all the enemy's plan of debarkation, driving the ships foul of each other, and from their anchors in utter confusion, and thus put a stop to the intended operation."

Meanwhile, the American work party kept at the job of improving and strengthening the fortifications on Dorchester Heights. Washington repeatedly inspected the works and the readiness of his troops. While on an inspection tour on Friday, the eighth of March, he somehow lost one of his pistols and later, in a notice issued from his headquarters, offered a reward for its recovery: "Whoever will bring it to him or leave it with General Thomas shall receive two dollars reward and no questions asked; it is a screwed barreled pistol mounted with silver and a head resembling that of a pug dog at the butt."

About 2 p.m. on Friday a flag of truce was seen raised at the British advance position on Boston Neck, and Colonel Ebenezer Learned of Massachusetts, commanding the American unit opposite that position, the 3rd Continental Regiment, stepped out from his lines and strode forward to meet the four men who were walking toward him. One wore the uniform of a British officer; the three others were dressed as civilians. When they were within greeting distance, the officer introduced himself as Major Henry Bassett. The men with him were Thomas Amory, Jonathan Amory, and Peter Johonnot, evidently a committee of Boston residents. One of them held out to Colonel Learned a letter, said to be from the selectmen of Boston, the city's governing body. Colonel Learned accepted the letter, and the four men turned and walked back to the British lines.

Colonel Learned immediately sent the letter to Washington, who promptly examined and read it:

> As his Excellency General Howe is determined to leave the town with the troops under his command, a number of the respectable inhabitants, being very anxious for its preservation and safety, have applied

to General Robertson for this purpose, who at their request have communicated the same to his Excellency Genl. Howe, who has assured them that he has no intention of destroying the town, unless the troops under his command are molested during their embarkation or at their departure, by the armed forces without, which declaration he gave Genl. Robertson leave to communicate to the inhabitants; If such an opposition should take place, we have the greatest reason to expect the town will be exposed to entire destruction. As our fears are quieted with regard to Genl. Howe's intentions, we beg we may have some assurances that so dreadful a calamity may not be brought on by any measures without. As a testimony of the truth of the above, we have signed our names to this paper, carried out by Messrs. Thomas and Jonathan Amory and Peter Johonnot, who have at the earnest entreaties of the inhabitants, through the Lt. Governor, solicited a flag of truce for this purpose.

The letter bore the signatures of John Scollay, Timothy Newell, Thomas Marshall, and Samuel Austin.

Washington wasn't sure what he should make of it. He sent for whoever of his generals was nearby and available. When they came to his headquarters, he had them read the letter and asked for their opinions. All were wary, as was Washington. It was agreed, though, that the letter should be answered. The reply stated that since there was no written promise of anything by General Howe, the Americans would reserve to themselves all the rights of war. The reply letter was taken to Colonel Learned for him to sign and have delivered to the British lines.

The days dragged by with neither a British attack on the American positions nor a British departure from Boston. On Friday, March 15, eight days after he had received the selectmen's letter, Washington, in a new attempt to force a showdown with Howe, issued orders for his troops to occupy and fortify Nook's Hill, on a salient near Dorchester Heights and almost literally within a stone's throw of the Boston harbor. With Knox's artillery emplaced on Nook's Hill, the British and their ships would truly be sitting ducks. General Howe would have to take action against the American position or else make good on his stated intention of evacuating his army from Boston.

On the night of March 16–17 the Americans, under the cover of darkness, as on the hills of Dorchester Heights, constructed the works for the emplacement of their artillery and for the defense of Nook's Hill. Sounds of their labors brought an ineffectual artillery response from the British just across the water. No American was hurt by the cannonade.

The rising sun on Sunday, March 17, Saint Patrick's Day, revealed the long awaited British response. The Boston docks were swarming with red-coats, lining up to enter the lighters that were ferrying men to the fleet of transports lying at anchor outside the harbor. General Howe and his British army were giving up their hold on Boston and their threat to Massachusetts. An eyewitness recorded the event in his diary:

> This morning the British army in Boston, under General Howe, consisting of upwards of seven thousand men, after suffering an ignominious blockade for many months past, disgracefully quitted all their strongholds in Boston and Charlestown, fled from before the army of the United Colonies, and took refuge on board their ships. . . . To the wisdom, firmness, intrepidity and military abilities of our amiable and beloved general, his Excellency George Washington, Esquire, to the assiduity, skill, and bravery of the other worthy generals and officers of the army, and to the hardiness and gallantry of the soldiery, is to be ascribed, under God, the glory and success of our arms, in driving from one of the strongest holds in America, so considerable a part of the British army as that which last week occupied Boston.[10]

On that same Sunday, Washington attended services at the Congregational church in Cambridge. The minister's sermon that morning was from the text found in Exodus 14:25, ". . . the Egyptians said, Let us flee from the face of Israel; for the Lord fighteth for them against the Egyptians."

Washington was less than jubilant over the British withdrawal. In a letter to his brother John he wrote, "That this remarkable interposition of Providence is for some wise purpose, I have not a doubt; but as the principal design of the manouvre was to draw the enemy to an ingage-ment under disadvantages . . . and seemed to be succeeding to my utmost wish . . . I can scarce forbear lamenting the disappointment."[11]

The British army, still intact, was gone, but to where? Washington now could only wonder.

CHAPTER Three

The King's Volunteer

Charles Cornwallis—a peer of the realm and a major general in the king's army—decided he would do something about what he was feeling. It would mean temporarily depriving himself of the comforts of his estates and the company of his beloved family, but the rebellion in the colonies was to him a matter so grave and so wrong that sacrifice was warranted. Besides that, the war in America offered opportunities for distinction that any ambitious professional soldier would find extremely hard to pass up. What Charles Lord Cornwallis was feeling was a call to glory as well as to duty.

Though ambitious, Cornwallis was not the sort to push himself out front or unnecessarily call attention to himself. He was too much the gentleman for that. He was a mild-looking man, fleshy faced and portly, with a sadness in his expression when his face was in repose. His habits were as bland as his personality. Not a gambler, not a heavy drinker, not a womanizer, not particularly social, he seemed more a stuffy, sobersided country squire than a titled, privileged friend of the king and a general in the king's army.

He had never had to push and claw his way up, never had to scheme and manipulate to get what he wanted. He had been born into a distinguished English family, the eldest son of the first Earl Cornwallis, and was Viscount Brome (the hereditary title of eldest Cornwallis sons) until he succeeded his father as earl when his father died in 1762. He had been schooled at Eton (where he was struck in the face playing field hockey, suffering a permanent disfigurement that, some said, gave him a quizzical look) and at Cambridge. After deciding, as a teenager, on a career in the

army, he had attended military college in Turin, Italy (England then having no military academy except for engineers) in order to prepare himself
as well as possible.

He had acquired his first commission, as an ensign, in 1756 when he
was seventeen years old. A year later he purchased a captaincy in the
85th Foot Regiment and was promoted to lieutenant colonel in the 12th
Foot in 1761. In 1766 he became colonel of his own regiment, the 33rd. He
saw action in several battles in Germany during King George II's defense of
his German properties and received a number of commendations. His rapid
advancement, however, apparently owed more to who he was than what he
had accomplished in the field. In 1775 he was appointed a major general.

Not concerned with marrying well—he had no need to—he fell in love
with Jemima Jones, the daughter of Colonel James Jones, a regimental
commander of modest means and background, and in 1768 married her
because he loved her.

In politics Cornwallis didn't precisely fit the mold of a king's man. At
times he seemed sympathetic toward the American colonists. As a member
of the House of Lords he had voted with the Whig faction that opposed
many of the Tory government's policies that offended the colonists. He
had opposed taxing the colonists and opposed military action to constrain
their protests. But at the same time, he felt a deep sense of loyalty to the
crown, which had been faithfully served by members of his family for four
centuries or more. Furthermore, as could be expected of any landed, titled
aristocrat, born to position and privilege, Cornwallis was resolutely keen
on preserving his society's status quo, to which any revolution could be
considered a threat.

Well known to be of strong character and inflexible principles,
Cornwallis believed the American colonists had gone too far in their resistance to their sovereign's will. They had crossed the line when at Lexington
and Concord they took up arms against His Majesty's troops, who in their
splendid scarlet-and-white uniforms formed the living symbol of British
law and order and were the royal guardians of Britain's status quo. Those
despicably treasonous actions by the Americans had cost them whatever
sympathy Cornwallis might have felt for their interests. Armed rebellion
could not be countenanced. It must be contested and defeated, and as a
general officer in His Majesty's army, Cornwallis felt that he could, that he
should, contribute to that defeat.

On Sunday, November 26, 1775, he sent a friend to see Lord George
Germain, the newly appointed British Secretary of State for American

Colonies. The friend carried with him an offer from Cornwallis. Despite the fact that Cornwallis knew he would have to serve under two generals senior to him—General William Howe, the British army's commander in chief in America, and Lieutenant General Henry Clinton, Howe's second-in-command—Cornwallis nevertheless was willing, he let Germain know, to go to America to serve his king.

On the same day that Cornwallis's friend took his offer to Germain, Germain met with King George III and relayed Cornwallis's offer to him. The king of course knew Cornwallis well. He had given him several royal appointments over the past few years. He was delighted that a general of Cornwallis's ability and character was volunteering. The king quickly accepted the offer and gave him the 33rd Regiment, Cornwallis's own regiment, to take to America with him.

Countess Jemima Cornwallis was aghast at what her husband had done. She sought the help of Cornwallis's uncle, the archbishop of Canterbury, Frederick Cornwallis, in a vain effort to have her husband's orders rescinded. Devoted as he was to Jemima, Cornwallis nevertheless was determined to go serve his king and his career in America. Her pleadings went for nought.

In December, Cornwallis, who would observe his thirty-eighth birthday on the last day of the month, said goodbye to Jemima and their two children and traveled to Cork to take charge of seven infantry regiments and two artillery companies that were also embarking for America. Their departure had been scheduled for December 1, but one administrative blunder after another kept delaying them, even after Cornwallis's arrival. It was not until February 12, 1776 that the fleet of forty-four warships and transports bearing the troops and their equipment and supplies finally set sail.

On the first day out of port the fleet ran into an Atlantic storm that hurled nine of the ships back to England. The fleet's losses continued throughout the long voyage. After three weeks at sea only fourteen of the forty-four vessels remained. The winds, Cornwallis wrote in a letter to Germain, were almost always contrary and the fleet suffered from violent gales during the entire crossing.

The first ships of the fleet reached the mouth of the Cape Fear River in North Carolina on April 18. The ship bearing Cornwallis, the *Bristol*, the fleet's flagship, after three hard and perilous months at sea, arrived on May 3. The last ship of the fleet to arrive straggled in on May 31.

The mission of the fleet, under the command of Commodore Sir Peter Parker, was to link up with an army commanded by Lieutenant General

Henry Clinton and a force of North Carolina loyalists and together overwhelm the rebels in the southern colonies and re-establish royal government there. That mission was part a new British strategy to take the war to the southern colonies. It was based on a belief, popular in London, that hundreds of thousands of loyal colonists would rally to the king's cause behind a show of force by the king's army. The royal governors of Virginia, North Carolina, South Carolina, and Georgia, all of whom had been deposed by the rebels, had been urging the deployment of British troops in those colonies, insisting that not much force would be needed to rally the loyalists and regain control. Clinton had been ordered by Howe, who was responding to instructions from London, to take a contingent of about 1,500 regulars from besieged Boston, rendezvous with Cornwallis in the Cape Fear River and from there, supported by Commodore Parker's fleet, move to restore the king's law and order in the southern colonies.

By the time Cornwallis arrived, much of the plan had already foundered. An army of about 2,000 impatient loyalists, mostly immigrants from the Highlands of Scotland, without waiting for help from Clinton's British regulars, on February 27 had attacked a rebel position at Moore's Creek Bridge, about 18 miles north of Wilmington, North Carolina, and had been decisively defeated and scattered, with losses in killed and captured amounting to nearly half their numbers.

Clinton and his army had sailed from Boston on January 20 and had arrived at the Cape Fear River on March 12, too late to aid the loyalists and well ahead of Cornwallis. When Cornwallis finally did arrive, his sea-weary troops were joined to an army weakened by a lack of provisions while its wait for the fleet stretched into unplanned weeks. Cornwallis's orders were to place himself and his troops under Clinton's command, which he did.

Commodore Parker, meanwhile, having met with Clinton, took part of his fleet and sailed off to reconnoiter the strategic port of Charleston, South Carolina and assay its defenses. He returned May 26 to report to Clinton that Fort Sullivan, guarding the entrance to the vast Charleston harbor, was still under construction and could be taken and held without much effort. The capture of Charleston, thought to be assured once its protective harbor forts were seized, would provide an ideal base for British operations against the rebels in the southern colonies. Clinton bought the idea. Accepting Parker's assessment, he planned to take the fort, leave a small garrison to man it with the support of a couple of Parker's frigates, and then take the rest of his army, including Cornwallis, back up north. Cornwallis was consulted, but left out of the planning of the operation.

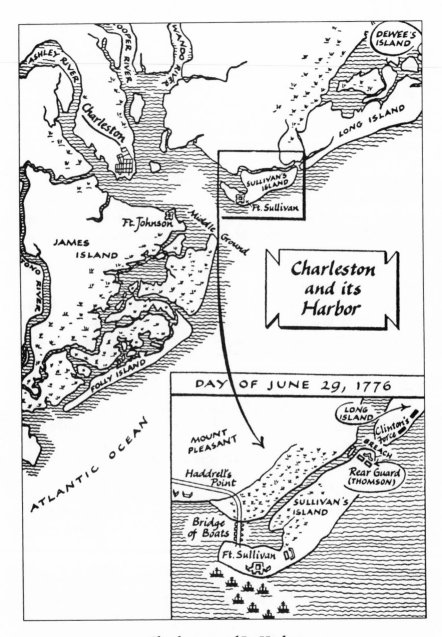

Charleston and Its Harbor

The city of Charleston stood at the tip of a seven-mile-long peninsula that dangled between two rivers and into a bay where the Ashley, Cooper, and Wando Rivers flowed together. The bay, a magnificent natural harbor, was approached from the Atlantic Ocean through an inlet between two low, sandy islands: Sullivan's Island on the northeast side of the inlet and James Island on the southwest side. Forts had been erected, or were being erected, on the harbor ends of both islands—Fort Johnson on James Island and Fort Sullivan on Sullivan's Island.

Fort Johnson mounted twenty heavy guns, and a twelve-gun battery was mounted out from the fort, nearer the city of Charleston. Fort Sullivan, the construction of which had begun in January, was only half completed. It was designed as a square redoubt with bastions at each corner. The rebels were building it with the materials at hand, raising two parallel palmetto-log walls, sixteen feet apart, and filling the space between them with sand. By the last week of June, only the south- and east-facing walls and the two southernmost bastions were finished. On the other half of the fort the walls were built to a height of seven feet, and breastworks had been hastily raised atop them. On the completed walls were mounted twenty-five guns ranging in size from nine-pounders to twenty-five-pounders. Six twelve-pounders were mounted on the unfinished walls, to offer protection from the rear, the north side. The harborside of the city itself was also defended by fortifications on which artillery was mounted.

Any ship trying to reach Charleston would first come under the guns of James and Sullivan's islands. Clinton and Parker drew up a plan to take Fort Sullivan, regarded as the more threatening and more vulnerable of the two forts, and silence its guns. That done, Clinton and Parker believed, Charleston would quickly become the king's.

With Clinton and Cornwallis and their troops aboard, Parker's fleet sailed out of the Cape Fear River on May 31 and reached the islands off Charleston harbor the next day. Bad weather that persisted over the next several days prevented the ships from entering Five Fathom Hole, the channel that led between sandy shoals into Charleston harbor, and Clinton, seeking an alternative route to force his way into the fort, boarded one of Parker's sloops and made a reconnaissance of the harbor islands.

Lying at the northernmost end of Sullivan's Island and extending northeastward along the mainland's slanting coastline was Long Island, separated from Sullivan's Island by a narrow, shallow pass called the Breach, where at low tide, Clinton was told, the water was only eighteen inches deep. Now Clinton made a fateful change in his plans.

Instead of landing his troops on Sullivan's Island, he would land them on Long Island, which would make an easier landing because of that island's gentler surf and because the island was undefended, allowing the troops to land unopposed. While the guns of Parker's warships assailed Fort Sullivan from the south and west, Clinton's troops would go ashore on Long Island, march to its southernmost end, ford the Breach at low tide and assault the fort from the northeast.

It took eight days to disembark the troops, but by June 16 Parker's ships had put ashore on Long Island most of the 2,000 infantrymen and 500 seamen who would attack the fort. They began their march to the Breach as Parker's warships waited for a change in the wind so they could maneuver to begin their bombardment of the fort. The first men to enter the water at the Breach waded only a short distance before they plunged into depths well over their heads. Instead of being eighteen inches deep, the waters of the Breach, they were surprised to discover, were seven *feet* deep. Fording was impossible. With no boats to carry them across, Clinton's army was stuck on desolate Long Island and soon came under harassing artillery fire from Fort Sullivan.

On June 18 Clinton dispatched Brigadier General John Vaughan to inform Parker that the ground force was unable to cross to Sullivan's Island and, while Clinton futilely sought new alternatives, to ask how else might the army aid Parker's fleet in overcoming Fort Sullivan. Vaughan returned to Clinton on June 21 with Parker's response, which to Clinton seemed to imply that the commodore believed he could handle the destruction of the fort with his ships alone, that the assistance of Clinton and Cornwallis's soldiers was not needed.

Parker had planned to commence his bombardment on June 23. Persistent adverse winds, however, prevented his maneuvering his ships into position, and forced him to keep delaying the assault. Shortly after dawn on the morning of June 28, in the cool air that brought relief after days of scorching heat, Parker's men-of-war loosed their topsails and made for the fort. H.M.S. ship *Thunder*, a bomb-ketch, opened fire at a distance of a mile and a half from the fort, blasting the southeast corner with ten-inch mortars while covered by the frigate *Friendship*, carrying twenty-two guns. Parker's flagship *Bristol*, with fifty guns, along with the *Experiment*, also carrying fifty guns, the *Active*, a twenty-eight-gun frigate, and the *Solebay*, also with twenty-eight guns, dropped anchor some 400 to 800 yards south of the fort and commenced firing. Behind them, the *Acteon*, *Syren*, and *Sphinx* maneuvered to form a second line and opened fire, all three of them, like the others, still standing outside the harbor. By ten o'clock, as the day itself grew hot, the guns of all of Parker's warships had come to bear on the fort, filling the damp air with the sound, smell, and smoke of artillery fire. The shot and shell of more than a hundred guns fell unrelentingly on the crude American fort.

Then the ships of the second line started moving into the harbor, to position themselves west of the fort, but as they attempted the maneuver, all three vessels, *Acteon*, *Syren*, and *Sphinx*, ran hard aground on a huge sandbar called the Middle Ground, which partially blocked the entrance into the harbor. After several hours, the *Syren* and *Sphinx* were at last floated free, but both had to withdraw from action to undergo repairs. The *Acteon* remained fast on the sandbar and was finally abandoned and set ablaze by her crew. While the ship was burning, a party of rebels boarded her, turned her guns toward the other ships and fired on them before removing the ship's bell and scrambling overboard. Minutes later the ship blew up and burned down to the waterline.

The remaining ships of Commodore Parker's fleet were taking a punishing fire from the guns of Fort Sullivan. The flagship, the *Bristol*, on which the Americans for a time deliberately concentrated their fire, took seventy hits and lost her mizzenmast and main mast. Her captain, John Morris, had an arm torn off by a cannonball and lay mortally wounded. Parker had his breeches blown off by an explosion and was slightly though painfully wounded. Sixty-four of the crew were killed. The captain of the *Experiment*, Alexander Scott, also had an arm ripped away by shot and was feared to be dying. All of the frigates were damaged. Throughout its battering by the American guns, however, the fleet never slackened its assault.

The target, Fort Sullivan, despite the fierce and prolonged bombardment, suffered little significant damage. The spongy palmetto logs, instead of splintering as other kinds of wood would have done when hit, absorbed the shot, as did the sand that filled the space between the walls. Shells landing between the walls burst harmlessly, buried in the sand. Many of the shells that came into the fort landed in a morass in the center of the fort and were, as the fort's commander and builder, Colonel William Moultrie, put it, "swallowed up instantly." At one point as many as four broadsides struck the fort simultaneously, but when the smoke, sand, and dust cleared from the air, the wall could be seen still standing.

The fort's flag was shot away, disappearing from the view of Parker's seamen as well as the hundreds of spectators who were watching from the high vantage points near the water's edge in Charleston, six miles away.

Fearful that the absent flag might be misunderstood to mean the fort had struck its colors, a sign of surrender, a sergeant inside the fort, William Jasper of Georgia, shouted to Moultrie, "Colonel, don't let us fight without our color." When Moultrie explained that the flag's staff had been shot away, Jasper volunteered to replace it. He spotted the flag where it had fallen to the ground with its shattered staff and he climbed through an embrasure and retrieved it. He fashioned a makeshift staff, attached the flag to it, then stuck the staff onto a merlon of the bastion nearest the British ships. Standing defiantly beside the remounted flag, he shouted three huzzahs while the cannonades from the ships continued, then jumped down and returned to man his gun.

The firing, from the ships and the fort, continued throughout the sultry day, subsiding around sunset and at last ending about 9:30 p.m., the bright muzzle flashes vanishing from the night sky, the booming guns finally falling mercifully silent.

At 11 p.m. the ships of the British fleet slipped their cables and drifted out toward the sea on the ebbing tide. The sentries atop Fort Sullivan watched their lights recede as the fleet returned to its previous anchorage about three miles away. It would not return. The battle for Charleston was over. Its stout-hearted defenders had prevailed.

The British had suffered a defeat they regarded as so humiliating that it would, as one British officer remarked, "scarcely be believed in England." The British had taken some 225 casualties, killed and wounded, most of them aboard the *Bristol* and the *Experiment*. Among the wounded was the deposed royal governor of South Carolina, Lord William Campbell, who had volunteered to help man the *Bristol*'s guns. He later died of his wounds. The vessels of the fleet were so badly damaged that five British seamen who deserted to the rebels reported that the ships' carpenters were "all hard at work, and that we need not expect another visit from them [the British ships] at present." One observer described the ships as in a "very shattered condition."

The numbers vary on the American casualties. The worst of them put the American losses as twelve killed and twenty-five wounded, five of whom later died of their wounds.

After three weeks on mosquito-infested Long Island with little to eat and short of fresh water, the frustrated Clinton and Cornwallis and their troops were retrieved, and the fleet sailed away for New York on July 21.

As his ship carried him away from the disaster, Cornwallis had time to reflect on his first experiences as a British officer at war in America. His impressions could not have been good, either of the operation he had just witnessed or of the two senior officers who had planned and executed it. The inadequacies of the preparations, the intelligence, the logistics, and the plan itself were glaring to a general such as Cornwallis, who knew what such an operation required to be successful.

Being associated with the defeat surely would have galled Cornwallis and perhaps left him wondering about its possible effect on his career. What had been defeated at Charleston harbor was more than the British military forces; it was the southern strategy that had been initiated in London. News of the failure would not be cheerfully received by Parliament, Lord George Germain, or the king.

Still more bothersome must have been Cornwallis's newfound realization that he was having to serve under an officer whose competence as a soldier failed to equal his own. That fact alone was sufficient to preoccupy Cornwallis as his ship bore him north to a new mission that lay worrisomely ahead.

CHAPTER Four

The Battle of Long Island

O n Thursday, August 1, 1776, the forty remaining vessels of Commodore Parker's damaged fleet, one of them bearing Cornwallis, arrived in New York harbor and disembarked some 3,000 troops on Staten Island, in friendly, loyalist territory. The arrival of those vessels set off mixed feelings—apprehension among the rebels, dismay among some of the British. One of the latter, observing Parker's limping flagship, the *Bristol*, remarked that "the arrival of a crippled ship and a defeated officer at this time was very unwelcome; for it infused fresh spirits into the rebels and showed them that ships were sometimes obliged to retreat from batteries."[1]

Already gathered in the harbor were some 150 ships, many of which in March had evacuated General Howe's army from beleaguered Boston and transported it first to Halifax, then to New York, arriving at Staten Island in mid-July. All were vessels of the fleet commanded by Admiral Richard Howe, the commander of all British naval forces in America and brother of General William Howe. Also, there were the vessels that had brought British reinforcements for Howe's Boston veterans, as well as an army of 7,800 Hessian mercenaries under the command of General Leopold Philip von Heister, the crippled veteran of many European campaigns. Altogether the army under Howe's command totaled some 30,000 troops, martialed on Staten Island for a massive assault on Long Island.

The British strategy now was to divide and conquer, cutting off the colonies of New England from the rest of the American colonies by seizing and controlling the Hudson River (known then as the North River), which divided them. The capture of the Hudson River valley would also provide the British with an invasion route from Canada, down the chain of rivers and lakes that led into the heartland of the northern colonies. The first step in that strategy was to force the rebels out of New York, at the mouth of the Hudson, and occupy the city. The best way to do so, the British brass had decided, was to put ashore on Long Island an overwhelming force that would sweep the American defenders from their positions and capture the western end of the island, especially including Brooklyn, which would give access to the East River, across from which stood the mile-square city of New York. Once the western end of Long Island had been captured, the city of New York and all of Manhattan would be vulnerable to another massive British landing.

Washington had long suspected that the city of New York was the object of British intentions. As early as February, while his troops still stood before Boston, he had sent Major General Charles Lee to organize the defense of New York and had ordered reinforcements into defensive positions in New York and on Long Island. In March Lee had been ordered to take charge of the American forces in the south and had been in command at the Battle of Charleston. To replace Lee in preparing for New York's defense, Washington had sent Brigadier General William Alexander, the self-proclaimed earl of Stirling, or Lord Stirling, as he was popularly known. About a month later, following the British withdrawal from Boston, Alexander was succeeded by Major General Israel Putnam, who arrived in New York on April 4. A few weeks later Washington himself came to take command.

The rebels' first line of defense from an attack coming from Long Island was their positions on the Heights of Guan, a thickly wooded, five-mile-long ridge stretching diagonally from southwest to northeast between Flatbush and Brooklyn nearly all the way across the island. Four roads led to Brooklyn, one at the western end of the ridge, the three others through natural passes between the series of hills that made up the ridge. The westernmost road, called the Narrows Road or Gowanus Road, started at Gravesend on the coast and ran along Gowanus Bay as it proceeded to Brooklyn. The next road to the east ran through Flatbush Pass and then forked, Port Road splitting off from Flatbush Road, both leading northwest into Brooklyn. Before Flatbush Road passed through the heights, another road split off from it toward the east; that road turned north, went through Bedford Pass and continued on to the village of Bedford. The fourth road ran northward from Flatlands Village on Jamaica Bay, then eastward to Jamaica Pass, through the heights, then curved westward, passing through Bedford and continuing on to Brooklyn.

About a mile and a half behind the Heights of Guan, to the west, the rebels had built a series of works that formed the main line of Brooklyn's defense. It extended from Gowanus Creek on the southwest to the marshy edges of Wallabout Bay on the northeast. The Americans manning that line would be fighting with their backs to the town of Brooklyn and to the East River.

Before dawn on Thursday, August 22, 1776, after a night of violent, deadly, and perhaps ominous storms, three British frigates and two bomb-ketches maneuvered into position in the Narrows, between Staten Island and Long Island, to join the frigate *Rainbow*, which was already anchored in the Narrows, to support the invasion. At 8 a.m. some 4,000 troops, redcoats, green-uniformed Hessian jagers, and blue-uniformed Hessian grenadiers, the first contingent of the invasion force, boarded an assortment of bateaux, galleys, and miscellaneous small craft and, under the protection of the guns of the *Rainbow*, were swiftly rowed across the Narrows from Staten Island to Denyse Point on the southwestern shore of Long Island. After disembarking their troops, the craft returned to Staten Island to ferry the next contingent across, a 5,000-man force that landed near Gravesend. By noon nearly 15,000 men, the horses of the dragoons, and more than forty pieces of artillery had been carried across the Narrows and landed on Long Island. The landings were unopposed.

Cornwallis had been given command of Howe's reserve, comprising ten light infantry battalions and a corps of Hessian jagers and grenadiers commanded by Colonel Emil Kurt von Donop. Encountering only scattered resistance, Cornwallis's troops drove about four miles inland before encamping at Flatbush. During the night of Monday, August 26 and Tuesday, August 27, Howe set his troops in motion to begin the execution of his plan of attack. The first action occurred on the British left, where a 5,000-man British column, under the command of the vehemently anti-American Brigadier General James Grant, began advancing on the Gowanus Road and ran up against rebel defenders in a skirmish in which the American unit's commanding officer, Major Edward Burd, was taken prisoner and most of his unit withdrew to higher ground.

Howe's plan, reportedly first proposed by Lieutenant General Clinton in an effort to redeem himself after the Charleston disaster, was to engage the Americans on their right and center and keep them occupied there while Howe took his main force of about 10,000 men around the American left to get behind the rebel line. The British column under Grant, its advance guard having pushed past the first American outposts, now encountered rebel units commanded by the so-called Lord Stirling, some 1,600 troops that had been ordered into position on the far side of a creek and a marsh. Grant's force opened up on the rebels with cannon and mortar fire at a distance but made no move to continue its advance. Grant was keeping the American right engaged until he received a signal from his right that Howe had turned the American left flank.

At the American center, whose defenders were commanded by Brigadier General John Sullivan of New Hampshire, a force of Hessians and Highlanders under the command of General von Heister had taken positions on either side of the Flatbush Road, facing Flatbush Pass. They had moved out of Flatbush at 6 a.m., and before daylight they had begun cannonading the rebel positions on the heights there.

Washington himself, meanwhile, stood commanding the line outside Brooklyn, rallying his troops and holding them firm at their posts. One eyewitness reported seeing Washington "walk along the lines and give his orders in person to the colonels of each regiment. . . . I also heard Washington say, 'If I see any man turn his back today, I will shoot him through. I have two pistols loaded, but I will not ask any man to go further than I do. I will fight so long as I have a leg or an arm.' He said the time had come when Americans must be free men or slaves. Quit yourselves like men [he told us], like soldiers, for all that is worth living for is at stake."[2]

Howe's main force, with twenty-eight pieces of artillery, had started moving out from Flatlands about 9 p.m. on Monday, August 26. Howe himself commanded the vanguard. Cornwallis and his units followed the main body. They made a hurried, quiet, nine-mile night march, first heading north up the road from Flatlands, then swinging right before reaching the heights and then again turning north on the Jamaica Road, heading for Jamaica Pass. By 8:30 a.m. on Tuesday, August 27 the leading elements, guided by three loyalists who knew the area, had reached Bedford, directly behind the left end of the American line. Captain Francis Rawdon of the British 63rd Regiment, described the action in a letter: "General Howe . . . marched with the greatest silence towards a pass some miles to the right of Flatbush, which being but little known we thought would be but weakly guarded. The advanced guard under General Clinton consisted of light dragoons, light infantry, grenadiers, and six battalions with some light guns. We got through the pass at daybreak without any opposition, and then turned to the left towards Bedford. When we were within a mile of that town, we heard firing in that part of the mountain where General Grant was expected. We fired two pieces of cannon to let him know we were at hand."

Brigadier General Sullivan, commanding the American center, heard the firing of the signal guns and guessed what it meant—the American left had been turned and the British were now behind his line and to his left while he still faced the enemy in front of him. Sullivan was standing at Flatbush Pass with a force of about 1,000 men, with four artillery pieces, behind a rough works built of felled trees. About a mile to his left, at Bedford Pass, were 800 troops from Connecticut, and just east of them were 400 Pennsylvania riflemen. All now were in jeopardy. Sullivan quickly decided to fall back to the main line of defense outside Brooklyn, wheeling first to face the British advance on his left and leaving a small force that would briefly defend his rear and then fall back as the Hessians and Highlanders began to rush through Flatbush Pass.

British dragoons and light infantry swiftly smashed into Sullivan's new front, overwhelming it. As Sullivan's troops recoiled from the onslaught they were fallen upon by von Heister's troops sweeping through Flatbush Pass. The slaughter began. One of the Hessian colonels recounted it: "The enemy was covered by almost impenetrable brushwood, lines, abatis, and redoubts. The greater part of the riflemen were pierced with the bayonet to the trees. These dreadful people ought rather to be pitied than feared; they always require a quarter of an hour's time to load a rifle, and in the meantime they feel the effects of our balls and bayonets."

Without bayonets of their own, the rebels were unable to defend themselves once they had fired their weapons. Some futilely turned their muskets and rifles into clubs in an attempt to fend off the steadily advancing enemy. Many broke and ran, singly and in groups, frantically trying to escape the trap between Hessians and British. Urged by the British to give no quarter to the rebels who faced their bayonets, the Hessians were merciless. A British officer boastfully recorded the massacre:

> The Hessians and our brave Highlanders gave no quarters, and it was a fine sight to see with what alacrity they despatched the rebels with their bayonets after we had surrounded them so that they could not resist. Multitudes were drowned and suffocated in morasses—a proper punishment for all rebels. . . . It was a glorious achievement, my friend, and will immortalize us and crush the rebel colonies. Our loss was nothing. We took care to tell the Hessians that the rebels had resolved to give no quarter to them in particular, which made them fight desperately, and put all to death that fell into their hands. You know all stratagems are lawful in war, especially against such vile enemies to

their king and country. . . . I expect the affair will be over this campaign, and we shall all return covered with American laurels and have the cream of American lands allotted us for our services.[3]

Many of the rebels, fleeing up Port Road, managed to make it to the American lines outside Brooklyn. General Sullivan, though he escaped death, became a prisoner when the British surrounded him and a large number of other Americans in heavy fighting.

By 11 a.m. Howe's army had swept the ridges clear of rebels, except for the 1,600 troops of Lord Stirling (Brigadier General Alexander) on the American far right, and was within two miles of the defenders' lines outside Brooklyn. Stirling's Maryland and Delaware regiments were being pressed by Hessians moving toward them from the east. The units under Cornwallis's command, the 71st Regiment (Fraser Highlanders) and the 2nd Grenadier Battalion, had moved behind Stirling while Grant's 5,000-man force, reinforced by 2,000 British marines, was attacking Stirling's front.

When Stirling attempted a retreat up the Gowanus Road toward Brooklyn, he found that escape route blocked by Cornwallis's troops and he was then forced to try to ford Gowanus Creek, an 80-yard-wide tidal stream with a swift, now ebbing current that flowed through a broad salt marsh. One of the American fighters later reported the debacle:

> . . . we stood from sunrise till 12 o'clock, the enemy firing on us the chief part of the time, when the main body of the British, by a route we never dreamed of, had surrounded us and driven within the lines or scattered in the woods all our men except the Delaware and Maryland battalions, who were standing at bay with double their number. Thus situated, we were ordered to attempt a retreat by fighting our way through the enemy, who had posted themselves and nearly filled every road and field between us and our lines. We had not retreated a quarter of a mile before we were fired on by an advanced party of the enemy, and those in the rear playing their artillery on us.
>
> Our men fought with more than Roman valor. We forced the advanced party which first attacked us to give way, through which opening we got a passage down to the side of a marsh, seldom before waded over, which we passed, and then swam a river, all the while exposed to the enemy's fire. . . . The whole of the right wing of

our battalion, thinking it impossible to march through the marsh, attempted to force their way through the woods, where they, almost to a man, were killed or taken.[4]

As Grant's force pushed ahead in Stirling's front, Stirling's troops fell under an assault from the east by von Heister's Hessians, and Cornwallis was at their rear. It was that entrapping movement the Americans were desperately fighting and fleeing to evade. Another eyewitness, 15-year-old Private Joseph Plumb Martin of Massachusetts, gave this account:

We were soon called upon to fall in and proceed. . . . Our officers . . . pressed forward towards a creek, where a large party of Americans and British were engaged. By the time we arrived, the enemy had driven our men into the creek, or rather mill pond (the tide being up), where such as could swim got across; those that could not swim and could not procure anything to buoy them up sunk.

The British having several fieldpieces stationed by a brick house were pouring the canister and grape upon the Americans like a shower of hail; they would doubtless have done them much more damage than they did but for the twelve pounder . . . the men having gotten it within sufficient distance to reach them, and opening fire upon them, soon obliged them to shift their quarters.

There was in this action a regiment of Maryland troops (volunteers), all young gentlemen. When they came out of the water and mud to us, looking like water rats, it was a truly pitiful sight. Many of them were killed in the pond and more were drowned. Some of us went into the water after the fall of the tide and took out a number of corpses and a great many arms that were sunk in the pond and creek.[5]

In an attempt to dislodge Cornwallis's troops and to relieve the pressure being applied by them on the fleeing Americans, Stirling ordered Major Mordecai Gist of the 1st Maryland Regiment to lead a 250-man detachment in a thrust at Cornwallis's position athwart the Gowanus Road to the rebels' rear. Gist's courageous Marylanders five times threw themselves against Cornwallis's line and each time were repulsed by Cornwallis's enormously superior numbers. A sixth American assault was defeated when Cornwallis received reinforcements that routed the rebel force. The survivors of Gist's detachment abandoned the fight and fled into the woods. Only Gist and nine of his men managed to escape.

All rebel resistance along the Heights of Guan now ended. The American troops who still had life and legs to do so were scurrying toward their lines outside Brooklyn. Of the estimated 3,500 rebels who had manned the defenses along the heights, at least 312 were believed killed and 1,186 captured, including 89 officers, Stirling and Sullivan among them. Stirling had been surrounded as he attempted to flee and had surrendered himself and his sword to von Heister. Victory had come so quickly that Cornwallis wrote to his mother, Elizabeth, the dowager Countess Cornwallis, saying he was "blessed with the prospect of being soon restored to my family."

Total losses among the estimated 31,625 British and Hessian troops were placed at 377, including 61 British officers and men killed and 288 wounded. The Hessians reported two men killed and three officers and twenty-three men wounded.

The Heights of Guan and their outnumbered defenders had been swiftly, easily overcome, and the overwhelming British force now was poised to flood over the Americans' line of defense—its last—on the eastern edge of Brooklyn. There General George Washington and some 9,500 rebel fighters, the best hope for the survival of the American cause, tensely awaited the massive, decisive assault of redcoats and hired Hessians they believed must soon come.

CHAPTER Five

The Fall of New York

The peril that Washington and his army now faced was annihilation. Confronted by overpowering numbers in his front, Washington was also in danger of having British warships sail up into the East River and block a retreat across the river to New York while bombarding his positions from his rear. In that catastrophic event, Washington and his army, and perhaps the revolution, would be lost.

Throughout the afternoon of August 27, while winds from the north continued to prevent the British men-of-war from sailing northward into the East River, Washington and his army kept an anxious vigil over the ground before their lines, expecting at any moment to see a red-coated enemy horde advancing toward them. The day passed into darkness, and now the fear was a dreaded nighttime assault. Slowly the night also passed, and still no British attack. Across the breadth of the American lines the vigil continued while reinforcements were ferried over from New York to help man the rebel defenses.

During the afternoon of Wednesday, August 28, a steady northeasterly wind brought a cold rain falling from the dreary gray skies into the exposed, already sodden trenches of the American defenders, increasing their discomfort and making it extremely difficult to keep their weapons dry. Following a miserable though uneventful night, daylight crept in on the morning of Thursday, August 29, allowing Washington and his troops to see the reason the British assault had not yet come.

Not more than 600 yards in front of them, on the American left, the unmistakable shape of a redoubt was clearly visible through the continuing rain, its muddy earthworks newly rising from the rain-soaked ground

45

on a site well chosen. Washington instantly realized what it meant. Howe was not going to attempt an immediate massive assault against the American lines. Instead, he was preparing to lay siege to the American position. Probably still pained by the inordinate losses his troops had suffered in their naked assault on the American positions on Breed's Hill, Howe apparently had decided he would not again attempt to overrun American riflemen dug into fortified positions. He had learned a lesson the hard way.

Washington's realization of Howe's present intentions did little to calm his fears. The probability that British warships would sail up the East River as soon as wind and tide permitted remained an enormous threat. Furthermore, with his army divided between New York and Brooklyn, Washington knew he had placed himself at a dangerous disadvantage, unable to concentrate his maximum strength at the point of attack, which he now worried might come from a repositioning British army moving against New York, in his rear, while he was held in check by the besieging force to his front. He had already received reports that British ships were in Flushing Bay, where the East River widens into Long Island Sound, and he wondered if Howe meant to land troops on the mainland and advance on New York from the north, entrapping the divided American army simultaneously in New York and Brooklyn. He must not risk such a possibility. He would have to make a move very soon to avoid it.

On the afternoon of August 29, as the rain continued, Washington assembled the seven generals then commanding in the Brooklyn defenses and held a council of war in the country house of Philip Livingston, the wealthy New York civic leader who had placed his signature on America's Declaration of Independence exactly eight weeks earlier. Washington's big question to his generals, as stated in the minutes of the meeting, was whether "under all circumstances, it would not be eligible to leave Long Island and its dependencies, and remove the Army to New York."

The response of Washington's war council was clear and unanimous: Evacuate.

The daunting task now would be to remove upwards of 10,000 men without being discovered by the enemy who faced them some 600 yards away and who would likely instantly swarm over their abandoned positions and smash into their rear as they retreated toward the Brooklyn ferry landing. With preparations for a withdrawal quickly put into effect following the council of war, the troops, under the cover of darkness, started pulling out about 10 p.m. The evacuation plan called for the units manning posts closest to the enemy to be kept in position until the last possible moment and then be the last units to be ferried across the river.

Even before his council of war met, Washington had ordered Major General William Heath and the army's assistant quartermaster general to collect all available boats and move them to the East River by dark. Those boats, which were gathered at the Brooklyn ferry landing around dusk, would supplement the flotilla of craft the army had been using for weeks to transport men and materiel back and forth across the river. As the wet, weather-weary, dispirited American troops quietly boarded the boats to be rowed across the river in the darkness, Washington himself stood for a time at dockside overseeing their embarkation.

One potentially disastrous hitch developed, giving a frightening shock to the commander in chief. Brigadier General Thomas Mifflin of Pennsylvania had been given command of what would become the rear guard of the evacuating army. His orders were to man the steadily weakening lines right up to the last minute, lest the British detect the withdrawal. About two o'clock on the morning of Friday, August 30, Mifflin received an order to pull his troops back from the line and hurry to the Brooklyn ferry landing to be embarked. The order, which Mifflin questioned, was delivered to him in person by one of Washington's aides-de-camp, Major Alexander Scammell. The incident was later described by Colonel Edward Hand, a regimental commander under Mifflin, who witnessed it:

> Scammell told him [Mifflin] that the boats were waiting, and the Commander-in-Chief anxious for the arrival of the troops at the ferry. General Mifflin said he thought he must be mistaken, that he did not imagine that the General could mean the troops he immediately commanded. Scammell replied he was not mistaken, adding that he came from the extreme left, had ordered all the troops he had met to march; that in consequence they were then in motion and that he would go on and give the same orders. General Mifflin then ordered me to call my advance pickets and sentinels, to collect and form my regiment, and to march as soon as possible, and quitted me.
>
> I obeyed, but had not gone far before I perceived the front had halted, and, hastening to inquire the cause, I met the Commander-in-Chief, who perceived me and said, "Is not that Colonel Hand?" I answered in the affirmative. His Excellency said he was surprised at me in particular, that he did not expect I would have abandoned my post.

I answered that I had not abandoned it, and I had marched by order of my immediate commanding officer. He said it was impossible. I told him I hoped, if I could satisfy him I had the orders of General Mifflin, he would not think me particularly to blame. He said he undoubtedly would not.

General Mifflin just then coming up and asking what the matter was, his Excellency said: "Good God! General Mifflin, I am afraid you have ruined us by so unseasonably withdrawing the troops from the lines."

General Mifflin replied with some warmth: "I did it by your order."

His Excellency declared it could not be.

General Mifflin swore: "By God, I did," and asked, "Did Scammell act as an aide-de-camp for the day, or did he not?"

His Excellency acknowledged that he did.

"Then," said Mifflin, "I had orders through him."

The General replied it was a dreadful mistake and informed him that matters were in much confusion at the ferry and unless we could resume our posts before the enemy discovered we had left them, in all probability the most disagreeable consequences would follow. We immediately returned and had the good fortune to recover our former stations and keep them for some hours longer, without the enemy perceiving what was going forward.[1]

The hours of darkness passed all too quickly for the retreating American troops who, while still embarking for their flight across the East River, were caught in the process by a rising sun on the morning of the 30th. As if by an act of Providence, however, daylight brought with it a dense gray fog, shielding the exodus from the eyes of the enemy. Major Benjamin Tallmadge recounted the final minutes of the evacuation:

As the dawn of the next day approached, those of us who remained in the trenches became very anxious for our own safety, and when the dawn appeared there were several regiments still on duty. At this time a very dense fog began to rise and it seemed to settle in a peculiar manner over both encampments. I recollect this peculiar providential occurrence perfectly well, and so very dense was the atmosphere that I could scarcely discern a man at six yards distance.

When the sun rose, we had just received orders to leave the lines, but before we reached the ferry, the Commander-in-Chief sent one of his aides to order the regiment to repair again to their former station on the line. Colonel Chester immediately faced to the right about and returned, where we tarried until the sun had risen, but the fog remained as dense as ever.

Finally, the second order arrived for the regiment to retire, and we very joyfully bid those trenches a long adieu. When we reached the Brooklyn ferry, the boats had not returned from their last trip, but they very soon appeared and took the whole regiment over to New York, and I think I saw General Washington on the ferry stairs when I stepped into one of the last boats that received the troops. . . .

In all the history of warfare, I do not recollect a more fortunate retreat. After all, the providential appearance of the fog saved a part of our army from being captured, and certainly myself among others who formed the rear guard.[2]

At last, the evacuation was complete. Washington had lost an important battle and the whole of Long Island, including Brooklyn, but more important, he had saved an army. He had managed to remove more than 10,000 men, their provisions and equipment, most of their artillery and their horses, all under the enemy's nose, without being detected. When the fog finally dissipated, the British discovered they now faced no enemy, but only empty trenches. Dismayed by the escape, the British were nevertheless impressed by it. Charles Stedman, a British officer, recorded words of admiration for the Americans' accomplishment: "Driven to the corner of an island, hemmed in within a narrow space of two square miles, in their front . . . near twenty thousand men, in their rear an arm of the sea a mile wide . . . they secured a retreat without the loss of a man."[3]

Criticism of General Howe for failing to press the attack on August 27, while the rebel defenders were reeling from the loss of the Heights of Guan, now rose among British officers and men. Commodore George Collier, captain of the frigate *Rainbow*, expressed in scathing sarcasm the feelings of many of his comrades:

The having to deal with a generous, merciful, forbearing enemy, who would take no unfair advantages, must surely have been highly satisfactory to General Washington, and he was certainly very deficient in not expressing his gratitude to General Howe for his kind behavior towards him. Far from taking the rash resolution of hastily passing over the East River . . . and crushing at once a frightened, trembling enemy, he generously gave them time to recover from their panic, to throw up fresh works, to make new arrangements, and to recover from the torpid state the rebellion appeared in from its late shock.

For many succeeding days did our brave veterans, consisting of twenty-two thousand men, stand on the banks of the East River, like Moses on Mount Pisgah, looking at their promised land, little more than half a mile distant. The rebel's standards waved insolently in the air from many different quarters of New York. The British troops could scarcely contain their indignation at the sight and at their own inactivity; the officers were displeased and amazed, not being able to account for the strange delay.[4]

If Cornwallis felt he was serving under not one general but two less competent than himself, he kept that opinion to himself and did not join Howe's critics. He reserved his criticism for the Americans. "These unhappy people," he wrote to his mother, "have been kept in utter darkness by the tyranny of their wicked leaders and are astonished to hear how little is required of them by Great Britain."

In New York the residents saw a returned army different from the one they had seen go to defend Long Island. The pastor of New York's Moravian church, a Mister Shewkirk, described it in his diary:

In the morning [of August 30], unexpectedly and to the surprise of the city, it was found that all that could come back was come back; and that they had abandoned Long Island, when many had thought to surround the King's troops and make them prisoners with little trouble. . . . It was a surprising change: the merry tones on drums and fifes had ceased, and they were hardly heard for a couple of days. It seemed a general damp had spread, and the sight of the scattered people up and down the streets was indeed moving. Many looked sickly, emaciated, cast down, etc.; the wet clothes, tents—as many as they had brought away—and other things were lying about before the houses and in the streets to dry. In general everything seemed to be in confusion. . . .[5]

The defeat and dejection aroused feelings of discontent among some in Washington's army and a questioning of Washington's ability as a general. Like his British counterpart, General Howe, Washington drew criticism from his countrymen. They found fault with his positioning of his troops in the failed defense of Long Island, with his rejection of cavalry, whose mounted patrols, if used, would have discovered Howe's flanking movement at Jamaica Pass before Howe and Cornwallis were able to reach the rear of the American lines. His critics also faulted him for the unwise division of his troops between Long Island and New York. Colonel John Haslet, commander of the Delaware Regiment that had fought so doggedly and so well under Stirling, openly wished for a replacement for Washington. "The General I revere," Haslet wrote in a letter to Caesar Rodney, a congressional delegate from Delaware and a signer of the Declaration of Independence. "His character for disinterestedness, patience, and fortitude will be had in everlasting remembrances, but the vast burden appears too much his own. Beardless youth and inexperience regimentated are too much about him. The original scheme for the disposition of the army appears to have been on too narrow a scale, and everything almost sacrificed or endangered for the preservation of New York and its environs. . . . We have alarm after alarm. Orders now issue, and the next moment reversed. Would to Heaven General Lee were here, is the language of officers and men."[6]

Griping and second-guessing, a natural part of army life, would continue, Washington probably realized, but he faced so many other problems that he had little time to worry about what had already occurred. The American army's discipline had shattered, and many of the troops who were now crowded into the wet, muddy streets of New York turned to robbery and pillaging of residents and their homes, including the home of the captured Stirling. In some cases, frustrated or aggrieved enlisted men attacked their officers. Washington lamented the contemptible behavior of the men. "The General is sorry to see soldiers, defending their country in time of imminent danger," he wrote, "rioting and attempting to do themselves justice."[7] Many of the troops, he reported, completely disregarded "that order and subordination necessary to the well-being of an army."

Still more alarming were the departures that were presumably precipitated by the defeat and retreat. Washington described to Congress the loss of militiamen:

> The check our detachment sustained [on Long Island] . . . has dispirited too great a proportion of our troops and filled their minds with apprehension and despair. The militia, instead of calling forth their utmost efforts . . . in order to repair our losses, are dismayed, intractable, and impatient to return. Great numbers of them have

gone off, in some instances by whole Regiments, by half ones, and by companies at a time.[8]

New militiamen were arriving from Connecticut and Massachusetts, taking the places of those who had decamped, but the new recruits came reluctantly and without adequate weapons or sufficient equipment. Washington recognized that, as a group, these diffident defenders would probably prove no more dependable than those they replaced. Although his returns indicated he still had under his command in New York some 20,000 effectives, at least one of his chief officers, Brigadier General Hugh Mercer, doubted that Washington could muster from them more than 5,000 reliable fighters.

Most worrisome of all his concerns was the next move of the British, about which Washington could only guess. His first reaction to the rising expectation of an attack on New York was to reorder the city's defenses by restructuring his army, which he now organized into three divisions. One division, composed of five brigades, was posted facing the East River and placed under the command of Israel Putnam. A second division, composed of six brigades, was positioned from Putnam's left flank northward to Harlem Heights. Its command was given temporarily to Joseph Spencer, newly promoted from brigadier general to major general. He would head the division until Major General Nathanael Greene, who had missed the action on Long Island because of illness, was well enough to return to duty. The third division, comprising two brigades, was posted where it could keep watch over Kings Bridge, which spanned Spuyten Duyvil Creek and provided an approach to New York from the Bronx. The third division would also keep watch over the Westchester County shore of Long Island Sound. That division Washington placed under the command of William Heath, also recently promoted to major general.

Particularly troubling to Washington was the enormous advantage their warships provided the British, allowing them to land troops wherever Howe chose. Within a week of the reorganization of his army to defend New York, he was having second thoughts about the worthwhileness of the attempt. Major General Nathanael Greene, sufficiently recovered from his illness to return to duty by September 5, let Washington know that he thought they should not try to defend it, that the city should be put to the torch and abandoned. Two-thirds of the property in New York belonged to Tories anyway, Greene argued. Colonel Rufus Putnam, Washington's chief engineer, thought that trying to fortify the city was a waste of time and energy, since there were so many places where the British might land their forces, from either the East River or the Hudson, or both. Besides that consideration, which Washington realized was hugely important, he wondered about his troops' willingness to fight to save the city. "Till of late," he said, "I had no doubt in my mind of defending this place, nor should I have yet if the men would do their duty, but this I despair of."[9]

He let the Congress know that sooner or later he would have to abandon the city, and Congress let him know that it wanted New York preserved, even if it fell to the British. In a resolution conveyed to Washington, Congress informed him that "General Washington be acquainted that the Congress would have especial care taken, in case he should find it necessary to quit New York, that no damage be done to the said city by his troops on their leaving it." Believing that was a mistaken policy that would eventually give aid and comfort to the enemy, Washington nevertheless set about to do the best that he and his generals, who agreed that the city was indefensible, thought could be done to protect it and stave off its ultimate capture. It was now, on September 8, that Washington wrote to Congress a letter setting forth the danger of making an all-out effort to defend New York, thereby placing in jeopardy other sections of the country—a let's-not-put-all-our-eggs-in-one-basket argument—and also revealing his supreme strategy for the conduct of the war. "History, our own experience, the advice of our ablest friends in Europe . . . ," he wrote, "demonstrate that on our side the war should be defensive . . . that we should on all occasions avoid a general action or put anything to the risk unless compelled by necessity, into which we ought never to be drawn."[10]

To protect Kings Bridge and guard the passage from the Bronx onto Manhattan Island, also known as New York Island, a fortification named Fort Independence had been built just north of the bridge. On a cliff just south of the bridge and overlooking the Hudson River, opposite Fort Constitution on the New Jersey side of the river, Washington's troops were constructing a large earthworks that would come to be called Fort Washington. Washington considered Kings Bridge essential to the defense of New York and his army, for he was now sure that General Howe intended another massive flanking maneuver, the same tactic he had employed so successfully against Washington on Long Island, which would place the redcoats at the Americans' rear and trap them between Kings Bridge and New York.

On September 10 the British landed on Montresor's Island (later renamed Randalls Island), at the mouth of the Harlem River, and occupied it, providing them a base from which to move troops onto the Harlem plains, on Manhattan Island, and into Morrisania, in the lower Bronx, thereby menacing Washington's army with a possible two-pronged assault. The Americans' situation was growing graver by the day.

On September 12 Washington called a new council of war. All but three of the thirteen generals (Joseph Spencer, George Clinton, and William Heath) concurred that they should evacuate all of Manhattan Island except for Fort Washington, where 8,000 troops would be left posted, and do so as quickly as possible. The situation, the majority agreed, was extremely perilous.

What was possible was not quick. There were many tons of supplies and equipment to be removed, plus the sick, who amounted to a quarter of the total American troops on the island, and there were far too few wagons. On September 14 Washington wrote to Congress about the evacuation: "I fear we shall not effect the whole before we shall meet with some interruption."

The feared interruption came the next day, September 15. With wind and tide now in their favor, four British ships ran the American batteries at Fort Constitution and Fort Washington and anchored in the Hudson River above the two works, preventing the evacuation of American troops and supplies by water and threatening to land enemy troops behind the American lines.

At the same time, around dawn, on the other side of the island, five British frigates sailed into Kip's Bay, a wide indentation in Manhattan's east side, several hundreds yards long. Behind them, on the Long Island side of the river, stood six British transports, anchored near the mouth of Newtown Creek. About 10 a.m. 84 flatboats carrying 4,000 British and Hessian troops moved out of the creek and took cover behind the hulls of the transports. About an hour later the frigates began a furious bombardment of the shallow entrenchments the Americans had dug along the river. For over two hours more than seventy guns aboard the frigates pounded the American position while, concealed by the clouds of smoke given off by the cannon fire, the boats bearing the enemy troops glided toward the shore of Kip's Bay.

From his command post in Harlem Washington could clearly hear the fierce bombardment and immediately mounted his horse and galloped off to the sound of the guns. He later reported to Congress what he found when he reached the American lines at Kip's Bay.

> As soon as I heard the firing, I road with all possible despatch towards the place of landing, when to my great surprize and mortification, I found the troops that had been posted on the lines retreating with the utmost precipitation, and those ordered to support

them . . . flying in every direction. . . . I used every means in my power
to rally and get them into some sort of order, but my attempts were
fruitless and ineffectual and on the appearance of a small party of the
enemy . . . they ran away.[11]

About 1 p.m. the cannonade had stopped and the flatboats had put
ashore the 4,000 British and Hessian troops, landing at both ends of the bay's
shore. Panicked, the militiamen posted along those lines frantically fled without firing a shot, completely routed. Five Connecticut militia regiments abandoned their posts and retreated northward. Two brigades that were intended
to support the units in the lines failed to come within a half mile of the Kip's
Bay shore. Young Private Joseph Plumb Martin of Massachusetts, who was
at the site of the action, described the scene and the flight:

> We kept the lines till they were almost leveled upon us, when our offi-
> cers, seeing we could make no resistance, and no orders coming from
> any superior officer and that we must soon be entirely exposed to the
> rake of their guns, gave the order to leave the lines.
>
> In retreating we had to cross a level, clear spot of ground, forty or
> fifty rods wide, exposed to the whole of the enemy's fire. And they
> gave it to us in prime order. The grapeshot and langrage flew merrily,
> which served to quicken our motions. . . .
>
> We had not gone far [along the road] before we saw a party
> of men, apparently hurrying on in the same direction with ourselves.
> We endeavored hard to overtake them, but on approaching them we
> found . . . they were Hessians. We immediately altered our course and
> took the main road leading to King's Bridge.
>
> We had not long been on this road before we saw another party
> just ahead of us, whom we knew to be Americans. Just as we overtook
> these, they were fired upon by a party of British from a cornfield, and
> all was immediately in confusion again. I believe the enemy's party was
> small, but our people were all militia, and the demons of fear and dis-
> order seemed to take full possession of all and everything on that day.
> When I came to the spot where the militia were fired upon, the ground
> was literally covered with arms, knapsacks, staves, coats, hats. . . .[12]

Colonel George Weedon, with the newly arrived 3rd Virginia Regiment,
witnessed Washington's futile attempts to halt the flight of the militiamen
and rally them:

... they were not to be rallied till they had got some miles. The General was so exasperated that he struck several officers in their flight, three times dashed his hat on the ground and at last exclaimed, "Good God! Have I got such troops as those?" It was with difficulty his friends could get him to quit the field, so great was his emotions. . . .[13]

Major General Putnam was sent hurrying southward to retrieve the units of his command and other American units still in New York, including Henry Knox's artillery battalions. After assembling those troops, Putnam found that his planned escape route, the Post Road, was already blocked by a British and Hessian force that greatly outnumbered him. His aide-de-camp, Aaron Burr, then informed him of an alternate route, the Bloomingdale Road, which led northward up the west side of Manhattan, along the Hudson River, and he hastily took the retreating Americans up that road, fleeing north as enemy troops poured into Manhattan from the East River, on the opposite side of the island.

General Howe's plan had been to strike the rebel line at one of its weakest points—Kip's Bay—with 4,000 troops under the command of Lieutenant General Clinton, seize and hold the landing site area, known as Murray's Hill, and then, joined by reinforcements, march south to New York to place themselves at the Americans' rear and, at the same time, with a second force, march west across the breadth of Manhattan to seal off all avenues of escape. The reinforcements, however, some 9,000 troops, did not all arrive until 5 p.m., causing a delay fortunate for the Americans. Howe himself had reached Murray's Hill with his vanguard about 2 p.m., and there he waited idly (some reports said he was detained by a patriotic Quaker housewife who purposefully plied him and his generals with Madeira and cake) till the rest of his force was landed, giving Putnam time to lead some 3,500 rebel troops safely out of New York, which now, abandoned, fell to the British without a fight.

The British assault at Kip's Bay had cost the Americans the loss of 17 officers and an estimated 350 men, most of them believed captured. Many of the Americans who were killed were slaughtered by the Hessians, who shot them or bayoneted them when they tried to surrender.

The British suffered no losses. By the end of the day, Sunday, September 15, 1776, they had gained their objective, the strategic city of New York, its buildings left intact, ready to shelter the enemy army throughout the coming winter. And they had done so without cost.

CHAPTER Six

From Harlem Heights to White Plains

A fter marching north with his troops on the Post Road, paralleling the path of the fleeing Americans to the west of him, General Howe had ended the day (September 15) encamped at McGowan's Pass, a defile where the road passed between two steep hills before rapidly descending to Harlem Plains. His delay, whatever its cause, had not only permitted Putnam and the rebel troops in New York to escape capture but had allowed Washington time to regroup and maneuver.

Early in the morning on September 16, from his command post at Harlem Heights, where he had formed new defensive lines, Washington sent out reconnaissance patrols to discover where the British were and what they were doing. Reports quickly came back to him that the British were about two miles below his forward units and moving toward him. He mounted his horse and set out to see for himself. By the time he reached his advance outposts, he could hear musket fire to the south.

A British advance party, about 300 strong, from the 42nd Highlanders Regiment, the famed Black Watch, had come upon the patrol commanded by Lieutenant Colonel Thomas Knowlton, a detail of 150 Connecticut Rangers, and had fired on them. The Americans had stood and returned the fire until, pressed by the superior British numbers, they were forced to fall back.

The engagement was witnessed by Colonel Joseph Reed, Washington's adjutant general, who was returning from his reconnaissance. He hurried to report it to Washington and later described the incident that followed:

I went over to the General to get some support for the brave fellows, who had behaved so well. By the time I got to him [Washington], the enemy appeared in open view, and in the most insulting manner sounded their bugle horns as is usual after a fox chase. I never felt such a sensation before. It seemed to crown our disgrace.[1]

The bugle call was the one that fox hunters sounded when a fox had been run down; it signaled the end of a triumphant chase. Perhaps angered by the British insolence, Washington ordered a demonstration in the enemy's front, where the redcoats were coming out from the woods, and ordered Knowlton to take his Connecticut Rangers and three rifle companies from the 3rd Virginia Regiment and, while the British were distracted by the demonstration in their front, slip around their left flank and hit them in their rear.

The attack failed to go according to Washington's plan. After a time, he could hear rifle fire, but it came from too far left of the redcoats' position to indicate Knowlton had got behind the enemy. One of Washington's aides-de-camp, Tench Tilghman of Philadelphia, recounted the fight:

Unluckily, Colonel Knowlton and Major [Andrew] Leitch [commanding the Virginia rifle companies] began their attack too soon; it was rather in flank than in rear. The action now grew warm. Major Leitch was wounded early in the engagement and Colonel Knowlton soon after, the latter mortally. He was one of the bravest and best officers in the army. Their men, notwithstanding, persisted with the greatest bravery.

The General [Washington], finding they wanted support, ordered over part of Colonel Griffith's and part of Colonel Richardson's Maryland regiments. These troops, though young, charged with as much bravery as I can conceive; they gave two fires and then rushed right forward, which drove the enemy from the wood into a buckwheat field, from whence they retreated. The General, fearing (as we afterwards found) that a large body was coming up to support them, sent me over to bring our men off. They gave a "huzza" and left the field in good order. . . .

The prisoners we took told us they expected our men would run away as they did the day before, but that they were never more surprised than to see us advancing to attack them. . . .[2]

For the first time, American soldiers had stood up to the vaunted red-coats and bested them in an eyeball-to-eyeball exchange. The fight went into the annals as, in Washington's words, a "brisk little skirmish," but its psychological effect on the American troops was immense. Colonel Reed described it to his wife: "You can hardly conceive the change it has made in our army. The men have recovered their spirits and feel a confidence which before they had quite lost."

Washington, too, noticed. "The affair," he reported to Congress, ". . . seems to have greatly inspirited the whole of our troops." And to his army he wrote this message in his general order for the next day:

> The behavior . . . was such a contrast to that of some troops the day before as must shew what can be done where officers and soldiers will exert themselves. Once more, therefore, the General calls upon offi-cers and men to act up to the noble cause in which they are engaged.[3]

Both the British and the Americans having withdrawn to their lines after the skirmish, the dead of both armies were left on the ground where they had fallen, in the woods and the fields. The Americans had lost an estimated 30 killed and 100 wounded or missing. The British, who in the late stages of the fight had been reinforced by Hessians, lost an estimated 14 killed and 154 wounded, including the Hessian casualties. On the fol-lowing day, September 17, burial parties were sent out from the American lines to handle the grim task of interring friend and foe alike, in the places where they lay.

All was quiet now between the armies. Washington and his generals were divided in their opinions about what Howe would do next. Some believed he would make an all-out effort to take Fort Washington and eliminate every American presence on the island of Manhattan. Having learned, through the recent events on Long Island and at Kip's Bay, of Howe's penchant for flanking maneuvers, others among Washington's generals guessed Howe would make a similar move now, landing a force from Long Island Sound at Morrisania, Hunt's Point, or Throg's Neck (also called Frog's Point) in order to get behind the American lines of defense. Though not at all persuaded that Howe would attempt a frontal assault, Washington nevertheless prepared for it, establishing three paral-lel lines of redoubts and trenches at Harlem Heights, a mile's distance between each. Into those lines he posted 10,000 troops. He ordered another

10,000 to defend against a flanking attack to the east and sent 5,000 troops, under the command of Nathanael Greene, across to the west bank of the Hudson to help with the defense of Fort Constitution, considered vital to the defense of the river. With those deployments in place, Washington and his army vigilantly awaited Howe's next move.

On the night of September 20–21, shortly after midnight, a fire broke out in a wooden building on a wharf in New York and, fanned by a stiff breeze from the south, quickly spread northward, destroying 493 houses before the wind died and the flames were brought under control. New shelter would have to be found for the British and Hessian troops billeted in those houses. The British immediately called the fire the work of rebel saboteurs, though no evidence was found to substantiate the accusation. Commenting on the fire to his brother Lund, Washington didn't conceal his satisfaction. "Providence, or some good honest fellow," he wrote, "has done more for us than we were disposed to do for ourselves."[4] Unfortunately, he pointed out, enough of the city's buildings remained to answer the housing needs of the enemy army.

Lacking a legitimate suspect to arrest and try for the fire, the British vented their wrath on a 21-year-old American officer captured and accused of spying—Nathan Hale, an artillery captain in Colonel Knowlton's Connecticut regiment. Hale apparently had volunteered to slip behind the enemy lines, posing as a schoolteacher (which he had been before the war), and gather intelligence. He had left the American lines at Harlem Heights about September 12 and by a circuitous route had made his way to Long Island. He had acquired sketches of the British fortifications on Manhattan and Long Island and had made notes about them and about the disposition of British troops. On the night of September 21, while in civilian clothes and on his way back to his own lines, he was betrayed by his cousin, Samuel Hale, a Tory and General Howe's deputy commissioner of prisoners. He was arrested and searched and found to be carrying information concerning British army defenses and activities. Taken to Howe on Manhattan, he identified himself as an American officer and admitted he had been gathering intelligence.

Without so much as a token trial, Howe ordered him hanged the next morning. As he stood on the gallows, Captain Hale made a statement that ended with words that were to make him immortal to Americans: "I only regret that I have but one life to lose for my country." He was then hanged.

Washington learned of Hale's execution when in the evening of that same day, September 22, British Captain John Montresor, an aide to General

Howe, came to Washington under a flag of truce to arrange an exchange of prisoners. The British were seeking to exchange Stirling (William Alexander) and Sullivan, both captured during the Battle of Long Island, for loyalist official Montfort Browne, Major Courtlandt Skinner, and Brigadier General Richard Prescott. In passing, Montresor happened to mention that an American officer, Nathan Hale, had been caught spying and hanged that morning. Although Washington perhaps had never known Captain Hale or known of his mission, the young officer's hanging would stick in Washington's memory for months to come.

Washington no doubt, at least temporarily, had taken new heart from his troops' behavior in the skirmish at Harlem Heights, but he nevertheless persisted in his appeals to Congress to improve and strengthen the entire army by eliminating its crippling dependence on militias, whose military value he continued to question and who too often served mostly as bad examples to the Continentals, the regular soldiers of the Continental Army. It was vital to the revolution, he argued in repeated letters to Congress, that militiamen be replaced by soldiers who were recruited, trained, and paid to be professionals, men whose terms of enlistment would extend for years if not for the duration of the war and who would be subject to a discipline necessarily stricter than currently existed. Furthermore, he contended, the army absolutely must have better officers. Good officers, he insisted, were the key to a good army; ". . . the very existence . . . the well doing of every army," he wrote, "depends upon good officers." His army, he asserted, "never had officers, except in a few instances, worth the bread they eat."

Moved by his pleading (and probably by appalling reports received from others), Congress sent a three-man delegation to meet with Washington and his generals where they were encamped. The delegation arrived on or around September 25 and held a series of conferences, from which emerged more candor than Washington had desired to express in writing. As a result, in the end, Congress gave Washington most of what he had been asking. It authorized a standing army of 88 battalions, whose troops would be enlisted, according to the resolution passed by Congress, "to serve during the present war." Enlistment quotas were assigned to each of the 13 provinces. Weapons and other necessities were to be provided by the provinces, instead of by the troops themselves. An enlistment bonus of $20 cash and 100 acres of land were to be given to privates and noncommissioned officers who enlisted for the duration. A clothing allowance was to be paid to them, instead of having the cost of clothing deducted from the soldiers' pay. New standards and higher pay for officers were approved. Congress also approved a new, sterner code of military justice.

All of that was done in hopes of turning Washington's unruly, unreliable troops into an effective army, a hope of which he often despaired. "Such is my situation," he wrote to his brother Lund, "that if I were to wish the bitterest curse to an enemy on this side of the grave, I should put him in my stead with my feelings. . . . I see the impossibility of serving with reputation, or doing any essential service to the cause by continuing in command, and yet I am told that if I quit the command, inevitable ruin will follow. . . . In confidence I tell you that I never was in such an unhappy, divided state since I was born. . . ."[5]

September passed into October without a new move by the British. Howe had gained a reputation for hypercaution and delay, and his refusal to react to the skirmish at Harlem Heights, perhaps owing to a now ingrained reluctance to test the American defenses head on, had only added to it. Indeed, in a report that Howe wrote to Lord George Germain on September 25, he claimed that "The enemy is too strongly posted to be attacked in front, and innumerable difficulties are in our way of turning him on either side." In that report, as he had evidently done before, Howe asked Germain for more troops. On October 12 he received them, British and Hessian, increasing his estimated total troop strength to almost 70,000 men.

On that same day he at last sent his army back to do battle. Under the cover of fog, he embarked a large force on some eighty boats of various sizes, sailed up the East River about 9 a.m. and later began landing some 4,000 men on Throg's Neck, a peninsula that stuck like a bony finger into Long Island Sound at its southernmost end and which, at high tide, became an island when it was severed from the mainland by a tidal creek and marsh.

The move onto Throg's Neck, the apparent spearhead of another flanking maneuver, was one that Washington had anticipated, and the vanguard of Howe's force soon ran into fire from a unit of Colonel Edward Hand's command that had watched the British come ashore. Hand's men had removed the planking from the bridge that spanned the tidal creek, and some thirty Pennsylvania riflemen, firing from concealment behind a pile of wood and later joined by an 1,800-man reinforcement, stymied the entire British landing force. Howe then halted, made camp, inexplicably dallied for six days, then withdrew, re-embarked, sailed up the Westchester County coastline about three miles, and on October 18 came ashore at Pell's Point. Generals Cornwallis and Clinton were each commanding units of Howe's invasion force.

American resistance delayed the British advance from the Pell's Point landing site for an hour and a half or more, but the rebel units eventually had to fall back in the face of immensely superior numbers. Three days later, on October 21, the British had secured a foothold and had occupied the town of New Rochelle, north of Pell's Point.

Receiving reports of the British movements, Washington concluded that, as suspected, Howe intended to contain him between the Hudson River and Long Island Sound and get behind him to attack his rear and cut off a retreat to the north. Howe's next immediate objective, Washington surmised, would be the village and the vicinity of White Plains. Washington quickly ordered his main force northward, and while the British were taking over New Rochelle, the Americans were abandoning their positions on Harlem Heights and hurriedly marching and hauling equipment to White Plains to secure it before Howe and his army of redcoats and Hessians could get there.

Washington's sudden shift of his strength now left Fort Washington and its 3,000-man garrison isolated and on their own. Washington's generals, in view of the fort's strategic importance to the defense of the river and Congress's wish that the river be barred to British ships, had determined that the fort should be held as long as possible. The obstructions that the Americans had placed in the river to prevent British warships and transports from sailing up the Hudson had been proved an insufficient defense when three enemy vessels on October 9 managed to get past them, thereby placing even greater importance on the forts being held. Major General Greene, whom Washington had left in charge of the Hudson River forts when he marched off to White Plains, believed they could be held.

Washington deployed his troops on a three-mile-wide front that ran through the village of White Plains and extended, on its right side, to Chatterton's Hill, an eminence that rose 180 feet above the plain before it. On October 27, after a British advance party had approached the American lines, Washington decided he would have to strengthen his position on Chatterton's Hill, it now seeming critical to his defense of White Plains. He put Colonel Joseph Reed in charge of fortifying the hill, and some 1,600 men, supported by two artillery pieces, were quickly positioned there, in hastily dug trenches. Meanwhile, a force of some 1,500 Continentals and militiamen under Major General Joseph Spencer was ordered out to discover the location of the British and do whatever was possible to delay their approach. That scouting detachment hurried back to the American lines to report that the British were just behind them, advancing up the road from New Rochelle.

Howe's army soon came into view. Howe apparently quickly decided to take Chatterton's Hill and he arrayed his force in front of it. His troops would have to cross the Bronx River, little more than a stump-choked creek, then climb the hill's steep, wooded slopes to gain the top, where the Americans waited in their entrenchments dug into cultivated fields and behind low, stone walls. The British artillery opened fire along the American lines, sending many of the defenders running from their posts. The British cannonade intensified as the redcoats and Hessians formed up on their left and started fording the Bronx River, preparing to storm the hill. Colonel John Haslet of Delaware described the action:

> I received his Excellency's [Washington's] orders to take possession of the hill beyond our lines, and the command of the Militia regiments there posted, which was done. We had not been many minutes on the ground when the cannonade began, and the second shot wounded a militia-man in the thigh, upon which the whole regiment broke and fled immediately, and were not rallied without much difficulty.
>
> Soon after, General McDougall's brigade took post behind us. Some of our officers expressed much apprehension from the fire of our friends so posted. On my application to the general, he ordered us to the right, formed his own brigade on the left and ordered Brooks's Massachusetts Militia still farther to the right, behind a stone fence.
>
> The troops being thus disposed, I went up to the top of the hill, in front of our troops, accompanied by Major McDonough, to reconnoitre the enemy. I plainly perceived them marching to the White-Plain, in eight columns, and stop in the wheat fields a considerable time. I saw their General Officers on horseback assemble in council, and soon their whole body face about and in one continued column march to the hill opposite to our right.
>
> I then applied to General McDougall again to vary his disposition and advised him to order my regiment farther onward and replace it with Colonel Smallwood's, or order the colonel forward, for there was no dependence to be placed on the Militia. The latter measure was adopted.
>
> On my seeing the enemy's march to the creek begin in a column of their main body, and urging the necessity of bringing our field-pieces immediately forward to bear upon them, the general ordered one, and that so poorly appointed that myself was forced to assist in dragging it along the rear of the regiment. While so employed, a cannon-ball struck

the carriage and scattered the shot about, a wad of tow blazing in the middle. The artillerymen fled. One alone was prevailed upon to tread out the blaze and collect the shot. The few that returned made not more than two discharges, when they retreated with the field-piece.

At this time the Maryland battalion was warmly engaged, and the enemy ascending the hill. The cannonade from twelve or fifteen pieces, well served, kept up a continual peal of reiterated thunder. The Militia regiment behind the fence fled in confusion, without more than a random, scattering fire. Colonel Smallwood in a quarter of an hour afterwards gave way also. The rest of General McDougall's brigade never came up to the scene of action.

Part of the first three Delaware companies also retreated in disorder, but not till after several were wounded and killed. The left of the regiment took post behind a fence on the top of the hill with most of the officers, and twice repulsed the Light Troops and Horse of the enemy; but seeing ourselves deserted on all hands, and the continued column of the enemy advancing, we also retired. Covering the retreat of our party, and forming at the foot of the hill, we marched into camp in the rear of the body sent to reinforce us.[6]

Washington pulled in his collapsed right flank. Howe didn't pursue, but instead began positioning his artillery to be able to rake the entire American line. Washington, as quickly as he could move his supplies and equipment, began evacuating White Plains. He also shifted some of his troops to higher ground above White Plains, and on the night of October 31 he withdrew his army to North Castle, a stronger defensive position, about five miles farther north of White Plains, across the Croton River. There the rebels dug in and awaited a new British assault. For several days neither side moved, each guardedly eyeing the other.

On the morning of Tuesday, November 5, American forward sentries, who had heard the sounds of gun carriages rumbling off during the night, discovered that Howe's army had vanished. Two nights earlier an American deserter, William Demont, an English immigrant who had become a lieutenant and adjutant of a Pennsylvania regiment, had stolen out of Fort Washington and come to Howe's headquarters with a plan of the fort and the details of its defenses. With Demont's information in hand, Howe had abruptly decided it was time to capture that rebel stronghold and so had swiftly withdrawn from the engagement at White Plains, having accomplished nothing.

CHAPTER Seven

The Shattered Army

Fort Washington was a crude, five-sided earthworks surrounded by abatis that covered an area of about four acres. It was built on a hill called Mount Washington, atop a heavily wooded plateau that rose nearly vertically about 100 feet above the Hudson and Harlem Rivers. Its occupation by rebels remained a strategic obstacle to British dominance of Manhattan and the city of New York and to the British plan to command the Hudson River.

Among the things the fort lacked were protective casemates, a defensive palisade, barracks to shelter its garrison, and an independent source of water, but its commander, Colonel Robert Magaw, believed it could be held against the enemy until the end of December and, before it was yielded, its garrison and stores could be removed and ferried safely across to the New Jersey side of the Hudson.

Washington had his doubts. If British ships could evade the obstructions in the river and the guns of the fort, as they had done on November 5, Washington wondered about the worthwhileness of trying to hold the fort, but left it up to Nathanael Greene, commanding the two river forts from his position on the New Jersey side, to decide on its evacuation. In a letter written on November 7, Washington warned Greene to expect an attack upon the fort and possibly a move into New Jersey. The next day, in another letter, Washington urged Greene to remove or destroy all of Fort Washington's stores and provisions not needed for its immediate defense, lest they fall into the hands of the enemy.

Greene demurred. "I cannot help thinking," he replied to Washington on November 9, "that the garrison is of advantage and I cannot conceive it to be in any great danger. The men can be brought off at any time, but the stores may not so easily be removed. Yet I think they can be got off in spite of them, if matters grow desperate. . . ."[1]

On the morning of Sunday, November 10, Washington moved from his position outside White Plains. He ordered odd Major General Charles Lee, recently returned from service in Charleston and Philadelphia, to command the 7,000 troops that would be left at North Castle to guard against the possibility that Howe's movement was merely a feint. He posted Major General William Heath with a force of some 4,000 troops to Peekskill, New York, to defend against a British advance up the Hudson River valley. Taking with him about 2,000 Virginia and Maryland troops, which he believed could be reinforced by New Jersey militia and the so-called Flying Camp, a mobile strike force already in New Jersey, Washington crossed the Hudson. After reconnoitering the Hudson highlands, he turned south and reached Hackensack, New Jersey, west of Fort Lee (the recently renamed Fort Constitution) on the evening of November 13. There he conferred with Greene, who again assured him that Fort Washington could be held and informed him that he had not removed the stores but had strengthened the garrison. Greene reminded Washington of Congress's directive to hold the fort as long as possible. Against his better judgment, and probably with more confidence in Greene's abilities than in Greene's assurances, Washington acceded.

On the morning of Friday, November 15, Howe sent his adjutant general, Lieutenant Colonel James Paterson, along with a drummer who beat the signal for a parley and a soldier bearing a white flag, to deliver an ultimatum to Fort Washington's commanding officer, Colonel Magaw. Howe demanded that Magaw surrender the fort and its garrison within two hours or be wiped out, with every defender to be put to the sword. Magaw sent Paterson back to Howe with a blunt message of refusal.

During the night of November 14–15, the British, using some thirty flatboats, had transported a force up the Hudson, into Spuyten Duyvil Creek, and down the Harlem River to an assembly area east of the fort. On the morning of the 15th, Lieutenant General Wilhelm von Knyphausen, commanding a force of 3,000 Hessians, crossed Kings Bridge from the north. Behind him came two light infantry battalions commanded by Brigadier General Edward Mathews. Cornwallis, commanding two guards battalions, two battalions of grenadiers, and his own 33rd Regiment, crossed behind Mathews around noon. General Hugh Percy, commanding the troops that Howe had left posted at McGowan's Pass, moved toward the fort's outposts from the south.

The attack began from the north, whence two columns of Hessians, the left column under the command of Knyphausen, the right one commanded by Colonel Johann Gottlieb Rall, approached the fort along the ridges that led from the Harlem River. The two columns merged in front of the north face of the fort and scaled the rocky precipice to launch their assault with artillery and musket fire. At the same time, the force of redcoats and Hessians under General Percy swept quickly through the first line of American defenders on the south, but ran into stubborn resistance from the rebels entrenched in their second line of defense. Cornwallis shifted two battalions southward to reinforce Percy and to strike the flank of that rebel line, which he soon overcame with his superior numbers, sending the surviving defenders dashing for the protection of the fort.

While the combat raged, Washington, accompanied by Generals Greene, Putnam, and Hugh Mercer, commander of the Flying Camp, crossed the Hudson and climbed up into Fort Washington to get an onsite view of the battle. Apparently deciding there was nothing they could do to help, Washington and his three generals withdrew and recrossed the river to Fort Lee, leaving Colonel Magaw to do the best he could.

Fifteen minutes later, according to one report, British troops occupied the spot where Washington and his generals had stood to overlook the battle. Knyphausen's Hessian regiments, meanwhile, despite having come under heavy fire from the fort, had driven the rebel defenders from their positions behind the breastworks on the north side of the fort. By the next morning, Sunday, November 17, the fort had suffered a furious, wall-crushing artillery bombardment and stood virtually surrounded by redcoats and Hessians, poised with fixed bayonets to charge the fort's smashed earthworks.

The Hessian Colonel Rall called for a temporary ceasefire and ordered one of his officers to tie a white cloth onto a musket barrel, go up to the fort with a drummer beating for a parley and deliver to the Americans a new demand for their surrender. Braving the rebels' fire, the officer, a Captain Hohenstein, did so, reaching the American lines safely despite scattered musket fire. He was led by rebel soldiers to the fort's second-in-command, Colonel John Cadwalader. Hohenstein reported on the meeting:

> I made the following proposal: He should immediately march out of
> the fort with the garrison, and they should lay down their arms before
> General von Knyphausen. All ammunition, provisions, and whatever

belonged to Congress should be faithfully made known. On the other hand, I gave him my word that all, from the commanding officer down, should retain their private property. Finally, a white flag should be immediately hoisted to put a stop to hostilities.[2]

When Hohenberg's proposal was related to Colonel Magaw, Magaw asked for four hours to consider it. Hohenberg refused, allowing him but thirty minutes to confer with his officers. Hohenberg then offered to take Magaw to Knyphausen himself, who, he said, was just a hundred paces away, to whom Magaw might appeal for better terms. Magaw accepted the offer, but received nothing more from Knyphausen. Magaw then accepted the terms and at three o'clock that afternoon capitulated. About an hour later his troops began coming out of the fort.

Two long rows of Hessian soldiers, one the regiment of Colonel Rall and one the regiment of Colonel Lossberg, were formed up facing each other outside the fort to receive the American colors and to have the American troops pass between them and give up their weapons. A British officer who witnessed the event described the Americans as they dejectedly streamed out:

> The rebel prisoners were . . . very indifferently clothed. Few of them appeared to have a second shirt, nor did they appear to have washed themselves during the campaign. A great many of them were lads under fifteen and old men, and few had the appearance of soldiers. Their odd figures frequently excited the laughter of our soldiers.[3]

As the Americans trooped from the fort, many of them were stripped of their meager belongings, including the clothes they were wearing, in violation of the Hessians' assurances.

Following the surrender, General Howe reported that 2,818 American officers and men had been captured and 53 killed. An estimated 250 were wounded, presumably all of them taken prisoner. The entire garrison had been lost, along with artillery, muskets, ammunition, tents, entrenching tools, and other equipment.

Of some 8,000 British and Hessian troops that took part in the engagement, the British lost 20 killed and 102 wounded, and the Hessians lost 58 killed and 272 wounded.

Three days later, on Wednesday, November 20, Howe gave Cornwallis 4,500 men and ordered him across the Hudson to seize Fort Lee. Cornwallis now, for the first time since he had arrived in America, would be operating on his own. It was an opportunity to show what he could do, perhaps do better than others, and it was, no doubt, more like what he imagined when he volunteered.

His crossing was made in the rain during the hours before dawn on Wednesday, his troops pushing out into the river from a point below Dobbs Ferry and landing on the opposite bank about six miles above Fort Lee. The stealth of the attack was lost, however, when the leading elements of Cornwallis's force, moving south on the road to the fort, encountered an American mounted patrol, which hurriedly wheeled and galloped back to the fort to warn Greene.

Roused from his bed, Greene quickly ordered an evacuation of the fort, the troops moving out so swiftly that they left their kettles heating over their fires and their tents standing. Cornwallis's troops arrived in time to capture some 150 stragglers outside the fort and 12 rebels who were too drunk to flee with their comrades, but the great bulk of the garrison had escaped. Left behind in their haste were several hundred muskets, about 50 pieces of artillery, all their entrenching tools, much of their baggage, 1,000 barrels of flour, and about 300 tents. The flight of those who escaped, between 2,000 and 3,000 men, took them west as they raced for the Hackensack River, where, on the west side, Washington was trying to regroup his shattered army.

Desperate for reinforcement, Washington dispatched orders to Major General Charles Lee, commanding the force left outside White Plains, to turn over the defense of the Hudson highlands to Major General Heath and hurry across the Hudson with his force of about 7,700 troops, urgently needed to replenish Washington's disintegrating army. Faced with an imminent attack from Cornwallis, Washington fell back to the southwest, across the Passaic River to Newark, giving up the flat country between the Hackensack and Passaic Rivers in search of ground that offered more protection for defenders who had lost their entrenching equipment.

Having gained possession of Fort Lee and having been reinforced by nine battalions, Cornwallis now turned his force to the southwest, intent on overtaking Washington and the tattered, retreating rebel army. On Tuesday, November 25, in weather turned suddenly wintry, he marched his long column doggedly toward Newark, hoping to succeed at a task where his superior had failed.

He reached the outskirts of Newark on Friday, November 28, his advance units arriving in Newark just as Washington's rear guard scurried out on the other side of town, headed south toward New Brunswick. Enlivened by the growing prospect of at last catching Washington in flight, Cornwallis ordered his troops to press on. The march was not unhindered. Rebel snipers fired on the British troops from concealment in the woods on either side of the line of march. When detachments of redcoats were sent into the woods after the rebels, the Americans ran off, refusing an engagement. Then after the detachments had rejoined the march, the rebels would reappear and open fire on the marchers once more, harassing them as much as possible in an attempt to slow their progress. Cornwallis cautiously put flankers out on both sides of his column to seek out possible ambushes. It was also necessary for him to form work details to clear the road of trees the rebels had felled to impede the British wagons and artillery carriages. The rebels had also torn up bridges that had to be hastily repaired.

After some twenty additional miles of pursuit in bad weather over worse roads, Cornwallis's army reached New Brunswick on Monday, December 1. There Cornwallis discovered that his quarry had outrun him and his troops, who, like the stout horses drawing their baggage wagons and artillery, were now exhausted by the chase. In their haste to run down the rebels, Cornwallis's men hadn't even taken time to bake bread to feed themselves. They were subsisting on raw flour.

Further frustrated by the rebels' destruction of the bridge over the Raritan River, Cornwallis at New Brunswick ordered his ill-fed, weary, and cold army to a halt. Actually, his orders from Howe were to proceed no farther than New Brunswick, but few doubted his willingness to interpret those orders to suit his purpose had he the stomach for further pursuit deeper into unfriendly country, particularly at a time of year when it was normal for professional soldiers to be thinking not of fighting but of holing up in comfortable winter quarters. In giving those orders, Howe perhaps thought Cornwallis's force would not be strong enough to defend itself if it were drawn any deeper into enemy territory. It would be safer for Cornwallis to wait till Howe's reinforcements could reach him.

In any case, the halt proved controversial. Cornwallis later defended it against critics who were certain that if he had sought a ford of the Raritan and continued to press the pursuit, he would have caught Washington and the rebels with their backs to the Delaware River. "I could not have pursued the enemy from Brunswick with any prospect of material advantage or without greatly distressing the troops under my command," Cornwallis insisted. "But had I seen that I could have struck a material stroke by moving forward, I certainly should have taken it upon me to have done it."[4]

On December 6, a week after Cornwallis had halted, a column led by Howe caught up to him at New Brunswick, and Howe assumed command of the reunited army. The next day, Saturday, December 7, Howe ordered the entire force to resume the southwestward march, sending Cornwallis's units ahead of his to form the vanguard.

About 4 p.m. on Saturday the lead elements of the long British column arrived in Princeton, scarcely an hour after the rebels' rear guard had pulled out. Howe commandeered the buildings on the campus of the college to house his troops and ordered them to bed down there for the night. At about nine o'clock the next morning, Sunday, December 8, they were back on the road, resuming the march.

Around 2 p.m. that Sunday, after a wearing march through the intensifying cold, Cornwallis's vanguard reached Trenton, on the banks of the Delaware River, just in time to see the last elements of Washington's bedraggled army slipping away to the Pennsylvania side of the river in the only available boats. Washington, with notable forethought, had seized or destroyed every usable boat within 75 miles. Once again he had escaped, but narrowly. Some thought it uncanny. One of Howe's officers, Charles Stedman, commented that it was as if Howe "had calculated . . . with great accuracy the exact time necessary for his enemy to make his escape."

Howe was satisfied that the chase was over and decided to call it a year. The British campaign of 1776 was ended. The bulk of Howe's army could now march off to their winter quarters. Left posted along the route they had just come would be 3,000 Hessians in Trenton and Bordentown, facing the Americans across the Delaware, and 3,000 redcoats in Princeton, New Brunswick, and Amboy, all of whom could be moved quickly toward a rebel army that might decide to recross the Delaware. The rest of Howe's army would return to New York for the winter. No one was more eager than Howe to get back to New York, where his mistress, the pretty, young, blond wife of Joshua Loring, Howe's commissary of prisoners, was waiting to share a snug bed with the forty-seven-year-old general.

Feeling expansive, Howe in his general orders for Saturday, December 14, saluted Cornwallis's efforts in the campaign, declaring that the earl's pursuit of Washington was "much to the honor of his lordship and the officers and soldiers under his command."

Also presumably pleased to call it quits for the year, a homesick Cornwallis asked permission to return to England. Leave was granted, and he started for New York, there intending to board a ship for home.

On the Pennsylvania side of the Delaware, behind a thin defensive line strung out along the river some thirty miles, Washington brooded in near despair. At one point he spoke to his adjutant, Colonel Joseph Reed, about continuing the retreat all the way to Virginia and if defeat seemed inevitable, he would attempt to escape the British hangman by crossing the Allegheny Mountains. His army had diminished to fewer than 4,000 effectives, including Nathanael Greene's troops who had fled from Fort Lee. Furthermore, his little army was about to become still smaller, for enlistment terms were about to run out. The enlistments of nearly all the Continental regiments except those from Virginia and Maryland would expire at the end of December. For days he had hoped, even expected, to be reinforced by Charles Lee's force, but every communication from Lee gave some new excuse for delay.

Washington felt sure that the British plan was to cross the Delaware and drive on to Philadelphia, which, he believed, was Howe's objective. Only the lack of boats, he assumed, was holding Howe back. One report he received said that Howe was bringing boats with him. With winter deepening, it was only a matter of time, Washington further feared, before boats would be unnecessary, for the Delaware River would freeze over and the British could march across it on solid ice. The situation was absolutely desperate. Unless Lee and his troops arrived soon, Washington's army, or the residue of what had been an army, would be forced into a final flight and would cease to be a fighting force. The light of American freedom was flickering dangerously, and Washington, better than anyone, knew it.

Having repeatedly ordered Lee to bring his army from White Plains, and having repeatedly been insubordinately ignored or refused, Washington now humiliatingly turned to pleading for Lee to come. "Do come on," he wrote to him. "Your arrival may be happy, and if it can be effected without delay, may be the means of preserving a city, whose loss must prove of the most fatal consequences to the cause of America."[5]

It was December 4 when Lee at last crossed the Hudson and marched, inexplicably for someone who should have been hurrying southward, north to Pompton, very much out of the way, then south to Morristown. By December 12 he had reached a spot several miles southwest of Morristown, not far from Basking Ridge. With his army encamped there for the night, Lee decided he would seek more pleasurable arrangements at a tavern run by a widow in Basking Ridge, about three miles distance from his troops' camp. He took with him a six-man personal guard and some of the members of his staff and apparently caroused far into the night.

The next morning, December 13, while his troops struck their tents and resumed their march, Lee languished at the widow's tavern in his dressing gown and slippers, writing a complaining letter about Washington to Horatio Gates. About 10 a.m. he was finishing the letter as breakfast was served. One of the officers at the table with him was Captain James Wilkinson, who described what then occurred:

> I had risen from the table and was looking out of an end window down a lane about one hundred yards in length which led to the house from the main road, when I discovered a party of British dragoons turn a corner of the avenue at a full charge.
>
> Startled at this unexpected spectacle, I exclaimed, "Here, Sir, are the British cavalry!"
>
> "Where?" replied the general, who had signed his letter in the instant.
>
> "Around the house;" for they had opened files and encompassed the building.
>
> General Lee appeared alarmed, yet collected, and his second observation marked his self-possession: "Where is the guard? Damn the guard, why don't they fire?" and after a momentary pause, he turned to me and said, "Do, Sir, see what has become of the guard."
>
> The women of the house at this moment entered the room and proposed to him to conceal himself in a bed, which he rejected with evident disgust. I caught up my pistols which lay on the table, thrust the letter he had been writing into my pocket, and passed into a room at the opposite end of the house, where I had seen the guard in the morning. Here I discovered their arms, but the men were absent. I stepped out of the door and perceived the dragoons chasing them in different directions, and receiving a very uncivil salutation, I returned into the house.
>
> Too inexperienced immediately to penetrate the motives of this enterprise . . . and from the terrific tales spread over the country of the violence and barbarity of the enemy, I believed it to be a wanton murdering party, and determined not to die without company. I accordingly sought a position where I could not be approached by more than one person at a time, and with a pistol in each hand I awaited the expected search, resolved to shoot the first and second person who might appear, and then to appeal to my sword.
>
> I did not remain long in this unpleasant situation, but was apprised of the object of the incursion by the very audible declaration,

"If the general does not surrender in five minutes, I will set fire to the house;" which after a short pause was repeated with a solemn oath; and within two minutes I heard it proclaimed, "Here is the general. He has surrendered."

A general shout ensued, the trumpet sounded the assembly and the unfortunate Lee mounted on my horse, which stood ready at the door, was hurried off in triumph, bareheaded, in his slippers and blanket coat, his collar open, and his shirt very much soiled from several days' use.[6]

A mounted British patrol commanded by Lieutenant Colonel William Harcourt (who had served under Lee in Portugal when Lee was a British lieutenant colonel) had been tipped off that Lee was lodging at the tavern and had sped to capture him. The swift charge up to the building had been led by a twenty-two-year-old officer named Banastre Tarleton.

Washington learned of Lee's capture in a report from Major General John Sullivan, Lee's second in command. Washington wrote back to Sullivan an "oh well" response. "The event has happened," he said in his letter. Now Sullivan was in command, which was obviously for the best, and, Washington hoped, Sullivan would speed his troops southward to join him. Washington also continued to plead with Congress for additional new troops.

Sullivan arrived at Washington's camp on Saturday, December 20, with 2,000 troops, all that remained of a 7,700-man force diminished by desertions and enlistment expirations. When Sullivan's troops were added to the 500 troops of Horatio Gates (all that remained of seven regiments), who had arrived at almost the same time as Sullivan, and Washington's own force, Washington's army at the moment amounted to 7,659 effectives, according to regimental returns, a figure that included the militiamen who had joined Washington during his march through New Jersey. Washington had repeatedly urged the governments of New Jersey and Pennsylvania to send him troops, without much success.

Howe had offered pardon to all citizens who would renounce their American leaders and declare their allegiance to the king, and colonists disheartened by the ineffectualness of their army were accepting the offer in significant numbers. British and Hessian troops, without restraint, were terrorizing the populace in New Jersey, marauding, raping, and stealing indiscriminately among loyalists and patriots alike. In the face of those atrocities and the apparent indifference of many of his countrymen, who had repeatedly spurned calls to service or had cowardly fled at the first exposure to danger, Washington became exasperated.

Now winter was deepening, and the American army was nearly destitute, many of the men without boots or shoes, lacking warm clothes and blankets, posted out in the snow and freezing temperatures along a tenuous line of defense. The terms of enlistment of most were less than two weeks from expiring. The situation was altogether bleak. Thomas Paine, who had made a name for himself with the publication of *Common Sense*, had endured the long retreat with his comrades from Fort Lee, and now at Washington's camp on the Delaware he penned new eloquence that might rouse from apathy a needed new army to carry on the fight:

> These are the times that try men's souls. The summer soldier and the sunshine patriot will, in this crisis, shrink from the service of their country; but he that stands it *now* deserves the love and thanks of man and woman. Tyranny, like Hell, is not easily conquered; yet we have this consolation with us, that the harder the conflict, the more glorious the triumph.[7]

As if in response, Washington, far from being a summer soldier, was thinking new thoughts. He had grown tired of running, of losing, and of criticism. After so many defeats and failures, after so much frustration and hopelessness, what he fervently desired—what he and his countrymen desperately *needed*—was a victory. He began planning one.

CHAPTER Eight

The Raid on Trenton

The 3,000 Hessian troops that General Howe had posted on the banks of the Delaware River were nearly evenly divided between Trenton and Bordentown, a village about five miles downriver from Trenton. The 1,400-man garrison posted in Trenton included three regiments plus a detachment of jagers (an elite infantry corps), an artillery company with six three-pounder field guns, and twenty British dragoons. The three regiments were those of Colonel Rall, Colonel von Lossberg, and General von Knyphausen.

It was Rall's and Lossberg's regiments that had formed parallel lines between which the defeated American troops pouring out of Fort Washington were forced to pass to surrender their colors. They were the regiments whose men, among others, had laughed at the ragged Americans and had stripped from many of the prisoners the clothes they were wearing.

Rall, fifty-six years old, was a veteran of European conflicts and had gained a reputation as a hard fighter and a hard drinker. He was in command of the garrison at Trenton. At Bordentown the garrison was commanded by Colonel Carl Emil Kurt von Donop, who was in overall command at both Bordentown and Trenton.

Despite orders to do so, Rall had not bothered to build fortifications at Trenton, feeling confident enough against the "country clowns," as he called the American troops, to turn them back without his men having to go to the trouble of digging entrenchments in the frozen ground and heaping up muddy breastworks or redoubts. "Let them come," he boasted in German, disdaining to learn any English. "We want no trenches. We will go at them with the bayonet."

Apparently without worry that the Americans might dare face his Hessians, Rall had not posted sentries outside Trenton, nor had he troubled himself to inspect his troops' defenses. Neither had he positioned his six field pieces to defend likely avenues of approach to Trenton. Instead, he had mounted two of them outside his headquarters building as martial ornaments. He satisfied himself of his troops' readiness by having them assembled in parade formation and ceremonially inspecting them as they stood at rigid attention.

Washington had received intelligence on the disposition of the Hessians across the river from his lines and although he believed the strength of the garrison at Trenton to be greater than it was, between 2,000 and 3,000 troops, he thought, he believed his plan to attack it would work. It was of extreme importance, though, that the attack be made quickly. His army was melting away at the same time plummeting winter temperatures were freezing the waters of the Delaware, which meant he would soon lose a large part of his fighting force and the protection of the river as well. Now was the hour. He wrote to his adjutant, Colonel Joseph Reed, then in Philadelphia, telling what he planned to do:

> Christmasday at night, one hour before day, is the time fixed upon for our attempt on Trenton. For Heaven's sake keep this to yourself, as the discovery of it may prove fatal to us, our numbers, sorry am I to say, being less than I had any conception of; but necessity, dire necessity, will, nay must, justify an attempt. . . . If I had not been fully convinced before of the enemy's designs, I have now ample testimony of their intentions to attack Philadelphia so soon as the ice will afford the means of conveyance.[1]

Washington's plan called for a three-pronged attack involving river crossings at three different points. He would take the main force of 2,400 men across the river at McKonkey's Ferry, about nine miles above Trenton, then divide his army into two paralleling columns, one commanded by Nathanael Greene and one by John Sullivan, and march on Trenton from the north. This main force would include six batteries of artillery equipped with eighteen field pieces, under the command of Colonel Henry Knox, the former Boston bookseller.

At the same time, Colonel John Cadwalader would take a 1,900-man force, mostly militia and including two artillery companies, across the river near Bristol, Pennsylvania, landing below Bordentown and attacking von

Donop's positions in a diversionary move to prevent von Donop from reinforcing Rall at Trenton.

Between that southernmost crossing and Washington's crossing a third force, 700 Pennsylvania and New Jersey militiamen under the command of Brigadier General James Ewing, would cross at Trenton Ferry and seize the bridge over Assunpink Creek, on the south side of Trenton. They would establish a line on the south bank of the creek and seal off Rall's escape route south to Bordentown.

The timing and coordination of the three separate crossings and attacks would have to be near perfect if all was to go according to plan. All three divisions of the assault forces would have to be across the river by midnight of Christmas, in order to allow Washington enough time to march an estimated five hours through the night to reach Trenton and deploy his main force to strike the Hessians an hour before daybreak on December 26.

The success of the raid depended on, first of all, sufficient boats and boat handlers to swiftly ferry Washington's 2,400-man assault force across the Delaware. The job of providing both boats and boatmen fell to Colonel John Glover of Marblehead, Massachusetts, whose infantry regiment included a large number of commercial fishermen skilled at handling boats. It was Glover's fishermen-soldiers who in August had rescued Washington's army in the remarkable overnight evacuation of Brooklyn, rowing them across the East River to New York. It was also Glover's fishermen-soldiers who had brought the present rebel army across the Delaware to escape Cornwallis. Now Washington and the American cause were once again depending on them.

As part of his preparations for the raid, Washington called in surgeons who would be needed to tend the wounded. He had ordered Doctor William Shippen, stationed at the army hospital in Bethlehem, Pennsylvania, to come immediately. He also called in Doctor Benjamin Rush of Philadelphia (a signer of the Declaration of Independence) and conferred with him three days before the raid was scheduled to occur. Doctor Rush wrote about that meeting with Washington:

> On the [23rd] of December, I visited General Washington . . . at
> the General's quarters about ten miles above Bristol and four from the
> Delaware. I spent a night at a farmhouse near to him, and the next
> morning passed near an hour with him in private. He appeared much
> depressed and lamented the ragged and dissolving state of his army
> in affecting terms. . . .

While I was talking to him, I observed him to play with his pen and ink upon several small pieces of paper. One of them by accident fell upon the floor near my feet. I was struck with the inscription upon it. It was, "Victory or Death.". . . I believe . . . he had been meditating upon his attack upon the Hessians . . . for I found that the countersign of his troops at the surprise of Trenton was, "Victory or Death."[2]

On the evening of Tuesday, December 24, Christmas Eve, Washington assembled a group of his chief officers for a council of war at the house of Samuel Merrick, where Nathanael Greene was staying, not far from where Washington's main force would cross the Delaware. There he laid out the plan for them. Those present were Generals Greene, Stirling (William Alexander), Sullivan, Hugh Mercer, Arthur St. Clair, Adam Stephen, Matthias Alexis de Roche Fermoy, and Colonels Henry Knox (who would be promoted to brigadier general three days later), John Glover, Paul D. Sargent, and John Stark. Also attending were two of Washington's military secretaries and a preacher, a Mister McWhorter, who apparently was something of a chaplain to some of the generals and whose opinions were evidently valued by them. Over a dinner of cold meat and beer, Washington handed out the assignments to his commanders. Written orders would be dispatched to the two other division commanders, Cadwalader and Ewing.

When the council concluded, Washington, his mind still clear after several rounds of Madeira, stayed on to dictate detailed orders to his brigade commanders. It was well after midnight before the generals and colonels left, and even later when Washington left. Snow had begun falling on Monday afternoon, December 23, and had continued throughout the night so that on Christmas Eve it was obvious there was going to be a white Christmas, the snow already covering the ground. Washington and the members of his war council rode off into a picturesque world from the Merrick house to seize as many hours of sleep as they could before they would have to marshal their troops preparatory to boarding the boats awaiting them at the river's edge.

Around 2 p.m. on Wednesday, Christmas Day, with the temperature at about thirty degrees and a stiff wind blowing a mix of snow and rain, the troops of the main force broke camp and assembled in their company areas. Many were ill clad, some without boots or shoes, their feet swathed in cloths to keep them from freezing. They carried their rifles or muskets, bayonets, forty rounds of ammunition each, and, if they had followed Washington's general orders, a three-day supply of cooked food and one or more blankets. Their officers checked to see if they had everything. About 3 p.m. they marched off across the snow to their rendezvous at McKonkey's Ferry.

The boats they would board there were flat-bottomed Durham boats, used to haul freight between the port of Philadelphia and communities up the river. Variously described as forty to one hundred feet in length and eight to twelve feet in the beam, they were pointed at each end, like huge canoes, usually painted black and drew but two to two and a half feet of water when fully loaded. The largest of them could carry fifteen tons or more, and their ordinary cargoes were iron ore, grain, and other bulk freight. They were usually crewed by four or five men and were either poled or sailed. A sort of catwalk ran atop the gunwales on both sides of the boat to provide platforms for the crewmen propelling the boat with long push poles. A removable steering sweep allowed the boat to be steered from either end. Designed for river transport, they were a type of craft with which Glover's Massachusetts fishermen had had no familiarity until they were used to carry the fleeing rebel army across to Pennsylvania some two weeks earlier.

Now, reaching the water's edge at McKonkey's Ferry, the troops of Washington's main force encountered the first sign of unforeseen trouble. On the upper reaches of the Delaware days earlier the temperature had fallen far below freezing and the river had frozen over there; then the weather suddenly had warmed somewhat and the ice had started breaking up. Enormous chunks of ice were being carried downstream by a swift current, menacing any craft sent out into it. Glover's boatmen would have to contend with that icy assault, immense and jagged pieces now rushing past their launching point at the McKonkey's Ferry landing.

Daylight vanished early on that winter day, and the boarding of the boats began in the darkness of late afternoon, sometime after 4:30. The men waiting for their turn to board huddled in groups for warmth as the wind picked up and night brought on a deepening chill. Some stood or crouched in the lee of McKonkey's Inn, built beside the landing and now serving as Washington's temporary headquarters, from which to oversee the boarding operations. Washington was in and out of the building repeatedly as the evening wore on.

The advance guard of Brigadier General Stephen's brigade was first to enter the boats. They were mostly Virginia troops, Washington's most trusted, and would secure the landing site on the opposite side of the river. Artillerymen with four of the eighteen guns were next, pushing and

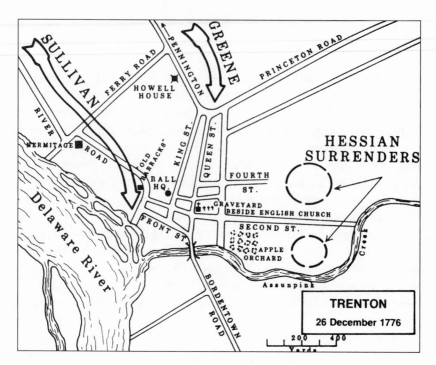

Trenton, 26 December 1776

hauling their gun carriages aboard, leading and coaxing the carriages' draft horses. Their loading was overseen by Colonel Knox, who shouted orders to his men and Glover's alike in a distinctively loud voice. The artillery pieces, nine assigned to each of the two columns that would advance on Trenton, were Washington's foul-weather weapons. They could be loaded and fired in the field despite the rain, sleet, and snow. Hand-held weapons, vulnerable to rain, could not, unless kept dry by extraordinary means.

When fully loaded, the boats were poled over to the New Jersey side, then returned to accept another load of men, horses, and equipment. Those who made the first crossings immediately discovered the effects of the immense chunks of floating ice. The struggle to avoid them or overcome their diverting, broadside crashes and pushes against the boats was adding precious, unplanned minutes to each crossing. Meanwhile, the snow and freezing rain continued, necessitating greater exertion and caution and further slowing the loading and unloading of the boats. The entire process was falling farther and farther behind schedule.

Down the river, at the points where Ewing's and Cadwalader's divisions were to cross, conditions were no better. Cadwalader was managing to get his men across, but not his artillery. After some 600 of his troops had been ferried over, he despaired of getting his artillery across. He then ordered the 600 men on the New Jersey side to get back into the boats, and they crossed back to Pennsylvania. Ewing, whose troops were expected to block the Hessians' escape over Assunpink Creek, studied the river at his crossing point, Trenton Ferry, and decided it was so clogged with floating ice that it was uncrossable. He gave up on his assignment. Washington didn't know it, but there would be no American troops at the Assunpink Creek bridge or at Bordentown.

The schedule called for all troops to be across the river by midnight. At midnight, there were still troops of Washington's main force standing in the cold beside McKonkey's Inn, waiting to board Glover's boats. Washington, who had been standing on the river bank, wrapped in his long cloak, superintending the embarkation, made himself one of the last to board. The boat into which he stepped was commanded by Captain William Blackler, one of Glover's Massachusetts fishermen. Twenty or so enlisted men and about a dozen officers were already in the boat when Washington boarded; among them was his stocky young chief of artillery, Colonel Henry Knox, and Major General Nathanael Greene. Washington picked his way along the length of the boat, past gloomy soldiers hunched over where they crouched or sat, their heads ducked against the snow and sleet. When he reached the spot where Knox was sitting, where he apparently intended to take a seat also, Washington lifted his foot and prodded Knox's wide bottom with the toe of his boot. "Shift that fat ass, Harry," he told him, loud enough for the men to hear. "But slowly, or you'll swamp the damn boat."[3] Down the rows of gloomy troops, wet, cold, and miserable, laughter broke out for a few bright moments.

It was not until 3 a.m. that the last troops of the main force and the remainder of their artillery and horses were landed on the New Jersey side of the river, and it took another hour to form up a marching column. Washington's plan to commence his raid before dawn had already failed. The attack force would not be able to reach Trenton till well after sunup. The element of surprise may have been altogether lost. The question now was, should Washington abort the mission?

He had received no word from Cadwalader or Ewing and had no way of knowing what their situation was. Those close to him saw no anxiety in him, however. "He is calm and collected," one of his officers said of him on that night, "but very determined."[4] Even so, he evidently was feeling some anxiety. The three-hour delay, he conceded in a report to Congress, "made me despair of surprizing the town, as I well knew we could not reach it before the day fairly broke, but . . . I determined to push on."[5]

The entire force having formed up on the road, Washington's little army began its march through the cold, blustery night down the rutted, frozen roadway. Near the community of Birmingham, about four miles from the landing site, the road forked, and there the columns of Sullivan and Greene split from each other. Sullivan led his column down the river road, which roughly followed the course of the Delaware. His column would approach Trenton from the north. Greene and his column took the Pennington Road, some 700 to 800 yards farther to the north. They would advance on Trenton from the west. Since the northern route was slightly longer than the river road, Sullivan was instructed to halt his march when he reached Howland's Ferry, on the outskirts of Trenton, and pause about twenty minutes, so that both columns could deploy simultaneously. Washington, on horseback, rode with Greene's column.

Although there was a full moon, it was obscured by the cloudy overcast and the constant snow. Through the darkness the troops of the two columns made their way by the light of the torches of the artillery pieces, mounted on the guns, flaring and sparkling through the snowy gloom. The rough, frozen surfaces were inflicting a painful toll on the men who were bootless and had only cloth wrappings to cover their feet. Hours of trudging over the icy ruts had their feet bleeding from lacerations, and behind them in the snow was left a crimson trail of blood.

As the march continued, Captain John Mott, in Sullivan's column, made an informal inspection of his men's weapons and discovered the rain and snow had dampened the powder in the muskets' priming boxes to the extent that the weapons could not be fired. He so informed his superiors, Colonel John Stark and Major General Sullivan. Sullivan dispatched one of his aides to ride across the fields separating the river road from the Pennington Road, find General Washington, report to him that the men's muskets could not be fired, and receive the general's orders.

Washington's orders were brief. "Tell General Sullivan," he said, "to use the bayonet. I am resolved to take Trenton."[6]

At daylight, around 7:30 a.m., Greene's column halted momentarily. Elisha Bostwick of the 7th Connecticut Regiment was one of the soldiers in that column. He reported what then occurred:

... his Excellency and aids came near to front on the side of the path where the soldiers stood. I heard his Excellency as he was comeing on, speaking to and encouraging the soldiers. The words he spoke as he passed by where I stood and in my hearing were these:

"Soldiers, keep by your officers. For God's sake, keep by your officers!" Spoke in a deep and solemn voice.[7]

Minutes later the column reached the edge of Trenton about 7:45 a.m. Now Brigadier General Stephen's brigade, the leading element of Greene's column, had in sight the first Hessian outpost, the Richard Howell house on the Pennington Road north of the town. About sixty of Stephen's troops immediately rushed toward the house on the double, while several Hessian sentinels, seeing them, ran toward the house shouting, "*Der feind! Heraus! Heraus!*" ("The enemy! Turn out! Turn out!") One of Washington's aides, Colonel John Fitzgerald, recorded the action that followed:

Looking down the road, I saw a Hessian running out from the house. He yelled in Dutch and swung his arms. Three or four others came out with their guns. Two of them fired at us, but the bullets whistled over our heads. Some of General Stephen's men rushed forward and captured two. The others took to their heels, running toward Mr. Calhoun's house, where the picket guard was stationed, about twenty men under Captain Altenbrockum. They came running out of the house. The captain flourished his sword and tried to form his men. Some of them fired at us; others ran toward the village.

The next moment we heard drums beat and a bugle sound, and then from the west came the boom of a cannon. General Washington's face lighted up instantly, for he knew that it was one of Sullivan's guns.

We could see a great commotion down toward the meetinghouse, men running here and there, officers swinging their swords, artillerymen harnessing their horses. Captain Forrest unlimbered his guns. Washington gave the order to advance, and we rushed on to the junction of King and Queen streets. Forrest wheeled six of his cannon into position to sweep both streets. The riflemen under Colonel Hand and Scott's and Lawson's battalions went upon the run through the fields on the left to gain possession of the Princeton Road. The Hessians were just ready to open fire with two of their cannon when

Captain [William] Washington and Lieutenant [James] Monroe with
their men rushed forward and captured them.[8]

The Hessians, totally surprised, were blocked and thwarted at every
turn. Once formed up in the street, they attempted to counterattack to the
north, but their formation was riddled by head-on artillery fire from the
north and the fire of Brigadier General Mercer's men into their right
flank. Sullivan's column, meanwhile, had attacked from the north and
rushed down the river road to the south side of town, overrunning all
opposition and seizing command of the west and south of Trenton, all the
way to the bridge at Assunpink Creek. The Hessian garrison at Trenton
was trapped. In a letter to his wife written two days later, Colonel Knox
described the Hessians' predicament:

> The hurry, fright and confusion of the enemy was [not] unlike that
> which will be when the last trump shall sound. They endeavored to
> form in streets, the heads of which we had previously the possession
> of with cannon and howitzers; these, in the twinkling of an eye,
> cleared the streets. The backs of the houses were resorted to for shel-
> ter. These proved ineffectual; the musketry soon dislodged them.
> Finally, they were driven through the town into an open plain
> beyond. Here they formed in an instant.
>
> During the contest in the streets, measures were taken for
> putting an entire stop to their retreat by posting troops and cannon
> in such passes and roads as it was possible for them to get away by.
> The poor fellows after they were formed on the plain saw themselves
> completely surrounded; the only resource left was to force their way
> through numbers unknown to them. The Hessians lost part of their
> cannon in the town; they did not relish the project of forcing, and
> were obliged to surrender upon the spot, with all their artillery, six
> brass pieces, army colors, etc.[9]

Colonel Rall, the garrison's haughty commander who despised
Washington's soldiers, had spent Christmas afternoon consuming a grand
dinner at the Trenton Tavern and when that was done, he had passed the
evening and most of the early morning drinking wine and playing cards.
He had been in bed only a short time when the fighting broke out. His
aide, Lieutenant Piel, had come rushing into his bedroom to rouse him,
but had difficulty doing so, shaking him repeatedly to wake him up.

"What's the matter?" he had asked Piel. Piel told him, and that report jolted him awake.

He took time to remove his nightshirt and put on his uniform and emerged from his quarters fully dressed. He mounted his horse and began shouting orders to rally his troops. He drew his sword, ordered his men to fix bayonets and to charge the advancing Americans as he moved out in front of the formation to lead the charge. No sooner had he done so than one of the Pennsylvania riflemen who had managed to shield his gunpowder from the rain, fired at what was an easy target, the mounted colonel, his dark-blue uniform outstanding against the gray sky and snow. Rall lurched, and his sword fell from his hand as he cried out that he had been hit. His troops halted and watched him slump in his saddle. Many of his men then broke and ran; others held out their muskets to the oncoming rebels in a sign of surrender.

Two Hessian officers and two Hessian enlisted men were permitted by Major General Sullivan to carry Rall to the home of Stacey Potts, a Quaker and tavernkeeper who, like many other pacifist Quakers, had stayed in Trenton after the Hessians had occupied it. Potts instructed the Hessians to take their colonel upstairs and lay him on the bed in Potts's own bedroom. There Potts's wife and daughter did what they could for him. He was obviously seriously wounded.

Washington was informed by Nathanael Greene that Rall was dying. Greene asked Washington to go with him to see Rall so they could pay their respects to a fellow officer. Washington balked at the idea, feeling no sympathy for the Hessian. Greene urged him to go, however, and Washington finally consented. He and his aide, Colonel Fitzgerald, then went with Greene and stood beside the bed as Rall asked Washington, in German that had to be translated, for kind treatment for his men. Washington promised they would be well cared for, and the American officers then turned and left. Rall died the next day, December 27.

The Hessians' surrender had come at 9:30 a.m., an hour and forty-five minutes after the fight had started. Washington's victory—America's victory—had been nearly complete. Although some 500 of the enemy had escaped, 918 had been taken prisoner, 22 killed, 84 wounded. Two enemy regiments had been eliminated. All of the Hessians' muskets and accouterments were captured, along with six pieces of artillery, artillery ammunition, and all of their supply wagons. When the Hessian prisoners were rounded up, bootless and coatless rebel soldiers helped themselves to what the enemy was wearing. It was fitting retribution for the men of the same regiments that had stripped surrendering Americans at Fort Washington six weeks earlier.

Remarkably, no Americans had been killed in the fight. Only four had been wounded.

It was exactly the victory that Washington and America needed. Reflecting on it, Henry Knox told his wife that "Providence seemed to have smiled upon every part of this enterprise."

Washington had planned to march on to Princeton once Trenton had been taken, but when he learned that he was without the 2,600 men of Cadwalader's and Ewing's divisions, that they were still on the other side of the Delaware, he met with his senior officers and decided to take his weary 2,400 troops and their Hessian prisoners and their artillery and march back the way he had come, recrossing at McKonkey's Ferry.

After a rest of about two hours, Washington's army of raiders and the captured Hessians moved out of Trenton at a little past noon. The snow was still coming down, and now the biting, frigid wind was in their faces as they trudged north toward McKonkey's Ferry. When they reached it, they found the crossing even harder and slower this time, the river more choked with ice, and the cold so intense that three men froze to death. The crossing again was made in darkness, and it was morning when the last of the troops reached their camps in Pennsylvania.

Most of Washington's valiant little army was now utterly exhausted. The regimental morning reports showed that barely 60 percent of his soldiers were fit for duty. Yet, he had more in mind for them.

CHAPTER Nine

The Battle of Princeton

C ornwallis was still waiting for a ship to England when the appalling news reached New York that Washington had nearly wiped out the Hessian garrison at Trenton. Howe quickly recalled Cornwallis from his leave and gave him orders to hurry to Princeton, assume command once more of the British and Hessian forces in New Jersey, and forestall any other move by Washington and his rebels.

Early on New Year's Day, 1777, Cornwallis mounted his horse and rode some fifty miles from New York to Princeton, gathering his forces as he traveled southward. He arrived in Princeton that evening and immediately assembled his army, which now, including the garrison at Princeton, amounted to some 8,000 troops. The next morning, Thursday, January 2, he and his army set out for Trenton, about ten miles to the southwest. Left behind in Princeton as a rear guard was a force of 1,200 men, the 4th Brigade, composed of three infantry regiments under the command of Lieutenant Colonel Charles Mawhood. Cornwallis ordered his main baggage train back to New Brunswick, site of a large British supply depot.

The weather had changed overnight, warming winds from the south bringing rain, which continued through the day. The icy, snow-covered roads, which had been frozen hard, gradually turned into muddy quagmires in which Cornwallis's artillery carriages and supply wagons repeatedly bogged down, slowing his advance. Anxious over the delays, Cornwallis split his force into three divisions and had them move ahead in parallel columns.

About 10 a.m., as they reached the community of Maidenhead (later renamed Lawrenceville), the columns of redcoats came under fire from

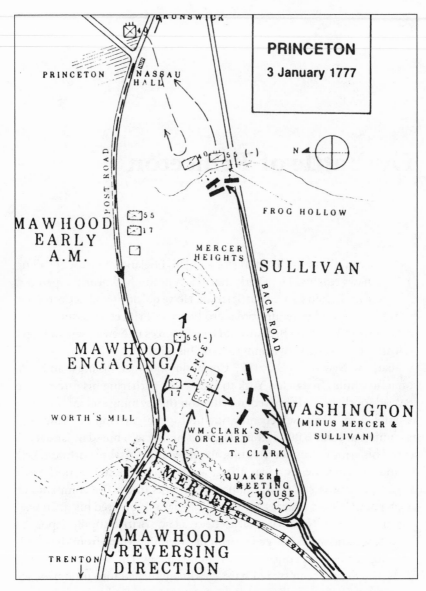

Princeton, 3 January 1777

rebels concealed among the trees on either side of the line of march. From Maidenhead onward, as the road passed through woods, the British troops were continually harassed by snipers firing into their flanks.

Washington's army, Cornwallis had discovered, was again on the New Jersey side of the Delaware. Colonel John Cadwalader, who had been unable to get his artillery across the river on the night of December 25, had crossed on December 27, expecting to find Washington still in Trenton. Brigadier General Thomas Mifflin, who had been in Philadelphia recruiting new troops while Washington was encamped along the river, had also crossed, leading a force of 1,800 Pennsylvania militiamen and expecting to join Washington. On that news, Washington had recrossed and moved back into Trenton.

Knowing all too well that the enlistments of many of his men were going to expire in a day or two, Washington had made an emotional appeal for the men to stay on, offering a bonus of ten dollars (the money would have to be quickly raised by Washington, since there was none on hand) to every man who would extend his enlistment. A sergeant who heard him related the earnest entreaty made by Washington to his troops:

> General Washington, having now but a little handful of men and many of them new recruits in which he could place but little confidence, ordered our regiment to be paraded and personally addressed us, urging that we should stay a month longer. He . . . told us that our services were greatly needed and that we could now do more for our country than we ever could at any future period; and in the most affectionate manner entreated us to stay.
>
> The drums beat for volunteers, but not a man turned out. The soldiers, worn down with fatigue and privations, had their hearts fixed on home and the comforts of the domestic circle. . . .
>
> The General wheeled his horse about, rode in front of the regiment and addressing us again said, "My brave fellows, you have done all I asked you to do, and more than could be reasonably expected; but your country is at stake, your wives, your houses and all that you hold dear. You have worn yourselves out with fatigues and hardships, but we know not how to spare you. If you will consent to stay only one month longer, you will render that service to the cause of liberty and to your country which you probably never can do under any other circumstances."

A few stepped forth, and their example was immediately followed by nearly all who were fit for duty in the regiment, amounting to about two hundred volunteers.[1]

When his troops were joined by those of Cadwalader and Mifflin, Washington's new army totaled some 5,000 men. That was enough to decide him to return to his plan and resume the New Jersey campaign. It was more than a morale boost that he now sought; the victory at Trenton had already accomplished that much. Washington considered Princeton and the Delaware River crossings below it vital to the defense of Philadephia, the new nation's capital, headquarters of the Continental Congress. If at all possible, Washington believed, the route that the British must take to Philadelphia, through Princeton and across the Delaware, must be closed to the enemy army.

Cornwallis meant to keep it open, and Trenton was his first objective. To combat the harassing sniper fire as he continued his slow march on Trenton, Cornwallis ordered detachments from his columns to clear the woods of rebels, who reacted by withdrawing into the woods to avoid a confrontation. At Five Mile Run, near the outskirts of Trenton, Cornwallis's advance guard met and scattered the first rebel outposts they encountered, manned by a large contingent under the command of Brigadier General de Roche Fermoy, who inexplicably abandoned his position and hurried back toward Trenton, along the road from Princeton.

After that, Cornwallis's advance units were repeatedly halted by rebel resistance. At Shabbakonk Creek the fire from the Americans was so heavy, inflicting such a toll of British casualties, that Cornwallis mistook the line set up by what was only Fermoy's covering force as Washington's main line of battle. He ordered his artillery to saturate the rebel positions with shot, then called in two Hessian battalions to assault the rebel line on the opposite side of the creek. The Americans had destroyed the bridge that spanned the creek, and when the Hessians managed to ford it and charge the rebel line, they found their enemy gone, withdrawn to a new position.

The covering force, under the command of Colonel Edward Hand of Pennsylvania, a former medical officer in the British army, then took a position in a ravine about a half mile northeast of Trenton as the American army fell back to the south and southeast side of the town. When Cornwallis marshaled his force to make a massive assault on Hand's position, the Americans once more withdrew, falling back to the streets and alleys of Trenton. By then it was 4 p.m. and growing dark. The rebels continued to fire from inside and behind houses as they slowly retreated through the town, giving up ground stubbornly. Then, reaching the south edge of the town, they swiftly retreated across the stone bridge spanning Assunpink Creek, where Washington had established a strong line of defense on the south bank. An immediate effort by Cornwallis's advance guard to take the bridge was promptly turned back by the rebels.

In the face of the enemy's withering artillery fire, Cornwallis called a halt. It was dark now, and he could see the lights of the rebel campfires beyond the creek. He called a council of war and solicited the advice of his chief officers. Brigadier General William Erskine urged him to press the attack now. "If Washington is the general I take him to be," he told Cornwallis, "he won't be there in the morning."

Brigadier General James Grant was the officer who had commanded the British forces in New Jersey while Cornwallis was recently on leave. He had written Colonel Rall five days before Rall was mortally wounded, telling him that the Americans were nothing to worry about, since "the rebel army in Pennsylvania . . . have neither shoes nor stockings, are in fact almost naked, dying of cold, without blankets and very ill supplied." He now assured Cornwallis there was no need for a night attack on the rebels. They were dug into their positions and presumably meant to hold them, and besides, there was no escape for them. They had no boats at hand to take them across the Delaware and though the river was frozen over, the ice was not thick enough to support an army.

Cornwallis's troops, it was pointed out, had slogged through mud and slush and enemy fire practically the entire day and they were exhausted. Let them rest. Washington's army would still be there in the morning, and Cornwallis could then, in the light of day, find the rebels' right flank and turn it, forcing them up against the river with nowhere to go. An end would be put to the war then and there.

With conflicting advice, Cornwallis was forced to choose between a frontal assault against the rebel lines now, since locating the rebel right flank would be prohibitively difficult in the darkness, and waiting till morning to launch an attack on the flank in daylight. He decided on the latter. "We've got the old fox safe now," he told his generals as the war council concluded. "We'll go over and bag him in the morning."

Through the night Cornwallis's forward sentries could see the rebels' campfires glowing, the Americans' forward sentries patrolling their posts, and troops with picks and shovels working on the earthwork fortifications.

But the American camp was not as it appeared from a distance. Washington described what he had done:

> Having by this time discovered that the enemy were greatly superior in numbers and that their drift was to surround us, I ordered all our baggage be removed silently to Burlington soon after dark, and at twelve o'clock (after renewing our fires and leaving guards at the bridge in Trenton and other passes on the same stream above) marched by a roundabout road to Princeton, where I knew they could not have much force left and might have stores.[2]

Aided by a great stroke of fortune—a shift in the wind that brought frigid air streaming out of the north, dropping the temperature into the twenties and refreezing hard the wet, muddy roads—Washington's army silently stole away in the dark, carriage and wagon wheels wrapped in rags to make them as noiseless as possible. A decoy force of about 500 men stoked the fires, patrolled and dug earthworks till they, too, withdrew. Washington's entire force slipped around the left flank of the British advance troops and turned northeast onto the Princeton road, avoiding the main body of Cornwallis's army, encamped on the north side of Trenton. One eyewitness remarked that Washington's men had moved out so quietly that the rebels' own rear guard and many of their sentries never missed them.

The ten-mile march to Princeton became a nightmare for Washington's weary troops, plodding and stumbling in fits of exhausted sleep through the cold darkness. "We moved so slow," one of those who made the march commented, "on account of the artillery frequently coming to a halt or stand still, and when ordered forward again, one, two or three men in each platoon would stand, with their arms supported, fast asleep."[3] Some of the troops were virtually walking in their sleep, their pace slowing as they dozed while moving; and the night was so dark that their comrades behind them, maintaining their pace, walked into them, bowling them over.

At sunrise on Friday, January 3, British sentries along Assunpink Creek discovered they were keeping watch over an empty position, the enemy having flown away while Cornwallis's army slept. Brigadier General Erskine had been proved right; morning had come and Washington was gone, just as Erskine had told Cornwallis he would be. If the first rule of warfare was "never underestimate your enemy," Cornwallis had violated it. As a consequence, the fox would not be bagged this morning.

Probably angry with himself, Cornwallis immediately issued orders for his army to break camp and begin a new chase, back up the road to Princeton, where he assumed Washington was headed.

Washington wasn't fleeing this time. He was attacking. Provided with a map gained from intelligence, he planned to divide his army into two forces as they approached Princeton. A couple of miles outside Princeton, toward the southwest, the Post Road—the main road between Trenton and Princeton and points beyond—forked. Soon thereafter, the right fork, known as Quaker Road, crossed a stream called Stony Brook and paralleled the stream as both continued northward on the west side of Princeton. A bit farther Quaker Road forked, the right fork, known as the back road, turning east and running past the town on the south side, the left fork proceeding northward until it intersected with the Post Road. Just west of that intersection the Post Road crossed Stony Brook over a bridge.

Washington's entire force would cross Stony Brook on the Quaker Road bridge. Brigadier General Hugh Mercer would take 350 men and continue north on Quaker Road to its intersection with the Post Road and there destroy the Post Road bridge over the brook, thereby impeding Cornwallis, who, Washington assumed, would soon be in pursuit of him. The destruction of that bridge would also prevent the British garrison at Princeton from escaping southward toward Trenton. Meanwhile, the main body of Washington's force would take the back road, approaching the town from the rear, from the side that was least guarded, and attack across a wide front.

Not all went according to Washington's simple plan. Cornwallis had changed his mind about keeping Lieutenant Colonel Mawhood in Princeton and had ordered him to march to Maidenhead with two of his three regiments, the 17th and the 55th Foot, there join Brigadier General Alexander Leslie's 1,200-man brigade and march on to Trenton to reinforce Cornwallis. Left behind in Princeton to guard the British supplies was the 40th Foot. About 8 a.m, as Mawhood's men trooped out of Princeton along the Post Road and across the Stony Brook bridge, his soldiers could see, to their left, on the other side of the brook, Mercer's rebel contingent marching on Quaker Road, heading for the bridge that Mawhood's regiments had just crossed.

In the morning fog Mawhood at first mistook the Americans for Hessians. He then decided they were not Hessians, but Americans retreating from Trenton. He quickly led his column in a U-turn and hurried back across the Stony Brook bridge to intercept the rebels.

At that point, Washington had reached the Quaker Road fork, where the back road branched off, and the main force, led by Major General Sullivan, was advancing up the back road toward Princeton. Behind Washington, still on Quaker Road, was the brigade commanded by Colonel Daniel Hitchcock.

Mercer ordered his men off Quaker Road and into woods and a field, beyond which was the orchard of William Clark. His first intention apparently was to attack Mawhood's flank as the column of redcoats rushed back toward Princeton. Realizing he was facing substantially superior British numbers, Mercer evidently then decided to turn back to the southeast, cross through the orchard, cross over a hillock, and rush to join Sullivan's main force. As Mercer's men reached the orchard, they came under fire from troops of the 17th Foot Regiment, which had left the Post Road after recrossing the brook, wheeled to their right and had taken a position behind a fence on the left of Mercer's men, who were crossing the orchard from west to east.

Mercer then turned his troops to the left to face the 17th Foot, returned the redcoats' fire and drove them from their position. The British reformed a line of battle, bringing up two artillery pieces, and poured a devastating fire into Mercer's line, then charged it with bayonets and collapsed it, driving the Americans back in a rout. Mercer was killed in that assault, beaten with the butt of musket and bayoneted to death, stabbed seven times, after his horse was felled by a gunshot. Also among those killed was Colonel John Haslet, shot in the head; he had earlier commanded the valiant Delaware Regiment. Haslet had been ordered home for recruiting duty, but he had put off following the order so he could stay and fight.

Washington, coming up the back road, could see Mercer's troops were in trouble, and not just Mercer's but Cadwalader's, who had turned off the back road to assist Mercer. All were in full flight. The British were restrained only by the fire of two artillery pieces commanded by Captain Joseph Moulder, which poured continuous shot into the line of redcoats. Washington ordered Hitchcock's brigade, marching on the double to the sound of battle, to take a position to the right of Cadwalader's broken line, which was now reforming. To the right of Hitchcock, Washington positioned the 1st Pennsylvania Regiment, commanded by Colonel Edward Hand. The Americans' line now faced Mawhood's in a semicircle that threatened to turn Mawhood's left flank and envelop his redcoats.

Mounted on a white horse, Washington rode out in front of the American line, calling for Mercer's men to halt their flight and regroup to help form a new line. The sergeant who had found Washington's entreaty to extend enlistments so appealing was one of those fleeing rebels. He told what occurred next:

> I looked about for the main body of the army, which I could not discover, discharged my musket at part of the enemy, and ran for a piece of wood at a distance where I thought I might shelter.
>
> At this moment, Washington appeared in front of the American army, riding towards those of us who were retreating, and exclaimed, "Parade with us, my brave fellows, there is but a handful of the enemy, and we will have them directly." I immediately joined the main body and marched over the ground again.[4]

Washington rode to a spot directly in front of Cadwalader's men, then gave the command to advance on the British line. The entire American front began moving forward then. When it came to within thirty yards of Mawhood's line, Washington ordered his troops to commence firing, and from both sides the gunfire raged, the air quickly filling with gunsmoke and the sounds of volleys of intense musket and rifle fire. Washington's aide, Colonel John Fitzgerald, could see his commander out in front, in an exposed position, conspicuous astride the white horse, and so feared for Washington's life, certain he would be shot at any moment, that he briefly held his hand over his eyes, so as not to witness his death.

The weight of the rebel force was too much for Mawhood's redcoats, the troops of the 17th Foot. They broke and ran, some toward Maidenhead, some toward New Brunswick, the rest eastward into Princeton.

Meanwhile, Sullivan's troops had been stalled on the back road. On their left flank was the hillock that rose east of William Clark's orchard, where the battle was being fought. From the road, Sullivan could see redcoats on the hillock's high ground. They were troops of the 55th Regiment, which had been in Mawhood's column moving south on the Post Road to join Cornwallis and had raced to the hillock (later named Mercer's Heights) to take the high ground between Washington's army and the town of Princeton. Not knowing the strength of the British force, Sullivan had stopped his advance to Princeton along the back road, fearful of exposing his flank to unknown numbers. The commander of the British 55th, at the same time, was afraid to turn west to aid the beleaguered 17th lest he expose his flank and rear to Sullivan's rebels. The two forces had reached a standoff.

Now, however, with the 17th in flight, the 55th moved toward Princeton to reinforce the British 40th, the regiment that Mawhood had left behind to defend Princeton and the British stores stockpiled there. The 40th had taken a position in a ravine (Frog Hollow) about three quarters of a mile southwest of the center of the town, and there the 55th joined it to make a stand. When Sullivan led his force off the back road and attacked the British position, sending two regiments to assault the British left, nearest the road, the redcoats soon abandoned the ravine and fell back to Princeton proper.

Many of the retreating redcoats took refuge in Nassau Hall, a large, brick building on the college campus. They smashed the glass out of the windows and meant to turn the building into a defensive fortress. Captain Moulder and Captain Alexander Hamilton swiftly rolled their field pieces into position and commenced firing on the building. "Cannon were planted before the door," the re-enlisted sergeant related, "and after two or three discharges, a white flag appeared at the window and the British surrendered. . . ."[5]

Another eyewitness, an eighty-five-year-old civilian resident of Princeton, told what he saw:

> The battle was plainly seen from our door. . . . Almost as soon as the firing was over our house was filled and surrounded with Genl Washington's men, and himself on horseback at the door. They brought in with them on their shoulders two wounded Regulars; one of them was shot in the hip and the bullet lodged in his groin, and the other was shot through his body just below his short ribs. He was in very great pain and bled much out of both sides, and often desired to be removed from one place to another, which was done accordingly, and he dyed about three o' [clock in the] afternoon. . . .
>
> Immediately after the battle Genl Washington's men came into our house. Though they were bo[th] hungry and thirsty some of them [were] laughing out right, others smileing, and not a man among them but showed joy in his countenance. It really animated my old blood with love to those men that but a few minutes before had been couragiously looking death in the face in ravages of a bold and dareing enemy. . . .[6]

The Battle of Princeton had lasted approximately forty-five minutes. The Americans lost about forty men, killed or wounded, including the significant loss of Mercer and Haslet. Estimates of British losses varied, from 28 killed, 58 wounded, and 187 missing, to nearly 500 killed, wounded, or taken prisoner, the figure Washington reported to Congress. A more accurate, and still hugely impressive, total was probably 400 killed, wounded, or captured.

About two hours after the British surrender at Princeton, Washington received news that Cornwallis was on the march, his column advancing up the Post Road from Trenton. Washington had already abandoned the part of his plan that called for an attack on New Brunswick to capture the British supply depot and a treasury that contained some 70,000 British pounds. His troops, he and his war council decided, were too few and too exhausted. In the face of Cornwallis's advance with superior numbers, Washington had his troops tear up the Stony Brook bridge and he pulled his victorious little army out of Princeton, marching swiftly northward to Somerset Courthouse, about fifteen miles away, taking his prisoners with him and arriving around dusk. Cornwallis did not follow him, but instead, after arriving in Princeton, hurried on toward New Brunswick, evidently fearing it was Washington's next objective.

The next day, Saturday, January 4, Washington led his troops on to Pluckemin, New Jersey before completing the final leg of his march. On Sunday, January 5, doubtless feeling surer of himself and of his army, he took time to write a report to Congress, telling of his intentions now and of the gratifying progress of the American army:

> The militia are taking Spirit and, I am told, are coming fast from this State [New Jersey]; but I fear those from Philadelphia will scarce sub-mit to the hardships of a Winter Campaign much longer, especially as they very unluckily sent their blankets with their baggage to Burlington; I must do them justice however to add that they have undergone more fatigue and hardship than I expected Militia . . . would have done at this inclement season.
>
> I am just moving to Morristown where I shall endeavour to put them under the best cover I can, hitherto we have lain without any.[7]

Morristown would provide Washington's army a safe haven for the win-ter, protected as it was by natural defenses, a swamp on the east and moun-tains on the south. The weary American troops arrived there on January 6, about 5 p.m., and immediately made camp in the woods on snow-covered ground. Washington moved into Jacob Arnold's tavern, on the north side of the village green, and set up his headquarters, soon settling in for the winter.

Cornwallis, having marched his troops to New Brunswick to defend it, established a headquarters and remained there, evidently satisfied to stay comfortable in winter quarters rather than pursue Washington's outnumbered army through the snow and cold into disadvantageous territory. General Howe, alarmed at Washington's successes, soon after withdrew all of his troops from New Jersey, except for the defensive and communications line that extended along the Raritan River from New Brunswick to Amboy.

In the twelve days since Christmas, Washington and his army, with extraordinary effort, had reversed the awful course of the war and at the last desperate minute had revived the dying American cause. Whatever plans the British had had for New Jersey, for Philadelphia, too, had been thwarted for now.

Unable to afford idleness, no matter how deserved a respite, Washington now concentrated much of his effort on trying to solve administrative woes, grappling with the continuing problems of procuring clothing, equipment, provisions, and troops—and money to pay for them all. Adding to those problems, an outbreak of deadly smallpox threatened to devastate his army encamped at Morristown. He quickly ordered inoculation for all his troops and, under the nearly dictatorial power newly granted him by Congress, he commandeered the houses of Morristown's residents to shelter his afflicted soldiers.

Washington could not spare a man. Of the 1,000 to 1,200 men who in December had agreed to stay on when Washington offered them a ten-dollar bonus, only about 800 were still with his shrinking army on January 19. New recruits would be coming in April, but he anguished that his army would not last that long. "How we shall be able to rub along till the new Army is raised," he wrote to his stepson, Jack Custis, "I know not."

He couldn't believe that Howe was unaware of his diminished numbers. He couldn't help believing that a new British offensive would soon come. To cope with that danger, he ordered Brigadier General William Heath, whom he had left posted to guard the Hudson River highlands, to move down toward Kings Bridge, at the northern tip of Manhattan island, and make a show of an attempt on the British position there, hoping to force Howe to shift troops from New Brunswick to New York and thereby provide Washington with an opportunity to strike Cornwallis's garrison while the redcoats' force was reduced. Heath, however, made an ineffective attempt, and Howe refused to take the bait.

At the time, it seemed to Washington that the British, far from being weakened and driven from their purpose in New Jersey, remained strong and still bent on a march through New Jersey to attack Philadelphia. The big question in Washington's mind was, how soon?

CHAPTER Ten

The Burgoyne Fiasco

That some credit for the American success in the field must be awarded to the British themselves was bitterly obvious to those who believed Britain's generals were less than completely competent. Some British officers said as much. One of them was Lieutenant Colonel Allan Maclean, who from winter quarters in New York on February 19, 1777 wrote a complaining letter to his friend Alexander Cummings:

> Poor devils as the Rebel generals are, they out-generaled us more than once, even since I have been here, which is only six weeks, and it is no less certain that with a tolerable degree of common sense, and some ability in our commanders, the rebellion would now be near ended.
>
> Indeed, I find our mistakes in the campaign were many and some very capital ones; but I know I am writing to a friend who has some prudence and will not expose me, tho' I write real truths. . . .
>
> After what I said it would be unjust not to say that General Howe is a very honest man, and I believe a very disinterested one. Brave he certainly is and would make a very good executive officer under another's command, but he is not by any means equal to a C. in C. I do not know any employment that requires so many great qualifications either natural or acquired as the Commander in Chief of an Army. He has, moreover, got none but very silly fellows about him— a great parcel of old women—most of them improper for American service. I could be very ludicrous on this occasion, but it is truly too serious a matter that brave men's lives should be sacrificed to be commanded by such generals.

For excepting Earl Percy, Lord Cornwallis, both Lt. Generals, and the Brigadier Generals Leslie and Sir William Erskine, the rest are useless. Lord Percy is greatly distinguished with Gen. Howe; Lord Cornwallis is, I believe, a brave man, but he allowed himself to be fairly out-generaled by Washington, the 4th Jan. last at Trenton, and missed a glorious opportunity when he let Washington slip away in the night.

Men of real genius cannot long agree with Howe; he is too dull to encourage great military merit—and our great men at home seem to be as little anxious about encouraging true military abilities as our commanders here....[1]

The major blame for the British lack of success was laid by many on Howe. Justice Thomas Jones, a New York loyalist who had become discouraged by British army failures, expressed the criticism that doubtless was in the minds of many (and coincided with Washington's expectations of Howe):

Their [the British] numbers were sufficient to have driven Washington out of New Jersey with the greatest ease. But orders were wanting. Cornwallis commanded at Brunswick, [Brigadier General John] Vaughn at Amboy, both generals of spirit. Nothing could be done without the directions of the Commander-in-Chief [Howe], who was diverting himself in New York in feasting, gunning, banqueting and in the arms of Mrs. Loring....[2]

For all Howe's flagrant deficiencies, though, none of the British generals engaged in the war attracted more notoriety to himself than did Major General John Burgoyne. Son of a wastrel British army captain from an aristocratic family, Burgoyne had turned the good fortune of attending a proper school, Westminster, into a lifelong advantage. At Westminster he had become the close friend of fellow student Edward Stanley, son and heir of the earl of Derby. After school, he chose the army for a career, managing to purchase his first commission, as a dragoon lieutenant, at age eighteen. At age twenty he eloped with Edward's sister, Charlotte (over her father's objections), thus wedding himself to the wealth and influence of the Stanley family.

During the Seven Years' War Burgoyne won distinction for himself through boldness and daring. Apparently with the influence of his father-in-law, he advanced from captain to lieutenant colonel in 1759 and was given command of a regiment. In 1761, with the help of a fellow officer, he was elected to the House of Commons. In 1762 he went with his regiment to fight the French and Spanish in Portugal, where Charles Lee served with him as a subordinate. Returning to Parliament, he used his own political position as well as that of his in-laws to gain additional promotions, becoming a major general in 1772.

Whatever talents he possessed as a soldier were overmatched by his powers of expression, particularly in written form. He was fond of spinning out proposals and comments on a range of military and political matters. When his proposals were rebuffed or ignored, he frequently turned a caustic pen on whoever had caused the rebuff or slight, including superior officers. So capable was he at words that he became a playwright, authoring a drama called "Maid of the Oaks," which was produced in London theaters in 1774 and 1775. By then he had also become an amateur actor.

He was well known in London's clubs, having become a member of several, and had acquired a reputation as a reckless gambler, but also one who preyed on fellow club members who became too drunk to play a winning hand of cards. He was widely seen as a charming (sometimes cruel) wit, a man of fashion, a connoisseur, and a *bon vivant*. Either because of the admiration he commanded from his troops, who found him endearingly less abusive and more considerate than was the average army officer, or because of his flair for elegance and his love of the high life, he gained the sobriquet of Gentleman Johnny.

In February 1775, King George III himself picked Burgoyne for duty in America. Burgoyne sailed for the colonies on April 20, 1775, aboard H.M.S. *Cerberus* and in the company of two other generals also on their way to service in the war. One was Major General William Howe; the other was Major General Henry Clinton. Both were senior to Burgoyne, a fact that bothered Burgoyne a great deal. What would be his chances for glory and reward when he was junior to those with whom he must compete for command?

Informing the Continental Congress of the assignment of the three British generals, Arthur Lee, Congress's diplomatic agent in London, gave his evaluation of them:

> The first [Howe] is an honorable man, respected in the Army & trained in the late American War [French and Indian War]. He goes reluctantly.

The second [Clinton] is a man of very fair character. He served all the late War in Germany. His abilities, tho not brilliant, are yet respectable.

General Burgoyne is of a very different character. A man of dark designs, deep dissimulations, desperate fortunes, & abandoned of principles. He is closely connected with the Bedford Party in this Country. No Banditti were ever bent on blood & spoil, & on more desperate principles than this Bedford Party. . . . They are as ready to sacrifice this Country as America to the arbitrary views of a tory, tyrannical Court. Among the worst of their Party is Gl. Burgoyne. . . . To finish his character of dissimulation, tho an abandond & notorious Gambler & engaged in every scene abhorrent from true religion & virtue, he has always effected to be exemplary in religious Worship. . . . You will judge however from what I have said, that he is a dangerous character; & therefore be on your guard. If he is solicitous to commune with you, it will be to betray you.[3]

Burgoyne landed in Boston in late May 1775 and almost immediately began to complain about the minor role he had been assigned to play in America. On June 14 he wrote the British prime minister, Frederick North, grousing that his position was "too humble" to be of any substantial military help to the king's cause. He had commanded more troops as a lieutenant colonel, he complained, than he did in America as a major general. When action came, at the Battle of Bunker Hill, he sat it out, claiming that "the inferiority of my station as the youngest Major-General on the staff left me almost a useless spectator."[4] He was particularly critical of General Gage, as he was toward most officers under whom he served. In a letter to Lord George Germain, the secretary of state for American colonies, Burgoyne wrote that Gage was "an officer totally unsuited for command."[5]

In December 1775 Burgoyne returned to England, as the king had promised he could, and stayed till spring, taking the opportunity to assert his ideas while the government was planning the army's actions for the summer of 1776. His big idea, not original with him, was for a campaign that would be launched from Canada and that would drive British troops down the Lake Champlain–Hudson River corridor, while another force would push northward up the Hudson River valley to meet with the southbound force, cleaving New England from the lower colonies and forcing Washington into a decisive battle.

Germain approved much of the plan; at the same time that he appointed William Howe to succeed Gage as the British commander in chief, he appointed Burgoyne to be second in command to Major General Guy Carleton, whom he named to lead the southward offensive from Canada. With Burgoyne criticizing and second-guessing him most of the way, Carleton managed to push his force down Lake Champlain, past the American defenders, and by October 1776 had reached Crown Point (which Carleton later abandoned). There the drive ended for the year: The redcoats went into winter quarters, and Burgoyne headed back to England.

He arrived there on December 9 and the very next day went to see Germain. He criticized Carleton's handling of the campaign, having already made known his displeasure with being placed in "a secondary station in a secondary command," and gave Germain his ideas of how it should be done.[6] In an elaborate document titled *Thoughts for Conducting the War from the Side of Canada*, Burgoyne spelled out his detailed plan for a new campaign to be launched from Canada. Partly owing to that document, and partly to his political influence and importunings, Burgoyne won approval for his plan and was given command of the British force that would conduct the proposed campaign into New York.

The plan called for Carleton to remain in Canada with a force of some 3,700 troops while Burgoyne commanded a two-pronged offensive into New York. The main force, composed of some 7,000 men, would be led by Burgoyne himself and would move down Lake Champlain, capture strategic Fort Ticonderoga, on Lake Champlain, near the north end of Lake George, then drive on to Albany. A secondary force of about 2,000 men, under the command of Lieutenant Colonel Barry St. Leger (with the temporary rank of brigadier general), would create a diversion by moving down Lake Ontario to Oswego, New York, then driving eastward to the Mohawk River and proceeding down the Mohawk to join the main body at Albany. Burgoyne assumed that the approved plan also called for Howe to move up the Hudson River valley from New York City and link up with Burgoyne's army at Albany, completing the line that would separate the New England colonies from those below the Hudson. In a letter of instructions to Carleton, Germain made it clear that Burgoyne and St. Leger "must never lose view of their intended junctions with Sir William Howe as their principal objects."

After a forty-day voyage, Burgoyne arrived in Quebec on May 6, 1777 and, with the assistance of his former commander, Guy Carleton, began to assemble his troops, as well as their equipment and provisions. Burgoyne's

army of more than 8,000 men included a main force of 3,700 British regulars and 3,000 Germans (some Hessians, but mostly Brunswickers) under
the command of Major General Friedrich Adolphus von Riedesel, supported by nearly 600 artillerymen with 138 guns, plus 150 Canadians,
100 American loyalists, and about 400 Indians.

Neither Burgoyne nor Carleton had had the foresight to gather sufficient wagons to haul that army's provisions and equipment, nor horses to
draw them. As a result, the bulk of the army's supplies would be carried in
500 hastily built two-wheel carts. The shortage of horses was such that
Riedesel's 250 dragoons, the army's only cavalry, would march dismounted,
like infantry, but in heavy, thigh-high jackboots, their swords dangling
from their waists.

On June 13—Friday the 13th—Burgoyne's army set out aboard a flotilla
of assorted vessels that carried it down Lake Champlain and on June 27
landed it at Crown Point, eight miles north of Fort Ticonderoga. On
July 1 the army re-embarked and the next day began its siege of Fort
Ticonderoga. When the American defenders saw that Burgoyne's artillerymen had managed to haul two twelve-pounder field pieces up Sugar Loaf
Mountain and place them in firing position above the fort, Major General
Arthur St. Clair, commanding the fort's garrison, ordered a nighttime
withdrawal and abandoned the fort to Burgoyne. The rear guard of the
retreating Americans was overtaken and defeated by Riedesel's jagers at
Hubbardton, east of Lake George, but the main body of St. Clair's fleeing
troops made it to Fort Edward, on the Hudson River, about fifteen miles
southeast of the southern tip of Lake George.

Believing that Lake George would be heavily patrolled by American
gunboats and that he would have to run the risk of having his troop-laden
bateaux attacked by them, and because he didn't want to reverse his march
in order to reach Lake George, Burgoyne decided to take the overland route
to Fort Edward from Skenesborough (later renamed Whitehall), a distance
of about twenty-three miles.

The route took Burgoyne's troops on rough roads, and even where
there were no roads, through forests and marshlands. The retreating
Americans had felled hundreds of trees to impede Burgoyne's progress,
and these had to be removed to allow the carts and artillery carriages to
pass. Bridges had to be built, or rebuilt, and causeways constructed across
stretches of track that disappeared beneath the clear waters of creeks and
the murk of marshes. Forty such bridges and causeways were built. On
those rugged, wilderness roads and trails the hastily carts began breaking

down and had to be repeatedly halted for repairs. Progress was made at the rate of a mile per day.

Besides the delays in his march, Burgoyne was suffering other problems. His Indians proved uncontrollable, wreaking terror throughout the countryside, robbing, raping, murdering, and scalping. Their rampages roused the citizenry, who were appalled by the savagery and blamed Burgoyne. Burgoyne had hoped to rally loyalist citizens to the king's cause and recruit them to his expedition, but virtually none joined him.

Burgoyne finally reached Fort Edward on July 30. It had taken him and his army twenty-four days to travel twenty-three miles.

To acquire horses for Riedesel's dragoons and augment his dwindling provisions, and to draw loyalists to his expedition, Burgoyne decided to conduct a raid on Bennington, where 100 horses were said to be kept, along with stores of rebel ammunition and food. On August 6 he detached a force of about 800 men, mostly Brunswicker mercenaries, but also including 80 Indians and about 200 Canadians and American loyalists, and ordered German Lieutenant Colonel Friedrich Baum, the dragoon commander, to lead it and round up the horses and capture the stores. The operation was expected to take about two weeks.

On July 16, Baum's force was met and overcome by 1,500 New Hampshire militiamen led by Brigadier General John Stark, who inflicted heavy casualties on the raiders. Among those mortally wounded was Lieutenant Colonel Baum. Another contingent, sent to reinforce Baum, was also defeated, though most of those troops managed to escape. In those two engagements, Burgoyne lost 207 men left dead on the field and an estimated 700 who were taken prisoner. He also lost nearly all his Indians (who escaped into the woods and disappeared), four brass artillery pieces, and several tons of weapons and supplies.

When the defeats became known, Burgoyne immediately came under intense criticism. He was not spending enough time and thought in planning and preparation, his critics said. Instead, he was preoccupied with enjoying the perks of his command. He was spending too much time at elaborate dinners with his officers and their wives (who were among the authorized camp followers), too much time sipping claret and listening to the music provided by his army bands, too much time with his mistress, the wife of one of his officers. "It was only too true," the Baroness von Riedesel wrote, "that General Burgoyne liked to make himself easy, and that he spent half his nights in singing and drinking, and diverting himself with . . . his mistress who was as fond of champaign as himself."[7]

In the meantime, things were not going well with other parts of the plan. St. Leger's diversionary force had left Montreal on June 23 and reached Oswego on July 25. After making good progress, on August 2 the vanguard reached the first big obstacle, Fort Stanwix, at the head of navigation on the Mohawk River. After beating off an attempt by the Americans to reinforce the fort's garrison, St. Leger laid siege to the fort.

On August 10 a relief column of 800 troops under Brigadier General Benedict Arnold left Stillwater, New York, 110 miles to the east, to assist the Stanwix defenders. One of Arnold's officers in his advance guard, Lieutenant Colonel John Brooks, devised a ruse to cause St. Leger's Indians, nearly half of his force, to desert. The ruse worked, and not only did the Indians desert but they attacked their former comrades before fleeing. At that development, St. Leger gave up the siege, turned his remaining force around, and began a retreat.

Arnold arrived at the fort on the evening of August 23 and the next day sent a force in pursuit of St. Leger. The swiftest of Arnold's troops reached Lake Oneida in time to see the last of St. Leger's rear guard sail out of reach in their flight back to Canada.

At the other end of the province, General Howe was still at his headquarters on Staten Island, waiting to learn of Burgoyne's progress. When he heard about the easy capture of Fort Ticonderoga, Howe concluded that Burgoyne was doing well enough without him and he then began to implement his own plan, the design of which was to take him not to Albany but to Philadelphia.

Burgoyne was now on his own, dangerously so. It wasn't too late for him to save his endangered army by aborting his mission and retreating back up Lake George and Lake Champlain. But Burgoyne was stubbornly determined to follow the plan, and dead set on reaching Albany, even though the plan was now somewhat pointless. Howe had decided against joining him to seal off the Hudson or to force Washington into a showdown to prevent its being sealed off; thus, the plan had little strategic bearing.

Burgoyne was on the east side of the Hudson. Albany was on the west side. The farther Burgoyne traveled southward the more problematic a river crossing became. He decided to cross at Saratoga, about thirty miles above Albany. He stopped to accumulate a thirty-day supply of food and had a bridge of rafts built across the Hudson. On Saturday, September 13, he and his army, now about 6,000 men, started crossing the Hudson. Once on the west bank, they dismantled the bridge.

Resuming their march, and using the few Indians who remained with him as scouts, Burgoyne soon discovered that between him and Albany, obstructing his army's march, lay a strong rebel defensive position at Bemis Heights, about five miles south of Burgoyne's crossing site. The rebels' fortified position had been designed by the Polish engineer, Colonel Thaddeus Kosciusko. Burgoyne drew up a plan to attack it.

Aware of Burgoyne's movements, Washington had ordered a brigade under Major General Benjamin Lincoln and 500 sharpshooters from Pennsylvania, Maryland, and Virginia, commanded by Colonel Daniel Morgan, to reinforce the army of the Northern Department, which now stood facing the enemy with 7,000 troops at Bemis Heights. Command of that army on August 4 had passed from Major General Philip Schuyler to Major General Horatio Gates, named to the post by a Congress disappointed by the defeat at Fort Ticonderoga. Assisting Gates was Benedict Arnold, back from his pursuit of St. Leger.

Burgoyne's plan was to advance on the rebel position with three columns. Brigadier General Simon Fraser would command the column on the right, a force of 2,200 men that would attempt to sweep the Americans' left flank in a clearing known as Freeman's Farm. Fraser would be supported by Lieutenant Colonel Heinrich von Breymann's riflemen and a contingent of loyalists, Canadians, and Indians. Baron von Riedesel would command the column on the left, 1,100 men supported by artillery and the troops of Major General William Phillips. Burgoyne himself would command the center column, 1,100 troops who would advance through woods and then turn to their left to link up with Riedesel's column, which would be advancing along the river road that led to Albany. The purpose apparently was to draw out the Americans, or at least concentrate their efforts on the center and their right side while Fraser swept around the rebels' left side.

At Bemis Heights the sun rose on a cold and foggy morning the day of the assault, Friday, September 19, 1777, but by 11 a.m. the fog had vanished and the air had warmed in the bright sunshine. A signal gun was then fired to start the simultaneous advance by the three columns.

American patrols alerted Gates to Burgoyne's approach, and Arnold, eager to act and seeing the center column at a disadvantage in the woods, unable to employ either artillery or the fearsome bayonet charge, urged Gates to let him burst out of the fortifications and hit Burgoyne's center. Gates, characteristically slow to act, at first refused, but with repeated urgings by Arnold, finally gave orders to attack. By then the main chance had been lost. Fraser's column was in position on Burgoyne's right, and when Arnold attempted to turn Burgoyne's right, Fraser's column prevented him from doing so. Arnold then shifted his assault to the center, in the clearing of Freeman's Farm.

The fighting became fierce there, the battle raging for hours. The British tried repeated bayonet charges, but each time were repulsed as Arnold brought up more men to pour musket fire into the advancing scarlet ranks. The American sharpshooters, trained to pick off the enemy's officers, did so with devastating efficiency. In one British contingent, every officer but one was killed or wounded. From both sides the firing was continuous. "The crash of cannon and musketry," British Lieutenant William Digby of the Shropshire Regiment reported, "never ceased till darkness parted us."[8]

The terrible sights and sounds of battle panicked many of Burgoyne's men. "The Indians were running from wood to wood," British Lieutenant Thomas Anburey wrote in his account of the battle. "As to the Canadians, little was to be depended upon their adherence, being easily dispirited with an inclination to quit as soon as there was an appearance of danger. Nor was the fidelity of the [American loyalists] who had joined our army to be relied on, as they withdrew on perceiving the resistance of [the American patriots] would be more formidable than expected."[9]

By the time the fighting ended at nightfall, Burgoyne had suffered considerable losses. Of the 800 troops in the three regiments that had been in the thickest of the fighting, 350 had been killed, wounded, or captured. One of those, the 62nd Regiment, lost all but 60 of its 350 men. Total losses to the British were put at 600, about 10 percent of Burgoyne's army.

American losses were 8 officers and 57 men killed, 21 officers and 197 men wounded, and 36 missing, a total of 319.

Up above the Hudson, at the southern tip of Lake George, an American force had surprised the three British infantry companies guarding Burgoyne's flotilla of transports and armed vessels and had captured all of the boats and taken the three companies of infantry prisoner. Another American force, under Colonel John Brown, had surprised the British garrison at Fort Ticonderoga on September 18 and freed 100 American prisoners and captured 300 British troops. Brown lacked the siege guns big enough to smash the fort's walls and after four days of futile cannonading, withdrew. The British were still in possession of the fort, but it was obvious they were vulnerable.

Informed of those events while dug in at his position above Bemis Heights, Burgoyne realized a retreat back the way he had come was no

longer possible. His army was now reduced to about 5,000 men, and desertions were further shrinking it daily. Food was so short that his troops
were subsisting on a steady diet of salt pork and flour—but even that was
running out, and the rations had to be cut further. The army's draft horses
were dying of starvation. Burgoyne was in desperate straits, but he had one
last hope.

That was that Lieutenant General Henry Clinton, left by Howe in command of the 7,000-man garrison in New York City, would strike out to take
the rebel strongholds along the lower Hudson and divert American strength
away from Gates, or even entrap Gates between Clinton advancing to his rear
while Burgoyne remained to his front at Bemis Heights. Clinton at last did
so, capturing Forts Montgomery, Clinton, and Constitution in the Hudson
highlands with a force of some 3,000 troops. But after that he halted, then
turned around and abandoned the three forts, returning to New York
apparently in response to Howe's request for reinforcements to help him
in his Philadelphia campaign.

Clinton dispatched a message to Burgoyne informing him of his latest move and notifying him that he could not relieve Burgoyne. The
courier, however, an American loyalist, was captured by rebel troops, made
to vomit up the message, contained in a silver bullet that he swallowed
upon his capture, and then was hanged as a spy. Burgoyne was left wondering what was happening with Clinton's relief army.

Meanwhile, Gates's army standing before Burgoyne had been reinforced, and on October 7 it totaled 11,000 men, mostly militia. It was well
supplied with ammunition and was constantly harassing Burgoyne, pick-
ing off his sentries and patrols, and preventing him from gaining any intelligence on the American positions or strength.

Burgoyne decided he could wait no longer in his present position.
Riedesel advised him to withdraw to Fort Miller, about 12 miles up the
river, on the east bank, where they could try to re-establish contact with
Canada and await Clinton. Burgoyne, however, was still determined to
reach Albany, for whatever good might come from doing so.

On Tuesday, October 7, he launched another three-column attack on
the American fortification at Bemis Heights, intending to probe the rebel
front to discover its weakest point, then move his strength to take advantage of the rebel weakness. The advance toward the American line started
sometime between 10 a.m. and 11 a.m.

Profiting by the lessons of the earlier fight, Gates ordered Morgan's
sharpshooters to the right flank of the westernmost British column in

hilly, wooded terrain that suited the rebel riflemen and denied the British the use of a bayonet attack (which Burgoyne had earlier urged his commanders to employ). The main body of the British, 1,500 men, was extended over a front of about 1,000 yards, supported by artillery.

The artillery pieces had to be fired from a slope down onto Brigadier General Enoch Poor's brigade, and the shot flew harmlessly over the heads of the rebels as the gun barrels were not sufficiently depressed. The British infantry's bayonet charge was repulsed by heavy fire from rebel muskets and rifles. The Americans then swept over the position of the British grenadiers, wounding and capturing their commander, Major John Acland.

On orders from Benedict Arnold, Morgan's sharpshooters shot the gallant British Brigadier General Simon Fraser from the saddle of his gray horse, mortally wounding him. Arnold became like a berserker in the heat of battle, galloping about with sword waving, urging his men on, shifting them as the need dictated. He ordered a charge on the British redoubts behind the British line of attack, assaulting one fortification, then another, denying Burgoyne's troops a retreat and effectively ending the battle. The British had lost about 600 men, the Americans about 150.

Back in his command post with the remainder of his army, Burgoyne held a war council with his chief officers. They unanimously recommended that Burgoyne ask Gates for terms. Gates, having never set foot on the battlefield while the fight raged, but rather letting Arnold take command and the risks of battle, showed no more spirit in negotiation than he had in combat. Being the son of an English housemaid, he now, as if in proper deference to his social betters, allowed Burgoyne to dictate the terms of surrender, which, along with other remarkable concessions, permitted Burgoyne and his army to return to England, on the promise they would not again participate in the war. (Except for Burgoyne, however, they did not return, the indignant citizens of Massachusetts disavowing the odious surrender document and confining the prisoners outside Boston, to which they had been marched to board ships for England.)

Lieutenant Digby of the Shropshire Regiment described the surrender ceremony, held October 17, 1777, and his own feelings about the defeat:

> About 10 o'clock we marched out, according to treaty, with drums beating and the honours of war, but the drums seemed to have lost their former inspiriting sounds, and though we beat the Grenadiers

march, which not long before was so animating, yet then it seemed by its last feeble effort as if almost ashamed to be heard on such an occasion.

As to my own feelings, I cannot express them. Tears (though unmanly) forced their way, and if alone, I could have burst to give myself vent. I never shall forget the appearance of their troops on our marching past them; a dead silence universally reigned through their numerous columns, and even then they seemed struck with our situation and dare scarce lift up their eyes to view British troops in such a situation. I must say their decent behaviour during the time (to us so greatly fallen) meritted the utmost approbation and praise.

The meeting between Burgoyne and Gates was well worth seeing. He paid Burgoyne almost as much respect as if he was the conqueror; indeed, his noble air, tho prisoner, seemed to command attention and respect from every person. A party of light dragoons were ordered as his guard, rather to protect his person from insults than any other cause.

Thus ended all our hopes of victory, honour, glory, etc. Thus was Burgoyne's Army sacrificed to either the absurd opinions of a blundering ministerial power, the stupid inaction of a general [Howe], who, from his lethargic disposition neglected every step he might have taken to assist their operations, or lastly, perhaps, his [Burgoyne's] own misconduct in penetrating so far as to be unable to return, and tho I must own my partiality to him [Burgoyne] is great, yet if he or the army under his command are guilty, let them suffer to the utmost extent, and by an unlimited punishment in part blot out and erase, if possible, the crime charged to their account.[10]

Burgoyne's surrender at Saratoga sent shock waves across the Atlantic, creating dismay in London, joy in Paris. Because of his disgrace in defeat, Burgoyne for a while became a pariah in his country, and his active military career was ended forever.

Because of the Americans' victory over Burgoyne, French authorities, whom Benjamin Franklin had been officially courting, on December 17, 1777, notified American envoys in Paris that France would at last recognize the independence of the American states. That recognition, hugely important, led to America's military alliance with France, which brought to the American cause assistance that would prove crucial in the days ahead.

CHAPTER Eleven

The Philadelphia Campaign

Except for the annoyance of intermittent rebel raids on his outposts, Cornwallis spent a quiet winter and early spring in his quarters at New Brunswick. At one point he became so annoyed by a raid made on the outpost at Bonhamtown, where his own 33rd Regiment was posted, that he took a force of 2,000 troops from his 8,000-man garrison and on April 13 sallied out to retaliate against the American outpost at Bound Brook, about seven miles northwest of New Brunswick, up the Raritan River.

Militia who were supposed to be on guard along the river failed to warn the American outpost, and the 500 rebel troops posted there under the command of Benjamin Lincoln were taken by surprise. Cornwallis's attempt to encircle them was only partly successful, for most of the rebel troops managed to escape. The American losses in the engagement were put at six killed and, according to varying reports, as many as eighty captured. Also lost were the outpost's three pieces of artillery. Cornwallis then withdrew back to New Brunswick, before Nathanael Greene could reach Bound Brook with reinforcements.

Washington remained at his quarters in Morristown, ordering occasional raids in New Jersey and New York, but mostly maintaining a defensive position while keeping up with reports on Burgoyne's expedition and trying to divine Howe's next move. During the winter Washington's army had shriveled to about 3,000 effectives. By late spring, however, new enlistees had brought his strength up to nearly 9,000.

On June 26, 1777, Washington received intelligence that Howe was leading a large force out of Amboy, just across the lower end of Arthur Kill

117

from Staten Island, and was moving northwestward in two columns. Washington concluded that Howe had one or more of three possible objectives in mind: the capture of the force commanded by Stirling (William Alexander), which was posted near Metuchen Meeting House, about six miles northwest of Amboy; or to bring Washington's main army to battle; or to take over the high ground around Middle Brook and thereby place his army between the rebels and their mountain refuge. The reports to Washington said Howe's force was moving rapidly, indicating that Howe meant to overwhelm Stirling and/or seize the heights of Middle Brook before Washington could get there.

Washington's main force was then at Quibbletown (later renamed New Market), about six miles northwest of Metuchen. He immediately led it back toward Middle Brook and sent orders to Stirling to pull out from his post near Metuchen Meeting House. Howe's army, however, with Cornwallis in command of the lead units, had begun its march at one o'clock that morning and was already engaging Stirling.

For a while Stirling thought of making a stand, ordering his troops into parade-ground formation to exchange volleys with Cornwallis's redcoats. He soon changed his mind and decided to withdraw. Cornwallis pressed the attack, inflicting as many as one hundred casualties and taking an estimated seventy prisoners before the rebels could get away. The Americans' rear guard suffered the loss of three field pieces during the retreat. Cornwallis pursued Stirling for five miles, in the direction of Westfield, before giving up the chase.

The American forces were then beyond a point where Howe wanted his redcoats to go. Once again Washington had seen through Howe's plan and had refused to be drawn into battle at a time and place not of his choosing. On June 28 Howe frustratedly ordered Cornwallis and the rest of his army back to Amboy, with very little having been accomplished.

The engagement came to be known as the Battle of Short Hills, although it might be more appropriately called the Battle of Metuchen Meeting House. Minor as it was, it brought new praise for Cornwallis. In his reports to London, Howe repeatedly commended Cornwallis. Reading Howe's extravagant praise of Cornwallis, Lord George Germain was moved to remark to Howe how fortunate he was to have the services of "an officer in whose zeal, vigilance and active courage you can so safely confide."[1]

Having thwarted the British again, Washington won high praise, too, not from an American this time but from Nicholas Cresswell, the British civilian traveling in America and observing events. He wrote:

Washington is certainly a most surprising man, one of Nature's geniuses, a Heaven-born general, if there is any of that sort. That [he] . . . should with a ragged banditti of undisciplined people, the scum and refuse of all nations on earth, so long keep a British general at bay . . . with as fine an army of veteran soldiers as ever England had on the American continent, to retreat, it is astonishing. . . .

He certainly deserves some merit as a general that he . . . can keep General Howe dancing from one town to another with such an army as he has. . . .Washington, my enemy as he is, I should be sorry if he should be brought to an ignominious death.[2]

On July 1 Washington received word that the British had evacuated Amboy the day before and had withdrawn across Arthur Kill to Staten Island. Howe apparently had given up on holding any part of New Jersey and had cleared out completely. His attention was turned elsewhere.

Washington realized that Howe, unlike the Americans, need not march his troops overland to reach an objective. The British navy, its American fleet commanded by Howe's brother, Admiral Richard Howe, could move troops to any new point of attack accessible by water. In the first week of July 1777, Washington still felt Howe might sail or march up the Hudson to join Burgoyne on his southward march. But he knew that Philadelphia might also be Howe's objective. Still unable to be certain of Howe's intentions, Washington on July 3 withdrew his troops back to their previous position at Morristown, where he could quickly move toward the Hudson or toward Philadelphia. If he received prompt intelligence on Howe's embarkation and southward sailing from Staten Island, Washington figured he could beat the British to Philadelphia and be in position to defend it before Howe and Cornwallis could reach it via Delaware Bay and the Delaware River.

On July 11 Washington received the fearful news of the loss of Fort Ticonderoga to Burgoyne. More clearly than ever, probably, he imagined a link-up between Burgoyne and Howe and the severing of the provinces. He marched his army to a spot near Clove, New York, in Orange County, beside the New Jersey border, and halted there on July 22, awaiting Howe's next move. British ships had been reported off Sandy Hook, but the direction of their movement wasn't yet known. On July 24 Washington decided those ships must be carrying Howe's army toward Philadelphia. He ordered his light cavalry unit to begin a march to Philadelphia and he began moving the bulk of his force to the Delaware River crossings near

Trenton, a position from which he could still quickly reach the Hudson if Howe's maneuvers were merely deceptive.

On July 27 Washington received a report that seventy British ships had been sighted off Egg Harbor, far down the New Jersey coast, clearer evidence than ever that Howe was aiming at Philadelphia. Yet Washington was unconvinced, unable to believe that Howe was turning his back on Burgoyne. "Howe's in a manner abandoning General Burgoyne," Washington wrote, "is so unaccountable a matter that till I am fully assured it is so, I cannot help casting my eyes continually behind me."[3]

On July 30 the British fleet was sighted off the capes of Delaware Bay and apparently was preparing to enter the bay. Washington now felt fully assured of Howe's intention. He ordered Major General John Sullivan to march with his force to Philadelphia by the fastest possible route, so that they would arrive on August 1. Washington himself, along with his staff, rode quickly for Philadelphia to prepare for the positioning of his troops to defend the city. He was in Chester, Pennsylvania, on the southwest side of Philadelphia, when on the evening of August 1 he was met by a rider hurrying from Cape May, New Jersey to report that the British ships— 228 vessels, presumably the entire British fleet in America—had not entered Delaware Bay, but on July 31 had sailed away.

Perplexed, thinking the fleet's move to Delaware Bay might have been an elaborate feint, Washington now ordered Sullivan's units to turn back and march to Peekskill, New York to be in position to defend the Hudson. Washington stayed on in Philadelphia for several days.

While there, he attended a dinner at which a nineteen-year-old Frenchman was introduced to him. The young man was not a tourist; he was, surprisingly, a major general—and not in the army of France, but in Washington's Continental Army. The rank had been bestowed on him on July 31, by a Congress influenced by the young man's French connections and the promises made to him by the American agent in Paris, Silas Deane. The young man was Marie-Joseph-Paul-Yves-Roch-Gilbert du Motier, Marquis de Lafayette, and he had agreed to serve in the American army without pay, merely for the romance and glory of it all and to contribute to a noble cause. Congress had agreed to make him a major general with the understanding that his position in the American army was an honorary one, that there was no command to go with the rank. Washington was meeting him for the first time.

Remarkably enough, Washington was not at all resentful or scornful. He took an immediate liking to the marquis, a young man of extraordinary charm and brilliance, being at once modest, tactful, and winsome. Lafayette seemed from the first to hold Washington in both awe and affection, becoming an instantaneous devotee, to the point of developing what became almost a father-son relationship. Lafayette had lost his own father, a colonel of French grenadiers, killed in action against the British and Germans at Minden, when he was a year old. His mother had died when he was thirteen, and his grandfather, from whom he had inherited a considerable fortune, had died several weeks later. When he was sixteen, he married Marie-Adrienne-Françoise de Noailles, thereby becoming part of one of the most powerful families in France. He had entered the French army when he was fourteen, but had seen no action and gained little military experience. He came as a volunteer to America because his imagination had been caught by the American cause and by the chance to make a name for himself fighting his nation's old enemy, the British.

The only problem was, what to do with him? Congress had left the problem to Washington to solve, which he would soon do.

On August 22 he learned that the British fleet was in the Chesapeake Bay, heading north. Howe's objective was indeed Philadelphia, but not by either route that Washington had supposed him to take, overland through New Jersey or by sea via Delaware Bay. Washington quickly moved to meet him. He recalled Sullivan, feeling more confident to do so after hearing news of the American victory at Bennington. He marshaled his troops on the north side of Philadelphia about three o'clock on the morning of Sunday, August 24, and marched his army, estimated at 16,000 men, southward through the streets of Philadelphia in a parade that began around seven. John Adams, the Massachusetts lawyer and member of Congress, watched the troops pass and recorded the spectacle in a letter to his wife:

> The rain ceased, and the army marched through the town between seven and ten o'clock. The wagons went another road. Four regiments of light horse, Bland's, Baylor's, Sheldon's and Moylan's. Four grand divisions of the army and artillery . . . marched twelve deep and yet took up above two hours in passing by. General Washington and the other general officers with their aides on horseback. The colonels and other field officers on horseback. . . .
>
> The army . . . I find to be extremely well armed, pretty well clothed, and tolerably disciplined. . . . Our soldiers have not yet quite the air of soldiers. They don't step exactly in time. They don't hold up

their heads quite erect, nor turn out their toes so exactly as they
ought. They don't all cock their hats; and such as do, don't all wear
them the same way. . . .[4]

Reaching Wilmington, Washington halted his army, and it made camp
while he made a reconnaissance.

On August 25, Howe's army, numbering about 12,500 troops, started
disembarking near Elkton, Maryland, at the northernmost tip of Chesapeake
Bay, about 45 miles below Philadelphia. The four companies of rebel militia that had been posted to contest their landing quickly fled, and the
British began an unopposed march northeast on the road to Christiana
and Wilmington.

Advance units of the two armies made contact, as each side felt the
other out and attempted to learn the movements of each other. Howe had
divided his army into two divisions, one commanded by Cornwallis and
the other by the German, Knyphausen. The troops of both divisions
needed fresh meat to eat and horses to replace the estimated 300 lost on
the voyage from Staten Island. For the next several days the British army
established camps, Cornwallis at Elkton, Knyphausen near Cecil Courthouse,
and foraged and pillaged in the nearby countryside.

On the morning of September 3, advance units of Cornwallis's
division, moving northeast up the road from Elkton, came under fire
from the troops of Brigadier General William Maxwell, lying in ambush
in the woods along the road. Cornwallis's vanguard was soon reinforced,
and a skirmish known as the Battle of Cooch's Bridge followed, ending
when the Americans, afraid of being outflanked, withdrew to the position of Washington's outposts along White Clay Creek, about four
miles away.

Washington ordered a line of defense established on the east side, the
Philadelphia side, of Brandywine Creek, a stream that might well have
been called a river, varying in width from 50 to 150 yards but fordable in a
number of places along its wooded banks. It flowed from the northwest to
the southeast, emptying into the Delaware River near Wilmington. The
best and likeliest place for an army to cross it was Chadd's Ford, where the
road from Kennett Square to Philadelphia crossed. Above Chadd's Ford
were at least six other possible crossings, and below Chadd's Ford was
another crossing, all of which Washington would have to guard.

In his general orders issued on September 5, Washington attempted
to rally his troops to a grand effort. He told them that the British were

making a final try to take Philadelphia, their previous attempts, overland from New Jersey, having twice been defeated by the valiant American army. American defenses in and along the Delaware River, he said, had forced Howe to launch his present attack from Chesapeake Bay. Now, Washington told his men, they would make a stand and if they were victorious here, "the war is at an end. . . . One bold stroke will free the land from rapine, devastations and burnings, and female innocence from brutal lust and violence. . . . If we behave like men, this third Campaign will be the last. . . ."⁵ On the other hand, although he didn't say it, if his army failed at the Brandywine, Philadelphia in all likelihood was lost.

On September 9 the two armies were separated by a mere two miles. That same day Washington began deploying his army on the east side of the Brandywine. His left flank would be at Pyle's Ford, below Chadd's Ford, where the wooded, hilly terrain favored a defensive position. There, where no attack was expected, Washington posted Brigadier General John Armstrong and 1,000 Pennsylvania militiamen.

The main body of his army Washington concentrated at Chadd's Ford. Those units included Nathanael Greene's division and Brigadier General Anthony Wayne's brigade, which were posted along the Brandywine from Chadd's Ford southward and were supported by most of Washington's artillery. Brigadier General William Maxwell's 800-man light infantry unit was posted on the west side of the creek, at the approaches to Chadd's Ford.

From Chadd's Ford north, to protect all the crossing points above Chadd's Ford, Washington posted Major General Sullivan and his division. Some short distance east of the line of defense was Stirling's division, positioned to support Sullivan or Greene, and Major General Adam Stephen's division, positioned to support the defense of Chadd's Ford.

Howe's army had camped at Kennett Square, about eight miles west of Chadd's Ford. At dawn on September 11, around five o'clock on a warm and foggy morning, it began moving toward the American lines. Howe's plan was for Knyphausen, with 5,000 men, to assault the rebel defense at Chadd's Ford while Cornwallis and Howe, leading a main force of 7,500 men, turned left onto Great Valley Road, which roughly paralleled the creek at a distance ranging from two to four miles. The main force would cross the Brandywine above Chadd's Ford and dash around Washington's right flank. When Washington reacted to the threat from behind, Knyphausen would then come crashing across at Chadd's Ford. It was the same plan that Howe had employed so successfully on Long Island—a demonstration at the center, a main attack on the flank.

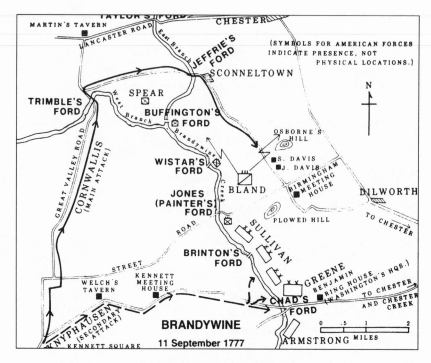

Brandywine, 11 September 1777

The British advance was reported to Washington early that morning, and he immediately alerted his commanders. The fog had lifted by seven, and around eight, the forward units of Knyphausen's command made contact with Maxwell's light infantry. Knyphausen maneuvered to confront Maxwell and the Virginia regiments that had come up to reinforce him. Knyphausen drove them back across the creek. By 10:30 a.m. Knyphausen was in his planned position along the west bank of the Brandywine and was cannonading the American artillery emplacements on the east side.

Around eleven, Washington received a report sent from Colonel Moses Hazen, who was guarding Jones Ford, upstream of Chadd's, saying that a large enemy force was moving toward the point above his position where the creek forked into two streams. That report, delivered by Major Lewis Morris, Sullivan's aide-de-camp, was confirmed by a report from Lieutenant Colonel James Ross, who wrote to Washington from his position on the Great Valley Road at 11 a.m.:

Dear General,

A large body of the enemy, from every account five thousand, with sixteen or eighteen field-pieces, marched along this road just now. . . .

We are close in their rear with about seventy men, and gave them three rounds within a small distance. . . .[6]

If the information was correct, Washington realized, Cornwallis was on his way to turning Washington's right flank; but the reports also meant that Howe had divided his army and Knyphausen's units across the creek at Chadd's Ford could be overwhelmed by a charge with Washington's superior numbers.

Washington alerted his commanders and instructed Alexander and Stephen to take their divisions to Birmingham Meeting House, about three miles directly north of Chadd's Ford, on the east side of the creek and on the road that Cornwallis would likely take if indeed he was trying to get behind Washington. At the same time, Washington prepared to launch an assault to crush Knyphausen. He sent orders to Sullivan, posted above Chadd's Ford, to cross the Brandywine and assault Knyphausen's positions in a concerted attack with Greene's division at Chadd's Ford.

Before Greene's troops could move out into the stream, Washington received back from Sullivan a disconcerting message:

Since I sent you the message by Major Morris I saw some of the Militia who came in this morning from a tavern called Martins on the forks of the Brandywine. The one who told me, said he had come from thence to Welches Tavern and heard nothing of the Enemy above the forks of the Brandywine and is Confident that [the enemy] are not in that Quarters. So that Colonel Hazen's Information must be wrong. I have sent to the Quarter to know whether there is any foundation for the Report and shall be glad to give your Ex'y the earliest information.[7]

Washington now became extremely cautious, careful to avoid taking a precipitous action that would later prove a mistake. Preferring Sullivan's contradictory, secondhand report to the firsthand reports of Hazen and Ross, he called off the attack on Knyphausen, fearful that Howe's army was still intact and facing him across the creek, when in fact Cornwallis was racing toward his rear.

Howe and Cornwallis crossed the Brandywine at Jeffries Ford, about five miles upstream of Chadd's Ford and beyond the farthest position of the right side of Sullivan's line. The going there was slow as the redcoats passed through a wooded area, and it was early afternoon by the time they emerged from the woods on the north side of a prominence called Osborne's Hill. Crossing the hill, they completely surprised Sullivan and were suddenly threatening his rear, having formed into two lines with a reserve behind them.

Sullivan swiftly reacted and ordered his division to shift its front from the creek to the right to face the advancing British and Hessians. As Sullivan's units scrambled into a new defensive formation, Cornwallis halted his infantry and opened fire with his artillery, pouring an awesome cannonade into the rebel positions as Cornwallis's front line of guards on his right, grenadiers in the center, and light infantry and jagers on his left, stood watching the effects of the fire, ready to commence a bayonet charge following the cessation of the cannonade. Cornwallis and Howe, resplendent in their scarlet coats with bright gold epaulets, sat mounted on their horses, also watching.

Then the artillery fell silent, and the red-coated band struck up "British Grenadiers," a lively martial tune that floated across the smoky air. On the signal to charge the rebel line, the redcoats and Hessian mercenaries moved forward down the south slope of Osborne's Hill in precise formation, their polished steel bayonets glinting in the mid-afternoon sun. The rebel troops fired and fell back, and soon Sullivan's entire division began to give way as the ranks of bayonets came relentlessly onward. A reinforcement by Greene's division saved them from slaughter and allowed them to retreat in order, but the battle had been lost, the field abandoned to Cornwallis and Howe.

The American defeat was recounted in the diary of Joseph Clark of Princeton, a witness to the battle that day:

> At the upper ford the enemy sent a great part of their force about noon. Three divisions of our army were sent immediately to oppose them, viz.: Sterling's, Sullivan's and Stephens'; but as there were no heights at this ford, on our side, to prevent their landing by cannon from batteries, we were obliged to oppose them after they had crossed; but as their number was larger than was expected, they stretched their line beyond ours and flanked our right wing shortly after the action began.

This occasioned the line to break, to prevent being surrounded, though the firing, while the action lasted, was the warmest, I believe, that has been in America since the war began; and as our men on the left of the line were pretty well stationed, they swept off great numbers of the enemy before they retreated, and from the best accounts I could collect from the officers in the action, the enemy must have suffered very much from our people before they broke, though indeed our people suffered much in this action, and would have suffered more if Gen'l Green had not been detached to their assistance, by whose timely aid they made a safe retreat of the men, though we lost some pieces of artillery; he, however, got up too late to form in a proper line and give our party that was broken time to recover. Notwithstanding this repulse, which was the most severe upon the 3d Virginia Regiment, who, through mistake, was fired upon by our own men, our whole body got off with but an inconsiderable loss in men, though something considerable in artillery.

When the action began at the upper ford, the batteries at the middle ford opened upon each other with such fury as if the elements had been in convulsions; the valley was filled with smoke, and now I grew seriously anxious for the event. For an hour and a half this horrid sport continued, and about sunset I saw a column of the enemy advance to one of our batteries and take it. Under cover of their cannon they had crossed at the ford, and were advancing in a large body. What we lost at our batteries I have not yet heard. As all our militia were at the lower ford, where [there] was no action, and Gen'l Green sent to reinforce at the upper ford, we had not a very large party to oppose the enemy at the middle ford. The body stationed across the valley drew off to the right, and formed farther back on an eminence, when an engagement began with musketry, and the enemy gave way; but as night was spreading its dusky shade through the gloomy valley, and our army was something broke, it was necessary to leave the field of action and take care of the troops.

Accordingly, after sunset, the party at the middle ford drew off and marched down to Chester, where the whole army, by appointment, met. The sun was set when I left the hill from whence I saw the fate of the day. His Excellency I saw within 200 yards of the enemy, with but a small party about him, and they drawing off from their station, our army broke at the right, and night coming on, adding a gloom to our misfortunes, amidst the noise of cannon, the hurry of the people, and wagons driving in confusion from the field, I came off with a heart full of distress. In painful anxiety I took with hasty step the gloomy path from the field and travelled fifteen miles to Chester, where I slept two hours upon a couple of chairs. . . .[8]

The failure of Washington's attempt to stop Cornwallis at the Birmingham Meeting House was described by Major John Andre, then an aide to Major General Charles Grey:

> Sir William Howe, drawing near Birmingham, found the Rebels posted on the heights to oppose him. Washington had drawn part of his army here about two hours before, on receiving the first intimation of General Howe's approach. At about 4 o'clock the attack began near the Meeting House. The Guards were formed upon the right, the British Grenadiers in the centre, and the Light Infantry and Chasseurs on the left. . . .
>
> The Guards met with very little resistance and penetrated to the very height overlooking the 4-gun battery of the Rebels Chad's Ford, just as General Knyphausen had crossed. . . .
>
> The Rebels were driven back by the superior fire of the troops, but these were too much exhausted to be able to charge or pursue. . . . Night and the fatigue the soldiers had undergone prevented any pursuit. . . .[9]

At midnight that same night, Washington, at new quarters in Chester, also wrote about the battle, his letter addressed to the president of the Continental Congress:

> Sir: I am sorry to inform you that in this day's engagement we have been obliged to leave the enemy masters of the field.
>
> Unfortunately the intelligence received of the enemy's advancing up the Brandywine, and crossing at a ford about six miles above us, was uncertain and contradictory, notwithstanding all my pains to get the best. This prevented my making a disposition adequate to the force with which the Enemy attacked us on the right; in consequence of which the troops first engaged were obliged to retire before they could be reinforced. In the midst of the attack on the right, that body of the Enemy which remained on the other side of Chad's Ford, crossed it, and attacked the division there under the command of

General Wayne and the light troops under General Maxwell who, after a severe conflict, also retired. The Militia under the command of Major Genl. Armstrong, being posted at a ford about two miles below Chad's had no opportunity of engaging.

But though we fought under many disadvantages, and were from the causes above mentioned obliged to retire, yet our loss of men is not, I am persuaded, very considerable, I believe much less than the enemy's. We have also lost about seven or eight pieces of cannon, according to the best information I can at present obtain. The baggage having been previously moved off, is all secure, saving the men's Blankets, which being at their backs, many of them doubtless are lost.

I have directed all the Troops to Assemble behind Chester, where they are now arranging for this Night. Notwithstanding the misfortune of the day, I am happy to find the troops in good spirits; and I hope another time we shall compensate for the losses now sustained.

The Marquis La Fayette was wounded in the leg, and Gen. Woodford in the hand. Divers other Officers were wounded and some Slain, but the number of either cannot now be ascertained.[10]

Contrary to Washington's remarks about the casualties of both sides, the American losses were put by Major General Greene at 1,200 to 1,300, about 440 of those being taken prisoner. Also lost were eleven pieces of artillery.

Howe's losses were reported as 577 killed or wounded and six missing. Forty of the killed or wounded were Hessians, the rest British.

Washington marched his army out of Chester the next morning, Friday, September 12. They crossed the Schuylkill River and proceeded to the outskirts of Germantown, on the northwest side of Philadelphia, where they encamped.

Fearing that Howe would again try to turn his right flank and back him into a corner between the Schuylkill and Delaware Rivers, Washington decided to preempt a British attack by blocking Howe's advance to the Schuylkill. He repositioned his troops athwart the Lancaster Road, by which he expected Howe to come, and waited.

On September 16, Howe's troops drew near to the American line, moving as Washington had anticipated. Before the armies could engage, however, the storm that had been a threat for several days finally blew in, bringing strong winds, falling temperatures, and a torrent of rain. Fields and roads were turned into a morass in which men sank up to their calves in mud. The movement of equipment wagons and artillery carriages became impossible. Washington then moved out of his position and marched through the evening and night to Yellow Springs, about eleven miles away.

The next day, September 17, apparently to replenish his supply of gunpowder at a storage depot, Washington moved farther west, to Warwick, about twelve miles west of the Schuylkill, then two days later turned his army around and recrossed the Schuylkill at Parker Ford, some thirty miles northwest of Philadelphia, once again placing the river between him and Howe.

The British threat to Philadelphia now became so dire that on Thursday, September 18, Lieutenant Colonel Alexander Hamilton, Washington's young aide-de-camp, presumably on Washington's instructions, urgently warned members of Congress that the city could not be successfully defended against Howe's army and that they should immediately leave town to avoid possible capture. Hamilton's warning came in the middle of the night, and many Congress members quickly heeded it, some of them angry, dismayed, and complaining, fleeing for safety into the darkness, heading for Lancaster, where they had previously agreed to reconvene in the event Philadelphia fell to the enemy.

When he recrossed the Schuylkill at Parker Ford, Washington left behind the 1,500-man division commanded by Brigadier Anthony Wayne with orders to harass Howe's army and impede the British advance. Wayne positioned his force, which included four pieces of artillery, near Paoli and planned to attack the British flank or their baggage train as Howe pursued Washington. Howe received intelligence about Wayne's mission and his location. (Pennsylvania's population included a percentage of loyalists higher than any other province's, and to some extent, Washington's army was operating in enemy territory in the environs of Philadelphia.) Howe instructed Major General Grey to take a detachment of two regiments and a light infantry battalion and make a night attack on Wayne's camp.

The British attack was made shortly after midnight, on the morning of September 21, taking the Americans completely by surprise and routing those who did not fall victim to the British bayonets. Wayne managed to escape with most of his force and his artillery pieces in a hurried retreat to Chester, but he lost at least 150 men, killed, wounded, or captured. British losses were put at six killed and twenty-two wounded. The engagement became known as the Paoli Massacre.

The Continental Army had a large supply depot at Reading, some fifty miles northwest of Philadelphia, where the bulk of its stores were warehoused, and Washington, continually conscious of a possible attack on the depot, was anxious to protect it.

On September 21 Howe seemed to be planning such an attack. He moved his army to Valley Forge, then proceeded northwestward along the south bank of the Schuylkill River, headed toward Reading. Washington countered by marching parallel to him on the opposite side of the river. Suddenly Howe reversed his march, quietly turning around under cover of darkness and backtracking down the river, crossing it at two fords below Washington's position.

Howe's apparent threat to Reading had been merely a feint to draw Washington away from Philadelphia, and the ruse succeeded. On Friday, September 26, Howe's army marched into Philadelphia unopposed. One of the thousands who witnessed the triumphant entry was loyalist Robert Morton. He described the British arrival:

> About eleven o'clock a.m., Lord Cornwallis with his division of the British and auxiliary troops, amounting to about three thousand, marched into this city, accompanied by Enoch Story, Joseph Galloway, Andrew Allen, William Allen, and others, inhabitants of this city, to the great relief of the inhabitants who have too long suffered the yoke of arbitrary power, and who testified their approbation of the arrival of the troops by the loudest acclamations of joy.
>
> Went with Charles Logan to headquarters to see his Excellency General Sir William Howe, but he being gone out, we had some conversation with the officers, who appeared well disposed towards the peaceable inhabitants, but most bitter against and determined to pursue to the last extremity the army of the United States.
>
> The British army in this city are quartered at the Betterling House, State House, and other places, and already begin to show the great destruction of the fences and other things, the dreadful consequences of an army, however friendly....[11]

Mrs. Henry Drinker of Philadelphia, evidently *not* a loyalist, succinctly recorded the same event in her diary:

> *Sept. 26.*—Well! here are the English in earnest! About two or 300 came in through Second Street with opposition. Cornwallis came with the troops. Gen. Howe has not arrived.[12]

Howe had stopped in Germantown and there had encamped the greater part of his army while he sent a 3,000-man occupation force, headed by Cornwallis, to Philadelphia. He sent another 3,000 troops across the Delaware River into New Jersey, opposite Philadelphia, apparently in an attempt to open the Delaware River to British ships, which were barred by rebel fortifications and obstructions placed in the river.

Washington now determined to redeem himself, his generals, and his army following their humiliating defeat at Brandywine. By the end of September the army that Washington had at hand had been reinforced by the units of Brigadier General Alexander McDougall, formerly posted at Peekskill, by Maryland militia under the command of Brigadier General William Smallwood, and by New Jersey militia under the command of Brigadier General David Forman. Washington's forces now totaled some 11,000 men, including 8,000 Continental regulars and 3,000 militamen. With a tone of confidence he wrote to Major General William Heath in Boston and told him, "I am in hopes it will not be long before we are in a situation to repair the consequences of our late ill success. . . ."

On September 29 Washington moved his army from Pennypacker's Mill to a position five miles closer to Philadelphia. On October 2 he moved it to a position in Worchester Township, within fifteen miles of Germantown, and encamped there, knowing from intelligence reports that the main body of Howe's army was at Germantown, facing Chestnut Hill, its left flank against the Schuylkill, its right flank near Lucken's Mill and Old York Road. Conferring with his generals in a council of war, Washington decided to attack with his superior numbers.

An elaborate attack plan was devised, calling for coordinated assaults on the British position from several directions. Nathanael Greene, commanding three divisions, would lead a wide, enveloping movement against the British right. Smallwood and Forman would lead their militias down Old York Road, on Greene's extreme left, to turn and get behind the British right flank. The divisions of Sullivan and Anthony Wayne would make the frontal assault along the Skippack Road, and Brigadier General John Armstrong's Pennsylvania militiamen would attack the British left from Manatawny Road, which ran alongside the Schuylkill on its way to Philadelphia. Two brigades under the command of Stirling (Alexander) would be held in reserve behind Sullivan's division.

All columns were to march fifteen miles through the dark over different routes and be within two miles of the British position by two o'clock on the morning of the attack. Then, all were to launch their assaults simultaneously at 5 a.m. The clearest element of the plan was its complexity, which was captured in Washington's orders:

> The divisions of Sullivan and Wayne to form the right wing and attack the enemy's left; they are to march down the Monatawny road. The divisions of Green and Steven to form the left wing and attack the enemy's right; they are to march down the Skippack Road, General Conway to march in front of the troops that compose the right wing, and file to attack the enemy's left flank. General McDougall to march in front of the troops that comprise the left wing, and file off to attack the enemy's left flank. General Nash and General Maxwell's brigade to form the corps de reserve and to be commanded by Major General Lord Stirling. The Corps de reserve to pass down the Skippack Road. General Armstrong to pass down the ridge road, pass by Leverings Tavern and take guides to cross the Wissahickon creek up the head of John Vandeering's mill-dam so as to fall above Joseph Warner's new house. Smallwood and Forman to pass down the road by a mill formerly Danl. Morris and Jacob Edges mill into the White marsh road at the Sandy run: thence to Whitemarsh Church, where take the left hand road, which leads to Jenkin's tavern, on the old York road, below Armitages, behind the seven mile stone, half a mile from which turns off short to the right hand, fenced on both sides, which leads through the enemys incampment to German town market house. General McDougall to attack the right of the enemy in flank. General Smallwood and Forman to attack the right wing in flank and rear. General Conway to attack the enemy's left flank and General Armstrong to attack their left wing in flank and rear.[13]

The rebel columns began moving slowly forward in the darkness at 7 p.m. on Friday, October 3, and reached Chestnut Hill the next morning at dawn. The first contact with the enemy came about 6 a.m. when Captain Allen McLane's light horse company, riding ahead in the center of the American advance, ran into a British outpost near Mount Airy, between Chestnut Hill and the British front line, and drove it back through the morning fog.

Behind McLane's cavalry came Sullivan's column, steadily advancing and sending the forward British troops reeling in flight through the streets of Germantown and into their camp beyond. Then, from the windows of a large, three-story stone house on the rebels' left came concentrated musket fire. It was the home of Benjamin Chew, Pennsylvania's chief justice, and it had been commandeered by British Lieutenant Colonel Thomas Musgrave, who with six companies of infantry, some 120 men, was attempting to stand off the rebel advance.

Instead of having his brigade stay out of musket range and bypass the house, Brigadier General William Maxwell ordered it taken with artillery fire and an assault by infantry. In so doing, his troops needlessly lost half an hour in a battle that depended on timing. Colonel Thomas Pickering, Washington's adjutant general, gave his account of the incident:

> The other brigades drove the enemy before them a mile or two to the very centre of Germantown. All this time we could not hear of the left wing's being engaged, for the smoke and fog prevented our seeing them, and our own fire drowned theirs. (General Washington went with the right wing, attended by his aides-de-camp and myself.)
>
> But the left wing [Greene's divisions] had engaged, and both wings met almost in the same point, which was at Mr. Chew's house, into which the enemy had thrown a party (we since find them to have been six companies, with a colonel to command them) that annoyed us prodigiously and absolutely stopped our pursuit—not necessarily, but we mistook our true interest; we ought to have pushed our advantage, leaving a party to watch the enemy in that house. But our stop here gave the enemy time to recollect themselves and get reenforced, and eventually to oblige us to retreat. . . .[14]

On Washington's left things were not going as planned. Brigadier General John Peter Gabriel Muhlenberg, the Lutheran minister who had laid down the cloth to take up the sword and had inspired 300 men of his congregation to join him, sent his brigade on a bayonet charge that penetrated the British line, but having driven into a pocket of the British defenders and becoming outnumbered, had to fight his way back to the position of Greene's main body. The 9th Virginia Regiment, which had led Muhlenberg's charge and had penetrated deepest into the enemy position, was surrounded before it could disengage and was captured.

The fog that had shielded the entire American advance from the redcoats' observation and had given the rebels an advantage, now worked to their disadvantage. From the far left came sounds of firing and shouting, men yelling to be heard, and others yelling back in response. The situation seemed one of complete confusion. Then, to the front of Sullivan's units, rebel troops came running from the left, through the fog, panicked, shouting that the enemy had turned their flank and was behind their line. Adam Stephen's troops, confused and partially blinded by the fog (and commanded by a general too rum-soused to see or think clearly), had fired on their comrades, and their comrades, troops of Anthony Wayne, had returned the fire. The scene was chaos. Colonel Pickering called the battle a disaster and mostly blamed the fog and smoke:

> . . . the enemy advanced, and our troops gave way on all sides and retired with precipitation. This retreat surprised every body (all supposing victory was nearly secured in our favor). . . . Another circumstance also contributed to it: the foggy, still morning (the air moving very little, but what there was bringing the smoke and fog in our faces) and the body of smoke from the firing absolutely prevented the two wings, and even the different brigades, of the same wing, from seeing each other and cooperating in the best manner; nay, I am persuaded they sometimes fired on each other, particularly at Chew's house, where the left wing supposed the cannon-balls fired by the right at the house came from the enemy.
>
> In a word, our disaster was imputed chiefly to the fog and the smoke, which, from the stillness of the air, remained a long time, hanging low and undissipated. But, on the other hand, it must be remembered that the fog blinded the enemy as well as ourselves, though it certainly injured us most.[15]

Washington's officers, for all their efforts, found the frightened flight of their troops impossible to stem. Rebel soldiers crowded the roads and fields over which they had just traveled to reach the enemy, running to safety. Although Cornwallis came from Philadelphia with three battalions, the British did not pursue the fleeing rebels.

Many minutes later order was reimposed on the retreat. By mid-morning the whole horrible affair was over. Washington led his exhausted army back to Schwenksville, more than twenty miles to the north.

American losses were reported as 152 killed, 521 wounded, and more than 400 taken prisoner. British losses were put at 537 killed or wounded and 14 captured. One odd survivor of the battle was taken captive and then two days later was returned to the British lines with a note written by Washington: "General Washington's compliments to General Howe. He has the pleasure to return him a dog, which accidentally fell into his hands, and by the inscription of the Collar, appears to belong to General Howe."

Turning to Congress, Washington put the best face possible on another failure in the field. Having become perhaps more adroit at public relations than at warfare, he reported to Congress:

> Upon the whole, it may be said the day was rather unfortunate than injurious. We sustained no material loss of Men and brought off all our Artillery, except one piece which was dismounted. The enemy are nothing the better by the event; and our Troops, who are not in the least dispirited by it, have gained what all young troops gain by being in action.[16]

Washington's troops, admirably enough, were feeling far from losers, despite the disaster. "Tho we gave away a complete victory," one Continental officer, Will Heth, wrote, "we have learned this valuable truth: [we are able] to beat them by vigorous exertion. . . . We are in high spirits. Every action [gives] our troops fresh vigor and a greater opinion of their own strength. Another bout or two must make their [the British] situation very disagreeable."[17]

If most of Washington's fighters felt the same way, their buoyant spirit might prove to be the American army's salvation, for bitter and disheartening hardship lay just ahead.

CHAPTER Twelve

The Winter at Valley Forge

The city of Philadelphia lay in the hands of the British, but the American defenses that had been raised to protect it still had to be removed before Howe and his occupying army could feel secure. The remaining defenses were mainly two forts below Philadelphia—Fort Mercer, at Red Bank, New Jersey, and Fort Mifflin, southeast of Philadelphia, on the Pennsylvania side of the river. Until those rebel fortifications were captured or destroyed, Howe's army in Philadelphia could not be reliably supplied by ships coming up the Delaware and would continue to be dependent on the overland route by which it had come from Elkton, Maryland, a supply line subject to continual harrying attacks by the rebels.

The rebel defenses also included underwater chevaux-de-frise, devices adapted (apparently by Benjamin Franklin) from a hellish instrument used to stop men and horses and to form roadblocks and otherwise obstruct passage in land warfare. The land version was made of portable wooden beams traversed with iron-pointed spikes or spears up to six feet long, fearsome to see, lethal to engage. The underwater version was a gigantic wooden box bristling with timbers as large as a ship's mast, tipped with iron points. The boxes were filled with tons of rock and sunk to the river bottom, leaving the pointed timbers projecting upward at an angle, menacing the wooden underbelly of any craft attempting to pass over them. Ships of any considerable draft would have their hulls ripped open by the chevaux-de-frise or else be impaled upon them and rendered immobile.

Howe determined to remove all the obstacles blocking British shipping on the Delaware. On October 22 he sent Hessian Colonel Carl von Donop to attack Fort Mercer with a detachment of 2,000 troops. The fort, which mounted 14 artillery pieces, was manned by 400 troops under the command of Colonel Christopher Greene, Nathanael Greene's cousin. Donop's troops were repulsed with heavy casualties, an estimated 400 being killed, wounded, or captured. The casualties included Colonel von Donop, who was mortally wounded. The Americans lost 14 killed and 23 wounded.

The next day, October 23, the batteries of Fort Mifflin, supported by rebel river craft, severely damaged six British vessels attempting to sail through a gap the British had made in the chevaux-de-frise. Two of the British warships ran aground and were abandoned and blown up by their crews.

More determined than ever, Howe ordered his shore batteries to join a flotilla of British warships in a fierce, prolonged bombardment of Fort Mifflin. On the night of November 15–16, after five days and nights of unrelenting cannonading, some 200 American survivors, less than half the fort's original garrison, abandoned the ruined structure and withdrew across the river to Fort Mercer under the cover of darkness.

Howe then ordered Cornwallis to command a 2,000-man force in a new assault on Fort Mercer. Upon Cornwallis's approach, the loss of Fort Mifflin having substantially reduced the usefulness of Fort Mercer and rendered it vulnerable to a combined attack from land and river, Colonel Greene on the night of November 20–21 evacuated the fort and slipped away with his garrison.

Washington, however, was still unwilling to concede Philadelphia to the British. On November 25, at his army's encampment about twenty miles northwest of Philadelphia, Washington proposed an attack on the city. His generals strongly opposed the idea. Perhaps guessing Washington's main reason for wanting to recapture the city was to win back a perceived loss of respect by his countrymen, Brigadier General Henry Knox, who had joined the other generals in voting against an attack, wrote reassuringly to his commander in chief on November 26:

> I know . . . the people of America look up to you as their Father, and into your hands they entrust their all, fully confident of every exertion on your part for their security and happiness and I do not believe there is any man on earth for whose welfare there are more solicitations at the Court of Heaven, than for yours.[1]

Howe, meanwhile, had not given up trying to lure Washington into a fight. First he moved his army from its position at Germantown into

Philadelphia. Washington reacted by moving to White Marsh, about twelve miles outside Philadelphia, then moved again, eastward. As he did, Howe moved toward him. A skirmish on December 5 was followed by a major movement by the British on the night of December 6–7. Howe took the main body of his army to Jenkintown, north of Philadelphia, intending to attack Washington's left flank, but found it stronger than he had supposed and withdrew back into Philadelphia.

Cornwallis had returned from his mission into New Jersey and on December 11 led a 3,500-man foraging party into the farmlands along the south bank of the Schuylkill. On that same morning Washington began moving his army to a winter cantonment at Valley Forge. The vanguard of the rebel army encountered Cornwallis's foragers at an area known as the Gulph, near Matson's Ford (West Conshohocken), shortly after the Americans had crossed the river. Refusing an engagement, the Americans withdrew and recrossed the Schuylkill, tearing up their hastily built bridge after they had crossed again. Cornwallis's troops continued on their foraging mission, managing to round up some 2,000 sheep and cattle to feed Howe's army and returned to Philadelphia on December 12.

That action was Cornwallis's last of the year. The leave that had been revoked a year earlier he was now able to take, and on December 16, 1777, he boarded H.M.S. *Brilliant* and sailed home to England.

After waiting several days in the vicinity of the Gulph, Washington set out again for Valley Forge. In his general orders of December 17 he explained to his troops his choice of Valley Forge as a place to spend the winter:

> The General ardently wishes it were now in our power to conduct the troops into the best winter quarters. But where are these to be found? Should we retire to interior parts of the State, we should find them crowded with virtuous citizens who, sacrificing their all, have left Philadelphia. . . . To their distresses, humanity forbids us to add. This is not all, we should leave a vast extent of fertile country to be despoiled and ravaged by the enemy. . . . Many of our firm friends would be exposed to all the miseries of the most insulting and wanton depredation. A train of evils might be enumerated but these will suffice.
>
> These conditions make it indispensably necessary for the army to take such a position as will enable it most effectually to prevent distress and to give the most extensive security, and in that position we must make ourselves the best shelter in our power. With activity and diligence huts may be erected that will be warm and dry. In these

the troops will be compact, more secure against surprises than if in a divided state and at hand to protect the country.

These cogent reasons have determined the General to take post in the neighborhood of this camp. . . . He himself will share in the hardships and partake of every inconvenience.[2]

The site of the rebel encampment was an inhospitable, two-mile-long, heavily wooded slope that rose from the bank of the Schuylkill River, which curved to protect the rebels' rear and left flank. Their right flank was protected by a hill called Mount Joy. The encampment was well situated for defense, and the abundance of trees would provide timber for the construction of huts to house Washington's ill-clad, ill-shod, ill-fed troops. That was all the good that could be said about it. There was no nearby town or farms. The troops were in the middle of nowhere.

Major General Johann de Kalb, a volunteer to the American cause, wrote home to France about the site:

On the 19th instant [December 1777], the army reached this wooded wilderness, certainly one of the poorest districts in Pennsylvania; the soil thin, uncultivated and almost uninhabited, without forage and without provisions! Here we are to go into winter-quarters, *i.e.*, to lie in shanties, generals and privates, to enable the army, it is said, to recover from its privations, to recruit, to re-equip, and to prepare for the opening of the coming campaign, while protecting the country against hostile inroads. The matter has been the subject of long debates in the council of war. It was discussed in all its length and breadth—a bad practice to which they are addicted here—and good advice was not taken. The idea of wintering in this desert can only have been put into the head of the commanding general by an interested speculator or a disaffected man. . . .[3]

Brigadier General James Mitchell Varnum complained to Nathanael Greene about the site:

Many of the troops are destitute of meat, and are several days in arrear. The horses are dying for want of forage. The country in the vicinity of the camp is exhausted. There cannot be a moral certainty of bettering our circumstances while we continue here. What consequences have we rationally to expect? . . .

I have from the beginning viewed this situation with horror! It is
unparalleled in the history of mankind to establish a winter quarters in
a country wasted, and without a single magazine. . . . There is no alternative but immediately to remove the army to places where they can be
supplied, unless effectual remedies can be supplied upon the spot,
which I believe every gentleman of the army thinks impracticable.[4]

Nevertheless, there on that cold, wind-swept slope, the American army
on December 19 made camp, some twenty-two miles from where the
warm, well-clothed, well-fed enemy was settled in comfortable, commandeered houses in Philadelphia, ready to savor the winter's break in the hostilities. While they did, America's army suffered not only from want of
shelter but from want of clothing, of food, and of blankets to insulate their
bodies from the numbing cold. Colonel John Brooks of Massachusetts
wrote to a friend about the lack of clothing for the troops:

> With respect to the clothing, etc., etc., of our army, believe it, Sir, to be
> bad enough. Ever since our march from Albany our men have been suf-
> fering all the inconveniences of an inclement season and a want of
> cloathing. For a week past we have had snow, and as cold weather as
> I almost ever knew at home. To see our poor brave fellows living in tents,
> bare-footed, bare-legged, bare-breeched, etc., etc., in snow, in rain, on
> marches, in camp, and on duty, without being able to supply their wants
> is really distressing. Where the fault is I know not, but am rather inclined
> to think our General Court has not done every thing that might be
> expected of them. If it be for want of foresight in our rulers, the Lord
> pity us! But if it be through negligence or design, "is there not some cho-
> sen curse" reserved for those who are cause of so much misery? . . .[5]

A Connecticut private, James Sullivan Martin, also wrote about the
deprivation:

> The army was now not only starved but naked; the greatest part were
> not only shirtless and barefoot, but destitute of all other clothing,
> especially blankets. I procured a small piece of raw cowhide and made
> myself a pair of moccasons, which kept my feet (while they lasted)
> from the frozen ground, although, as I well remember, the hard edges
> so galled my ancles, while on a march, that it was with much diffi-
> culty and pain that I could wear them afterwards; but the only alter-

native I had was to endure this inconvenience or to go barefoot, as hundreds of my companions had to, till they might be tracked by their blood upon the rough frozen ground. . . .[6]

Albigence Waldo, a twenty-seven-year-old surgeon from Connecticut, poetically recorded in his diary the sufferings of the starving army:

December 21. Preparations made for hutts. Provisions scarce. Mr. Ellis went homeward—sent a letter to my wife. Heartily wish myself at home. My skin and eyes are almost spoiled with continual smoke. A general cry thro' the camp this evening among the soldiers, "No meat! No meat!" The distant vales echoed back the melancholly sound—"No meat! No meat!" Immitating the noise of crows and owls, also, made a part of the confused musick.

What have you for your dinners, boys? "Nothing but fire cake and water, Sir." At night: "Gentlemen, the supper is ready." What is your supper, lads? "Fire cake and water, Sir." . . .

December 22. Lay excessive cold and uncomfortable last night. My eyes are started out from their orbits like a rabbit's eyes, occasioned by a great cold and smoke.

What have you got for breakfast, lads? "Fire cake and water, Sir." The Lord send that our Commissary of Purchases may live [on] fire cake and water till their glutted gutts are turned to pasteboard.

Our division are under marching orders this morning. I am ashamed to say it, but I am tempted to steal fowls if I could find them, or even a whole hog, for I feel as if I could eat one. But the impoverished country about us affords but little matter to employ a thief, or keep a clever fellow in good humour. But why do I talk of hunger and hard usage, when so many in the world have not even fire cake and water to eat?[7]

Fire cake was a thin patty made of flour mixed with water and baked over an open fire—debilitatingly meager fare for men working strenuously in the cold, felling and hewing trees into log huts for their shelter.

While America's soldiers were undergoing such hardships, many of America's businessmen and farmers were enriching themselves by selling what Washington's men needed to the British at profiteering prices. The British in Philadelphia were paying hard cash for produce, and Pennsylvania farmers preferred cash to notes from America's government in refuge. Grain from New

York farms was also going to those who could pay, including New England civilians and to British troops posted around the city of New York. Private contractors reaped huge profits by using government wagons to haul food and raw goods north from Pennsylvania while meat meant for the American army spoiled in New Jersey waiting for wagons to carry it to the troops.

To cope, Washington sent out troops to forcibly requisition food from the farms closest to his cantonment and sent others on far-ranging foraging missions. Those foragers at times ran into British foragers and were forced to do battle, suffering losses at Quintan's Bridge, New Jersey; Hancock's Bridge, New Jersey; and Crooked Billet, Pennsylvania.

Washington also made a change in the office of quartermaster general. On October 1, 1776, he had replaced the incompetent Stephen Moylan with Thomas Mifflin, who proved to be not much better than Moylan and who bore the blame for the negligent management that resulted in the army lacking food and clothing at Valley Forge. Washington persuaded Nathanael Greene to take over as quartermaster general, which he did on March 23, 1778, and after that, things began to improve.

While at Valley Forge, Washington introduced another change for the better, one that improved the army significantly. Friedrich Wilhelm Augustin von Steuben was a former captain in the Prussian army and a self-styled baron in need of a new job and a change of scenery. While passing himself off as a lieutenant general, he had met a friend of Benjamin Franklin in Paris and had parlayed that connection into a position in the Continental Army. On February 23, 1778 he sought out the American commander in chief at Valley Forge and reported for duty.

Steuben could speak only German and a little French, but with a translator he instructed a hand-picked company of one hundred men on how to be soldiers in a well-disciplined army, applying European methods and standards to shape up the army of America. Those one hundred men then taught other troops assigned to them for training. What amounted to basic training was thus passed along to the Continental Army, turning recruits into soldiers and the army into a military organization worthy of the name. Steuben's detailed instruction covered every aspect of soldierly conduct, as shown in this excerpt from the exhaustive drill manual he authored:

Of the inspection of the Men, their Dress, Necessaries, Arms, Accoutrements and Ammunition.

The oftener the soldiers are under the inspection of their officers the better; for which reason every morning at troop beating they must inspect into the dress of their men; see that their clothes are whole and put on properly; their hands and faces washed clean; their hair combed; their accoutrements properly fixed, and every article about them in the greatest order. Those who are guilty of repeated neglects in these particulars are to be confined and punished. The field officers must pay attention to this object, taking proper notice of those companies where a visible neglect appears, and publicly applauding those who are remarkable for their good appearance.

Every day the commanding officers of companies must examine their men's arms and ammunition, and see that they are clean and in good order.

That the men may always appear clean on the parade, and as a means of preserving their health, the noncommissioned officers are to see that they wash their hands and faces every day, and oftener when necessary. And when any river is nigh, and the season favorable, the men shall bathe themselves as frequently as possible, the commanding officers of each battalion sending them by small detachments successively, under the care of a non-commissioned officer; but on no account must the men be permitted to bathe when just come off a march, at least till they have reposed long enough to get cool. . . .[8]

In recognition of the important contribution Steuben was making, Washington recommended to Congress that he be appointed inspector general of the Continental Army with the rank of major general. Congress approved his appointment on May 5, 1778.

Despite the hardships the troops were suffering at Valley Forge, their disgruntlement never manifested itself in any seriously harmful way. Throughout the worst days of the encampment there was fear of mutiny and mass desertions, but neither occurred. Men confident they were fighting for liberty endured the hardships, some with humor, others with grim resolve, most with respect for Washington's leadership warm in their breasts.

The hardships took their toll, however. Of the approximately 10,000 soldiers at Valley Forge during the six months the army encamped there, an estimated 2,500 died, an enormous loss. As Nathanael Greene put it to Washington, "God grant we may never be brought to such a wretched condition again!"

The army endured Valley Forge, but Washington would pay a price for allowing the circumstances that had placed it there.

CHAPTER Thirteen

The Conway Cabal

John Adams, the Boston lawyer, was a man who liked manipulating people to effect results that suited him. He had manipulated his congressional colleagues into adopting the New England militias as the Continental Army, and he had manipulated Congress into appointing Washington commander in chief. When Washington lost Adams's favor, Adams began new manipulations.

A member of the congressional Board of War, Adams, with no experience as a soldier, assumed he was entitled to give instructions to the commander in chief. In September 1776 he issued a directive that Washington should "call his troops in every day and discipline them,"[1] and Washington had let him know that was not a good idea and it would not be adopted. Taking umbrage at Washington's reply, Adams had complained to Colonel William Tudor that the generals of the Continental Army were not what they should be and the troops' lack of discipline and displays of cowardice were the fault of their officers. What the army needed, Adams told Tudor, was a great mind. In October 1776 Adams wrote to a Colonel Hitchcock that the army was being mismanaged. Adams complained to Congress about "the superstitious veneration that is sometimes paid to General Washington."[2] In October 1777, Adams was telling people that General Howe had only half the troops in Pennsylvania that he actually had. Adams criticized Washington for being timorous and defensive. On October 26, 1777, three weeks after the victory at Saratoga, for which Horatio Gates received the credit, Adams wrote to his wife that he was glad the victory was not "immediately due to the commander in chief. If it had been, idolatry and adulation would have been unbounded; so excessive as to endanger our liberties."[3]

Serious criticism of Washington was coming from other influential sources, including Richard Henry Lee of Virginia, a signer of the Declaration of Independence, James Lovell, a member of Congress from Massachusetts, Samuel Adams, and Major General Thomas Mifflin. Jonathan D. Sergeant, the attorney general of Pennsylvania, wrote accusingly of Washington:

> Thousands of lives and millions of property are yearly sacrificed to the insufficiency of our Commander-in-Chief. Two battles he has lost for us by two such blunders as might have disgraced a soldier of three months' standing, and yet we are so attached to this man that I fear we shall rather sink with him than throw him off our shoulders.[4]

Benjamin Rush, the army surgeon who had been a member of Congress from Pennsylvania and was also a signer of the Declaration of Independence, found John Adams a sympathetic listener to his complaints and found Horatio Gates a more acceptable leader than Washington. On October 21 Rush wrote to Adams:

> General Gates' unparalleled success gave me great pleasure, but it has not obliterated the remembrance of the disorders I have seen in the army in this department. . . . I have heard several officers who have served under General Gates compare his army to a well-regulated family. The same gentlemen have compared General Washington's imitation of an army to an unformed mob. Look at the characters of both! The one on the pinnacle of military glory . . . the other outgeneraled and twice beaten, obliged to witness the march of a body of men only half their number through 140 miles of a thick-settled country, forced to give up a city the capital of a state, and after all outwitted by the same army in a retreat. . . .[5]

In that same letter, Rush included a quote from a letter written by Thomas Conway, then a brigadier general in Washington's army:

> "A great and good God," says General Conway in a letter to a friend, "has decreed that America shall be free, or [Washington] and weak counselors would have ruined her long ago."

Conway was an Irish-born French army officer who had risen to the rank of colonel and who by December 1776 had decided to seek his fortune in America. With a letter of introduction from Congress's agent in Paris, Silas Deane, Conway had arrived in Morristown on May 8, 1777, and reported to Washington for an assignment. Washington's first impression of him was favorable. He wrote a letter of recommendation for Conway and sent him off to Congress with it. Conway was then appointed a brigadier general and served under Major General John Sullivan at the battles of Brandywine and Germantown.

Seeing opportunity in the growing dissatisfaction with Washington, Conway began promoting himself among certain members of Congress and among some army officers. He repeatedly wrote to Congress, practically insisting he be promoted to major general. By then Washington had formed a more accurate impression of Conway, having seen him as an opportunist, a schemer, and a shameless self-server and braggard. When Washington learned that Congress was thinking of giving Conway the promotion he had been importuning to receive, Washington wrote to Richard Henry Lee on October 17, 1777:

> If there is any truth in a report which has been handed me, Vizt., that Congress hath appointed, or, as others say, are about to appoint, Brigadier Conway a Major General in this Army, it will be as unfortunate a measure as ever was adopted. I may add (and I think with truth) that it will give a fatal blow to the existence of the Army.
>
> Upon so interesting a subject, I must speak plain: The duty I owe my Country; the ardent desire I have to promote its true Interests, and justice to Individuals requires this of me. General Conway's merit, then, as an Officer, and his importance in this Army, exists more in his own imagination than in reality: For it is a maxim with him, to leave no service of his own untold, not to want any thing which is to be obtained by importunity. But as I do not mean to detract from him any merit he possesses, and only wish to have the matter taken up upon its true Ground, after allowing him every thing that his warmest Friends will contend for, I would ask, why the Youngest Brigadier in the service (for I believe he is so) should be put over the heads of all the Eldest? and thereby take Rank, and Command Gentlemen who but yesterday were his Seniors; Gentlemen who, I will be bold to say (in behalf of some of them at least) of sound judgment and unquestionable Bravery?
>
> If there was a degree of conspicuous merit in General Conway, unpossessed by any of his Seniors, the confusion which might be

occasioned by it would stand warranted upon the principles of sound policy; for I do readily agree that this is no time for trifling. But at the same time, I cannot subscribe to the fact, this truth I am very well assured of . . . that they will not serve under him. I leave you to guess, therefore, at the situation this Army would be in at so important a Crisis, if this event should take place. These Gentlemen have feelings as Officers, and though they do not dispute the Authority of Congress to make Appointments, they will judge of the propriety of acting under them. In a Word, the service is so difficult, and every necessary so expensive, that almost all our Officers are tired out. Do not, therefore, afford them good pretexts for retiring: No day passes over my head without application for leave to resign. . . .[6]

Gates, who had become a rallying point for Washington's detractors, was that "friend" to whom Conway had written disparagingly of Washington. Washington, however, was apparently unaware of the double-dealing and conspiracies going on behind his back. But on October 27, 1777, Gates's aide, twenty-year-old Lieutenant Colonel James Wilkinson, entrusted by Gates to deliver to Congress the official report of the victory at Saratoga, stopped in Reading, Pennsylvania, en route to York, where the Congress was meeting. As a guest at the Reading headquarters of Major General Stirling (Alexander), Wilkinson, during rounds of drinks, passed along to Stirling's aide the gossip from Gates's headquarters, which included mention of the letter Conway had written to Gates.

When Stirling's aide relayed that information to Stirling, Stirling reported the matter to Washington. In response, Washington on November 9 sent Conway a terse note to let him know that he was aware of Conway's duplicity:

> Sir: A Letter which I received last Night, contained the following paragraph.
> In a letter from Genl. Conway to Genl. Gates he says: "Heaven has been determined to save your Country; or a weak General and bad Councellors would have ruind it."
> I am Sir Yr, Hble. Servt. G. Washington.[7]

Conway promptly replied in self-defense, explaining that he had sent a congratulatory letter to Gates after the Battle of Saratoga and in it:

I spoke my mind freely and found fault with several measures pursued in this army, but I will venture to say that in my whole letter the paragraph of which you . . . send me a copy cannot be found. My opinion of you, sir, without flattery or envy, is . . . you are a brave man, an honest man, a patriot, and a man of great sense. Your modesty is such that although your advice in council is commonly sound and proper, you have often been influenced by men who were not equal to you in . . . experience, knowledge, or judgment. . . .

I believe I can assert that the expression, *weak general*, has not slipped from my pen. . . . In order that the least suspicion should not remain . . . about my way of thinking, I am willing that my original letter to General Gates should be handed to you.[8]

By the time Wilkinson returned to Gates's headquarters, Washington's note to Conway had become a sort of *cause célèbre*, causing Gates enormous embarrassment. Gates was incensed not only over its harmful reflection on himself but on the breach of confidence that had made known to Washington the content of Conway's letter. Gates released his ill feelings to Washington and attempted to shift the guilt in a convoluted letter misdated November 8 and probably written on December 8, 1777:

I shall not attempt to describe what, as a private Gentlemen, I cannot help feeling on representing to my Mind the disagreeable Situation which confidential Letters, when exposed to public Inspection, may place an unsuspecting Correspondent to; but, as a public Officer, I conjure your Excellency to give me all the Assistance you can in tracing out the Author of the Infidelity which put Extracts from General Conway's Letters to me into your Hands. Those Letters have been Stealingly copied; but, of them, when, or by whom is to me, as yet, an unfathomable Search.

There is not one Officer in my Suite, nor amongst those who have a free Access to me, upon whom I would, with the least Justification to myself, fix the Suspicion; and yet my Uneasiness may deprive me of the Usefulness of the worthiest Men. It is, I believe, in your Excellency's Power to do me, and the United States, a very important Service by detecting a Wretch who may betray me and capitally injure the very Operations under your immediate Direction. For this reason, Sir, I beg your Excellency will favour me with the Proofs you can procure to that Effect. But, the Crime being eventually so important that the least

Loss of Time may be attended with the worst Consequences, and it being unknown to me whether the Letter came to you from a Member of Congress or from an Officer, I shall have the Honour of transmitting a Copy of this to the President [of Congress], that the Congress may, in Concert with your Excellency, obtain, as soon as possible, a Discovery which so deeply Affects the Safety of our States. Crimes of that magnitude ought not to remain unpunished.[9]

Seeing through Gates's ploy to present his exaggerated grievance and implicit accusation to members of Congress, Washington at Valley Forge on January 4, 1778 fired back with a letter that cut the contemptible Gates to shreds and did so in full view of the members of Congress, whom Gates had sought to win to his side:

Sir: Your Letter of the 8th. Ulto. come to my hands a few days ago; and, to my great surprize informed me, that a Copy of it had been sent to Congress, and for what reason, I find myself unable to acct.; but, as some end doubtless was intended to be answered by it, I am laid under the disagreeable necessity of returning my answer through the same channel, lest any Member of that honble. body should harbour an unfavorable suspicion of my having practiced some indirect means to come at the contents of the confidential Letters between you and General Conway.

I am to inform you then, that Colo. Wilkenson, on his way to Congress in the Month of Octobr. last, fell in with Lord Stirling at Reading, and, not in confidence that I ever understood, inform'd his Aid de Camp Majr. McWilliams that General Conway had written thus to you,

"Heaven has been determined to save your Country; or a weak General and bad Councellors[10] would have ruined it."

Lord Stirling from motives of friendship, transmitted the acct. with this remark.

"The inclosed was communicated by Colonl. Wilkinson to Majr. McWilliams, such wicked duplicity of conduct I shall always think it my duty to detect."

In consequence of this information, and without having any thing more in view than merely to shew that Gentn. that I was not unapprized of his intrieguing disposition, I wrote him a Letter in these Words.

"Sir. A Letter which I received last night contained the following paragraph.

In a Letter from Genl. Conway to Genl. Gates he says, 'Heaven has been determined to save your Country; or a weak General and bad Councellors would have ruined it.'

I am Sir &ca."

Neither this Letter, nor the information which occasioned it, was ever, directly, or indirectly communicated by me to a single Officer in this Army (out of my own family) excepting the Marquis de la Fayette, who, having been spoken to on the Subject by Genl. Conway, applied for, and saw, under injunctions of secrecy, the Letter which contained Wilkenson's information; so desirous was I of concealing every matter that could, in its consequences, give the smallest Interruption to the tranquility of this Army, or afford a gleam of hope to the enemy by dissentions therein.

Thus Sir, with an openess and candour which I hope will ever characterize and mark my conduct have I complied with your request; the only concern I feel upon the occasion (finding how matters stand) is, that in doing this, I have necessarily been obliged to name a Gentn. whom I am perswaded (although I never exchanged a word with him upon the Subject) thought he was rather doing an act of Justice, than committing an act of infidility; and sure I am, that, till Lord Stirlings Letter came to my hands, I never knew that General Conway (who I viewed in the light of a stranger to you) was a corrispondant of yours, much less did I suspect that I was the subject of your confidential Letters; pardon me then for adding, that so far from conceiving that the safety of the States can be affected, or in the smallest degree injured by a discovery of this kind, or, that I should be called upon in such solemn terms to point out the author, that I considered the information as coming from yourself; and given with a friendly view to forewarn, and consequently forearm me, against a secret enemy; or, in other words, a dangerous incendiary; in which character, sooner or later, this Country will know Genl. Conway. But, in this, as in other matters of late, I have found myself mistaken.

I am, etc.[11]

By now, Gates was president of the Board of War, having been appointed by Congress on November 27, 1777, in a move evidently meant to diminish Washington and possibly displace him. Furthermore, on December 13 Congress had appointed Conway inspector general of the Continental Army and, despite Richard Henry Lee's assurances to Washington that it wouldn't happen, had promoted Conway to the rank of major general, over the heads of twenty-three other brigadier generals.

Exercising his authority as inspector general, Conway had in December 1777 twice come to Washington's headquarters at Valley Forge to make inquiries and twice had been received with less cooperation than he felt was his due. He protested the cold treatment to Washington. When Washington answered him with a cool reply, he protested again. In a series of letters to Washington, Conway repeatedly protested Washington's attitude toward him. He protested Washington's objections to his having been promoted to major general, an "extraordinary promotion," Washington had called it. Conway replied that:

> What you are pleased to call an extraordinary promotion is a very plain one. There is nothing extraordinary in it, only that such was not thought of sooner. The general and universal merit, which you wish every promoted officer might be endowed with, is a rare gift. We see but few men of merit so generally acknowledged. We know but the great Frederick in Europe and the great Washington on this continent. I certainly was never so rash as to pretend to such a prodigious height. . . .[12]

Washington forwarded all that correspondence to the Congress on January 2, 1778, and wrote to the president of Congress, Henry Laurens, about Conway's complaints of a cool reception by Washington while attempting to perform his duties as inspector general:

> If General Conway means by cool receptions . . . that I did not receive him in the language of a warm and cordial friend, I readily confess the charge. I did not, nor shall I ever, till I am capable of the arts of dissimulation. These I despise and my feelings will not permit me to make professions of friendship to the man I deem my enemy and whose system of conduct forbids it. At the same time, Truth authorizes me to say that he was received and treated with proper respect to his official character and that he has had no cause to justify the assertion that he could not expect any support for fulfilling the duties of his appointment.[13]

Conway continued to protest. On January 10 he wrote to Washington:

> I remain in a state of inaction until such time as your Excellency will
> think fit to employ me. . . . I cannot believe, Sir, neither does any other
> officer in your army believe, that the objection to my appointment
> originates from any body living but from you.[14]

At that, Washington decided he would end his correspondence with
Conway. He wrote no more letters to him.

On January 12, Benjamin Rush, the contentious army doctor, wrote
to Patrick Henry, governor of Virginia and an influential member of
Congress, declaring his opinion that Washington should be replaced as
commander in chief either by Gates or by Conway. Rush was not bold
enough to sign his letter, but when Henry passed it along to Washington,
Washington instantly recognized Rush's distinctive penmanship.

At the same time, Washington received a letter of warning from his old
friend James Craik, the army's senior medical officer for the area between the
Hudson and Potomac Rivers. Craik cautioned Washington that a strong faction was forming against him in the Board of War and in the Congress, which
by now had so changed that only six of its members were members in 1776
when it appointed Washington commander in chief. Craik said that Richard
Henry Lee was the ringleader of the plot to get rid of Washington and that
Thomas Mifflin was very active in it. Their intention was to work through the
Board of War and so hinder Washington that he would be forced to resign.

Although Craik suspected Richard Henry Lee, no one could say for
sure who was the mastermind behind the move to depose Washington.
Many contributed to it, not least of which was John Adams, who deni-
grated Washington in letters and, presumably, in conversations. The
anonymous paper titled *Thoughts of a Freeman*, which was circulated among
congressional and other influentials to discredit Washington, impugned
Washington's ability and his popularity and did so echoing Adams's
words. "The people of America," it charged, "have been guilty of idolatry
in making a man their God."[15] Because Thomas Conway had become such
a prominent figure in the anti-Washington camp and in its cause, the plotters and detractors were lumped together and designated the Conway
Cabal, though Conway himself was more a tool than a manipulator.

The intemperate letters that Conway had written to Washington, and
that Washington had turned over to the Congress, became the instruments that scotched him. Members of Congress at last saw him, as

Washington had predicted, for what he was. They also saw, via a massive protest by the army's twenty-three brigadier generals, exactly how unpopular and unacceptable he was among the army's general officers, without whom the war could not be won. Support for Conway vanished, the prospect of his replacing Washington having become unthinkable.

Gates, the other darling of the cabal, seeing the anti-Washington tide ebb, let it be known that he was eager to patch things up with the commander in chief. Henry Laurens, the president of Congress, wrote to his son John, one of Washington's aides, that Gates was seeking a reconciliation. Washington was thus informed and was ready to effect the reconciliation, believing that Gates had merely been used for the purposes of dangerous men. (Nathanael Greene, however, one of Washington's most trusted confidants, believed that Gates, far from being merely used, was a party to the plot.) On February 23 Washington received a letter from Gates, saying:

> [I] earnestly hope no more of that time, so precious to the public, may be lost upon the subject of General Conway's letter. . . . I solemnly declare that I am of no faction; and if any of my letters taken aggregately or by paragraphs convey any meaning, which in any construction is offensive to your Excellency, that was by no means the intention of the writer. After this, I cannot believe your Excellency will either suffer your suspicions or the prejudices of others to induce you to spend another moment upon this subject.[16]

Washington wrote back to him the day after receiving the letter:

> I am as averse to controversy, as any Man and had I not been forced into it, you never would have had occasion to impute to me, even the shadow of a disposition towards it. Your repeatedly and Solemnly disclaiming any offensive views, in those matters that have been the subject of our past correspondence, makes me willing to close with the desire, you express, of burying them hereafter in silence, and, as far as future events will permit, oblivion. My temper leads me to peace and harmony with all Men; and it is peculiarly my wish, to avoid any personal feuds with those, who are embarked in the same great National interest with myself, as every difference of this kind must in its consequences be very injurious. . . .[17]

On March 23, 1778, Conway was directed by Congress to report to Major General Alexander McDougall, in charge of the forces posted in the Hudson highlands, and receive orders from him. On April 22 Conway wrote to Congress objecting that he had not been given a command of his own and threatening to resign from the army. His former friends in Congress by now had deserted him or turned against him, and his offer of resignation was accepted. Still in America in July, he got into an altercation with Brigadier General John Cadwalader, during which Cadwalader is reported to have called Conway a coward for his conduct in the Battle of Germantown. Conway promptly challenged Cadwalader to a duel. On July 4 the two met, and Cadwalader shot Conway in the mouth, inflicting a serious but not life-threatening wound. Perhaps believing the wound more consequential than it was and wishing to make peace, Conway wrote a letter to Washington on July 23:

> I find myself just able to hold the pen during a few minutes, and take this opportunity of expressing my sincere grief for having done, written, or said anything disagreeable to your Excellency. My career will soon be over; therefore justice and truth prompt me to declare my last sentiments. You are in my eyes the great and good man. May you long enjoy the love, veneration, and esteem of these States, whose liberties you have asserted by your virtues.[18]

Unmoved, Washington didn't respond to the letter. Conway recovered from his wound and sailed back to France to serve once again in the French army.

Having been ridded of Conway and been reconciled to Gates, Washington looked back on the affair and wrote his thoughts about it:

> That there was a scheme of this sort on foot, last fall, admits of no doubt; but it originated in another quarter . . . with three men who wanted to aggrandize themselves; but, finding no support, on the contrary that their conduct and views, when seen into, were likely to undergo severe reprehension, they slunk back, disavowed the measure, and professed themselves my warmest admirers. Thus stands the matter at present. Whether any members of Congress were privy to this scheme and inclined to aid it, I shall not take upon me to say, but am well informed that no whisper of the kind was ever heard in Congress.[19]

The plotters had been defeated. Washington had won. He could now fix his attention completely on the pursuit of victory not over adversaries who were his own countrymen, but rather over those who were the British enemy.

CHAPTER Fourteen

The Earl Goes Home and Returns

After a month at sea, Cornwallis arrived in England in mid-January 1778, coming home for the first time in two years. He owned two estates, both inherited from his father. One, in Suffolk, had been in the Cornwallis family since the fourteenth century, and its manor, Brome Hall, dated back to the sixteenth century. The other estate and its manor, Culford, larger than Brome Hall, came to the Cornwallis family through marriage in the seventeenth century. It was there that Cornwallis had lived as a boy and it was still his home. Upon his return from America, Culford was his destination.

First he would deliver the dispatches that he had carried to England from General Howe. After that, he would go home and become reacquainted with his ailing wife and son and daughter. He would have business matters to take care of, his properties requiring his attention. There was public business to be attended to also. Since 1770, when the king appointed him, he had served as constable of the Tower of London, a position he saw, to his credit, not as a sinecure but as a responsibility to be conscientiously discharged. As constable, he was the Tower's chief judicial officer, overseeing trials and punishments. On this visit he discovered that the Tower's courthouse and jail were in a state of severe decay. His bailiff, Richard Ruston, informed him that unless repairs were made, "all prisoners committed to the present prison will escape, and there will not be any court house for the justices to hold their session, or for the court of pleas, or court leet to sit, or any place of confinement for felons, and other persons committing misdemeanors as aforesaid, nor any place for debtors."[1]

Cornwallis conducted an inspection and confirmed the bailiff's report, then urged the treasury to authorize funds for the repairs, which it did. Another job taken on was the renovation of a house that was part of the Tower complex and intended to be the residence of the constable. It, too, was in disrepair. Cornwallis had never occupied the house, nor apparently had had any desire to, preferring to stay in an apartment or elsewhere when he was in London. Now he decided the dilapidated building should be remodeled or replaced and put to a good use. He recommended to the treasury that the structure either be torn down and two new residences be built for two of his deputy officials, or else the existing structure should be repaired and turned into residences for them. The decision was to do the latter.

He paid courtesy visits to the families of two fellow officers, Major General Charles Grey and Lieutenant General Henry Clinton, and he testified before the king's ministers about the conduct of the war. The Ministry subjected him to an intense questioning about Burgoyne's defeat, in an attempt, some said, to have Cornwallis pin the blame on Howe. Cornwallis deflected the ministers' questions about Howe, however, refusing to implicate his commanding officer in any way. As to his opinion about how the war was going and how soon it would be over, his wife, Jemima, may have revealed Cornwallis's pessimism when she wrote, "I am really so bilious as to think our army in America, Fleets everywhere, Possessions in the West Indies, &c., &c., &c., will be frittered away and destroyed in another Twelve months."

While in England, Cornwallis was promoted to lieutenant general and given a so-called dormant commission as "General in Our Army in America only." The commission was not only limited to the American theater of operations but it would become effective only if the British commander in chief were no longer able to command. The commission had resulted from Howe's resignation, which George III had accepted, and Henry Clinton's having been appointed to succeed him. Thus Cornwallis, upon his return to America, would be second in command, and his dormant commission would permit him to automatically succeed as commander in chief in the event of Clinton's resignation, death, or disability. It would also prevent Cornwallis from being outranked by one or more of the Hessian generals.

Parliament reconvened in mid-February, and Cornwallis attended several sessions of the House of Lords, keeping his political fences mended.

At the time, the British government was planning a new peacemaking attempt, but Cornwallis apparently did not take part in those discussions.

Following the American victory at Saratoga in September 1777, France had taken new interest in America's war with Britain. Before Saratoga, France had been hesitant to openly support the rebels, fearing that the British would crush the revolution and then turn angrily on France. Once the rebels had shown they could defeat an army of British regulars, as they did at Saratoga, the French government's attitude became bolder. King Louis XVI's foreign minister, Charles Gravier, *comte* de Vergennes, saw an alliance with the Americans as a way to avenge the losses France had suffered in the Seven Years' (French and Indian) War and an opportunity to win back the colonies France had had to cede.

The British prime minister, Frederick North (Lord North), who had opposed the war against the colonies in the first place and had been an unenthusiastic pursuer of it since the beginning, saw in a French–American alliance the final loss of the thirteen colonies and huge holdings in the West Indies as well, along with a bankrupting of the British economy in the effort to prevent those disasters. North proposed reaching out to the Americans in a conciliatory move that would patch up the quarrel and put everything right again with the colonies, which would remain colonies. To feel out the Americans, he had an old friend of Benjamin Franklin, James Hutton, contact Franklin, who was in Paris doing all he could to woo France into forming an alliance. Hutton wrote to Franklin on January 27 saying that the British government wanted to make peace and to do so it stood ready to yield "anything short of absolute independency."

Franklin replied with Poor Richard eloquence:

> You have lost by this mad war, and the barbarity with which it has been carried on, not only the Government and commerce of America, and the public revenues and private wealth arising from that commerce, but what is more, you have lost the esteem, respect, friendship and affection of all that great and growing people, who consider you at present, and whose posterity will consider you, as the worst and wickedest nation upon earth. A peace you may undoubtedly obtain by dropping all your pretensions to govern us. . . .[2]

Undeterred by Franklin's rebuke, the British government appointed a Peace Commission to sail to America with the Conciliatory Propositions that Parliament had approved and present them to Congress.

In the meantime, American representatives and French authorities on February 6 at last signed a treaty of alliance that would go into effect in the event of war between France and Britain, which all parties expected to occur soon. The treaty stipulated that the United States would not make peace with Britain without the concurrence of France. France promised to continue war with Britain until the United States won independence.

On April 21, 1778, Britain's party of peacemakers (called the Carlisle Peace Commission for its leader, the earl of Carlisle, Frederick Howard) embarked on its mission of peace, and Cornwallis began his return to war. Together the Peace Commission members and Cornwallis boarded H.M.S. *Trident* and sailed away, bound for British-occupied Philadelphia.

Cornwallis was going reluctantly. He was leaving behind a wife whose health was failing, which was a weighty personal concern to him. What's more, he realized that in front of him lay the distasteful task of helping lead the army of a country whose government now wanted peace more than victory. The situation had altogether changed since last Cornwallis set out for the conflict in America, full of confidence, strong motivation, and great expectation.

The *Trident* reached the mouth of the Delaware River on June 3 and not long after that tied up at the Philadelphia docks, where dozens of British ships lined the wharves. News of the American–French alliance had set off a defensive reaction in London, and Lieutenant General Henry Clinton, the new British commander, who had arrived in Philadelphia from New York on May 8 and taken over from Howe on May 24, had been ordered to evacuate Philadelphia and move his troops to New York, or even as far north as Nova Scotia if necessary to get them out of harm's way, before a French fleet could sever their supply lines.

Britain's government further feared the French would use their fleet to capture the treasured sugar-producing islands in the Caribbean and in anticipation of such a move ordered Clinton to sunder his army by sending 5,000 troops to Saint Lucia, in the Windward Islands, and 3,000 to Florida. What was left of the British force would then take on a defensive role, fighting to maintain its presence in the thirteen separated provinces.

Clinton was already gathering up his army for the march northward to New York when Cornwallis arrived back in Philadelphia. The city, Cornwallis found, was in an uproar. Some 10,000 British and Hessian troops were being drawn from quarters they had occupied since the previous September. Horrified at the withdrawal of the British troops with whom they had collaborated, loyalists were scurrying to get out of the city also, hoping to be carried to safety aboard a British fleet too small to transport Clinton's army. The loyalists realized that once the British troops were gone, they would be unprotected against the abuse they expected at the hands of patriots who had had to endure the British occupation of their city.

The evacuation and the sundering of the British army sorely disturbed Cornwallis. Furthermore, he would now be serving under Clinton instead of Howe, with whom he had got on well. Cornwallis and Clinton once had been friends, but the war doubtless had affected the friendship. The first strain had come following the Battle of White Plains, when Cornwallis passed along to Howe a critical comment that Clinton had made about Howe. The relationship seemed to have been repaired, though, and in March, when Cornwallis, still in England, learned that Clinton had been appointed to succeed Howe as commander in chief, he wrote to Clinton pledging his support:

> I must sincerely hope to find the war over [upon his return to America], but should that not be the case, I will do all in my power to contribute to your ease in a situation which I fear you will not find a bed of Roses. That health, happiness & success may attend you is the sincere wish of your very faithful servant and friend.[3]

Clinton, however, apparently remained guarded in his dealings with Cornwallis and was suspicious of his wanting to return to England at the end of the 1777 campaign. He believed Cornwallis had gone back, as he said, only because he wanted to "plan a command for himself similar to Burgoyne's, with a commission of genl. or at least Lt. g."[4] A new request by Cornwallis for permission to return home did nothing to overcome that suspicion. On the same day that the army began its evacuation of Philadelphia, Cornwallis wrote a letter to George Germain, the British secretary of state for American colonies, and asked to be relieved of command and be granted permission to return to England as soon as possible. He said he had no wish to serve in a theater where "no offensive operations can be taken." Although he wouldn't find out for weeks, permission was denied. Because he was Clinton's designated successor, like it or not, he would have to remain in America.

The British began moving out of Philadelphia on Tuesday, June 16, 1778, and by noon on Thursday had departed the city, all but the members of the Carlisle Peace Commission. After crossing the Delaware River at Philadelphia, the army formed a ponderous, twelve-mile-long column of marchers, riders, artillery carriages, 1,500 baggage and equipment wagons, and uncounted scores of camp followers, and headed for its first destination, Haddonfield, New Jersey. While the column plodded eastward toward Haddonfield, the army's invalids and its heavy equipment, along with an estimated 3,000 loyalists from the Philadelphia area, carrying large collections of their belongings, were being transported down the Delaware aboard ships of the British fleet.

Clinton was limited in a choice of roads leading to New York. The first leg of his march from Haddonfield would parallel the Delaware for about twenty-five miles, as far as Bordentown. There he would have to choose between two roads. One was the post road, which passed through Trenton, Princeton, and Brunswick. At Brunswick he could cross the Raritan River and turn eastward, keeping the river on his right to protect his right flank, and march to Amboy, where his army could be ferried to Staten Island. The other road ran northeastward to the vicinity of Sandy Hook, allowing his army to reach embarkation points between Sandy Hook and South Amboy and be transported by ship to Staten Island or New York.

Clinton realized that his long, cumbersome column would invite attacks by Washington and that the possibility of disaster lay waiting along either route. He would move out for Bordentown, keep his army's eyes and ears open for the movements of the rebels, and make his decision after reaching Bordentown, based on the disposition of Washington's forces at that time.

The British departure became known to Washington almost as soon as it had occurred, around noon on June 18. Also known was the direction of his march. The question in Washington's mind was, would Clinton turn south and head for an embarkation point on the east side of the Delaware or would he turn north and move overland toward New York? Washington already had troops in New Jersey who could track the redcoats. He had some 800 New Jersey militiamen under the command of Major General Philemon Dickinson and about 1,300 troops under the command of Brigadier General William Maxwell, posted at Mount Holly, about twenty miles east of Philadelphia.

Playing a hunch, Washington quickly marshaled his army at Valley Forge, now a disciplined force of some 13,500 troops, and ordered the division commanded by Major General Charles Lee to march for Coryell's Ferry on the Delaware, near Trenton, to put the rebel force in or near the presumed path of the retreating British. Lee's division included the brigades of Brigadier General Jedidiah Huntington, Brigadier General Enoch Poor, and Brigadier General James Varnum. A couple of hours later, around 3 p.m., the division under the command of Brigadier General Anthony (Mad Anthony) Wayne also set out from Valley Forge with three brigades. The divisions of Brigadier General Stirling (Alexander), Brigadier General DeKalb, and Major General Lafayette moved out in the same direction at 5 a.m. the next day, June 19.

At the same time that Washington's combat troops were setting out to pursue Clinton and Cornwallis, Major General Benedict Arnold, still recovering from his wounds suffered at Bemis Heights and unable to command in the field, was sent to re-establish an American government in Philadelphia, which had changed somewhat during the British occupation. One of the city's former residents who returned following the British evacuation described what he saw:

> The face of the suburbs on the North side is so much altered that people who were born here and have lived all their lives are much at a loss to find out the situation of particular houses. The houses themselves are destroyed and redoubts built in the neighborhood of the spots where some of them formerly stood. The timber has been all cut down and . . . the fine fertile fields are all laid waste. In short, the whole is one promiscuous scene of ruin. . . .
>
> Advancing near the city, you come to an abatis (chiefly if not entirely made of fruit trees) which extends from Delaware to Schuylkill. Redoubts are built at proper distances in this line. . . .
>
> Upon getting into the city, I was surprised to find that it had suffered so little; I question whether it would have fared better had our own troops had possession of it; that is, as the *buildings*, but the morals of the inhabitants have suffered vastly. . . .[5]

Days later the Congress moved back to Philadelphia from York, making the College Hall their new assembly hall because the British had left the State House, in the words of representative Josiah Bartlett of New Hampshire, "in a most filthy and sordid situation."

Washington's divisions, with the commander in chief riding among them, were slowed by a heavy rain on Saturday, June 20, rain that brought relief from scorching daytime temperatures but transformed the roadway into a virtual quagmire. Washington ordered camp made that evening at

Buckingham, Pennsylvania, about seven miles from Coryell's Ferry. The next day, June 21, Washington's troops reached Coryell's Ferry before noon. On June 23, after two more days of slow going in the rain and on sodden roads, Washington's army reached Hopewell, about eight miles northwest of Princeton. There Washington halted again and set up a head-quarters near the Baptist meeting house, intending later to move from there into Princeton.

Clinton and Cornwallis were also moving slowly, passing through woods and the New Jersey countryside, their ponderous train impeded by harassing New Jersey militia units and detachments of Continental regulars who destroyed bridges and chopped down trees to block the road and fired into their column. British and Hessian troops alike were suffering in their woollen uniforms and under heavy packs in heat that reached 100 degrees. Men fell out along the road, needing treatment for heat prostration and sunstroke. The march was exacting a toll in other ways, too. Hessians in particular were deserting, slipping away and turning themselves over to the Americans.

American units had been ordered to harass the enemy column as much as possible and to forward to Washington any pieces of information they might gain concerning the movement of the enemy. Washington was still trying to learn which route Clinton would take past Bordentown and he ordered outposts set up on every road available to Clinton.

On Wednesday, June 24, Washington called a council of war. He had learned the day before that Clinton's army was just south of Bordentown but still had given no clear indication of which route it would take after passing Bordentown. Even so, Washington wanted his generals' ideas about what the Americans should do now that the enemy, taking either route, would soon be within striking range. Attending the meeting were Generals Lee (who had been exchanged for British Brigadier General Richard Prescott), Greene, Stirling (Alexander), Lafayette, Steuben, Knox, Poor, Wayne, William Woodford, John Paterson, Charles Scott, and Le Begue de Presle DuPortail. Alexander Hamilton served as secretary. Lafayette later summarized the opinions of the council's most influential participants:

> The army of the United States, which was of nearly equal force [to the enemy] directed itself from Valley Forge to Coryell's Ferry, and from thence to King's Town, within a march of the enemy; it was thus left at the option of the Americans, either to follow on their [the enemy's] track or to repair to White Plains.

In a council held on this subject, [Major General Charles] Lee very eloquently endeavoured to prove that it was necessary to erect a bridge of gold for the enemy; that while on the very point of forming an alliance with them [the French], every thing ought not to be placed at hazard; that the English army had never been so excellent and so well disciplined; he declared himself to be for White Plains: his speech influenced the opinion of Lord Stirling and of the brigadiers-general.

M. de Lafayette, placed on the other side, spoke late, and asserted that it would be disgraceful for the chiefs, and humiliating for the troops, to allow the enemy to traverse the Jerseys tranquilly; that, without running any improper risk, the rear guard might be attacked; that it was necessary to follow the English, manoeuvre with prudence, take advantage of a temporary separation, and, in short, seize the most favourable opportunities and situations. This advice was approved by many of the council, and above all by M. du Portail, chief of the engineers, and a very distinguished officer. The majority were, however, in favour of Lee; but M. de Lafayette spoke again to the general [Washington] on this subject in the evening, and was seconded by [Alexander] Hamilton, and by [Nathanael] Greene. . . .[6]

Respectful of Lee and his years of experience, Washington nevertheless sided with his young protégé, who shared Washington's instincts. Soon enough, both Lafayette and Washington would get the action they sought.

CHAPTER Fifteen

The Battle of Monmouth Courthouse

Major General Charles Lee was convinced that the troops of Washington's army were no match for a European army. Defeat was a foregone conclusion, in his opinion, in the event of an engagement between equal numbers of America's sudden soldiers and the veteran professionals of the British and the Hessians. The wisest thing for Washington to do, he believed, was to wait for France's professionals to come and rescue the Americans from their fight.

Lafayette found Lee's opinions as objectionable as the man himself. "His visage was ugly," Lafayette said of him, "his spirit sarcastic, his heart ambitious and mean, his character inconsistent; on the whole a queer fellow."[1]

Alexander Hamilton's thoughts were like Lafayette's. Having listened closely to the arguments advanced at Washington's council of war on June 24, 1778, Hamilton later wrote about the decisions reached by the generals and revealed his own strong feelings:

> The General [Washington] unluckily called a council of war, the result of which would have done honour to the most honourable society of midwives, and to them only.
> The purport was that we should keep at a comfortable distance from the enemy and keep up a vain parade of annoying them in detachment. A detachment of fifteen hundred men was sent off under General Scott to join the other troops near the enemy's lines. General Lee was the *primum mobile* of this sage plan and was even

opposed to sending so considerable a force. The General [Washington],
on mature reconsideration of what had been resolved on, determined
to pursue a different line of conduct at all hazards.[2]

On the same day that Washington's council of war was held, Steuben
reported that Clinton had from Bordentown taken the road that led east
to Allentown and Monmouth Court House. After the meeting ended,
Washington ordered Daniel Morgan to take a detachment of riflemen and
move to Clinton's right flank as the British marched eastward. He ordered
another detachment, under William Maxwell, to Clinton's left flank, and
a third detachment, commanded by Charles Scott, to Clinton's left flank
and rear. Washington's orders to Scott presented a general idea of what
Washington wanted those detachments to do to the British column:

> You are immediately to march with the detachment, under your com-
> mand, towards Allen Town, in order to fall in with the enemy's left
> flank and rear, and give them all the annoyance in your power.[3]

To draw closer to the British column and place the main body of his
army in a position to support the detachments, Washington on June 25
moved the main body to Kingston, about four miles northeast of Princeton.
There he ordered a fourth detachment, a force of 1,000 men placed
under the command of Anthony Wayne, to harass Clinton's column.
Realizing that those detachments required coordination, he decided to
group them together as an advanced corps and name an overall commander for the corps.

As the senior general, Charles Lee was the logical officer to receive command of the corps, but Lee, in apparent disdain, declined in favor of
Lafayette. Then, when he learned that a reinforcement of 5,000 troops was
being added to the corps because Clinton had shifted his best troops to the
rear of his column, he changed his mind and decided he would like to command the corps after all. In a message to Lafayette, Lee claimed that his
honor was at stake. Ever the gracious gentleman, Lafayette replied that he
would cheerfully acquiesce to whatever change Washington wished to make.

Now Washington was on the spot. Lafayette had already moved out
with his troops, and Washington didn't want to recall him. Neither did he
want to unduly offend Lee. After wrestling with the dilemma, he at last
reached a compromise, not a good one, and wrote two letters, one to Lee,
one to Lafayette. To Lee he said:

Your uneasiness, on account of the command of yesterday's detachment, fills me with concern, as it is not in my power fully to remove it, without wounding the feelings of the Marquis de la Fayette. I have thought of an expedient which though not quite equal to either of your views, may in some measure answer both; and that is to make another detachment for this Army for the purpose of aiding and supporting the several detachments now under the command of the Marquis and giving you command of the whole, under certain restrictions; which, circumstances arising from your own conduct yesterday, render almost unavoidable. The expedient which I would propose is for you to march towards the Marquis with Scott's and Varnum's brigades. Give him notice that you are advancing to support him, that you are to have command of the whole advanced body; but as he may have formed some enterprise . . .which will not admit of delay or alteration, you will desire him to proceed as if no change had happened, and you will give him every assistance and countenance in your power.[4]

To Lafayette he said:

General Lee's uneasiness on account of Yesterday's transaction rather increasing than abating, and your politeness in wishing to ease him of it, has induced me to detach him from this Army, with a part of it, to reinforce, or at least cover, the several detachments under your command, at present. At the same time I felt for General Lee's distress of mind, I have had an eye to your wishes, and the delicacy of your situation; and have, therefore, obtained a promise from him, that when he gives you notice of his approach and command, he will request you to prosecute any plan you have already concerted for the purpose of attacking or otherwise annoying the Enemy. This is the only expedient I could think of to answer both your views. . . . I wish it may prove agreeable to you, as I am with the warmest wishes for your honour and glory, and with the sincerest esteem and affection.[5]

Washington ordered Lee to Englishtown, about fifteen miles southeast of Kingston, and when he moved out, Lee took with him two more regiments, further increasing the strength of the advanced corps, which would stand within five miles of Clinton's army. On Saturday, June 27, Lee took command of the corps.

On that same day, Washington called Lee to his headquarters, now five miles behind Lee's position, and ordered him to attack Clinton's column. Although a defeat of Clinton's army, coming within months of the defeat of Burgoyne's army, would probably mean the end the war, Washington was unwilling to gamble on an American victory in a general engagement. Rather, what he had in mind now was an assault upon the rear of Clinton's column while it was in motion and most vulnerable. He meant to strike, if not a fatal blow, at least a critical one. What he needed was an aggressive, confident general to plan and lead the assault and make it succeed. What he had instead was Charles Lee.

On the afternoon of June 27 Washington received reports that the enemy was still encamped in a strong defensive position at Monmouth Court House but was expected to move soon to Middletown, about ten miles to the northeast of its present position, as the next step on its line of retreat. Lee was ordered to confer with his general officers, secure his camp, and attack the rear of the enemy's column as soon as it moved out of Monmouth Court House.

From Lee came a reply as strange as the man. He told Washington that based on his personal knowledge of the British and Hessian senior officers, he believed that they would turn and strike back if the American troops were to attack; and furthermore, even if he were not so well acquainted with them, he would still expect such a reaction from such officers. His message seemed to be that he shouldn't attack the enemy because the enemy would fight back.

At four o'clock in the morning on Sunday, June 28, Major General Dickinson's New Jersey militiamen, posted to keep the enemy's movements under constant surveillance, reported that units under the command of Lieutenant General Knyphausen, together with the enemy's wagon train, had started moving out of Monmouth Court House, heading north toward Middletown. Dickinson immediately dispatched a courier to Washington's headquarters to inform him, and about 5 a.m. Washington was roused from his bed to receive the news. Washington quickly sent Colonel Richard Meade to tell Lee to have his men leave their packs in camp, set out immediately down the road behind the British column, and initiate an attack.

Lee in the meantime had done nothing during the night to observe the enemy, although he had received an order at 1 a.m. to send out a reconnaissance force to watch for any enemy movement. Five critical hours later, at 6 a.m., he at last complied with that order. On Saturday afternoon, the day before, he had met with his officers and told them that since he had no good intelligence on the enemy's disposition, he wouldn't prepare a plan of attack for Sunday, but instead would draw up a makeshift plan as the need arose. At 7 a.m. Sunday, lacking a previously prepared plan, he went into action.

Washington rousted his troops, formed them into a column, and began an advance on Monmouth Court House to support Lee's force. On the way, Washington received reports that the enemy was moving out at a quick pace, despite the soaring temperature, and that Lee was now in position to assault the rear of the British column, hoping to cut it off from the main body of the enemy.

Around noon, while on the march, Washington heard the sound of artillery fire coming from the vicinity of Monmouth Court House. Several rounds were fired, but no answering fire. Nor were there any sounds of rifle or musket fire.

Clinton had divided his army into two divisions, giving Knyphausen command of the first (lead) division, and giving Cornwallis command of the second (rear) division. In Cornwallis's division, with which Clinton rode, were the 16th Light Dragoons and fourteen battalions, including the 3rd, 4th, and 5th British infantry brigades, the 1st and 2nd British grenadier battalions, all the Hessian grenadiers, the British Guards, the 1st and 2nd British light-infantry battalions, the Queen's Rangers, and the 16th Dragoons. To further strengthen Cornwallis's division, Clinton ordered Knyphausen to send from his division an infantry brigade and the 17th Dragoons. All together, the troops under Cornwallis's command numbered some 6,000. The rest of Clinton's army, with its baggage train, continued its march toward Sandy Hook under Knyphausen's command.

Cornwallis's troops had broken camp and started following Knyphausen's line of march about 8 a.m. At 10 a.m. the rear guard of Cornwallis's division, nearly 2,000 men, had been attacked by the main force of Lee's advanced corps, and Cornwallis's other units had wheeled around to face the rebel front, establishing a line formed by the British Guards and three infantry brigades.

The formation of Cornwallis's line of defense deterred Lee from pressing an attack. He could see he would not be able to overwhelm the rear guard and cut it off from the remainder of Cornwallis's division. His moment of opportunity had been lost. Washington's aide, Alexander Hamilton, gave his account of the initial action:

The advanced corps came up with the enemy's rear a mile or two beyond the [Monmouth] Court House. I saw the enemy drawn up and am persuaded there were not a thousand men—their front from different accounts was then ten miles off. However favorable this situation may seem for attack, it was not made, but after changing their position two or three times by retrograde movements, our advanced corps got into a general confused retreat and even rout would hardly be too strong an expression. Not a word of all this was officially communicated to the General [Washington].[6]

In the confusion resulting partly from lack of a plan, partly from the inadequacy of communication between the detachments, and partly from the lack of leadership on the part of Lee, the Americans turned and fled from the enemy's rear guard when it was reinforced by the main body of Cornwallis's division. The detachments of Scott and Maxwell also fell back, either on orders from Lee, as some reports had it, or in response to the flight of Lee's main force, which was running without having fired a shot. By now the first of those in flight were reaching the forwardmost units of Washington's main body, marching eastward as those in retreat came toward them in the road. Lieutenant Colonel Richard Harrison, a member of Washington's staff, recounted the incidents that followed Washington's encounter with the retreating soldiers:

I marched with him [Washington] till we passed the Meetinghouse near Monmouth. . . . When we came to where the roads forked, His Excellency made a halt for a few minutes, in order to direct a disposition of the army. The wing under General Greene was then ordered to go to the right to prevent the enemy's turning our right flank.

After order was given in this matter, and His Excellency was proceeding down the road, we met a fifer, who appeared to be a good deal frighted. The General asked him whether he was a soldier belonging to the army, and the cause of his returning that way; he answered that he was a soldier and that the Continental troops that had been advanced were retreating. On this answer the General seemed to be exceedingly surprized, and rather more exasperated, appearing to discredit the account, and threatened the man, if he mentioned a thing of the sort, he would have him whipped.

We then moved on a few paces forward (perhaps about fifty yards) where we met two or three persons more on that road; one was,

I think, in the habit of a soldier. The General asked them from whence they came, and whether they belonged to the army; one of them replied that he did, and that all the troops that had been advanced, the whole of them, were retreating. His Excellency still appeared to discredit the account, having not heard any firing except a few cannon a considerable time before. However, the General, or some gentleman in the company, observed that, as the report came by different persons, it might be well not wholly to disregard it.

Upon this I offered my services to the General to go forward and to bring a true account of the situation of matters, and requested that Colonel Fitzgerald might go with me. After riding a very short distance, at the bridge in front of the line that was afterwards formed on the heights, I met part of Colonel Grayson's regiment, as I took it, from some of the officers that I knew. As I was in pursuit of information, I addressed myself to Captain Jones of that regiment and asked him the cause of the retreat, whether it was general or whether it was only a particular part of the troops that were coming off. I do not precisely recollect the answer that he gave me; but I think, to the best of my knowledge, he said, "Yonder are a great many more troops in the same situation."

I proceeded and fell in with Lieutenant-Colonel Parke. These troops were rather disordered. The next officer that I was acquainted with was Lieutenant-Colonel William Smith. I addressed myself to Colonel Smith and asked him what was the cause of the troops retreating, as I had come to gain information? who replied that he could not tell, that they had lost but one man. I then proceeded down the line, determined to go to the rear of the retreating troops, and met with Colonel Ogden. I asked him the same question, whether he could assign the cause or give me any information why the troops retreated. He appeared to be exceedingly exasperated and said, "By God! they are flying from a shadow. . . ."[7]

When Washington's aide was able to reach Lee and ask him why he wasn't pressing the attack, Lee replied, "Tell the general I am doing well enough."

Washington thought otherwise. Riding swiftly into the face of the impending new disaster, Washington met Lee and several of his officers leading the withdrawal of a detachment. Angrily confronting Lee, Washington demanded to know what was going on. Lee reeled out a series of excuses. He had received contradictory intelligence, he said, which had caused great confusion. He said he did not choose to meet the British in such a confused situation. He said that Brigadier General Charles Scott had given up a position favorable to the attack. He said his orders had not been properly executed. He said the whole idea of an attack was contrary to his opinion.

In crystalline clear terms Washington told Lee it didn't matter what his opinion was, that he was expected to obey orders. Furthermore, if Lee had no confidence in the operation, Washington told him, he should never have taken it on. Lee, by now apparently as furious as his commander in chief, told Washington, "Sir, these troops are not able to meet British grenadiers."[8]

"Sir," Washington shot back, "they are able and, by God, they shall do it!" He then ordered the column behind Lee to countermarch back to face the enemy. The man who had taken the blame for the losses on Long Island, at Fort Washington, Fort Lee, Brandywine, and Germantown was desperately determined that Monmouth Court House would not become another humiliation. Lieutenant Colonel Harrison, who had gone seeking the reason for the retreat, returned to report to Washington that the enemy was within a 15-minute march of where they stood. While Washington quickly thought of a plan to rally Lee's troops and regroup, Lieutenant Colonel Tench Tilghman, one of Washington's aides, told him that Lieutenant Colonel David Rhea of the 4th New Jersey Regiment had just passed their position and let Tilghman know that he was well acquainted with the area and he would be glad to assist if his help was needed. Washington immediately sent for Rhea.

The Americans' line of march and position in the field had taken them across three ravines, two cutting across the road just west of Monmouth Court House, and the third running east and west on the north side of the town. Between the westernmost ravine and the middle ravine was a ridge, on which Washington stood searching for a position at which to regroup. He spotted a hedgerow on the east-facing slope of the ridge, where Colonel Henry Beekman Livingston was already regrouping the men of his regiment. Washington instantly ordered his troops and all retreating troops, as they approached, to fall in behind the hedgerow. As the rebel soldiers began massing on the far side of the hedgerow, Tilghman returned with Rhea.

Rhea told Washington that he had picked a good position. The ridge on which they stood extended some distance in both directions, southwest to northeast, with swampy ground to the front, an eminence on the left, and woods to the rear. Pleased to hear Rhea's assessment, Washington began swiftly issuing orders to position his troops and to call for Henry Knox's artillery. The American army was going to stand and fight, here and now.

Washington marshaled the regiments of Henry Beekman Livingston, James Varnum, Walter Stewart, and Nathaniel Ramsay from their retreat and had them form a line to slow Cornwallis's advance while the bulk of Washington's force established a line behind those four forward regiments. Four pieces of artillery under the command of Colonel Eleazar Oswald were moved up in support of those forward regiments and later reinforced by additional guns.

Behind those regiments, five regiments under Anthony Wayne moved into position at the center of the line being formed on the slope of the ridge. The units under Stirling (Alexander) were posted on the high ground on the left, and Greene's force was posted on the right side of the line. Lafayette's detachment was positioned between and slightly to the rear of Stirling and Greene. Southwest of the hedgerow, within Greene's position, a hillock called Combs Hill rose to provide nearly ideal emplacements for artillery, as Rhea pointed out. Greene placed four guns on Combs Hill, allowing him to rake the enemy's left and center with enfilade fire.

Cornwallis's troops, though slowed in their advance, drove back the rebels' forward units, Ramsay's and Stewart's regiments being unable to withstand a mounted attack on their positions on the left flank. Varnum's and Livingston's regiments were then forced back by dragoons and grenadiers.

Once the rebels' first line of defense had been broken, Cornwallis ordered the Black Watch regiment, plus a detachment of British light infantry and several field pieces to assault the American left, where Stirling commanded. The assault continued for almost an hour in the enervating afternoon heat that reached 96 degrees.

In the midst of the action, Washington himself and Steuben and Stirling rode along the rebel line shouting encouragement and giving directions to the troops. The American line held as volley after volley streamed from the muskets of both sides. The 1st Continental Artillery Battalion responded to the British guns round for round. A counterattack by the 3rd New Hampshire and the 1st Virginia regiments, which sent rebel soldiers bursting from heavy woods on the left side of their line, at last drove the enemy back and took the pressure off Stirling's embattled infantrymen.

Cornwallis then led a massive assault on the Americans' right side, where Greene commanded. Cornwallis brought forward his elite units, the Coldstream Guards, the English and Hessian grenadiers, the 37th and 44th Foot regiments, another guards battalion, and a light-infantry detachment, and threw them at the rebel line. Continuous, merciless fire from the rebel artillery on Combs Hill riddled the enemy ranks, stopped Cornwallis's advance and finally drove him back.

As the American right was being assaulted, the center of the American line, where Anthony Wayne commanded, also came under attack. Cornwallis sent light infantry, dragoons, and grenadiers against the center, where Wayne's disciplined infantrymen waited till the redcoats were at close range before unleashing a devastating fire, cutting the redcoats down, bloodied bodies falling at the feet of comrades who continued to march forward until the heavy fire at last forced them to withdraw.

At the failure of the first charge against the center, Cornwallis ordered a second charge, with similar results. An hour later a third charge was attempted, this one led by British Lieutenant Colonel Henry Monckton who rallied his men within 500 yards of the American line, shouting, "Forward to the charge, my brave grenadiers!" His troops responded by rushing through the torturous heat and among their fallen comrades toward the steadfast rebel line, where the Americans again stood waiting till the enemy came within close range.

"Steady! Steady!" Wayne shouted to his troops. "Wait for the word, then pick out the kingbirds!" On command, at seemingly the last instant, the American line exploded in musket fire that spewed a deadly stream upon the attackers, scything through their ranks and dropping, among others, Lieutenant Colonel Monckton, who fell mortally wounded within several paces of the rebel position, close enough to allow his body and his battalion's fallen colors to be taken by the rebel defenders.

During the British assaults, the camp-following wife of an American artilleryman, a woman named Mary Ludwig Hayes, was not content to merely stand by and watch the intense artillery bombardment. She pitched in to help her husband man his gun and also carried drinking water to the sweltering artillerymen and to the wounded. She was noticed by Private Joseph Plumb Martin, the young Massachusetts journal keeper who recorded much of the war's action in fascinating detail:

> One little incident happened during the heat of the cannonade, which I was eyewitness to, and which I think would be unpardonable

not to mention. A woman whose husband belonged to the Artillery, and who was then attached to a piece in the engagement, attended with her husband at the piece the whole time. While in the act of reaching a cartridge and having one of her feet as far before the other as she could step, a cannon shot from the enemy passed directly between her legs without doing any other damage than carrying away all the lower part of her petticoat. Looking at it with apparent unconcern, she observed that it was lucky it did not pass a little higher, for in that case it might have carried away something else, and continued her occupation.[9]

The woman became known as Molly Pitcher, the stouthearted, rough-hewn American heroine.

Sixteen British field pieces continued pounding the American positions as the afternoon slipped into evening, but shortly after 5 p.m. Clinton and Cornwallis pulled back their infantry and dragoons. Their fight was finished. Now Washington ordered a counterattack. Brigadier General William Woodford brought his brigade down from Combs Hill, on the American right, and Brigadier General Enoch Poor came forward from the American left flank with his regiments and a North Carolina unit. Before those troops could be formed up for the counterattack, however, failing light and physical exhaustion prevented their moving out, many of the troops collapsing on the field.

Clinton retreated to a position a half mile on the Monmouth Court House side of the middle ravine and rested his men as night fell. Around midnight he and his troops quietly slipped away in the cool darkness. Unwilling to face Washington's army again, Clinton hurriedly marched his troops through the early morning of Monday, June 29, and caught up with Knyphausen's division and the baggage train around 6 a.m. The reunited army reached Middletown around 10 a.m. The next day, Tuesday, June 30, they arrived in Sandy Hook, and by July 5 they were in New York.

Although not as damaging to the British as Washington might have hoped, the battle had inflicted on Clinton and Cornwallis a heavy punishment. In so doing, the Americans suffered 356 casualties, including 72 killed, 161 wounded, and the rest missing. Washington reported that his men buried 249 of the enemy's dead and that total enemy casualties amounted to more than 1,200. The British suffered the loss of more than 600 deserters, including 440 Germans. They also lost an estimated 200 men taken prisoner.

The battle had proved just how wrong Charles Lee was. The American troops, vastly improved in discipline and fighting ability, which was largely attributable to Steuben's training regimen, had taken on the elite units of Britain's vaunted army and forced them from the field.

Washington had nothing but praise for his men and officers (with the exception of Charles Lee). In his official report of the action, he told the members of Congress:

> Were I to conclude my account of this day's transactions without expressing my obligations to the Officers of the Army in general, I should do injustice to their merit, and violence to my own feelings. They seemed to vie with each other in manifesting their Zeal and Bravery. The Catalogue of those who distinguished themselves is too long to admit of particularising individuals; I cannot however forbear mentioning Brigadier General Wayne whose good conduct and bravery thro' the whole action deserves particular commendation.
>
> The Behaviour of the troops in general, after they recovered from the first surprise occasioned by the Retreat of the advanced Corps, was such as could not be surpassed.[10]

Washington's officers reciprocated with praise for their commander in chief, probably none more eloquently than Lafayette, who later wrote:

> Never was General Washington greater in war than in this action. His presence stopped the retreat. His dispositions fixed the victory. His fine appearance on horseback, his calm courage roused by the animation produced by the vexation of the morning, gave him the air best calculated to arouse enthusiasm.[11]

Anthony Wayne, whose units had performed so well in the assaults by Britain's finest upon the center of the American line, had words to say to those who had so admired the British:

> Tell the Phil'a ladies, that the heavenly, sweet, pretty red coats—the accomplished gentlemen of the Guards and Grenadiers have humbled themselves on the plains of Monmouth.[12]

In the aftermath of the battle, Charles Lee was left to face the disgrace he had brought upon himself. On June 30, still seething over Washington's infuriated confrontation with him on the route of his retreat, he wrote to Washington:

> From the knowledge I have of your Excellency's character, I must conclude that nothing but the misinformation of some very stupid, or misrepresentation of some very wicked person, could have occasioned your making use of such very singular expressions as you did on my coming up to the ground where you had taken post. They implied that I was guilty either of disobedience of orders, or want of conduct, or want of courage. Your Excellency will therefore infinitely oblige me by letting me know on which of these three articles you ground your charge, that I may prepare for my justification which I have the happiness to be confident that I can do to the army, to the Congress, to America, and to the world in general. . . .
>
> I ever had, and I hope I ever shall have the greatest respect and veneration for General Washington; I think him endowed with many great and good qualities, but in this instance, I must pronounce that he has been guilty of an act of cruel injustice. . . . I have a right to demand some reparation for the injury committed and unless I can obtain it I must . . . retire from the service. . . .
>
> In justice to you, I must repeat that I from my soul believe, that it was not a motion of your own breast, but instigated by some of those dirty earwigs who will for ever insinuate themselves near persons in high office.[13]

As if to give further evidence of his despicability, Lee on July 3 wrote to Robert Morris, a signer of the Declaration of Independence, that "General Washington had scarcely any more to do in [the Battle of Monmouth] than to strip the dead."[14] And when his outrageous assertions failed to find an accepting ear, he complained that "no attack, it seems, can be made on General Washington but it must recoil on the assailant."[15]

On the same day that Lee accused Washington of a cruel injustice, Washington issued orders for Lee's arrest and court-martial. The charges were disobedience of orders, misbehavior, and disrespect to the commander in chief. Some six weeks later, in August 1778, the court-martial found Lee guilty of all three charges. His sentence was suspension from the army for one year. Before he had served the suspension, Lee wrote a characteristically sarcastic letter to the members of Congress, who thereupon dismissed him from the army.

Meanwhile, following the flight of Clinton's army to New York, Cornwallis, with seventeen servants to provide the amenities to which he was accustomed, moved into a country house on Long Island and settled into an uncomfortably idle summer, Clinton choosing to safely conserve his forces rather than risk another Monmouth Court House. Cornwallis grew increasingly restless in a role he didn't want to play and in a war that his commander seemed not to want to fight.

Washington and his army rested for two days in the vicinity of Monmouth Court House following the battle, then marched to Brunswick, where his ebullient troops on July 4 celebrated the second anniversary of the independence of the United States and their newest victory in the field.

On July 10 the Congress gave Washington its unanimous thanks for his "distinguished exertions in forming the line of battle; and for his great good conduct in leading on the attack and gaining the important victory at Monmouth over the British grand army."

More personally, the president of Congress, Henry Laurens, wrote prophetically to Washington that "Love and respect for your excellency are impressed on the heart of every grateful American, and your name will be revered by posterity."

CHAPTER Sixteen

The Newport Crisis

At his headquarters in Paramus, New Jersey, Washington received word that an eagerly awaited French fleet had arrived off Sandy Hook on July 11, 1778, three days after the fleet's commander, Vice Admiral Charles Hector Theodat, the Count d'Estaing, dispatched to Washington a letter effusively announcing his presence in American waters and declaring his devotion to the orders of his king to aid the American cause.

D'Estaing had left Toulon on April 13 and without knowing that the British had abandoned Philadelphia, he had sailed first to the mouth of the Delaware River. Then, on learning of the British withdrawal, he had turned north and made for the mouth of the Hudson. His fleet, carrying some 4,000 troops, anchored off Sandy Hook, in position to attack Admiral Richard Howe's vessels lying inside Sandy Hook, at the New York harbor entrance. The destruction or capture of Howe's fleet would be a huge strategic coup, since its loss would mean a death sentence for Clinton's army, which depended on Howe's ships for supply, support, and mobility.

Washington, however, was unsure what d'Estaing would do first, attack New York or attack Newport, Rhode Island, the other American port held by the British, which had been captured by Clinton two years earlier. The decision would depend on d'Estaing's assessment of his chances of defeating Howe's fleet. Putting his army in position to strike either at New York or at Newport, Washington promptly moved his troops from New Jersey to their former encampment outside White Plains.

He sent his French-speaking aide, John Laurens, aboard d'Estaing's flagship, *Languedoc*, to welcome him, then sent two pilots and four civilian

181

ship captains to assist d'Estaing in maneuvering his vessels in waters that were strange to him. He also sent Alexander Hamilton to serve as a liaison.

When the American pilots learned that the draft of the French vessels was five feet deeper than that of their British counterparts, they advised against attempting to cross the sandbar that stretched from Sandy Hook to Staten Island, fearing d'Estaing's fleet would run aground. D'Estaing ordered soundings of his own and satisfied himself that the water over the sandbar was indeed too shallow for his ships. The British fleet was unassailable inside Sandy Hook. D'Estaing would have to choose another objective.

In Newport the British occupation force totaled 3,000 men, commanded by Major General Robert Pigot. Opposing Pigot and his garrison was an American garrison of 1,000 Continentals posted at Providence and commanded by the notoriously hotheaded Major General John Sullivan. Anticipating an attack on Newport, Washington had authorized the call-up of more than 5,000 New England militiamen. Within thirty days of the call-up, some 7,000 militia troops, led by John Hancock, now a militia major general, showed up to do battle at Newport and win what they thought would be a quick, easy victory.

Washington sent Lafayette with the brigades of Brigadier General James Varnum and Brigadier General John Glover (the hero of Washington's escape from Brooklyn and of the crossing of the Delaware) to reinforce Sullivan's command in preparation for an allied attack on Newport. Also sent was the native Rhode Islander, Major General Nathanael Greene. Sullivan's forces, numbering about 10,000 men, including militia and regulars, would be organized into two divisions. According to Washington's orders, one would be commanded by Lafayette, the other by Greene. D'Estaing, who had been an army general before receiving a naval commission, commanded both the French naval and land forces.

On July 29 d'Estaing's fleet reached Point Judith, at the tip of a peninsula that dangled from the mainland southwest of Newport, and there he made contact with Sullivan. Without bothering to solicit d'Estaing's ideas or opinions, Sullivan forthrightly told d'Estaing what he wanted him to do. D'Estaing, unimpressed by the allies he had come to aid, was particularly disappointed by the lack of preparations they had made for him and his fleet, Sullivan having failed to supply the provisions and fresh water that d'Estaing was expecting.

D'Estaing sent his complaints to Washington, who on August 8 wrote to reassure and pacify him:

Engraving of Colonel George Washington (1732–1789) in 1772 by Charles
Willson Peale

Marquis Charles Cornwallis (1738–1805), Lieutenant General of the British Army, circa 1799 (*National Archives*)

Portrait of General Nathanael Greene (1742–1786) by J. Brown of the George Washington Bicentennial Commission (*National Archives*)

Henry Knox (1750–1806) (*Library of Congress*)

Count de Rochambeau (1725–1807), Lieutenant General of the French Army. When Cornwallis surrendered on October 19, 1781, Rochambeau was presented with one of the captured cannons. (*National Archives*)

American soldier Daniel Morgan (1736–1802) (*National Archives*)

Etching of Marquis de Lafayette (1757–1834), proponent of liberty in the American and French Revolutions, by Hillibrand

Colonel Banastre Tarleton (1754–1833), circa 1782 (*National Archives*)

Mrs. Martha Washington (1731–1802) by Woolaston

The Virginia delegation of George Washington, Patrick Henry (1736–1799), and Edmund Pendleton (1721–1803) travel to the first Continental Congress in September 1774. This nineteenth-century engraving was done by Henry Bryan Hall after a drawing by Felix O. C. Darley.

The surrender of Cornwallis to Washington in October 1781 is depicted in this copy of a painting by John Trumbull. (*National Archives*)

I most sincerely sympathize with you in the regret you feel at the obstacles and difficulties you have heretofore encountered. Your case has certainly been a case of peculiar hardship, but you justly have the consolation which arises from a reflection that no exertions possible have been wanting in you to insure success. . . . The disappointments you have experienced proceed from circumstances which no human foresight or activity can control. . . .[1]

Washington told d'Estaing that he had asked the governor of Connecticut to have fresh water provided to the fleet as soon as possible. He also warned d'Estaing that Admiral Howe was sailing for Newport with part of his fleet.

The town of Newport lay at the southern end of the island named Rhode Island, at the entrance to Narragansett Bay and the Providence harbor. To the west of Newport lay Conanicut Island. The channel between the two islands, which gave access from the Atlantic to Providence harbor, was called the Middle Passage. D'Estaing was to enter the Middle Passage on Saturday, August 8, and run past the British defenses at Newport. During the night of August 9–10 Sullivan would ferry his troops across Sakonnet Passage (the east passage) from Tiverton on the mainland and land them on the northeast tip of Rhode Island. Early Monday morning, August 10, d'Estaing was to land his troops on the west side of the island, then commence a bombardment of the British defenses with his fleet's guns while the American and French forces, on opposite sides of the island, moved south in unison to assault Newport's defenses by land. That was the plan.

The French vessels, following the plan, moved up the Middle Passage on Saturday, August 8, and ran past the British defenses, silencing two British batteries on the way. Early Sunday morning, August 9, after learning that the British had abandoned their position on the northern end of Rhode Island, Sullivan immediately sent his troops across from Tiverton to occupy the abandoned British works. That action placed Sullivan one day ahead of the schedule agreed upon. He sent word to d'Estaing to quickly land his French troops on the west side of the island, also ahead of schedule.

D'Estaing took offense at Sullivan's brashness in altering the plan without consulting him and then demanding an immediate adjustment by the French. However, events quickly overtook his offended feelings. Around noon on Sunday French lookouts reported a fleet approaching from the south. By 1:30 p.m. thirty-five ships had been sighted, flying British colors, making for Newport. D'Estaing's vessels now stood in danger of being trapped far up in the Middle Passage, with an unfavorable southerly wind that hindered their maneuverability.

D'Estaing instantly forsook the planned attack on Newport. As quickly as he could, he retrieved his troops that had already gone ashore on Rhode Island. He then picked up his crewmen and troops who, sick with scurvy, had been put ashore on Conanicut Island. With all his men once more aboard, he prepared to defend his fleet against a British attack.

As daylight faded, however, the British ships anchored without entering Narragansett Bay. That night, the wind shifted and began streaming from the north. About eleven o'clock the next morning, Monday, August 10, d'Estaing formed up his fleet and sailed out of the bay to do battle with the British fleet, about two-thirds the size of his own. Admiral Howe then maneuvered his ships to gain the weather gauge, whereby his ships would sail in the direction of the wind and not have to tack in order to close on the enemy. D'Estaing responded by also seeking the wind advantage, and for the next twenty-four hours both fleets maneuvered at sea, neither firing a shot.

On Tuesday night, August 11, the prevailing north wind brought a violent gale that raged for two days and scattered the two fleets over a large area of the Atlantic. A number of vessels suffered heavy damage, including d'Estaing's ninety-gun flagship, *Languedoc*, which lost her masts and rudder to the storm. The day after the storm ended, Wednesday, August 14, two smaller British vessels attacked *Languedoc* and another of d'Estaing's crippled ships, the *Tonnant*. With the coming of darkness, however, the British captains called off the fight.

The following day, August 15, having surveyed the storm's damage to his fleet, Admiral Howe decided to withdraw without further action. He turned south and sailed for New York for repairs. On the departure of the British, D'Estaing's fleet limped back toward Narragansett Bay.

The storm had delayed Sullivan's advance on Newport, having pounded troops exposed to the wind and rain, ruining much of their gunpowder. Sullivan had established a line across the top of the island while he waited for d'Estaing's troops to return and take a position on the west side of the line. On August 15, the east side of the line began advancing toward the British defenses, Sullivan apparently expecting d'Estaing at any hour to return and move into position.

The French vessels returned on August 20. D'Estaing, however, had no intention of attacking Newport. He had come only to inform Sullivan that he was sailing to Boston to have his ships repaired. Despite the urgings of Lafayette and Greene to stay, put his troops ashore to fight, and then have his ships repaired, d'Estaing took his fleet out of Narragansett Bay at midnight on August 21 and set sail for Boston.

Outraged that d'Estaing was deserting, infuriated with d'Estaing personally, and the French generally, Sullivan had his generals—with the exception of Lafayette—join in a protest of d'Estaing's behavior, asserting that he had done damage to the honor of France and injury to the alliance. Sullivan vented his anger in his general orders of August 24:

> The General [Sullivan] cannot help lamenting the sudden and unexpected departure of the French fleet, as he finds it has a tendency to discourage some who placed great dependence on the assistance of it. . . . He yet hopes the event [the attack on Newport] will prove America is able to procure with her own arms that which her allies refused to assist her in obtaining.[2]

Incensed by Sullivan's remarks, Lafayette reacted in hot defense of his countrymen, setting off recriminatory responses from his American comrades. Lafayette took the matter to Washington with a letter in which he remarked that "I am more upon a warlike footing in the American lines than when I came near the British lines at Newport." His heart was wounded, he said, "by that very people I came from so far to love and support."

Realizing the rift's potential for creating a wave of anti-French feeling throughout the army, Nathanael Greene saw disaster looming. Sullivan's censure of d'Estaing, Greene observed, "opened the mouths of the army in very clamourous strains." At last made to grudgingly see the danger himself, Sullivan issued a retraction of sorts in his general orders of August 26.

Washington quickly acted to put out the fire before it spread any farther. On August 28 he wrote to Sullivan:

> Should the expedition fail, through the abandonment of the French fleet, the officers concerned will be apt to complain loudly. But prudence dictates that we should put the best face upon the matter and to the world attribute the removal to Boston to necessity.
>
> The reasons are too obvious to need explaining. The principal one is that our British and internal enemies would be glad to improve the least matter of complaint and disgust against and between us and our new allies into a serious rupture.[3]

On September 1 he wrote again to Sullivan:

> The disagreement between the army under your command and the fleet has given me very singular uneasiness. . . . First impressions, you know, are generally longest remembered, and will serve to fix in a great degree our national character among the French. In our conduct towards them we should remember that they are a people old in war, very strict in military etiquette and apt to take fire where others scarcely seem warmed.
>
> Permit me to recommend in the most particular manner, the cultivation of harmony and good agreement, and your endeavours to destroy that ill humour which may have got into the officers. It is of the greatest importance, also, that the . . . soldiers and the people should know nothing of the misunderstanding. . . .
>
> I have one thing more to say. I make no doubt but you will do all in your power to forward the repairs of the French fleet.[4]

To the offended Lafayette on September 1 Washington wrote:

> I feel every thing that hurts the Sensibility of a Gentleman; and consequently, upon the present occasion, feel for you and for our good and great Allys the French. I feel myself hurt also at every illiberal and unthinking reflection which may have been cast upon Count D'Estaing or the conduct of the fleet under his command; and lastly I feel for my Country. Let me entreat you my dear Marquis to take no exception at unmeaning expressions, uttered perhaps without Consideration, and in the first transport of disappointed hope.
>
> Everybody, Sir, who reasons will acknowledge the advantages which we have derived from the French fleet, and the Zeal of the Commander of it, but in a free and republican Government, you cannot restrain the voice of the multitude; every man will speak as he thinks, or more properly without thinking, consequently will adjudge of Effects without attending to the Causes.
>
> The censures which have been levelled at the French fleet would more than probably have fallen in a much higher degree on our own (if we had one) in the same situation. . . .
>
> Let me beseech you therefore my good Sir to afford a healing hand to the wound. . . . I, your friend, have no doubt but that you will use your utmost endeavors to restore harmony, that the honour,

glory and mutual Interest of the two Nations may be promoted and cemented in the firmest manner.[5]

To Major General Heath, commanding the Eastern Department of the Continental Army, headquartered in Boston, where d'Estaing was headed and where there was talk of refusing help to the French fleet, Washington wrote a remarkable public relations brief:

> The unfortunate circumstance of the French fleet having left Rhode Island at so critical a moment, I am apprehensive, if not prudently managed, will have many injurious consequences, besides merely the loss of the advantages we should have reaped from succeeding in the Expedition.
>
> It will not only tend to discourage the people, and weaken their confidence in the new alliance, but may possibly produce prejudices and resentments, which may operate against giving the fleet such effectual assistance in its present distress, as the exigence of our affairs and our true interests demands. It will certainly be sound policy to combat these effects, and whatever private opinion may be entertained, to give the most favorable construction of what has happened to the public, and at the same time to put the French fleet, as soon as possible, in condition to defend itself and be useful to us.
>
> The departure of the fleet from Rhode Island is not yet publicly announced here, but when it is, I intend to ascribe it to necessity, from the damage suffered in the late storm. This, it appears to me, is the Idea which ought to be generally propagated.
>
> As I doubt not the force of these Reasons will strike you equally with myself, I would recommend to you to use your utmost influence to palliate and soften matters, and induce those, whose business it is to provide succours of every kind for the fleet, to employ the utmost zeal and activity in doing it.
>
> It is our duty to make the best of our misfortunes, and not to suffer passions to interfere with our interest and the public good.[6]

To the most offended party, Count d'Estaing, Washington wrote:

> If the deepest regret that the best concerted enterprise and bravest exertions should have been rendered fruitless by a disaster which human prudence is incapable of foreseeing or preventing can alleviate

disappointment, you may be assured that the whole Continent sympathizes with you; it will be a consolation to you to reflect that the thinking part of Mankind do not form their judgement from events; and that their equity will ever attach equal glory to those actions which deserve success, as to those which have been crowned with it.

It is in the trying circumstances to which your Excellency has been exposed that the virtues of a great Mind are displayed in the brightest lustre; and that the General's Character is better known than in the moment of Victory; it was yours, by every title which can give it. . . .

I exceedingly lament that in addition to our misfortunes, there has been the least suspension of harmony and good understanding between the Generals of allied Nations, whose views, like their interests must be the same. On the first intimation of it I employed my influence in restoring what I regarded as essential to the permanence of a Union founded on mutual inclination and the strongest ties of reciprocal advantage.[7]

Meanwhile, the battle for Newport was not going so well. Following the departure of the French ships and the 4,000 French troops aboard them, the militia that had turned out in gleeful anticipation of easy victory deserted en masse, abruptly reducing Sullivan's force to fewer than 3,000 troops. Major General Pigot, commanding the British garrison at Newport, seized the initiative and launched an attack against the American lines, which stubbornly held. The African-American regiment under the command of Colonel Christopher Greene was one unit in particular that distinguished itself in the attack, repelling three furious Hessian assaults.

On the night of August 30–31 Sullivan and his army, with the aid of Glover's Marblehead boatmen, who defended the left side of the rebel line by day and manned their oars that night, slipped away and crossed back to Tiverton, then returned to their post at Providence. The American withdrawal was well timed, for on September 1 British ships reached Newport with 5,000 redcoats to reinforce Pigot's troops. Although the outcome was seen by many as a defeat, what the Americans lost was an opportunity more than a battle. American casualties amounted to 30 killed, 137 wounded, and 44 missing. British losses totaled 38 killed, 210 wounded, and 12 missing.

The oil poured by Washington on troubled waters had the desired effect. Heath cooperated in getting repairs for d'Estaing's ships. Sullivan sent an apology to d'Estaing. Congress passed a resolution commending d'Estaing "as a brave and wise officer." Hancock and Greene traveled back to Boston to give d'Estaing and his fleet whatever help they could.

Not everything was brought under control, however. A bakery that the French had established in Boston to help feed d'Estaing's sailors and soldiers was attacked and pilfered by an anti-French mob, and a French lieutenant was killed trying to turn back the mob. The British crewmen of privateer vessels that operated out of Boston were blamed for inciting the riot. Even so, to make amends, the Massachusetts legislature voted to provide a monument to the lieutenant and have it placed on his grave. The gesture was prompt, but the monument itself came tardy. It was erected on May 24, 1917.

D'Estaing was apparently completely mollified by the extensive public relations effort. In a letter to Washington he drew a lesson from the affair:

> If during the coming centuries, we of America and France are to live in amity and confidence, we must banish recriminations and prevent complaints. I trust the two nations will not be forced to depart from moderation in their conduct but that they will reflect in all their public affairs that firmness and consideration for public interests necessary to unity between the two great nations.[8]

The breach repaired, Washington turned back to the larger scope of the war.

CHAPTER Seventeen

A Personal Tragedy

I n late September 1778 Cornwallis's spell of inactivity, which had lasted through most of the summer, was broken by Clinton's orders to take 5,000 men and cover the British foraging parties that were being harassed by rebel troops in the lower Hudson River valley. Cornwallis's assignment was to go up the west side of the Hudson—while Knyphausen led a force of 3,000 up the east side—and attack those units that Washington had detached from his main force to harass the British foragers.

Cornwallis learned, probably from loyalists living in the area, that Anthony Wayne, in command of the rebel units, had posted a detachment of New Jersey militiamen, commanded by Brigadier General William Winds, at Tappan, New Jersey; at the village of Old Tappan, about two miles to the southwest of Tappan, he had posted the 3rd Continental Light Dragoons, commanded by Lieutenant Colonel George Baylor. Hoping to cut off Wayne's entire force, Cornwallis planned simultaneous attacks on both rebel posts.

The plan called for British Lieutenant Colonel Archibald Campbell to detach the 71st Regiment and the Queen's Rangers from Knyphausen's force, cross the Hudson and attack the rebel position at Tappan from the east. At the same time, Cornwallis would attack the rebel units at Old Tappan with a detachment from his column. That detachment Cornwallis placed under the command of Major General Charles Grey, who twelve months earlier had gained the sobriquet "No Flint" after he ordered his men to remove the flints from their muskets (to prevent their being fired, accidentally or otherwise) and to use only their bayonets in their assault on a rebel post at Paoli, Pennsylvania. The attack caught the

191

rebels by surprise and resulted in the bloody slaughter of fifty-three of Wayne's soldiers.

Campbell's attack on Tappan, scheduled to take place during the night of Monday, September 28, failed when the boats needed to ferry his troops across the Hudson failed to show up on time and, warned by British deserters, Winds's militiamen fled from their encampment before Campbell's force could reach Tappan. Winds saved himself and his units, but apparently gave no thought to saving his rebel comrades encamped at Old Tappan, giving them no word of warning of the British advance.

Their silent approach covered by darkness, Grey's troops first surrounded the village. They then overwhelmed and bayoneted to death a twelve-man guard posted near the building that Baylor was using as his headquarters, then stole into the three barns where some 100 dragoons were sleeping and fell on them with their bayonets. About three dozen of Baylor's troops managed to escape; the rest were either stabbed to death or taken prisoner. Among the prisoners was Lieutenant Colonel Baylor.

The attack became known to Americans as the Tappan Massacre, the second such atrocity committed by "No Flint" Grey, this time under Cornwallis's command. Justification for it was found in the rules of war that allowed an attacking force to refuse quarter to the enemy if the attack was made at night, when it was difficult to tell friend from foe in the darkness.

Protecting foraging parties, even when it afforded opportunities to inflict significant losses on the rebel army, was not enough to hold Cornwallis's interest in the war. He was bored and restless, and the news from home was bad. His wife's condition was worsening. He decided he had had enough of the war, perhaps of soldiering, and he again requested permission to return to England. Clinton didn't object, believing that while in London Cornwallis would use his influence and his connections to get more troops.

Clinton's aide and apparent confidant, Captain William Sutherland, no admirer of the earl, was suspicious of Cornwallis's motives. "Lord Cornwallis is gone home to cock his eye in the House of Lords," he claimed, "insipid good natured Lord and the worst officer (but in personal courage) under the Crown."[1] Evidently disagreeing, Clinton approved the leave-taking. Cornwallis promised he would do Clinton the favor of looking in on his motherless children, and Clinton seemed not at all afraid to have Cornwallis present his views on the progress of the war to the king's ministers. It was in such high places, Clinton felt, that Cornwallis's "Knowledge of this Country and of our Circumstances may during this

Season be as Serviceable as I have found his Experience and Activity during the Campaign."

Cornwallis responded earnestly to Clinton's expression of confidence, telling him on the day before he sailed, "You may depend on my taking care of your letters and seeing your children, and obeying your commands in every respect." On November 27, 1778, Cornwallis, along with the members of the failed Carlisle Peace Commission, who had been his fellow passengers on the voyage to America months earlier, sailed from Sandy Hook, bound for Plymouth, England.

His ship reached Plymouth on December 19, and Cornwallis arrived in London on December 23. Apparently without discussing the matter with the secretary of state for American colonies, George Germain, or the king, Cornwallis turned in his resignation from the army. King George, probably sympathizing with him during the grave illness of Jemima, accepted the resignation. Cornwallis then left London and hurried to his Suffolk estate and the bedside of his wife, whom he found, as he said, in "a very weak state indeed," suffering apparently from a liver disease.

Through a cheerless Christmas and bleak January he remained with her, refusing to leave the manor to socialize with friends or to take care of business matters. Jemima's illness preoccupied him. "The very ill state of health in which I found Lady Cornwallis," he told Clinton in a letter, "has render'd me incapable of any attention but to her, and the thoughts of her danger is forever present in my mind."[2]

On February 14, 1779, St. Valentine's Day, Cornwallis's beloved Jemima died.

Deeply grieving and inconsolable, he shut himself off from friends, refusing to see or talk to anyone except his closest family members. His emotions, normally held in check by aristocratic reserve, poured onto the pages of letters he wrote to those closest to him. He told his brother William that Jemima's death had "effectually destroyed all my hopes of happiness in this world." Merely the thought of her, he wrote, would "harrow up" his soul.

It was hard to avoid thoughts of her. There were reminders of her everywhere—the children, the manor, the rolling meadows of the sprawling estate, everything they had shared. Besieged by sadness, he finally determined to leave everything behind, to remove himself from all those painful reminders. On April 4, 1779, he wrote to Clinton to tell him he wanted to return to the war in America. He had no desire to command, he said, and was reluctant to return, for fear that Clinton would resign and command of the king's American army would be thrust upon him. Nevertheless he wanted the escape that a return to action would provide him. In the event Clinton undertook a campaign in the south or in the French islands of the Caribbean, he said, he would "with great pleasure come out and meet you; This country [England] has now no charms for me, and I am perfectly indifferent as to what part of the world I may go."

By the time Cornwallis had decided he must go back to the army, Germain had picked someone else to succeed Clinton and didn't want to rescind that decision. He had given a dormant commission to Major General John Vaughan, who had first gone to America from Ireland with Cornwallis and had been through the same battles as Cornwallis. Getting over his stated reluctance to command and now bent on the reinstatement of his position in the king's American army, Cornwallis went over Germain's head and took his request for reinstatement directly to King George, who approved it.

"I am now returning to America," Cornwallis wrote to his brother William, "not with view of conquest & ambition, nothing brilliant can be expected in that quarter; but I find this country quite unsupportable to me. I must shift the scene. I have many friends in the [British] American Army. I love that Army, & flatter myself that I am not quite indifferent to them: I hope Sr. H. Clinton will stay, my returning to him is likely to induce him to do so. If he insists on coming away, of course I cannot decline taking the command, & must make the best of it, & I trust that good intentions & plain dealing will carry me through."

Before leaving England, Cornwallis appeared before the House of Commons to testify in the inquiry that was investigating the conduct of General Howe in his prosecution of the war, which had come under sharp criticism in Parliament. Cornwallis defiantly told the members of Commons that he would refuse to answer any questions that could be answered only with an opinion and that he knew Howe to be an officer who "deserved greatly of his country," having served it "with fidelity, assiduity and with great ability." His appearance, his manner, and his words all gave witness to Cornwallis's having emerged from the depth of his grief and reclusiveness. Shortly after completing his testimony, he boarded a ship bound for America. He arrived in New York harbor on July 21, 1779.

Clinton apparently had mixed feelings on seeing Cornwallis. He doubtless was disappointed that Cornwallis had not brought the additional troops Clinton had hoped and pleaded for. On the other hand, weary of the war and disgruntled over what he felt was a lack of support for it, he could now request relief from command in the hope that Cornwallis's return would make his request acceptable to Germain and the king. "I flattered myself," he wrote later, "that every objection to my request of being released from my very arduous and unpleasant situation must now cease, since His Majesty had upon the spot an officer of rank and experience upon whom to confer the command of his army."[3] It would take many weeks, however, for Clinton to get an answer to his request.

While he—and Cornwallis—waited for that answer, leadership of the king's army became uncertain. Neither of the two men, nor the officers who served with them, knew on any one day who would be in charge on the next. Feelings between Cornwallis and his commander grew tense. Despite his earlier having disclaimed interest in command, Cornwallis now sought a command of his own that would put distance between him and Clinton. In September 1779, when the governor of Jamaica asked Clinton to send troops to help him defend against an expected French attack, Cornwallis urged Clinton to grant the request and put him in charge of the expedition. Hesitant to reduce his army by sending reinforcements to Jamaica, Clinton nevertheless consented to it.

Cornwallis and 4,000 troops under his command embarked on a fleet commanded by Admiral Marriot Arbuthnot, the new British naval commander, and set sail for Jamaica in late September. Three days out, the British fleet received a report that the French fleet under d'Estaing, which had been in the Caribbean, was moving toward the North American mainland, destination unknown. Arbuthnot's fleet quickly turned around and headed back to New York. His mission aborted, Cornwallis would have to go back and suffer more inactivity under Clinton.

While Cornwallis was in Suffolk with Jemima, Washington had spent time in Philadelphia with Martha. Congress had called him there in December 1778 to talk about plans for the army's campaign of 1779. Martha came up from Mount Vernon to meet him in Philadelphia and was already there when he arrived shortly before Christmas. They were guests at the home of Henry Laurens.

After many months spent in the field with his officers and men and the enemy, Washington was appalled by what he found in Philadelphia, at the heart of the new nation. He wrote to Benjamin Harrison about it:

> I have seen nothing since I came here . . . to change my opinion of men or measures, but abundant reason to be convinced that our affairs are in a more distressed, ruinous, and deplorable condition than they have been in since the commencement of the war. . . .

If I was to be called upon to draw a picture of the times and of the men, from what I have seen, heard, and in part know, I should in one word say that idleness, dissipation, and extravagance seem to have laid fast hold of most them. That speculation, peculation, and an insatiable thirst for riches seems to have got the better of every other consideration....[4]

The want of zeal for America's cause Washington found not in civilians alone. In the army there were the continuing problems of discipline and desertion. To treat the discipline problem, Washington asked Congress to approve his recommendation for an increase in the number of lash strokes permissible for serious offenses. The maximum was then 100, which he felt was insufficient for some offenses. Washington's young fellow Virginian, Major Henry "Light Horse Harry" Lee, recommended much stronger measures to punish deserters. What he proposed was revealed in Washington's wise and tactful reply to his suggestion:

The measure you propose of putting deserters from our Army to immediate death would probably tend to discourage the practice. But it ought to be executed with caution and only when the fact is very clear and unequivocal. I think that that part of your proposal which respects cutting off their heads ... had better be omitted. Examples however severe ought not to be attended with an appearance of inhumanity otherwise they give disgust and may excite resentment rather than terror.[5]

Lee didn't wait for Washington's permission. On the day after Washington wrote to Lee, Brigadier General William Irvine, a physician turned soldier, reported that he had seen:

... the head of a corporal of the First Regiment who ... left us ... stuck up on the gallows. He was taken two nights ago by a party of Major Lee's, who it seems were at first determined to kill all, but on consultation or debate agreed to kill only one out of three. It fell to the corporal's lot, whose head was immediately carried to camp on a pole by the two who escaped instant death. These two villains were of the same regiment and have been tried here this day. Presume they will meet the same fate. I hope in future Death will be the punishment for all such. I plainly see less will not do.[6]

Despite the persistent problems, Washington's army was faring better in the winter of 1778–1779 than in previous winters. For one thing, it was a mild winter. For another, the troops were better clothed because of the uniforms supplied by the French, and they were generally better fed, although shortages still existed.

At his headquarters in Middlebrook, New Jersey, Washington waited to hear that Clinton had ended the winter respite and had bestirred himself to start a spring campaign. On May 31 Washington received a report that Clinton had moved a force to White Plains. Always wary that the British planned to try to take West Point, the fortress guarding the upper Hudson River valley—and therefore the key to control of the river and its crossings—Washington quickly shifted his army northeastward. While on the march to new positions at Springfield and Pompton, Washington learned that a 6,000-man British force had captured the fort at Verplanck's Point, on the east side of the river, and the unfinished fort at Stony Point, opposite Verplanck's Point, which gave the British control of the vital river crossing at King's Ferry.

Its loss by the Americans meant that supplies, communications, and troops moving between New England and the states to the south would be forced to take a route that crossed the Hudson farther north and was some sixty miles longer.

Nevertheless, Washington entertained no idea of retaking the King's Ferry river crossing. His force was insufficient for the task. "All we can do," he told Horatio Gates, "is to lament what we cannot remedy and to prevent a further progress on the river and to make the advantage of what they have now gained as limited as possible." Still believing West Point was the ultimate British objective, Washington positioned his force between Stony Point and West Point in rough, rocky country that provided a substantial advantage to a defending army.

Clinton made no attempt to move farther toward West Point. Instead, after lingering around King's Ferry till the end of June, he withdrew his army, leaving garrisons totaling some 1,100 troops at the two captured forts and ordering the works at Stony Point built into a strong fortress. If Clinton's intention was to tempt Washington into retaking King's Ferry and thus draw him into battle, as Clinton had been instructed by London to do, the ploy failed, for Washington refused the bait and kept his army in its defensive position on the Hudson.

Another apparent attempt to lure him into battle occurred when a British amphibious force in early July stormed ashore from Long Island Sound and made war on civilians by burning the defenseless Connecticut towns of Horse Neck (later renamed Greenwich), Norwalk, and Fairfield. What the raiders destroyed were houses, churches, barns, schools, and shops. Commenting on the Connecticut raids, Washington told Lafayette that:

> ... the intrepid and magnanimous [Major General William] Tryon who, in defiance of all the opposition ... by the Women and Children ... of these towns, performed this notable exploit with 2000 brave and generous Britons, adding thereby fresh lustre to their Arms and dignity to their King.[7]

Angered by the wantonness of the raids, Washington made plans to retaliate. He asked Anthony Wayne to somehow get one of his officers into the fort that the British were building on Stony Point and discover its defenses. Wayne chose Captain Allen McLane for the job. McLane had become unusually capable at reconnaissance and intelligence-gathering. Under a flag of truce to accompany a Mrs. Smith to see her sons, apparently being held as prisoners of war in the fort, McLane got a good look at the interior and exterior of the fort and the abatis protecting it. He reported his information to Washington's headquarters.

The fort's commandant was Lieutenant Colonel Henry Johnson of the British 17th Regiment; his garrison amounted to some 700 men. The point of land upon which the fort was built was a salient that jutted about a half mile into the Hudson. On the river sides of the salient the land rose steeply to a height of 150 feet above the water; on the third side the land dropped off into a marsh, across which a causeway had been built to give access to the point and to the ferry landing on the north side of the point. Two abatis protected the land side of the point and the artillery batteries that were emplaced near the top of the slope that rose from the marsh to the fort.

Washington decided on a nighttime assault and turned the operation over to Wayne, whose troops the British had massacred in night attacks at Paoli and Old Tappan. Wayne's attacking force would be made up of 1,350 troops that he divided into three assault columns. The main column would approach the fort along a sandbar on the south side of the salient, climbing the steep slope to reach the enemy. A second column would climb the north side, and the third column would cross the causeway and attack the front of the fort. The troops making the frontal assault would be the only ones carrying loaded muskets or rifles; their fire was intended to draw attention away from the attackers climbing the south and north sides, who were instructed to attack with bayonets.

The columns started moving toward the point about 11:30 p.m. on July 15. They made contact with the British outposts around midnight, overran them, and pressed on to the fort. The action that followed was described by Nathanael Greene in a letter written from Stony Point on July 17, the day after the assault:

> I wrote you a hasty account yesterday morning of a surprize Gen. Wayne had effected upon the garrison at this place. He marched about two o'clock in the afternoon from Fort Montgomery with part of the light infantry of the army, amounting to about 1,400 men. The garrison consisted of between 5 and 600 men, including officers. The attack was made about midnight and conducted with great spirit and enterprise, the troops marching up in the face of an exceeding heavy fire with cannon and musketry, without discharging a gun. This is thought to be the perfection of discipline and will for ever immortalize Gen. Wayne, as it would do honor to the first general in Europe. The place is as difficult of access as any you ever saw, strongly fortified with lines and secured with a double row of abatis. The post actually looks more formidable on the ground than it can be made by description, and, contrary to almost all other events of this nature, increases our surprize by viewing the place and the circumstances.
>
> The darkness of the night favoured the attack and made our loss much less than might have been expected. The whole business was done with fixed bayonets. Our loss in killed and wounded amounted to 90 men, including officers—eight only of which were killed. Gen. Wayne got a slight wound (upon the side of his head) and three or four other officers—among the number is Lieut. Col. Hay, of Pennsylvania—but they are all in a fair way of recovery.
>
> The enemy's loss is not certainly known, neither have we any certain account of the number of prisoners, as they were sent away in the dark and in a hurry, but it is said they amount to 440; about 30 or 40 were left behind unable to march, and upwards of 30 were buried.
>
> The enemy made little resistance after our people got into the works, their cry was, "Mercy, mercy, dear, dear Americans!"[8]

Other reports put the British dead at 63, most of them apparently bayoneted to death, and 543 captured. All of those in the British garrison were either killed or taken prisoner. The Americans suffered a loss of 15 killed and 84 wounded.

Wayne had fallen at the second abatis with a superficial head wound, but had shouted to his men, "Carry me to the fort, boys! Let's go forward!" At two o'clock on the morning of July 16 he dispatched a note to Washington: "Dear Genl. This fort & Garrison with Coln. Johnson are our's. Our Officers & Men behaved like men who are determined to be free."[9]

Paoli and Old Tappan had been avenged, though not with the terrible slaughter the British had inflicted on the Americans. When quarter was asked, the Americans at Stony Point granted it. Even the British commandant, Lieutenant Colonel Johnson, according to an account published in *The New York Journal*, acknowledged that "not a drop of blood was spilled unnecessarily."

Washington decided that the fort at Stony Point could only be held with more troops than he was willing to commit to it, and after dismantling the structure and carrying off the dozen or more pieces of British artillery and other matériel, Wayne and his troops abandoned it, withdrawing from the site on July 18. The British reoccupied it on July 19.

A lesson had been taught, however. The Americans could strike back successfully and, thanks to the training by Steuben, could do so with British tactics. Any position Clinton's army would take outside its refuge in New York would from now on be at risk. Stony Point was a warning to the British, in New York and in London, and it was a huge morale boost for Americans everywhere.

A month after the taking of Stony Point, shortly after midnight on August 19, a 400-man contingent under "Light Horse" Harry Lee attacked the British fort at Paulus (or Powle's) Hook, New Jersey, opposite the tip of Manhattan, and using the same tactics (and the reconnaissance of Allen McLane) as at Stony Point, captured it under the noses of Clinton and his redcoat army just across the Hudson River.

Again the British lost an entire garrison, with about 50 men being put to the bayonet during the fight and 158 men and officers taken prisoner. The American losses were put at two killed and three wounded. Lee quickly abandoned the fort before British relief columns could arrive.

Clinton became so depressed by the two defeats and by the criticism stemming from them that he once again offered his resignation to George Germain, suggesting that Cornwallis would be a suitable replacement. Germain refused to accept the resignation.

With winter still months away, Clinton called the British army's campaign of 1779 at an end and prepared for another hiatus.

CHAPTER Eighteen

The Benedict Arnold Treason

In March 1758, when he was seventeen years old, husky, swarthy Benedict Arnold ran away from his home in Norwich, Connecticut and enlisted in the New York militia during the French and Indian War. Fourteen months later he was reported as a deserter. In March 1760 he again enlisted and after serving briefly in upstate New York, he again deserted and returned home.

He served an apprenticeship to a druggist and after his parents died, he sold their property in Norwich and opened a drugstore/bookstore in New Haven. He later expanded into the shipping business, became successful at it and, seeking a proper place in New Haven society as a prospering businessman, husband, and father of three sons, he joined the Connecticut militia. Recognizing his leadership abilities, his company elected him its captain in December 1774, a month before his thirty-fourth birthday.

At that more mature age, Arnold had become serious about investing his restless energy in military enterprises. Within twenty-four hours of learning of the fighting at Lexington Green and Concord Bridge, Arnold on April 20, 1775 called out his militia company and began marching for Cambridge to join his compatriots. The New Haven selectmen, the town's governing body, at first refused to turn over to Arnold a needed supply of gunpowder for his militiamen, but Arnold told them they would either hand him the keys to the powder magazine or he would break open the doors and take what he needed by force. "None but Almighty God shall prevent my marching!" he warned them. The selectmen gave him the keys.

Shortly after reaching Cambridge and entering the American lines around Boston, Arnold proposed to the Massachusetts Committee of

Safety a plan to lead an expedition to capture Fort Ticonderoga and secure the fort's big guns for use in the siege of British-held Boston. On May 3 the committee authorized Arnold to conduct the expedition and to raise a force of up to 400 troops to accomplish the mission. It also commissioned him a colonel while he led the expedition. Arnold immediately set out for Ticonderoga, signing up recruits along the way.

The idea of capturing Fort Ticonderoga and its guns was so good that more than one person had thought of it. When Arnold reached Castleton, about twenty miles southeast of Ticonderoga, he caught up with an expedition, composed mostly of Green Mountain Boys, that had been authorized by Connecticut to take the fort. Arnold attempted to absorb those officers and men into his command, but they refused to serve under anyone but Ethan Allen. An arrangement to share command was worked out between Arnold and Allen, and together their forces overwhelmed Ticonderoga's weak garrison and captured the fort on May 10, 1775.

From that success Arnold went on to win fame for his heroic march through the rugged wilderness of Maine to invade Canada in the autumn of 1775. When Washington heard that he had managed to reach the St. Lawrence River with more than 600 troops, he wrote to Arnold and told him, "It is not in the power of any man to command success; but you have done more—you have deserved it. My thanks are due, and sincerely offered to you for your enterprizing and persevering spirit."[1]

Arnold's acclaim would have been far greater had his mission to capture Quebec succeeded, but he nevertheless earned a reputation for himself in conducting a daring, dogged, and courageous battle, suffering a severe leg wound in the process. His actions in the assault on Quebec gained him a commission as brigadier general in the Continental Army.

From Canada he moved on to his greatest achievement, the victory won against Burgoyne in the Battle of Saratoga, where he was again wounded. After the action at Saratoga, however, his reputation rapidly tarnished. He had been accumulating enemies ever since his attempt to take command of the Connecticut expedition at Castleton, and those enemies let none of his misbehavior go unnoticed. They harshly criticized him for his overzealous seizure of the goods of Montreal merchants and accused him of inflating his expenses in the account he submitted to Massachusetts for reimbursement. He had turned his quick and fiery temper on his commander, Horatio Gates, at Saratoga and had been relieved of his command for insubordination. He was passed over for promotion while five of his juniors were promoted to major general over him. In Philadelphia, where Washington in June 1778 had appointed him to command the troops garrisoned there, he became absorbed with social climbing and all the trappings of the good life, financing his extravagances with the sort of speculation and peculation that Washington found so appalling.

In April 1779, when he was thirty-eight years old, Arnold married Peggy Shippen, the vivacious, blond, eighteen-year-old daughter of Edward Shippen, a socially prominent and well-to-do Philadelphia judge whose family had loyalist leanings. Arnold's first wife had taken ill and died not long after the fall of Fort Ticonderoga. While the British occupied Philadelphia, fun-loving Peggy had become acquainted with and flirted with General Clinton's young aide, John Andre, then a captain. The new Mrs. Arnold's contact with Andre provided Arnold with an entrée to the British commander.

Moved by his anger and resentment and a need for money to support the lifestyle of his young, high-society wife, Arnold in May 1779 began talking to the British, at first through a Tory intermediary who made contact with Andre. Arnold let the British know what he might do for them and what he would expect them to do for him in return. The intermediary was Joseph Stansbury, a Philadelphia resident whose mild manner disguised his treachery. On May 10, 1779, in a verbose letter to Stansbury, Andre set forth in general terms the arrangement the British agreed to have with Arnold, who in the letter was referred to as "Monk," one of the code names used for him:

> ... On our part we meet Monk's ouvertures with full reliance on his honourable intentions and disclose to him with the strongest assurances of our sincerity that no thought is entertained of abandoning the point we have in view. That on the contrary powerfull means are expected for accomplishing our end. We likewise assure him that in the very first instance of receiving the tidings or good offices we expect from him, our liberality will be evinced; that in case any partial but important blow should by his means be struck or aimed, upon the strength of just and pointed information and cooperation, rewards equal at least to what such service can be estimated at will be given, but should the abilities and zeal of that able and enterprizing gentleman amount to the seizing an obnoxious band of men, to the delivering into our power or enabling us to attack to advantage and by

judicious assistance completely to defeat a numerous body, then would the generosity of the nation exceed even his own most sanguine hopes, and in the expectation of this he may rely on that honour he now trusts in his present advances. Should his manifest efforts be foiled and after every zealous attempt flight be at length necessary, the cause in which he suffers will hold itself bound to indemnify him for his losses and receive him with the honour his conduct deserves. . . .[2]

What Andre's beclouded prose was attempting to establish was that the British wanted Arnold to deliver into their hands an American army, or a substantial part thereof, and if he succeeded in doing so, he would be paid an amount that he would find more than acceptable. The Americans had become troublesome to fight, and the British were hoping Arnold would help them capture a rebel army without having first to fight it. They offered to pay him, in addition to other rewards for his betrayal, two guineas (about $10) for each American soldier he turned over to them. According to one report, so far every rebel soldier killed, wounded, or captured had cost the British Exchequer more than 3,000 guineas, or about $15,000 per American head.

While waiting to firm up some sort of deal with the British, Arnold found himself in more trouble with his countrymen. He drew the wrath of members of Congress and of the Council of Pennsylvania for his flagrantly lavish lifestyle and for consorting with Tories. The Council brought charges of misconduct against him. Four of the eight charges were later dismissed, but to decide the other charges, on Washington's advice, Arnold asked for and received a court-martial. The court-martial in early 1780 found him guilty on two of the counts. One concerned his issuance of a pass to a ship in which he subsequently held a financial interest; the other involved his use of government wagons to haul his own property to prevent its capture. His sentence was a reprimand from the commander in chief, which Washington in April 1780 wrote with precision and regret. Washington called Arnold's conduct concerning the ship pass "peculiarly reprehensible" and his conduct concerning the misuse of the government wagons "imprudent and improper."

Already seething with anger and resentment, Arnold was stung anew by the guilty verdicts and by Washington's reprimand. By now he had become completely alienated from the cause which he had earlier served with outstanding heroism and extraordinary energy. He felt his talents were unrecognized. He considered himself unappreciated for the substantial contributions he had made to the cause, for the wounds and suffering he had endured in its service. Besides that, he needed money.

Unaware of the depth of Arnold's feelings of alienation and resentment, Washington had not lost confidence in him as a general, despite his professional misconduct and questionable personal behavior. Following his court-martial, Arnold begged off being assigned the field command that Washington offered him, which at an earlier time would have pleased him. Instead, with his eyes on a British prize, he asked to be posted to West Point, citing his wounds as the reason for wanting a less strenuous assignment. Washington acceded to his request and gave him command of a section of the Hudson River valley that included West Point and the recaptured strongholds at Stony Point and Verplanck's Point.

As soon as he was certain the West Point post was his, Arnold, on July 15, 1780, resumed his stalled negotiations with the British and spelled out to Andre, for transmission to General Clinton, what his price was for handing West Point and its troops to the British:

> . . . On the 13th instant (July 1780) I addressed a letter to you expressing my sentiments and expectations, viz, that the following preliminaries be settled previous to cooperating. First, that S[ir] Henry [Clinton] secure to me my property, valued at ten thousand pounds sterling, to be paid to me or my heirs in case of loss; and, as soon as that shall happen,—hundred pounds per annum to be secured to me for life, in lieu of the pay and emoluments I give up, for my services as they shall deserve. If I point out a plan of cooperation by which S[ir] H[enry] shall possess himself of West Point, the garrison, etc., etc., etc., twenty thousand pounds sterling I think will be a cheap purchase for an object of so much importance. At the same time I request a thousand pounds to be paid my agent. I expect a full and explicit answer. The 20th I set off for West Point. . . .[3]

Arnold was asking for 10,000 pounds and an annual stipend whether or not his betrayal succeeded, and 20,000 pounds in the event it did succeed. In that same coded letter to Andre, who by then had been promoted to major and had become Clinton's adjutant general, Arnold asked that an officer in whom Clinton confided be appointed a liaison between Arnold and British headquarters to assist in planning the operation by which West Point would be yielded to the British. In a report Clinton later made to Lord George Germain, Clinton named the man he had picked to be that liaison officer:

. . . Many projects for a meeting were formed, and in consequence several appointments made, in all which General Arnold seemed extremely desirous that some person who had my particular confidence might be sent to him—some man, as he described in writing, of his own mensuration. I had thought of a person under this immediate description, who would have cheerfully undertaken it but that his peculiar situation at the time (from which I could not then release him) precluded him from engaging in it. General Arnold finally insisted that the person sent to confer with him should be the Adjutant General, Major Andre, who indeed had been the person on my part who managed and carried on the secret correspondence.[4]

Arnold's plot soon began to take form. His communication with the enemy became direct, as he sent messages straight to British headquarters in New York, instead of to his wife—who on September 6 left Philadelphia to join her husband at West Point—and from her to the Philadelphia intermediary and then on to Andre and Clinton. Eager to confer with Andre, whom he apparently had never met, Arnold proposed they meet on September 11. When a meeting on that date could not be effected, Arnold on September 16 proposed that they meet on September 20. A meeting on that date could not be worked out either. But around midnight on September 21 two men climbed down from the deck of the British sloop *Vulture*, which had anchored in Haverstraw Bay, a wide part of the Hudson River below Stony Point, and entered a small boat in which they were rowed to the west bank of the river, about fifteen miles below West Point. One was Joshua Hett Smith, who owned farmland near West Point and who believed he was aiding the American cause by acting as an agent for Arnold; the other was a man known to Smith as John Anderson, whose dark cloak failed to conceal the scarlet uniform coat beneath it.

John Anderson was actually John Andre, who was led by Smith to his rendezvous with Arnold. (Arnold explained Andre's red coat by telling Smith he was simply a businessman who liked to pretend he was a British officer.) While Smith and the two rowers, whom Smith had hired for the job, waited to return Andre to the *Vulture*, Arnold and Andre conferred in the woods below the town of Haverstraw until about 4 a.m. With daylight not far away, Arnold and Andre, who rode the spare horse Arnold had brought with him, rode off to Smith's house to conclude their conference, and Smith and the two rowers followed in their boat.

In the early light of the new day, Friday, September 22, 1780, the *Vulture*, riding at anchor in Haverstraw Bay, awaiting the return of Andre, became a conspicuous target for American guns. Lieutenant Colonel James Livingston, commanding the rebel fortifications at Stony Point and Verplanck's Point, ordered a four-pounder (some reports said two four-pounders) brought from Verplanck's Point and emplaced at Teller's Point, on the east side of the river. He then opened fire on the *Vulture*, pounding it for two hours, sending shot into the rigging, sails, and hull. Unwilling to take any more punishment, the *Vulture*'s captain weighed anchor and slipped downriver to get out of range.

Andre now could not get back to the ship that had brought him behind American lines. He would have to return to New York by land. Smith gave him civilian clothes to replace the British uniform he wore beneath his cloak. The documents that Arnold had given him, detailing West Point's defenses, Andre put in his boots. Arnold left him and boarded his barge to return to his headquarters.

Arnold had written a pass authorizing Smith and "John Anderson" passage across the Hudson and through the American lines, and Smith took Andre to Kings Ferry, on Stony Point, about three miles northeast of Smith's house, where they crossed the river to Verplanck's Point. After declining Colonel Livingston's invitation to have a drink with him, Smith led Andre northeast to Peekskill. They were stopped by an American patrol, which accepted Arnold's pass but warned them they should proceed no farther, since they were apt to run into Tory partisans patrolling the road.

Smith and Andre spent the night of September 22 at a nearby farmhouse. Early the next morning they were back on the road, riding east, then south to Pine's Bridge, where the road crossed the Croton River. There, Smith left Andre to make it the rest of the way on his own.

About twelve miles farther, just north of Tarrytown, around 10 a.m., Andre was stopped at gunpoint by three men whom he took to be loyalists. They were rough American militiamen, without uniforms. One of them, John Paulding, who wore a kind of ragged coat that usually distinguished loyalist fighters, four days earlier had escaped from a British prison in New York, where he had acquired the coat.

"I hope, gentlemen, you belong to the lower party," Andre told them, meaning they were British sympathizers, as differentiated from the so-called upper party, the rebels.[5]

"We do," one answered.

"So do I," Andre responded. "I am a British officer on business of importance and must not be detained."

He was then ordered to dismount and had his watch taken from him. Sensing he had made a mistake, he tried to undo it. "I am happy, gentlemen, to find I am mistaken. You belong to the upper party, and so do I. A man must make use of any shift to get along, and to convince you of it, here is General Arnold's pass. I am in his service."

"Damn Arnold's pass," one told him. "You said you was a British officer. Where is your money?"

"Gentlemen, I have none about me."

"You a British officer and no money?" one asked, then told the others, "Let's search him." They failed to find money in Andre's clothes, then decided he must have it hidden. "He has got his money in his boots."

In his boots they found not money, but Arnold's documents. They also searched his saddlebags for money and found none. At that, Andre attempted to bribe them to gain his release. The militiamen declined the bribe, apparently for no reason other than fear that any contact made by them to collect a bribe would result in their capture. They finally agreed among themselves to take Andre to their commanding officer and let him decide what should be done with him.

Arnold had not been careless about Andre's safety. He had issued notices to his commanders that they should be alert to John Anderson's coming into their areas from New York and if he were to enter their lines, he should be escorted to Arnold at his headquarters near West Point. Lieutenant Colonel John Jameson, commanding the militia to which Andre's captors belonged, was aware of Arnold's instruction, and so when the militiamen brought Andre to Jameson's headquarters at North Castle, along with the documents found in Andre's boots, Jameson ordered Andre to be taken to Arnold. But he sent the documents to Washington, who was thought to be somewhere west of Danbury on his way to Peekskill, along with this note:

Inclos'd you'll receive a parcel of Papers taken from a certain John Anderson who has a pass signed by General Arnold as may be seen. The Papers were found under the feet of his Stockings he offer'd the Men that took him one hundred Guineas and as many goods as they wou'd please to ask. I have sent the Prisoner to General Arnold he is very desirous of the Papers and every thing being sent with him. But as I think they are of a very dangerous tendency I thought it more proper your Excellency should see them.[6]

Major Benjamin Tallmadge, head of Washington's secret service, arrived at Jameson's headquarters later that day, Saturday, September 23. Informed about John Anderson, about the documents, and the suspicious fact that he was captured attempting to pass the American lines on his way *to* New York, not from it, Tallmadge suspected the truth. He persuaded Jameson to dispatch a detail to catch up with Andre and his escort and bring him back.

Jameson, however, by that same detail, sent a letter to Arnold, informing him that he had captured "a certain John Anderson going into New York. He had a pass signed with your name." Arnold would soon find out that his treason had been discovered.

Andre was brought to Lower Salem, New York, arriving there on Sunday morning, September 24, and placed under guard and in the care of a Lieutenant King, who described his experiences with Andre:

> . . . After breakfast, my barber came in to dress me, after which I requested him [Andre] to undergo the same operation, which he did. When the ribbon was taken from his hair, I observed it full of powder. This cicumstance, with others that occurred, induced me to believe I had no ordinary person in charge. . . .
>
> We were close pent up in a bedroom with a vidette at the door and window. There was a spacious yard before the door, which he desired he might be permitted to walk in with me. . . .
>
> While walking together, he observed he must make a confidant of somebody, and he knew not a more proper person than myself, as I had appeared to befriend a stranger in distress. . . . He told me who he was and gave me a short account of himself. . . . He requested a pen and ink and wrote immediately to General Washington, declaring who he was.[7]

Washington spent Sunday night at Fishkill, New York, instead of Peekskill as apparently previously planned. He sent word to Arnold's headquarters that he was on his way there and expected to arrive in time for breakfast on Monday (September 25). The rider who had been sent to give him Jameson's note and the documents found on Andre had not been able to find Washington, evidently because of the change in his travel route, and had returned to Jameson. Having now learned that Washington was enroute to Arnold's headquarters, Jameson sent another messenger to him, this time carrying not only Jameson's letter and the documents, but also the letter Andre had written to Washington.

Arnold had made his headquarters in the elegant home of Beverley Robinson, a notorious loyalist who had taken refuge in New York and who had helped arrange the meeting between Arnold and Andre. The house stood on the east side of the Hudson River, opposite West Point. Around nine o'clock Monday morning messengers from Washington arrived at the Robinson house to tell Arnold that Washington would be late. Arnold and his staff then started breakfast without waiting for the commander in chief.

While they were eating, the militia lieutenant who had been dispatched by Jameson arrived and delivered Jameson's letter to Arnold. Arnold read it, told the lieutenant not to mention it to the others, then calmly went upstairs to tell his wife, Peggy. As he was coming back downstairs, he was told that Washington would soon arrive. He called for a horse, left instructions for Washington to be told that he had an urgent matter to take care of at West Point, then rode to his barge, boarded it, and headed downriver to where the *Vulture* still lay at anchor.

Washington arrived at the Robinson house about 10:30 a.m., along with Lafayette, Henry Knox, Alexander Hamilton, and the others in his party. They were coming from a conference with the French army commander, Lieutenant General the Count Rochambeau, in Hartford. Washington was told about Arnold's having gone across the river to West Point and he then sat down to breakfast with his officers. After breakfast, he and his staff were rowed across the river so he could inspect the fortification and consult with Arnold.

The West Point commandant, Colonel John Lamb, was taken by surprise at Washington's visit. He apologized that he didn't know that Washington was coming and said that he hadn't seen Arnold in two days. Washington spent a couple of hours inspecting the works, which he found in serious disrepair. He then crossed the river again and returned to the Robinson house, perhaps expecting to find that Arnold had returned there.

The courier carrying Jameson's letter, the documents, and Andre's letter had finally made it to Arnold's headquarters, and following Washington's return from West Point, Alexander Hamilton put the packet of letters and documents into Washington's hands. Washington read the letter and studied the documents. They included returns on the strength of the rebel army and of the forces at and near West Point, a report on the fort's artillery, and the plans for deploying it in case of attack, a copy of the minutes of the council of war Washington had held with his commanders on September 6, and, among other information, Arnold's report on the defects in West Point's defenses.

Washington immediately ordered Hamilton to try to overtake Arnold, who, he now realized, was fleeing for his life. Racing along the eastern bank of the Hudson, Hamilton got as far as Verplanck's Point before discovering he was too late, the quarry had escaped. At Verplanck's Point he was given two letters addressed to Washington, one from Beverley Robinson, demanding that Andre be released, the other from Arnold, declaring Mrs. Arnold's innocence and asking consideration for her, both letters having been sent ashore from the *Vulture*, which after the delivery of the letters, had sailed off to New York. Hamilton turned around and headed back to Washington at the Robinson house.

Washington wrote an order to Jameson, instructing him to send Andre to headquarters at the Robinson house "under the care of such a party and so many officers as to preclude him from escaping." "Andre," he told Jameson, "must not escape."

Following the dispatch of that order, Washington quickly set about to adjust West Point's defenses and prepare for a possible British assault, which he feared might come as soon as that night. He called in the commanders of all the nearby forts and ordered them to put their garrisons on alert. He dispatched messages to all his chief commanders, putting his entire army on alert. He ordered Anthony Wayne to bring his division from Haverstraw to West Point as quickly as possible. Wayne responded by turning out his troops at two o'clock in the morning (Tuesday, September 26), hustling them up the dark, 16-mile road to West Point in four hours to arrive at West Point at daybreak. Nathanael Greene was instructed immediately to move his closest division to Kings Ferry. And fearing that some of Arnold's subordinate commanders were in on the plot, Washington made sure that only reliable officers were now in charge.

Not long after dawn, Benjamin Tallmadge and a hundred dragoons arrived with Andre. Also brought to headquarters as a prisoner was Joshua Hett Smith, whose dealings with Arnold had been reported to Washington by Arnold's aides, Major David S. Franks and Lieutenant Colonel Richard Varick, who themselves were placed under arrest until they could be cleared of complicity.

From Smith's accounts Washington was able to assemble many of the pieces of the plot. Washington refused to see Andre or hear his account, but did receive Tallmadge's report on the details of Andre's capture. Andre was sent across the river to West Point, then taken by barge to Stony Point and from there was taken to Tappan, New York, where Washington's main army was encamped and where Andre would be held prisoner at Mabie's Tavern.

Tallmadge was with Andre on the barge that transported him to Tappan. He later reported their conversation:

> As we progressed on our way to Tappan, before we reached the Clove, where we dined, Major Andre was very inquisitive to know my opinion . . . as to the light in which he would be viewed by General Washington and a military tribunal, if one should be ordered. I endeavored to evade this question, unwilling to give him a true answer.
>
> When I could no longer evade this importunity, I said to him that I had a much-loved classmate in Yale College by the name of Nathan Hale, who entered the Army with me in the year 1776. After the British troops had entered New York, General Washington wanted information respecting the strength, position, and probable movements of the enemy. Captain Hale tendered his services, went into New York, and was taken just as he was passing the outposts of the enemy. Said I, with emphasis, "Do you remember the sequel of this story?"
>
> "Yes," said Andre. "He was hanged as a spy, but you surely do not consider his case and mine alike."
>
> I replied, "Precisely similar, and similar will be your fate."
>
> He endeavored to answer my remarks, but it was manifest he was more troubled than I had ever seen him before.[8]

On September 29 a board of officers, with Nathanael Greene as its president, heard the case against Andre, heard letters from Beverley Robinson, Arnold, and Clinton read to them, and heard Andre's admission that he had not come ashore behind American lines under a flag of truce, contrary to what Robinson and Clinton said in their letters. "The unhappy prisoner gave us no trouble in calling witnesses," von Steuben, a member of the board, later commented. "He confessed everything." The board found Andre guilty of spying and determined that he should be executed.

On October 1 Washington issued an order that quoted the board's report and that ordered Andre be executed "in the usual way," that is, by hanging. Andre's appeal to be executed as a soldier by a firing squad was ignored, as Nathan Hale's had been. John Andre was hanged on October 2, 1780.

Benedict Arnold was commissioned a brigadier general in the British army and paid 6,315 pounds sterling by the British for the loss of his American property.

CHAPTER Nineteen

The Fall of Charleston

On the surface Cornwallis and his commander, Sir Henry Clinton, seemed to get along, and both had had good things to say about the other. However, their relations soured after Clinton learned that Cornwallis had violated his confidence, carrying to General William Howe the insubordinate remarks Clinton made about him while Howe was still commander of the British forces.

"I cannot bear to serve under him," Clinton had told Cornwallis as part of his complaint concerning Howe's actions during the Battle of White Plains, "and had rather command three companies by myself than hold my post [as] I have done [during the] last campaign in his army."[1] Ratting on Clinton, a despicably dishonorable thing to do, particularly to a superior officer, and behavior uncharacteristic of Cornwallis, reflected his low regard for Clinton.

The sort of frustration that Clinton had felt toward his commander now was duplicated in Cornwallis, who felt he could no longer bear to serve under Clinton, an officer of some ability in strategy and tactics but lacking leadership talents and at times showing signs of paranoia and other disagreeable personality disorders. Knowing, however, that Clinton had turned in his resignation, expecting that it would be accepted in London, and confident that he, Cornwallis, would replace him, Cornwallis bided his time, though not graciously.

With a touch of characteristic arrogance, Cornwallis assumed an attitude of command, which did not go unnoticed by either Clinton or other British officers. Clinton complained that Cornwallis was "regarded by a majority of the officers as actually possessed of the command: and so certain did his Lordship himself be of it that he made no scruples to declare he would assume it as soon as my leave should arrive. . . ."[2]

In December 1779, while still waiting to hear from London about his resignation, Clinton at last set out to do something other than spend a comfortable winter in New York. Lord George Germain months earlier had urged him to initiate a new campaign in the south, where the war effort now seemed more promising. Aware that the French fleet had moved out of American waters and buoyed by the British success in turning back an American–French attempt to recapture Savannah two months earlier, Clinton decided the time was right to launch that campaign, starting at Charleston.

Cornwallis was itching for action that would provide a diversion from the awkward standoff with Clinton and he welcomed the opportunity to sail away to battle. The German general, Wilhelm von Knyphausen, was left behind to command a 10,000-man garrison in New York while a force of 8,700 soldiers and 5,000 British sailors and marines sailed out of New York's icy harbor with Clinton and Cornwallis and passed Sandy Hook on Sunday, December 26, 1779. The fleet included 10 warships, bristling with some 530 guns, and 90 transports carrying the army's 400 horses, its supplies, and equipment as well as its men.

Two days out of New York, the fleet ran into the first of a series of storms that battered and scattered its vessels. Captain Johann Hinrichs of the Hessian jager corps recorded in his diary the torments of the weather:

> Jan. 3 [1780]. Today was no better than yesterday; in fact, it was worse. Left to the fury of wave and wind, we drifted southward with helm lashed and before one sail, the wind being westerly. Of the entire fleet we saw this morning only one man-of-war and seventeen sail. It may be safely said that the most strenuous campaign cannot be as trying as such a voyage; for (1) one cannot prepare a decent meal; (2) one takes every morsel with the greatest difficulty and discomfort; (3) one enjoys not a moment of sleep because of the fearful rolling and noise, which is worse in the cabin than in any other place in the ship. . . .[3]

The voyage took thirty-eight days, and Clinton reported that "scarcely a single day during the voyage passed without being marked by the foundering of some transport or other or the dispersion of the fleet."[4] The transport *Anna*, with some 200 Hessian troops aboard, lost its main mast and mizzenmast to the powerful winds and ended up at Cornwall, on the other side of the Atlantic. Another transport, loaded with artillery pieces, was sunk by the storm, and others were severely damaged. Lost, too, were nearly all of the army's horses, which had to be destroyed, and much of its supplies.

The plan called for the fleet's destination to be North Edisto Inlet, just south of Charleston, but instead the battered vessels sailed to British-held Savannah for needed repairs and to regroup in the haven of the Savannah River, some eighty miles below Charleston. By January 30 most of the fleet's ships had anchored in the river at Tybee Island, but many others were still straggling in days later.

On Thursday, February 10, 1780, Clinton's army sailed from Tybee and landed unopposed the next day at Johns Island, about twenty miles below Charleston. The Hessian diarist, Captain Hinrichs, described the events:

> *Feb. 11.* This afternoon the light infantry, the British grenadiers and two companies of Hessian grenadiers began the disembarkation. Rain and darkness prevented us from following. . . .
>
> The landing place was Simmons Point on Simmons Island, unmarked by name on any map. It is a part of Johns Island, desolate and salty, and full of cabbage trees. The landing was effected under the direction of Captain Elphinstone of the *Perseus,* who had demolished a battery here two years ago and had roamed all over Johns Island. The Commanding General [Clinton] and Lord Cornwallis were at the head of the light infantry. They advanced as far as Simmons' house and bridge, the generals remaining with the men as they marched through the woods in swamp and rain.[5]

Pushing inland, Clinton's forces established a beachhead on the mainland at Stono Ferry, then during the next several days occupied James Island, to the east of Johns Island, allowing them to take positions on the south shore of Charleston harbor and beside the mouth of the Ashley River. Clinton then halted his advance in order to secure his positions and wait for the British fleet's commander, Admiral Marriot Arbuthnot, to maneuver his vessels past the sandbar barrier at the entrance to Charleston harbor and sail into the harbor to begin bombardment of the town and its defenses. Also awaited from Arbuthnot were small craft and crews to ferry the British troops across the Ashley River for a land assault on Charleston.

Clinton had been careful to include Cornwallis in the planning of the siege that was intended to force the surrender of Charleston. Cornwallis apparently was pleased to be included, and for the same reason that Clinton had sought his consultation. Both men knew that any day now word could come from London that Clinton was relieved of command and Cornwallis was the new commander in chief of British forces in America. It was vital therefore that Cornwallis be fully informed about and participate in planning the operations against Charleston.

On Sunday, March 19, while still idly awaiting passage of Arbuthnot's warships into Charleston harbor and the commencement of the attack, Clinton received the long-awaited notification from Germain. It was not what he had hoped for or what Cornwallis had injudiciously anticipated. Clinton's resignation had been refused. He would continue to command.

That news sent Cornwallis into a monumental snit. He asked Clinton to consult him no longer about the campaign. He further asked Clinton for a separate command. He then withdrew completely from Clinton's councils and presence.

Clinton responded with anger. Ordering Cornwallis before him, he brought up old grievances, particularly the one that accused Cornwallis of turning junior officers against Clinton. He said Cornwallis should stop encouraging officers' complaints and charged that Cornwallis's doing so was "calculated only to make me enemies in the army." The meeting ended with nothing new having been decided.

Clinton's paranoiac tendencies were enlivened by the apparent friendship, or at least suspicious cordiality, between Cornwallis and Admiral Arbuthnot, whom Clinton disliked and distrusted. Clinton believed Arbuthnot was his enemy and was plotting against him. In Clinton's thinking, his army as well as Arbuthnot's navy hated him. Moved to take some measure to protect himself from those he thought were conspiring against him, he decided that a separate command for Cornwallis, one that would place him at a distance where he could not easily meddle or disrupt, was not a bad idea. It would take him awhile to find a suitable assignment for the earl.

In the meantime, the siege of Charleston began. On Monday, March 20, several of Arbuthnot's frigates managed to pass the sandbar and slip past the guns of the forts guarding the approach to the city. On March 28 and 29, navy crewmen at the oars of a fleet of seventy-five flatboats ferried the main body of the British army across the Ashley River, landing the troops about twelve miles north of the city. On Thursday, March 30, their march toward Charleston began. They swept south down the peninsula on which Charleston stands, encountering only minor resistance. When they

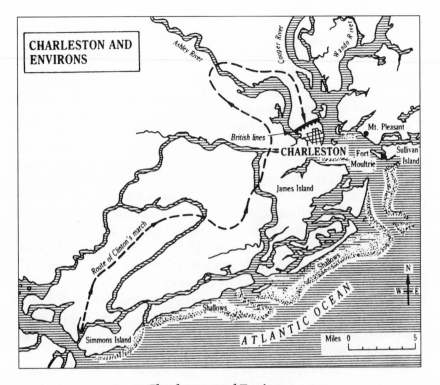

CHARLESTON AND ENVIRONS

Ashley River

Cooper River

Wando River

Mt. Pleasant

British lines

CHARLESTON

Fort Moultrie

Sullivan Island

James Island

Route of Clinton's march

Shallows

Shallows

ATLANTIC OCEAN

Simmons Island

N

W E

Miles 0   5

Charleston and Environs

were within 800 yards of the American defense lines north of the city, Clinton ordered the troops halted and the first siege line to be dug. The troops, reinforced by units summoned from Savannah, began digging on Sunday, April 1. On April 10, that first parallel was completed, and Clinton, together with Arbuthnot, sent the American commander in Charleston, Major General Benjamin Lincoln, a message demanding his surrender. Upon Lincoln's refusal, the British started digging their second parallel, moving still closer to the rebels' defense lines.

Charleston's defenders were virtually trapped. The British fleet commanded the harbor and the Ashley River, which flowed past the city on the west. Clinton's army was dug in athwart the peninsula on the north of the city, blocking an American escape by land. The only remaining escape route lay across the Cooper River, to the east of the city. The path across the Cooper was the defenders' only line of communication with the world outside Charleston, providing access to rebel arms and supply depots at Monck's Corner, about twenty miles north of Charleston, and Cainhoy, about thirteen miles northeast of Charleston, as well as allowing reinforcement of the defenders within Charleston.

Admiral Arbuthnot, whose warships had run past the rebel forts at the entrance to Charleston harbor, agreed to move his vessels into the Cooper to cut the defenders' last link, but Clinton, distrustful of him, planned a land operation to achieve the same goal. He ordered a force of 1,400 men under the command of Lieutenant Colonel James Webster to move north from the army's besieging main body and cross the Cooper where it forked into its west and east branches, about twelve miles above Charleston. Webster's force was composed of the 33rd Foot Regiment and the mounted unit of loyalists known as Tarleton's Legion, led by Lieutenant Colonel Banastre Tarleton, the zealous, then twenty-five-year-old dragoon commander who had taken Major General Charles Lee prisoner at a Basking Ridge, New Jersey tavern three years earlier.

On the night of April 13 Tarleton's troops, on horses seized from the countryside, along with Ferguson's Rangers, another loyalist unit, commanded by Major Patrick Ferguson, moved toward Monck's Corner, where 500 rebel troops, mostly cavalrymen, under Brigadier General Isaac Huger were posted. Huger and his men were taken by surprise as Tarleton's Legion and Ferguson's Rangers suddenly struck at about three o'clock on the morning of April 14. The Americans were completely routed, their horses and supplies captured.

With their victory at Monck's Corner, at the head of the Cooper River, the British had eliminated the only effective rebel defense force east of the river, and the force commanded by Lieutenant Colonel Webster had gained control of the area east of the river southward to within six miles of Charleston. On April 18 more than 2,000 British reinforcements, under Lieutenant Colonel Francis Rawdon, arrived from New York, bringing Webster's force up to sufficient strength to forestall any attempt by Charleston's defenders to retreat or receive reinforcement or supplies across the Cooper.

The noose around Charleston had grown tighter. On April 19 the besieging British army north of the city was within 250 yards of the defenders' lines and moving ever closer. On April 20 the American commander, Major General Lincoln, tried to extricate his trapped army. He sent Clinton a message proposing that he turn the city over to Clinton but be allowed to withdraw his men and cross the Cooper. Clinton, the next day, summarily rejected the proposal and, in harsh response, on the night of April 21 resumed bombardment of Charleston with, as one eyewitness reported, "greater virulence and fury than ever." The bombardment continued until daybreak on April 22.

Now Clinton sent the disgruntled Cornwallis across the Cooper River to take over from Webster and assume command of the forces east of the river, sealing off the last possible way out of beleaguered Charleston. He called Cornwallis in to receive his orders on the night of April 23, telling him he was to "seize the Rebel Communication." The next day Cornwallis crossed the Cooper and established his headquarters at St. Thomas' Church.

On that same morning, April 24, before dawn, 200 rebel troops charged out of their defensive position with fixed bayonets to make a desperate assault on the encroaching British lines and managed to inflict as many casualties as they received. The effects of the charge were insignificant. On April 25 Cornwallis's troops took possession of Mount Pleasant and Haddrell's Point on the river's east bank, where rebel artillery emplacements threatened Arbuthnot's vessels. On April 27 the rebels evacuated their last outpost east of the Cooper. On May 3 the British completed their third parallel, within rifle shot of the rebel lines. By May 6 the defenders were down to a week's supply of fresh provisions.

Early in the morning on May 8 the besiegers opened heavy fire on the defenders, pounding them with artillery and blistering them with small-arms fire. After daybreak Clinton sent Lincoln another note calling for his unconditional surrender. This time the American commander did not instantly refuse, but instead began negotiating in a lengthy session that continued until 9 p.m. the next day, when it ended inconclusively.

Clinton and Arbuthnot responded with this note to Major General Lincoln:

May 9th, 1780

Sir,
     No other motives but those of forebearance and compassion induced us to renew offers of terms you certainly had no claim to. The alterations you propose are all utterly inadmissable; hostilities will in consequence commence afresh at eight o'clock.

H. Clinton, M. Arbuthnot[6]

American Brigadier General William Moultrie later described the action that followed the receipt of the British commanders' terse note:

After receiving the above letter, we remained near an hour silent, all calm and ready, each waiting for the other to begin. At length we fired the first gun and immediately followed a tremendous cannonade, and the mortars from both sides threw out an immense number of shells. It was a glorious sight to see them like meteors crossing each other and bursting in the air; it appeared as if the stars were tumbling down. The fire was incessant almost the whole night; cannon-balls whizzing and shells hissing continually amongst us; ammunition chests and temporary magazines blowing up; great guns bursting, and wounded men groaning along the lines. It was a dreadful night! It was our last great effort, but it availed us nothing. After this our military ardor was much abated. . . .[7]

On Thursday, May 11, Charleston's defenders capitulated. Lincoln wrote this note addressed to Sir Henry Clinton:

Sir,

The same motives of humanity which inclined you to propose articles of capitulation to this garrison induced me to offer those I had the honor of sending you on the 8th inst. They then appeared to me such as I might proffer, and you receive, with honor to both parties. Your exceptions to them, as they principally concerned the militia and citizens, I then conceived were such as could not be concurred with; but a recent application from those people, wherein they express a willingness to comply with them, and a wish on my part to lessen as much as may be the distresses of war to individuals, lead me now to offer you my acceptance of them.

> I have the honor to be, etc.
> B. Lincoln[8]

The surrender of Charleston's defenders was described by Brigadier General Moultrie:

About eleven o'clock a.m. on the twelfth of May, we marched out between 1500 and 1600 Continental troops (leaving five or six hundred sick and wounded in the hospitals) without the horn-work, on the left, and piled our arms. The officers marched the men back to the barracks, where a British guard was placed over them. The British then asked where our second division was? They were told these were all the Continentals we had, except the sick and wounded. They were astonished, and said we had made a gallant defence.

Captain Rochfort had marched in with a detachment of the artillery to receive the returns of our artillery stores. While we were in the horn-work together in conversation, he said, "Sir, you have made a gallant defence, but you had a great many rascals among you" (and mentioned names) "who came out every night and gave us information of what was passing in your garrison."

The militia marched out the same day and delivered up their arms at the same place; the Continental officers went into town to their quarters, where they remained a few days to collect their baggage and signed their paroles, then were sent over to Haddrell's Point. The militia remained in Charleston. The next day the militia were ordered to parade near Lynch's pasture and to bring all their arms with them, guns, swords, pistols, etc., and those that did not strictly comply were threatened with having the grenadiers turned in among them. This threat brought out the aged, the timid, the disaffected and the infirm, many of them who had never appeared during the whole siege, which swelled the number of militia prisoners to, at least, three times the number of men we ever had upon duty.[9]

Missing from that account were significant details of the formal surrender, a ceremony with particulars ordinarily dictated by military tradition. Clinton humiliatingly brushed aside tradition, forbidding the surrendering American troops to display their colors or their band to play an English or American tune or their drummers to beat an English or American march. The tradition called for surrendering troops to play a march of the victorious army. But these despised rebels, undeserving of ordinary privileges, must neither be allowed to give honor to their own cause nor to sully the honor of those who had stood for the king's cause. So when at 11 a.m. the Continental soldiers moved out of their lines, their colors were furled and cased, and their band played "The Turk's March." To military men it was an insult, one that would be reported to and not forgotten by the Americans' commander in chief.

American losses in killed and wounded were placed at 90 killed and 140 wounded, practically all of them Continental regulars, the militia losing not more than a dozen or so. The number of captured, however, was staggering, the largest number captured in any battle of the war. The American Board of War officially placed that loss at 245 Continental officers and 2,326 noncommissioned officers and privates. Clinton's losses were estimated at 76 killed and 189 wounded, including Hessian and American loyalist troops.

On the day after the surrender of Charleston, Cornwallis wrote to Lord Jeffery Amherst, a military advisor to the government in London, saying that since Clinton had now resolved to stay in America, "my services here must be of less consequence." He asked to be transferred anywhere in the empire where there was action and where Clinton was not in command. Curiously, however, he had earlier written Clinton a letter when he heard that Clinton was considering storming Charleston's defenses. In the letter he asked Clinton to let him come back across the Cooper River and participate in the grand assault that he heard was being planned. Swallowing some pride perhaps in hopes of gaining some glory, he duplicitously told Clinton, "It is my hearty wish to attend you on that occasion."[10] The surrender came before Clinton had to make a decision on Cornwallis's request.

The action that Cornwallis sought came the week after the fall of Charleston, when he was ordered by Clinton to march to Camden, South Carolina and head off a rebel force that had been intended to reinforce Charleston's defenders but following the surrender was retreating northward to safety. The force was composed of some 350 troops of the 3rd Virginia Continental Regiment, commanded by Colonel Abraham Buford. On May 18 Cornwallis, with 2,500 troops and five guns, moved in pursuit of the rebel force.

After several days of pursuing, however, Cornwallis realized that his army was not closing on the American force, which remained about a ten-day march ahead of him, and he would not be able to catch up. He then turned the task over to Lieutenant Colonel Tarleton and his more mobile troops. On May 27 Tarleton, commanding a force of 40 men of the 17th Dragoons, 130 cavalry, and 100 infantrymen of Tarleton's Legion, many of them also mounted, charged after the retreating rebels, racing to cover 105 miles in 54 hours. On the afternoon of May 29 Tarleton's force caught up with Buford's rebels at Waxhaw Creek, about nine miles from Lancaster Courthouse in north central South Carolina.

Tarleton sent a messenger under a flag of truce to demand Buford's surrender. "If you are rash enough to reject the terms," Tarleton wrote to Buford, "the blood be upon your head."

Buford replied, "I reject your proposals and shall defend myself to the last extremity."

The battle that followed, which came to be known as the Massacre at the Waxhaws, was recounted in horrifying detail in an account written by Doctor Robert Brownsfield to William D. James:

In a short time Tarleton's bugle was heard, and a furious attack was made on the rear guard, commanded by Lieut. Pearson. Not a man escaped. Poor Pearson was inhumanely mangled on the face as he lay on his back. His nose and lip were bisected obliquely; several of his teeth were broken out in the upper jaw, and the under completely divided on each side. These wounds were inflicted after he had fallen, with several others on his head, shoulders and arms. . . .

This attack gave Buford the first confirmation of Tarleton's declaration by his flag. Unfortunately he was then compelled to prepare for action, on ground which presented no impediment to the full action of cavalry. Tarleton, having arranged his infantry in the centre and his cavalry on the wings, advanced to the charge with the horrid yells of infuriated demons. They were received with firmness and completely checked, until the cavalry were gaining the rear.

Buford, now perceiving that further resistance was hopeless, ordered a flag to be hoisted and the arms to be grounded, expecting the usual treatment sanctioned by civilized warfare. This, however, made no part of Tarleton's creed. His ostensible pretext for the relentless barbarity that ensued was that his horse was killed under him just as the flag was raised. He affected to believe that this was done afterwards, and imputed it to treachery on the part of Buford; but, in reality, a safe opportunity was presented to gratify that thirst for blood which marked his character in every conjuncture that promised probable impunity to himself. Ensign Cruit, who advanced the flag, was instantly cut down.

Viewing this as an earnest of what they were to expect, a resumption of their arms was attempted, to sell their lives as dearly as possible; but before this was fully effected, Tarleton with his cruel myrmidons was in the midst of them, when commenced a scene of indiscriminate carnage never surpassed by the ruthless atrocities of the most barbarous savages.

The demand for quarters, seldom refused to a vanquished foe, was at once found to be in vain; not a man was spared, and it was the concurrent testimony of all the survivors that for fifteen minutes after every man was prostrate they went over the ground plunging their bayonets into every one that exhibited any signs of life, and in some instances, where several had fallen one over the other, these monsters were seen to throw off on the point of the bayonet the uppermost, to come at those beneath. . . .

Capt. John Stokes . . . received twenty-three wounds, and as he never for a moment lost his recollection, he often repeated to me the manner and order in which they were inflicted.

Early in the sanguinary conflict he was attacked by a dragoon, who aimed many deadly blows at his head, all of which by the dextrous use of the small sword he easily parried; when another on the right, by one stroke, cut off his right hand through the metacarpal bones. He was then assailed by both, and instinctively attempted to defend his head with his left arm until the forefinger was cut off, and the arm hacked in eight or ten places from the wrist to the shoulder. His head was then laid open almost the whole length of the crown to the eye brows. After he fell he received several cuts on the face and shoulders. A soldier, passing on in the work of death, asked if he expected quarters. Stokes answered, "I have not, nor do I mean to ask quarters. Finish me as soon as possible." He then transfixed him twice with his bayonet. Another asked the same question and received the same answer, and he also thrust his bayonet twice through his body. . . .

Doctor Stapleton, Tarleton's surgeon . . . was dressing the wounds of [a British officer]. . . . Stokes, who lay bleeding in every pore, asked him to do something for his wounds, which he scornfully and inhumanely refused until peremptorily ordered by the more humane officer, and even then only filled the wounds with rough tow, the particles of which could not be separated from the brain for several days.[11]

Buford, whose military ability was called into question following the battle, particularly by Tarleton, lost nearly his entire force, 113 of his men having been killed, 203 captured. Of those captured, 150 were so badly wounded they couldn't be moved, many of them dying within a few days. Most of the 53 others who were captured were also wounded. Captain John Stokes amazingly managed to survive his wounds. Buford escaped, as did a few of his mounted troops and about 100 of his infantrymen who were among the leading elements of his retreating column and did not participate in the battle. Tarleton reported his losses as 19 men killed or wounded.

After the battle, Tarleton became a publicized hero in England. In America he became notorious. He was called Bloody Tarleton and the Butcher, and his butchery of surrendered soldiers became known as Tarleton's Quarter.

That mission accomplished, Cornwallis reported to Clinton that resistance in South Carolina had been eliminated. Satisfied with his success, Clinton wrote to Sir Charles Thompson in England to say that "we may have gained the two Carolinas in Charles Town."

On June 8, 1780, Clinton sailed for New York, turning the king's forces in the South over to Cornwallis. After four years of chafing under the command of others, Cornwallis at last had a command of his own.

CHAPTER Twenty

The Battle of Camden

U pon Clinton's departure for New York, Cornwallis, perhaps seeking popularity with his army, proved to be an indulgent commander, relaxing discipline and allowing his troops to loot the city of Charleston and its residents. Admiral Arbuthnot, whose seamen were permitted to join in the plundering, after a time apparently decided it had got out of hand. "This province," he wrote to Lord George Germain concerning the British troops, "with common prudence will submit & esteem it happiness to enjoy that freedom they once possessed if Lord Cornwallis can restrain their rapacity, etc."

Now with a free hand to choose his military associates, Cornwallis turned to four of his field-grade officers for companionship, showing them a cordiality missing from his dealings with others of his command. Those four were thirty-seven-year-old Lieutenant Colonel Nisbet Balfour, commandant of the British garrison at Ninety Six, South Carolina; twenty-six-year-old Lieutenant Colonel Francis Lord Rawdon, commander of the Volunteers of Ireland regiment, composed of immigrant Irish deserters from the American army; thirty-eight-year-old Major Alexander Ross, an aide to Cornwallis; and twenty-six-year-old Lieutenant Colonel Banastre Tarleton, commander of the British Legion. Curiously, all but Ross, the only one who was not a line officer, had, among Americans, a reputation for cruelty.

Cornwallis's forces held practically all of South Carolina under their control, which remained uncontested except by guerrilla groups until late July 1780. On July 13, Major General Horatio Gates, renowned in Philadelphia as the hero of the American victories at Saratoga, was commissioned by Congress, with no heed to Washington, who opposed the appointment, to take over the war effort in the South, succeeding Major General Benjamin Lincoln, who had become a British prisoner of war following his surrender at Charleston. On July 25 Gates arrived at Hillsborough, North Carolina, where Major General Johann de Kalb, commanding what remained of a force of some 2,000 rebel troops, had established a headquarters. De Kalb had been leading his troops to aid in the defense of Charleston when the city fell to the British. He then had quickly retreated and on Gates's arrival, with apparent relief, he turned his command over to Gates, greeting him with several rounds of artillery fire as a salute.

Gates's new army was composed of about 1,200 Continentals from Maryland and Delaware, plus three artillery companies and about 120 survivors of Brigadier General Casimir Pulaski's force of dragoons that had participated in the failed attack on British-held Savannah the previous October. It was an ill-fed, ill-supplied army of, as Gates put it, "multiplied and increasing wants." Among the most pressing wants were food and wagons. It was subsisting on its forage of green apples and green peaches and was carrying its baggage on the backs of its soldiers. Some days it went without food of any sort.

Nevertheless, calling it "the grand army," Gates ordered it into a state of readiness to march at a moment's notice, an order that astonished the officers who knew just how weak "the grand army" was. Through de Kalb, Gates had received intelligence from the partisan leader, Brigadier General Thomas Sumter, that Cornwallis's troops were spread thin and that the British garrison at Camden amounted to no more than 700 men. At Camden, Gates believed, his starving soldiers would find their fill of food and rum. He decided to march on Camden and seize it.

Gates could choose one of two routes to Camden. One would have "the grand army" approach Camden by circling west through Salisbury and Charlotte. It would lead through friendly country where Gates's troops could expect to find forage as well as protection. The other, a more direct route, was fifty miles shorter but passed through an uninviting land of pine barrens, sandy hills, and swamps, offering little hope of forage and harboring nests of hostile loyalists. Gates chose the shorter route. When de Kalb and other officers meeting in an unofficial counsel attempted to dissuade him, Gates ignored their advice.

Reassuring his hungry troops, Gates promised them they would find ample corn to eat along the banks of the Pee Dee River, which lay across their line of march, east of Charlotte. He ordered his army to move out before dawn on July 27. Colonel Otho Williams, Gates's deputy adjutant general, recounted the army's desperate attempt to feed itself along the way:

> The distresses of the soldiery daily increased. They were told that the banks of the Pee Dee River were extremely fertile, and so indeed they were; but the preceding crop of corn (the principal article of produce) was exhausted and the new grain, although luxuriant and fine, was unfit for use. Many of the soldiery, urged by necessity, plucked the green ears and boiled them with the lean beef which was collected in the woods, made for themselves a repast, not unpalatable to be sure, but which was attended with painful effects. Green peaches also were substituted for bread and had similar consequences. Some of the officers, aware of the risk of eating such vegetables and in such a state, with poor fresh beef and without salt, restrained themselves from taking anything but the beef itself, boiled or roasted. It occurred to some that the hair powder, which remained in their bags, would thicken soup, and it was actually applied.[1]

Gates's army crossed the Pee Dee River at Mask's Ferry on August 3 and on the far side was joined by some one hundred Virginia militiamen commanded by Lieutenant Colonel Charles Porterfield. On August 7 the grand army was substantially enlarged by the addition of about 2,100 North Carolina militiamen commanded by Major General Richard Caswell, recently the governor of North Carolina. On August 14, at Rugeley's Mill, about ten miles north of Camden, Gates's army was further increased by some 700 Virginia militiamen under the command of Brigadier General Edward Stevens.

Gates now, evidently feeling his grand army had sufficient strength to meet whatever task he would choose for it, decided that he could spare some troops. He detached 300 Maryland Continentals, 300 North Carolina militiamen, and one of his three artillery companies to aid Brigadier General Sumter in an attack on the British fortification at Wateree Ferry, South Carolina, whereby Sumter hoped to capture a British wagon train enroute between Charleston and Camden. Dividing his army that way was a breach of military fundamentals, a violation of the principle of economy of force. Gates did it anyway.

Cornwallis meanwhile had been warned by the garrison commander at Camden, Lieutenant Colonel Rawdon, that an army of 7,000 rebels was marching toward his positions. With a small force, Rawdon, on August 11, had briefly barred Gates's crossing of the bridge over Little Lynches Creek, fifteen miles northeast of Camden. Gates in broad daylight had turned his army to the right and forded the creek, and Rawdon, covered by Tarleton's Legion, had swiftly retreated back into Camden to avoid being flanked by the superior force of rebels. With that news in hand, Cornwallis hurried from Charleston to take personal command at Camden, arriving there during the night of August 13.

Gates's actual numbers were about 4,100 troops, of which only 3,052 were present and fit for duty. When Colonel Otho Williams reported those figures to Gates, who thought his strength was more than 7,000, Gates replied that "there are enough for our purpose."

By the time Cornwallis reached Camden, Rawdon's garrison had already been reinforced by four light infantry companies that Cornwallis had ordered moved from the British outpost at Ninety Six. The morning report on August 14 showed the British strength at Camden to be 122 officers and 2,117 men present and fit for duty. Those troops included Cornwallis's own regiment, the 33rd, as well as veterans from other units—three companies of the 23rd Regiment, five companies of the 71st, a detachment of the Royal Artillery, loyalist units brought by Clinton from New York, Rawdon's Volunteers of Ireland, and Tarleton's British Legion—comprising a formidable, experienced fighting force.

Although believing he was outnumbered three to one, Cornwallis decided to take the offensive against Gates's rebel army, an indication not only of his confidence in his own troops but perhaps his scorn for the Americans. Weighing the possible costly effects of a retreat, to the king's cause and possibly to his own career, Cornwallis concluded that there was "little to lose by a defeat and much to gain by a victory." He later wrote to Lord Germain that if he were to avoid a fight, "I must have not only left near 800 sick and a great quantity of stores at this place [Camden], but I clearly saw the loss of the whole province except Charlestown, and of all Georgia except Savannah, as immediate consequences, besides forfeiting all pretensions to future confidence from our friends in this part of America."

At ten o'clock on the night of Tuesday, August 15, the resolute Cornwallis began moving his troops out from Camden toward Gates's positions, planning to commence his attack on the rebels at dawn on the sixteenth.

On that same day, August 15, Gates summoned his chief officers to a meeting and announced that they would march that night for Saunders Creek, about five and a half miles north of Camden, where Gates planned to have his men dig a defensive position in preparation for an assault on the British garrison at Camden. Colonel Williams recorded the gist of the meeting:

> Although there had been no dissenting voice in the council, the orders were no sooner promulgated than they became the subject of animadversion. Even those who had been dumb in council said that there had been no consultation, that the orders were read to them and all opinion seemed suppressed by the very positive and decisive terms in which they were expressed.
>
> Others could not imagine how it could be conceived that an army, consisting of more than two-thirds militia, and which had never been once exercised in arms together, could form columns and perform other manoeuvers in the night and in the face of the enemy. . . .[2]

Nevertheless, Williams recalled, "the officers and soldiers, generally, not knowing or believing any more than the general that any considerable body of the enemy was to be met with out of Camden, acquiesced with their usual cheerfulness and were ready to march at the hour appointed."[3]

Before sending his men off into the darkness, unaware of the enemy advancing toward them, Gates had one more stupid thing to do. Colonel Williams described it:

> . . . one gill of molasses per man and a full ration of cornmeal and meat were issued to the army previous to their march. . . . The troops . . . had frequently felt the bad consequences of eating bad provisions; but at this time, a hasty meal of quick baked bread and fresh beef, with a dessert of molasses, mixed with mush or dumplings, operated so cathartically as to disorder very many of the men, who were breaking the ranks all night and were certainly much debilitated. . . .[4]

Gates's grand army began its march from Rugeley's Mill toward Camden at ten o'clock sharp on the moonless, muggy night of August 15. The mounted troops formerly commanded by Pulaski, now under the command of the French soldier of fortune, Colonel Charles Armand, led the column. The main body of troops plodded along the sandy road while the Virginia militia under Charles Porterfield and a force of North Carolina militia under John Armstrong groped through the piney woods on either side of the column to guard its flanks.

Shortly after 2 a.m. the lead elements of the main column and Porterfield's militamen on its right suddenly collided head-on with the lead elements of Cornwallis's column, forty of Tarleton's legionnaires, about midway between Rugeley's Mill (also known as Clermont Plantation) and Camden, on swampy ground near Saunders Creek. After an ineffectual exchange of musket and pistol fire and a bit of tactical maneuvering that lasted about fifteen minutes, both sides disengaged, but not before the Americans managed to take several prisoners, as did the British. Colonel Williams interrogated the captured British soldiers and later related what then transpired:

> From one of these [prisoners], the deputy adjutant general of the American army [Williams] extorted information respecting the situation and numbers of the enemy. He informed that Lord Cornwallis commanded in person about three thousand regular British troops, which were in line of march, about five or six hundred yards in front.
>
> Order was soon restored in the corps of infantry in the American army, and the officers were employed in forming a front line of battle when the deputy adjutant general [Williams] communicated to General Gates the information which he had from the prisoner. The general's astonishment could not be concealed. He ordered the deputy adjutant general to call another council of war. All the general officers immediately assembled in the rear of the line. The unwelcome news was communicated to them. . . .[5]

Gates was not only astonished, he was baffled, apparently having no clear idea of what he should do next. "Gentlemen," he now asked the very officers whose opinions earlier were by him unsought and later ignored, "what is best to be done?"

As if in mute testimony to a further failure of Gates's leadership, his generals sat silent, evidently unwilling to volunteer a suggestion that might prove unwelcome. There was one exception. After several moments, Brigadier General Stevens spoke up. "Gentlemen," he said to his colleagues, "is it not too late now to do anything but fight?"

No one else spoke. Before the meeting, de Kalb had let Williams know he thought Gates should order a retreat, but at the meeting, he held his tongue. With no voice to argue an alternative, the meeting concluded as Gates instructed his cowed generals to return to their units. They would fight, regardless.

The ground where the Americans stood was a mile-wide pine woods flanked on both sides by swamps. Behind them the woods broadened, so that if they were to fall back, they would lose the protection the swamps provided their flanks. Their position was slightly higher than that of the British and the path of possible retreat was clear. Cornwallis's army was at the disadvantage of having at their back, about a mile behind them, Saunders Creek, deep but fordable at one nearby spot, and about 200 feet wide. About 600 yards behind his front line Gates set up his command post and, apparently with no plan of his own, waited for Cornwallis to make the first move.

The battle's opening actions, and Gates's response to them, were described by Colonel Williams:

> Frequent skirmishes happened during the night between the advanced parties—which served to discover the relative situations of the two armies—and as a prelude to what was to take place in the morning.
>
> At dawn of day (on the morning of the 16th of August) the enemy appeared in front, advancing in column. Captain Singleton, who commanded some pieces of artillery, observed to Colonel Williams that he plainly perceived the ground of the British uniform at about two hundred yards in front. The deputy adjutant general [Williams] immediately ordered Captain Singleton to open his battery, and then rode to the general [Gates], who was in the rear of the second line, and informed him of the cause of the firing which he heard. He also observed to the general that the enemy seemed to be displaying their column by the right; the nature of the ground favored this conjecture, for yet nothing was clear.
>
> The general seemed disposed to wait events—he gave no orders. The deputy adjutant general observed that if the enemy, in the act of displaying, were briskly attacked by General Stevens' brigade, which was already in line of battle, the effect might be fortunate, and first impressions were important.
>
> "Sir," said the general, "that's right—let it be done."
>
> This was the last order that the deputy adjutant general received. . . .[6]

Cornwallis deployed his army in a line running perpendicular to the sandy road on which Gates's troops had been advancing. Rawdon commanded the British left, where his Volunteers of Ireland regiment and the

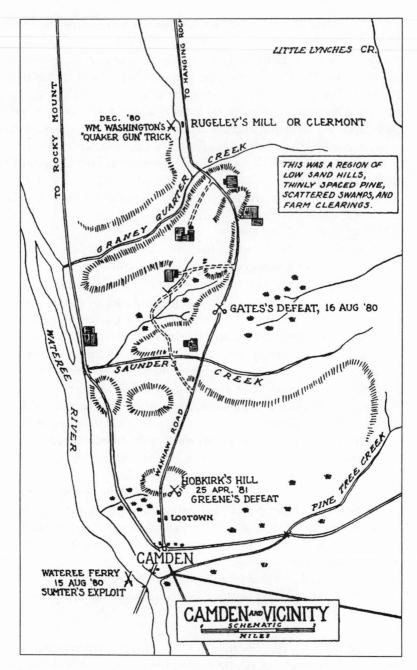

LITTLE LYNCHES CR.

TO ROCKY MOUNT

TO HANGING ROCK

DEC. '80
WM. WASHINGTON'S
"QUAKER GUN" TRICK

RUGELEY'S MILL OR CLERMONT

CREEK

GRANEY QUARTER

THIS WAS A REGION OF
LOW SAND HILLS,
THINLY SPACED PINE,
SCATTERED SWAMPS, AND
FARM CLEARINGS.

GATES'S DEFEAT, 16 AUG '80

WATEREE RIVER

SAUNDER'S CREEK

PINE TREE CREEK

WAXHAW ROAD

HOBKIRK'S HILL
25 APR. '81
GREENE'S DEFEAT

LOGTOWN

CAMDEN

WATEREE FERRY
15 AUG '80
SUMTER'S EXPLOIT

CAMDEN AND VICINITY
SCHEMATIC
MILES

Camden and Vicinity

infantry of Tarleton's British Legion were positioned, along with the Royal North Carolina Regiment, a loyalist unit commanded by Lieutenant Colonel John Hamilton, and the North Carolina Volunteers, a loyalist unit commanded by Colonel Morgan Bryan. On his right wing, the customary position of honor, Cornwallis placed the men of his own seasoned regiment, the 33rd Foot, plus the Royal Welsh Fusiliers and five companies of light infantry, all under the command of Lieutenant Colonel James Webster. At the center of the British line Cornwallis placed four guns of the Royal Artillery. He held in reserve two battalions of the kilted infantry of Fraser's Highlanders. Two artillery pieces were positioned on either side of the road where the Highlanders stood. Just to the rear of the Highlanders, astride their stolen mounts, waited Tarleton's dreaded dragoons.

Opposite those daunting units, on the British right, Gates placed his grand army's untested Virginia and North Carolina militiamen. On the American left stood the Virginia militiamen commanded by Stevens. Positioned behind them were the mounted troops commanded by Armand. The North Carolina militia commanded by Caswell stood at the center of the American line. The 2nd Maryland Brigade, composed of the 2nd, 4th, and 6th Maryland regiments and the Delaware Regiment and commanded by Brigadier General Mordecai Gist, was placed just west of the road, forming Gates's right wing. To the rear, straddling the road, the 1st Maryland Brigade, comprising the 1st, 3rd, and 7th Maryland regiments and commanded by Brigadier General William Smallwood, stood in reserve. The six guns of the 1st Virginia Artillery were positioned in front of the center of the line.

In telling contrast to Gates, Cornwallis placed himself near the front line, where he could see the action and issue orders to his commanders personally, rather than require the services of an adjutant, as Gates required from Otho Williams.

Cornwallis deployed into battle formation before Williams could get back to the line to order Stevens to strike the British right while it was in the act of deploying. Then Cornwallis ordered Webster to commence the attack on the American line, and immediately the British right wing moved out, advancing with fixed bayonets, marching steadily toward the rebel line, as Cornwallis reported to Lord Germain, "in good order and with the cool intrepidity of experienced British soldiers," some 800 strong, shouting as they moved forward.

The scarlet-coated ranks, firing and steadily advancing with gleaming steel bayonets, shot terror into rebel militiamen, who refused orders to fix their own bayonets, which they had never used, and then threw down their loaded weapons and dashed, panic-stricken, toward the rear of their lines. Colonel Williams, a horrified eyewitness to the debacle, reported that "a great majority of the militia (at least two thirds of the army) fled without firing a shot."

Gates attempted to halt the flight of his grand army. Major Charles Magill, one of Gates's aides, rode with his commander to within twenty yards of the rear of the American line, trying to rally the men. Magill described the scene in a letter to his father:

> About half a mile further, General Gates and Caswell made another fruitless attempt, and another was made at a still greater distance with no better success. General Smallwood on Stevens' advancing to the attack advanced to support him, and on the militia giving way, occupied the ground where the right of Stevens and the left of the North Carolina militia were drawn up. This made a chasm between the two brigades through which the enemy's horse came and charged our rear.[7]

As the rebel left disintegrated, Cornwallis's right, led by Lieutenant Colonel Webster, instead of pursuing the fleeing militias, wheeled to the left and began rolling up the Americans' exposed left flank.

Gates, meanwhile, failing to rally his troops back to the fight, let himself be swept along with the tide of terrified soldiers, which carried him farther and farther from the action. "The torrent of unarmed militia," Williams related, "bore away with it Generals Gates, Caswell and a number of others, who soon saw that all was lost."

On the right side of the American line the Maryland and Delaware Continentals held their ground against repeated assaults by Rawdon's Irishmen, and the intrepid Colonel Otho Williams, seeing the reserve's commander, Brigadier General Smallwood, swept away by the horde of fleeing militia, himself took command of the reserve units and attempted to stave off the British assault on the American left flank.

Cornwallis then ordered Webster to hit the front of the rebel reserve, and after twice driving the Marylanders back only to see them regroup and counterattack, Webster's redcoats finally forced them to withdraw from the field. De Kalb, the gallant old Bavarian warrior, unhorsed and streaming blood from a saber cut on his head as well as from several other wounds, also counterattacked, refusing to retreat without an order from Gates. His counterattack achieved momentary success, but finally he fell, mortally wounded, and the attack failed. When Tarleton and his dragoons quit their pursuit of the disintegrated rebel left wing and wheeled about to smash into the rebels' rear, the Battle of Camden was effectively ended.

The defeated American survivors now attempted to escape capture or, far worse, Tarleton's quarter. The largest group apparently was one of about sixty men, which retreated as a unit. The others scattered from the field either as individuals or in small groups. Gates's grand army was completely, abjectly routed, stampeded actually.

Probably none of the vanquished Americans fled from the field of battle faster than Gates himself. After falling back to Rugeley's Mill, he raced sixty more miles to Charlotte, arriving there before the end of the day of the battle. Not satisfied with that distance from the British, he then sped to Hillsborough on a succession of fast horses, arriving there on August 19. Alexander Hamilton, Washington's aide, was one of those who thought Gates's flight unseemly. "Was there ever an instance of a general running away as Gates has done from his whole army?"[8] Hamilton wrote in a letter to James Duane, a member of the Continental Congress. "And was there ever so precipitous a flight? One hundred and eighty miles in three days and a half! It does admirable credit to the activity of a man at his time of life. But it disgraces the general and the soldier."

The number of casualties suffered by the Americans varies from one account to another. Cornwallis put the figures at 1,000 killed and 800 captured. Gates reported 700 killed, wounded, or missing. Perhaps a more accurate count is the one that had 650 of the 1,000 Continentals either killed or captured, about 100 of the militia killed or wounded, and an additional 300 militiamen captured. Of the estimated 4,000 troops that comprised Gates's grand army, only 700 reached Hillsborough to regroup.

In any case, the Battle of Camden was a devastating defeat for the Americans—and a spectacular victory for Cornwallis and the British, made to seem all the more so because of the belief among the British that Cornwallis's army had been outnumbered three to one. Cornwallis's casualties totaled 324—2 officers and 66 men killed, 18 officers and 238 men wounded.

Although he managed to escape death, wounding, and capture, Gates nevertheless became a casualty of the battle. The congressional committee appointed to investigate Gates's conduct cleared him of any wrongdoing, but the public furor raised by the beating that his army suffered, as well as

by reports of his precipitous flight, made him a political pariah and effectively ended his military career. He retired to his farm in Virginia.

Having apparently lost confidence in its ability to choose military
leaders—and with good reason—Congress asked Washington to name a
replacement for Gates as commander in the south. Washington turned to
the man he had wanted to put in that position in the first place, Nathanael
Greene.

Late in the day of his victory at Camden, Cornwallis, determined to
suppress all organized resistance, ordered Tarleton to pursue Thomas
Sumter and his band of partisans, to whom Gates had detached a force of
Continentals and militia. With intelligence received by Cornwallis on
Sumter's whereabouts, Tarleton and about 350 men of his Legion, including cavalry and light infantry, left Rugeley's Mill early in the morning on
August 17, the day after the Camden battle. Tarleton caught up to Sumter
at Fishing Creek, North Carolina, on the east side of the Wateree River, on
the morning of August 18. Tarleton took Sumter's force by surprise at its
encampment, and Tarleton with his usual ferocity virtually annihilated it,
killing 150 and capturing 300. Sumter, however, managed to escape.
Tarleton also freed some 100 British troops that Sumter had taken prisoner at Wateree Ferry and recovered the British supply wagons that
Sumter had captured. With a keen regard for public relations, Cornwallis
dispatched his aide, Captain Alexander Ross, to bear all the good news to
Charleston, then by ship to carry it to London, where upon its dissemina-
tion, Cornwallis received widespread public acclaim for his success. The
news so gladdened the government that its bearer, Captain Ross, was
quickly promoted to major, simply for delivering it.

Events were going outstandingly well for Cornwallis. Total control of
the Carolinas was now within his reach. The southern campaign, under his
command, just might decide the war.

CHAPTER Twenty-One

The Battle of Kings Mountain

W ashington had not changed his mind about the importance of defending the Hudson River valley. During 1780 he was maintaining his base of operations at Morristown, New Jersey, in a position to quickly move troops to meet a British advance up the river. In early June of the year, while Clinton was besieging and conquering Charleston, von Knyphausen, commanding the New York garrison in Clinton's absence, had sent a force of 5,000 troops across the river, landed them near Elizabethtown, New Jersey, and had begun a march toward Morristown, about twenty miles to the northwest. Intelligence reports had come to von Knyphausen saying that Washington's army, short of food, money, clothing, and supplies, was understength, demoralized, and on the verge of mutiny. Von Knyphausen meant to take advantage of the Americans' weakened condition.

Despite all, including being outnumbered, Colonel Elias Dayton's New Jersey regiment, reinforced by New Jersey militia, halted the British and German advance with a furious defense at Springfield and drove the enemy back to Connecticut Farms (later renamed Union). Von Knyphausen had attempted a second attack on Washington's base in late June, but again was stopped at Springfield, this time by Continental regulars under Nathanael Greene, supported by New Jersey militia. The two failed attempts to reach Morristown had cost the British more casualties than they had suffered in their success at Charleston.

That was the good news at Washington's headquarters, where, amid shortages of all kinds, good news was hard to come by. On May 25 two Connecticut regiments, angered by having gone weeks without adequate rations and five months without pay, mutinied and were threatening to desert. They refused repeated commands by officers to disperse and return to their quarters and they inflicted a bayonet wound on one officer when he attempted to prevent them from arming themselves. A Pennsylvania unit was brought in to oppose them; the men dispersed and, following an appeal by officers of the Pennsylvania unit, the mutineers returned peacefully to their huts. Rations later were scrounged up from somewhere to feed them. With sympathy for their plight, Washington pardoned them all except a few of the bitterest leaders, who were arrested and held in custody.

Food was just one item in dangerously short supply. By July Washington was all but begging for French arms and gunpowder. "Another thing that gives me concern," he wrote to Lafayette, "is the non-arrival of our arms and powder. . . . With every effort we can make we shall fall short by at least four or five thousand arms, and two hundred tons of powder. We must, of necessity, my Dear Marquis, however painful it is to abuse the generosity of our friends, know of the French, whether they can assist us with a loan of that quantity."[1]

While Washington struggled to keep his army in the north fed, armed, and together, Cornwallis, buoyed by the British victory at Charleston and his own spectacular success at Camden, prepared to press his campaign to win the war by winning the south. His plan was to sweep through the Carolinas and into Virginia, where he would link up with Clinton's forces from the north as the two armies rolled up the rebel army like a carpet in repeated triumphs till at last Washington's army was annihilated and its cause forever vanquished.

Cornwallis's strategy was to divide the forces under his command into three divisions for its northward advance. The one on the right would move up along the Atlantic seaboard to Wilmington, North Carolina, at the mouth of the Cape Fear River, and secure it as a base for supply. A second division, the main force, under the direct command of Cornwallis, would drive northward from Camden to Charlotte to Salisbury and on toward Hillsborough, penetrating and capturing the North Carolina heartland. The third division, sweeping northward to the left of the main division and protecting its flank, was assigned the formidable task of squelching the harassment by rebel guerrilla groups that presented a constant threat of swift and sudden attack.

That westernmost third division was a tough aggregation of loyalists, many of them immigrants to America from Scotland. Their commander was Major Patrick Ferguson, a thirty-six-year-old Scotsman whom fellow officers called "the Bulldog." His right elbow had been shattered by gunshot at the Battle of Brandywine, permanently crippling his right arm and forcing him to learn to wield his saber left-handed. An arms expert and expert marksman, Ferguson had invented the Ferguson rifle, the first breech-loading rifle to be used in the British army. The standard firearm of the British infantryman was the Brown Bess, a .75-caliber, smooth-bore, muzzle-loading flintlock with a 39-inch barrel. Effective at a range of no more than 80 yards, its redeeming features were a tremendous stopping power and its use as an efficient mount for the British infantryman's fearsome 14-inch bayonet. The weapon that Ferguson developed from earlier breechloader designs was rifled, had greater range and accuracy than the Brown Bess, was faster to load and fire, could be loaded from a prone position (in contrast to muzzleloaders, which had to be loaded from a standing position), and could be fired in wet weather, unlike the Brown Bess and other flintlocks, which became unreliable in rain or snow.

Ferguson had tried to persuade the army to adopt his rifle, but had met with only limited success. The brass thought it should be tried in the field under battle conditions before mass producing and adopting it. To conduct the test, the army had armed a special unit with the rifles and placed Ferguson in command of the unit. At Brandywine the unit performed well enough, but General Howe, reportedly miffed that Ferguson's unit had been organized and armed without his participation in the test program, disbanded the unit and put the rifles in storage after Ferguson had been so severely wounded that he had to relinquish his command.

Ferguson's character differed from that of Cornwallis's favorite, the merciless Banastre Tarleton, who was considered a model British officer. Shortly after the Battle of Brandywine, Ferguson wrote a letter to one of his relatives, describing an event that occurred as the men of his unit lay concealed in the woods near the site of the imminent battle. According to Ferguson's telling, it was an event that could have changed the course not only of the war but of history:

> We had not lain long . . . when a rebel officer, remarkable by a hussar dress, passed towards our army within a hundred yards of my right flank, not perceiving us. He was followed by another dressed in dark

green or blue, mounted on a bay horse, with a remarkably large cocked hat.

I ordered three good shots to steal near . . . and fire at them, but the idea disgusted me. I recalled the order. The hussar in returning made a circuit, but the other passed again within a hundred yards of us, upon which I advanced from the woods towards him.

On my calling, he stopped, but after looking at me, proceeded. I again drew his attention and made signs to him to stop, but he slowly continued his way. As I was within that distance at which in the quickest firing [of the Ferguson rifle] I could have lodged half-a-dozen balls in or about him before he was out of my reach, I had only to determine. But it was not pleasant to fire at the back of an unoffending individual, who was acquitting himself very coolly of his duty, so I let him alone.

The day after, I had been telling this story to some wounded officers who lay in the same room with me, when one of our surgeons, who had been dressing the wounded rebel officers, came in and told us they had been informing him that General Washington was all the morning with the light troops and only attended by a French officer in a hussar dress, he himself dressed and mounted in every point as above described. I am not sorry that I did not know at the time who it was. . . .[2]

Moments after letting the man Ferguson believed to be Washington ride away to safety, Ferguson suffered his crippling wound. A dispute later arose over the actual identity of the officer Ferguson had refused to shoot in the back. John P. de Lancey, the New York loyalist officer who was with Ferguson when the incident occurred, said Ferguson was mistaken, that the officer who rode away was not Washington. Ferguson had never seen Washington, but de Lancey had. He had dined with him in Philadelphia in 1774. De Lancey believed the officer whose life Ferguson had spared was actually Count Casimir Pulaski, recognizable by his build and his uniform.

The point of the incident and what it reveals about Ferguson, however, is not the American officer's identity but that Ferguson, under the circumstances, refused to shoot him when he could have.

By his spectacular and successful attacks on rebel bases in New Jersey in October 1778, Ferguson had won the admiration of Clinton, who made him something of a protégé and took him with him to capture Charleston. Following the fall of Charleston, when he was making preparations for the southern campaign before returning to New York, Clinton on May 22, 1780, gave Ferguson the title of inspector of militia of the southern provinces and assigned him the task, the daunting challenge, of recruiting, equipping, and training a militia to be enlisted from among loyalist citizens in the Carolinas and forming them into an effective fighting force. Ferguson had met the challenge with commendable, though not complete, success, having enlisted some 4,000 loyalists into his militia. Their shortcomings as soldiers were the same as those of Washington's militiamen—a distinct lack of military discipline and a dangerous proneness to drift off to their homes when homesick or preoccupied with family concerns.

Ferguson's militia recruits came from the same stock as the rebel guerrillas fighting under the commands of such patriot partisan leaders as Colonel Charles McDowell and Colonel Isaac Shelby. They were rugged frontiersmen known as "over mountain men," drawn as they were from their lands amid and beyond the Blue Ridge Mountains of western South Carolina and North Carolina. They had their good qualities, which were described by Ferguson. He boasted that they were "very fit for rough & irregular war, being all excellent woodsmen, unerring shots, careful to a degree to prevent waste or damage to their ammunition, patient of hunger & hardship & almost regardless of blankets, cloathing, rum & other indulgences," which set them admirably apart from British regulars.[3]

The mission that Cornwallis gave to Ferguson and his militiamen was vital to the success of Cornwallis's drive through North Carolina. Yet Cornwallis gave indications that he lacked confidence in Ferguson's ability to carry out his mission. Lieutenant Colonel Nisbet Balfour, one of the members of Cornwallis's inner circle and commandant of the strategic British garrison at Ninety Six, South Carolina, wrote to Cornwallis in June 1780, saying about Ferguson, "I find it impossible to trust him out of my sight. He seems to me to want to carry the war into North Carolina himself at once."[4]

Cornwallis wrote back to Balfour on July 3 to say that "I am afraid of his getting to the frontier of N. Carolina and playing us some cussed trick."[5] And to Clinton Cornwallis on August 29 wrote, "Ferguson is to move into Tryon County [North Carolina] with some militia whom he says he is sure he can depend upon for doing their duty and fighting well; but I am sorry to say that his own experience as well as that of every other officer is totally against him."

Ferguson established a base on the Little River, a few miles east of Ninety Six and there he gathered his 4,000 loyalist militia recruits and formed them into seven regiments. He had given Balfour cause to believe he would start the northward push on his own, for by the end of June he was already sending his troops north of Ninety Six, mostly to recruit more loyalists to his army. Many of those he enlisted were already waging their own private war on their patriot neighbors, looting their houses, stealing their livestock, foraging off their crops, and then laying their fields waste. The depredations of those loyalist marauders, now Ferguson's militiamen, only served to drive outraged patriot sympathizers to more determined resistance.

Patriots responded to a call to arms that would let them strike back, and Colonel Charles McDowell and Colonel Isaac Shelby, rallying patriots to the cause, joined their forces of over mountain men to retaliate. Their numbers were swelled with the addition of a force of Georgia militiamen led by Colonel Elijah Clarke. On July 30, 1780, the combined forces of McDowell and Clarke, about 600 men, forced the surrender of the loyalist garrison at Thicketty Fort, on the Pacolet River, about ten miles southeast of Cowpens, South Carolina, without having to fire a shot. They then charged off after a band of Ferguson's marauding foragers.

At Cedar Spring, South Carolina, on August 8 they rode up against Ferguson's men and captured a number of them, but were unable to hold the field against them. On August 18 a force made up of rebels under the command of Clarke and Shelby, aided by the troops of Colonel James Williams, assaulted an encampment of Ferguson's men at Musgrove's Mill, South Carolina, on the Enoree River, far behind Ferguson's rear. The surprise attack that the rebels had planned failed to surprise the loyalists, and the rebel troops had to swiftly form into a defensive position to resist the loyalists' counterattack. In the battle that ensued, the rebels inflicted heavy casualties on Ferguson's troops, killing sixty-three, wounding ninety, and taking seventy of them prisoner. Rebel losses were four killed and eight wounded.

Emboldened by that success, rebel commanders then planned a daring, large-scale assault on the British post at Ninety Six. Just before they were to move out with their troops, however, word reached them that Gates's army had been routed at Camden two days earlier. The rebels then wheeled and headed north to seek refuge in the Blue Ridge foothills. Informed of the rebel retreat, Ferguson quickly ordered his loyalist militiamen to pursue and run down the fleeing patriots.

So hot was Ferguson's pursuit that at one point he was within thirty minutes of the rearmost element of the rebel column. Near Fair Forest, South Carolina, however, a rider dispatched by Cornwallis caught Ferguson and gave him Cornwallis's order to return to Camden.

It was at his meetings with Cornwallis, following Ferguson's return, that he was briefed on Cornwallis's grand plan to march through and subdue North Carolina en route to Virginia. In those meetings Ferguson received his assignment to lead his militiamen in covering Cornwallis's left flank and to raise additional loyalist troops as Cornwallis's entire army moved inexorably northward to an envisioned final triumph.

Ferguson's instructions were to penetrate into North Carolina as far north as Gilbert Town (later renamed Rutherfordton), about sixty-five miles west of Charlotte, and use his militia to pacify the area from western South Carolina up to Gilbert Town. When that was accomplished and he had raised additional recruits for his militia, he was to lead his loyalist army back toward Charlotte and rejoin Cornwallis there.

As the retreating over-mountain fighters of Shelby and McDowell reached the Blue Ridge, many of them scattered and headed for home, depleting their units. Intelligence came to Ferguson reporting on the break-up of rebel forces, and he decided his efforts to pacify the region were succeeding. On September 7, 1780 Ferguson and a force composed of seventy American Volunteers (loyalist regulars) and several hundred loyalist militiamen moved out from their South Carolina base, crossed into North Carolina, and occupied the little community of Gilbert Town. On September 8 Cornwallis's army moved out from its base at Camden, commencing the drive northward.

As part of his campaign of pacification, Ferguson announced to residents of the area that they and their property would be protected if they swore allegiance to the king, and many responded, strengthening Ferguson's belief that his campaign was working. He apparently did not suspect that the North Carolinians were pledging loyalty merely to save their cattle and crops from seizure, which they were.

To rebel fighters who would not submit he issued an ultimatum, delivered to Colonel Isaac Shelby. Shelby himself described it and its effect:

> In September 1780 Maj. Ferguson, who was one of the best and most enterprising of the British officers in America, had succeeded in raising a large body of Tories, who, with his own corps of regulars, constituted an effective force of eleven hundred and twenty-five men. With a view of cutting off Col. Clarke, of Georgia, who had recently made a demonstration against Augusta, which was then in the hands of the British, Ferguson had marched near the Blue Ridge and had taken post at Gilbert Town, which is situated but a few miles from the

mountains. Whilst there he discharged a Patriot, who had been taken prisoner on parole, and directed him to tell Col. Shelby (who had become obnoxious to the British and Tories from the affair at Musgrove's Mill) that if Shelby did not surrender he (Ferguson) would come over the mountains and put him to death, and burn his whole county.

It required no further taunt to rouse the patriotic indignation of Col. Shelby. He determined to make an effort to raise a force, in connection with other officers, which should surprise and defeat Ferguson....[6]

Shelby crossed to the west side of the Blue Ridge to meet with Colonel John Sevier, the veteran militia commander, and the two of them began to take action. They sent out a call for fighters, appealing to Colonel William Campbell in Virginia and to Colonel Charles McDowell and Colonel Benjamin Cleveland in North Carolina. The marshaling of the forces was scheduled for September 25 at Sycamore Shoals, on the Watauga River (near the present Elizabethton, Tennessee).

By the appointed day, more than a thousand men had gathered beside the Watauga, most of them on mounts and armed with their long hunting rifles. (The overall length of the so-called long rifle varied from 50 to 60 inches, its barrel 36 to 48 inches long. It was a flintlock muzzle-loader, usually .50-caliber, and was accurate up to 300 yards.) Shelby came with 240 men from Sullivan County, North Carolina. Sevier came with 240 men from Washington County, North Carolina. Campbell came with 440 men from Washington County, Virginia. McDowell came with 160 men from Burke and Rutherford Counties in North Carolina.

On September 26 the aggregation of rugged frontiersmen began their march through snowy Gillespie's Gap in the Blue Ridge and reassembled ninety miles away at Quaker Meadows on the Catawba River (near the present Morgantown, North Carolina). There they were joined by Colonel Cleveland and Major Joseph Winston and their 350 militiamen from Wilkes and Surry Counties in North Carolina. Ferguson's intelligence by now had revealed to him that a large and growing rebel militia force was moving toward him from north of his position, and on September 27 he started withdrawing southward. He had also been informed that Colonel Elijah Clarke's Georgia militiamen might be moving north toward him from Augusta. On September 30 Ferguson received additional, confirming information about the rebel force from two rebel deserters, and now his alarm grew. He dispatched urgent messages to Cornwallis and to Lieutenant Colonel John Cruger, who had succeeded Balfour as commander of the British post at Ninety Six, pleading for reinforcements.

The leaders of the rebel militias, meanwhile, realizing they needed someone to command the unified forces, sent Charles McDowell, the senior officer, to Hillsborough to ask Horatio Gates to appoint Brigadier General Daniel Morgan or Brigadier General William Davidson as commander. While McDowell was gone, the other militia leaders elected William Campbell temporary commander. Major Joseph McDowell took over command of his brother's regiment in his absence. The request for Gates to appoint a commander went unanswered, and so Campbell remained the leader of the rebel force.

Ferguson, meanwhile, issued a desperate call for volunteers, sending circulars out into the countryside: "I say, if you wish to be pinioned, robbed, and murdered, and see your wives and daughters, in four days, abused by the dregs of mankind—in short, if you wish and deserve to live and bear the name of men, grasp your arms in a moment and run to camp."[7] The appeal was largely ignored.

On October 1 Ferguson made an abrupt turn eastward toward Charlotte, apparently hoping to throw the rebel army off his trail, which the rebels would have expected to lead southward to Ninety Six. The maneuver did throw off the patriots. They reached Gilbert Town on October 3 and the next day, at Denard's Ford, where Ferguson had turned to the east, they lost his trail.

Ferguson continued his eastward march until he reached the plantation of a friendly loyalist named Tate, about ten miles west of Kings Mountain. Still hoping for reinforcements to catch up to him and wishing to give his men a break, he encamped at Tate's plantation for two days, October 4 and 5. On October 5 Ferguson wrote to Cornwallis, saying, "I am on my march towards you, by a road leading from Cherokee Ford, north of Kings Mountain. Three or four hundred good soldiers, part dragoons, would finish this business. [Something] must be done soon. This is their last push in this quarter and they are extremely desolate and [c]owed."[8] The 300 or 400 good soldiers, including dragoons, that Ferguson mentioned may have been what he was hoping to receive from Cornwallis as reinforcements.

On October 6 Ferguson again wrote to Cornwallis. "I arrived today at Kings Mountain," he reported, "& have taken post where I do not think I can be forced by a stronger enemy than that against us." Ferguson was apparently assuming that Cornwallis still would get reinforcements to him. Cornwallis on October 7 wrote a disappointing note back to Ferguson: "Tarleton shall pass at some of the upper Fords, and clear the Country; for the present both he and his Corps want a few days rest."

Cornwallis was putting a good face on the fact that Tarleton was unable to help. He had been seriously ill with malaria for two weeks. His second in command, Major George Hanger, commander of Tarleton's cavalry and cut from the same cruel cloth as Tarleton, had already died of malaria. Cornwallis himself was also sick with what he described as a "feverish cold." At the same time, word came from Ninety Six that Cruger would not be able to send reinforcements, his garrison being already weakened. Although he perhaps did not yet realize it, Ferguson was out on a dangerous limb, with no one else to look to now for aid.

Stymied, the rebel leaders sent out patrols to find Ferguson's trail and when the patrols found evidence that Ferguson had swung to the east, the next move was to detach a force of some 700 mounted men, handpicked for the swiftness of their horses, and send them speeding toward Cowpens, some twenty miles to the southeast, hoping to overtake Ferguson. The main body of rebel troops would follow the detachment. Colonel Shelby recounted the pursuit:

> Finding that Ferguson was retreating, and learning what was his real strength, it was determined on Thursday night the 5th of October, to make a desperate effort to overtake him before he should reach any British post or receive any further reinforcements. Accordingly, they [the officers] selected all who had good horses, who numbered about nine hundred and ten, and started the next morning in pursuit of Ferguson as soon as they could see.
>
> Ferguson, after marching a short distance towards Ninety Six, had filed off to the left toward Cornwallis. His pursuers never stopped until late in the afternoon, when they reached the Cowpens. There they halted, shot down some beeves [beef], ate their suppers and fed their horses. This done, the line of march was resumed and continued through the whole night, amidst an excessively hard rain. In the morning Shelby ascertained that Campbell had taken a wrong road in the night and had separated from him. Men were posted off in all directions and Campbell's corps found and put in the right road. They then crossed Broad River and continued their pursuit until twelve o'clock, the 7th of October. The rain continued to fall so

heavily that Campbell, Sevier and Cleveland concluded to halt, and rode up to Shelby to inform him of their determination. Shelby replied: "I will not stop till night, if I follow Ferguson into Cornwallis's lines!" Without replying, the other colonels turned off to their respective commands and continued the march. They had proceeded but a mile when they learned that Ferguson was only seven miles from there at King's Mountain.

Ferguson, finding that he could not elude the rapid pursuit of the mounted mountaineers, had marched to King's Mountain, which he considered a strong post, and which he had reached the night previous. The mountain, or ridge, was a quarter of a mile long, and so confident was Ferguson in the strength of his position that he declared the Almighty could not drive him from it. . . .[9]

Shelby and the other rebel leaders had first learned of Ferguson's position from a patriot named Joseph Kerr, a man apparently too crippled to serve as a soldier and who was instead serving as a spy for his country's cause. Ostensibly seeking shelter with Ferguson's troops, Kerr had been with them when they halted for a lunch break and had discovered they were headed for Kings Mountain and would encamp there. In Cowpens he reported his discovery to rebel leaders. Four hundred militiamen under the command of Colonel James Williams augmented the rebel force in Cowpens.

Kings Mountain is a ridge, nearly bald of trees and shaped roughly like a shoe print, that rises some 60 feet above the land around it. The toe of the shoe print points to the northeast, and the heel toward the southwest. The top of the ridge is about 600 yards long and 60 to 120 yards wide. The sloping sides of the ridge are heavily wooded and strewn with boulders and split open in spots by ravines. Ferguson considered it impregnable, so much so that he was careless about posting sentries on its approaches. The rebels drew within a quarter mile of its slopes before they were first challenged by gunfire from Ferguson's men. The rebel tactics and the ensuing battle were described by Colonel Shelby:

When the patriots came near the mountain they halted, tied all their loose baggage to their saddles, fastened their horses and left them under charge of a few men, and then prepared for an immediate attack. About three o'clock the patriot force was led to the attack in four columns. Col. Campbell commanded the right centre column, Col. Shelby the left centre, Col. Sevier the right flank column, and

Col. Cleveland the left flank. As they came to the foot of the mountain, the right centre and right flank columns deployed to the right,
and the left centre and left flank columns to the left, and thus sur-
rounding the mountain they marched up, commencing the action on
all sides.

Ferguson did all that an officer could do under the circumstances. His men, too, fought bravely. But his position, which he
thought impregnable against any force the Patriots could raise, was
really a disadvantage to him. The summit was bare, whilst the sides
of the mountain were covered with trees. Ferguson's men were drawn
up in close column on the summit and thus presented fair marks for
the mountaineers, who approached them under cover of the trees. As
either column would approach the summit, Ferguson would order
out a bayonet charge with fixed bayonet, which was always successful,
for the riflemen retreated before the charging column slowly, still firing as they retired. When Ferguson's men returned to retain their
position on the mountain, the patriots would again rally and pursue
them. In one of these charges Shelby's column was considerably broken; he rode back and rallied his men, and when the enemy retired to
the summit he pressed on his men and reached the summit whilst
Ferguson was directing a charge against Cleveland.

Col. Sevier reached the summit about the same time with Shelby.
They united and drove back the enemy to one end of the ridge.
Cleveland's and Campbell's columns were still pressing forward and
firing as they came up. The slaughter of the enemy was great, and it
was evident that further resistance would be unavailing. Still
Ferguson's proud heart could not think of surrender. He swore "he
never would yield to such a d—d banditti," and rushed from his men,
sword in hand, and cut away until his sword was broken and he was
shot down. His men, seeing their leader fall, immediately surrendered. The British loss, in killed and prisoners, was eleven hundred
and five. Ferguson's morning report [of that day] showed a force of
eleven hundred and twenty-five. A more total defeat was not practicable. Our loss was about forty killed. Amongst them we had to
mourn the death of Col. Williams, a most gallant and efficient officer. The battle lasted one hour.[10]

Shelby and his fellow commanders had been informed by a captured loyalist that Ferguson, the only man on Kings Mountain that day who was

not an American, would be conspicuous by the checked shirt or duster he wore over his uniform. He furthermore would be noticeable as the only officer wielding his sword in his left hand. Ferguson also wore a metal whistle around his neck, to whistle orders to his men, like a sheepherder to his dogs. Mounted on a white horse, he attempted to ride over and slash his way through Colonel Sevier's lines, leading a unit of his force into them, but came under a hailstorm of deadly rebel rifle fire. Every man in that unit fell from gunshot, killed or mortally wounded. Ferguson himself was shot from his horse. He dropped from the saddle onto the ground with not less than six bullets in his body. He was carried from the spot where he fell and died soon after and was buried on the southeastern slope of the mountain, in a grave marked by a cairn.

Ferguson had paid a terrible price for underestimating the fighting abilities of his rebel foe and overestimating the security of his position atop Kings Mountain. Not only had he lost his life but also through the loss of his army of loyalists he had cost Cornwallis a vital offensive arm. Cornwallis would now have to rethink his strategy for overcoming the south.

CHAPTER Twenty-Two

The Battle of Cowpens

C ornwallis was besieged by bad news. To his headquarters in
Charlotte came not only depressing tidings of the defeat at Kings
Mountain but reports of failure and imminent danger from
nearly every quarter of the embattled Carolinas.

From the British western outpost at Ninety Six, South Carolina,
Lieutenant Colonel Cruger, the commandant, wrote to Cornwallis saying
that he suspected his post would be the next objective of the rebel militia
force that had destroyed the protective left wing of Cornwallis's army and
had removed the shield that covered British-held territory, a possibility
already feared by Cornwallis. In that event, Cruger warned Cornwallis, he
would be facing a foe with menacingly superior numbers and his loyalist
militiamen, not liking the odds, would doubtless desert him.

From Camden, South Carolina, sixty-five miles south of Charlotte, in
the rear of Cornwallis's main army, word came that the loyalist militia,
upon learning of the Kings Mountain debacle, had already begun disintegrating. Furthermore, the Camden garrison's regular troops had run out
of flour and were without bread.

In Charlotte Cornwallis let it be known he was disgusted with the militia that once had been a vital part of his grand plan. Following the defeat
at Kings Mountain, he wrote in a letter to British Major General Alexander
Leslie that "it is throwing away good Arms, or what is worse helping the
Enemy, by giving them to the Militia."[1]

Of all the effects of the loss at Kings Mountain one of the most critical was a general dispiriting of loyalists, those who had already volunteered
for service in the militia and those who would otherwise have been

prospects for the king's cause. Most of the 700 or so prisoners taken by the rebels at Kings Mountain managed to escape and having done so, carried frightening stories of rebel ferocity to the troubled ears of their neighbors and kinsmen. The atrocities they reported were the equal of those committed by Tarleton's Legion. Indeed, it was Tarleton's notorious butchery that had set off the slaughter of many loyalist militiamen at Kings Mountain and of others who had been captured there and later marched away to detention. When the defeated loyalists threw down their arms and shouted for quarter, their pleas were answered by rebels with shouts of "Tarleton's quarter!" followed by merciless attacks on the unarmed men. In the minds of many of the Kings Mountain survivors and those who heard their accounts of the battle, the king's cause had become a hopeless one. Cornwallis would not be able to recruit loyalists as Ferguson had done before the Battle of Kings Mountain.

Cornwallis was also struggling to cope with illness in his camp at Charlotte. Exposure to inclement autumn weather, which had brought torrents of rain, plus a lack of adequate medical facilities had laid many of Cornwallis's troops low with fevers. Cornwallis himself had become a victim of the maladies pervading the camp.

On October 14, forced to abandon his plans for the 1780 campaign, he recalled Tarleton from his forward post and pulled out of Charlotte, headed for Winnsboro, South Carolina, about thirty miles northwest of Camden and about sixty miles east northeast of Ninety Six. There he would be in a position to help defend both Ninety Six and Camden. En route, he became so severely sick with what had apparently begun as a cold that he could not ride his horse or even hold a pen to write. Rawdon took over the command of Cornwallis's army during the remainder of its sixty-mile retreat to Winnsboro.

The march was a tour of horrors. The downpour of rain continued, nearly every day, soaking the troops, who lacked tents, transforming the mud roads into morasses, swelling streams over or through which Cornwallis's army had to pass. Militiamen were pressed into the task of helping fatigued horses pull baggage and artillery wagons through the clinging mud of the roadway. Food ran short. The troops lived on corn taken from the fields they passed, two and a half ears having to keep a man fed for twenty-four hours. Wanting water, the men drank muddy rainwater. The sick were transported in wagons that only exacerbated their misery. Major Hanger, who had been Tarleton's second in command, had fallen ill with what he called yellow fever, and he and five other officers suffering the same malady were placed in wagons for the trip to Winnsboro. All five of the others died during the first week of the retreat, their bodies quickly buried along the route of march. To make matters perilously worse, as Cornwallis's army plodded southward, it was continually harassed by rebels, firing into its flanks and its rear.

The army reached Winnsboro on Sunday, October 29. To prepare for winter, Cornwallis ordered his men to construct log huts that would serve as barracks, one of which he himself would occupy. There Cornwallis mulled over his reduced circumstances. His shortages were discussed in correspondence with Nisbet Balfour, commanding the British garrison at Charleston, and with Major Richard England, who became deputy quartermaster general under Cornwallis: ". . . the situation of the horses & gear is wretched beyond description." "Unless more carriadges [*sic*] can be got we shall be much distressed." "Upon the most accurate account I can get of our strength in waggons, I find it will be quite impracticable to go near supplying you with rum, salt & carrying up the necessities sent for." "Waggons were so scarce in these parts that the corn which was promised us, could not be brought to the mill."[2]

Shortages weren't the only problem affecting his chain of supply. The British quartermaster general's office was rife with corruption. Huge profits were being pocketed by staff officers quick to take capitalize on the shortages of horses and wagons. Officers bought horses and wagons for themselves, then hired them out to Cornwallis's army at exorbitant prices. The shortages were working to their advantage, and they had no interest in alleviating them. In fact, there were times when the quartermaster general's staff created shortages by withholding their horses and wagons, just when Cornwallis needed them most. He made some attempt to solve the problem. He told Balfour, "I hope by getting rid of everybody belonging to the Qr. Mr. Genl's department, & by paying conductors, drivers &c their wages, instead of putting them in our pockets, to procure a sufficient provision train to enable us to subsist."[3] He later issued directives to prevent his officers from owning wagons: ". . . the Quarter Master General should have no Property in either the Waggons or the Horses."[4] He also issued an order forbidding the quartermaster general from charging more for use of horses and wagons than had been paid for their acquisition. Those and other attempts to eliminate corruption and ease the shortage failed to solve the problem completely.

Meanwhile, the war in the south continued to go poorly for the British, adding to Cornwallis's distress. After receiving intelligence that Thomas Sumter had encamped with only 300 men just 30 miles from

Winnsboro, Cornwallis authorized Major James Wemyss to mount 100 infantrymen of the 63rd Regiment and detach 40 cavalrymen from Tarleton's British Legion for a surprise attack on Sumter at Moore's Mill, South Carolina. The attack was planned for dawn on November 9, 1780. Sumter, however, had shifted his troops to a new position five miles away, at Fishdam Ford, and when Wemyss stumbled onto Sumter's outposts about 1 a.m. on November 9, the surprised rebels opened fire on the equally surprised British regulars. Wemyss was hit twice and fell from his mount with a broken arm and a wounded knee.

After getting off only several shots, the rebel pickets withdrew, and Lieutenant John Stark, taking over for the fallen Wemyss, then led Tarleton's cavalrymen in a charge on Sumter's main bivouac, where the light of campfires made the mounted British easy targets for Sumter's riflemen. Sensing disaster, Stark dismounted his infantrymen and sent them against Sumter's defenses. Following a brief but intense exchange of fire, the troops of both sides broke off contact and withdrew into the darkness. The British lost an estimated five killed, and Cornwallis later reported that twenty-three of his men were left wounded on the ground. Accounts vary on the number lost by Sumter's force, from no losses to four killed and ten wounded. "The enemy on this event," Cornwallis reported, "cried victory."

Cornwallis's next move was to order Tarleton from his position on the lower Pee Dee River, where he was trying to hunt down Francis Marion's militiamen, and send him and his legion in pursuit of Sumter. Cornwallis's worry was that Sumter's 1,000-man force would threaten the British post at Ninety Six. He also sent Major Archibald McArthur to secure Brierly's Ferry on the Broad River, which reaches into northwestern South Carolina. McArthur's command included the 1st Battalion of the 71st Highlanders and the 80 surviving members of Wemyss's 63rd Regiment.

After a speedy forced march, Tarleton reached Brierly's Ferry on the morning of Saturday, November 18, and almost immediately came under rebel fire when his men went down to the river to bathe themselves and their horses. Tarleton quickly ordered his men to mount and led them across the river to pursue the withdrawing rebels.

Sumter had planned to attack a loyalist outpost on Little River, about fifteen miles from Ninety Six, and had gathered a force of some 1,000 militiamen for the assault. A deserter from Cornwallis's 63rd Regiment, however, made his way to Sumter's encampment around midnight on November 19–20 and warned Sumter that Tarleton was nearby and headed toward Sumter's position. Sumter quickly ordered a retreat.

By ten o'clock on the morning of November 20 Tarleton had learned of Sumter's retreat and urged his troops on in hot pursuit. Around 4 p.m. he concluded he would have to accelerate the pursuit if he was going to overtake Sumter, and so he left his foot soldiers behind and sped off with 190 of his dragoons and the 80 mounted infantrymen of the 63rd Regiment, whom he had collected at Brierly's Ferry.

Sumter had reached the Tyger River, which flows from northwest to southeast into the Broad, and in the fading daylight he halted at Blackstock's farm, on the steep hill that overlooks the river, 200 feet below. He would have no more than an hour to cross before darkness overcame him. The leading element of Tarleton's column had already caught up with the rear guard of Sumter's force, and Sumter knew he would have to make a hurried crossing or risk being caught by Tarleton in the process. Then came a stroke of American luck.

A woman who had seen Tarleton gallop off without his infantry and without his three-pounder and its crew rode into Sumter's temporary command post and informed him that Tarleton's infantrymen and his artillery piece had been left behind. Sumter quickly decided against crossing the Tyger. He would instead make a stand against Tarleton.

Sumter positioned the bulk of his force in thick woods on the hills above and to the left of the road by which Tarleton would approach. He placed a unit of riflemen in the farm's outbuildings, five unchinked log structures, on the right of the road.

When his column drew up near the Americans' position, Tarleton realized Sumter's position was too strong for him to attack and he decided to wait for the remainder of his infantry and his artillery to catch up to him. He dismounted the men of the 63rd Regiment and positioned them on his right, above a stream that flowed past Sumter's line of defenders. On his left he placed his 190 dragoons. Then he waited for the reinforcements that were moving up the road behind him.

Studying Tarleton's maneuvering, Sumter ordered Colonel Elijah Clarke to sweep around the British right flank and take a position that would block the road at Tarleton's rear, barring reinforcements from reaching him. Sumter then took personal command of a force of 400 of his militiamen and prepared to assault Tarleton's right. They crossed the creek and started up the hill toward the troops of the 63rd.

The veteran regulars of the 63rd, outnumbered five to one, took the first volley of the advancing rebels, then counterattacked and drove the rebels back past the farm's outbuildings. While attempting to rally the men in flight, Sumter ordered Colonel Edward Lacey to slip through the woods and hit the left flank of Tarleton's green-coated dragoons, who were idling in position, their attention absorbed by the action of the 63rd's infantrymen pursuing the fleeing rebels.

Lacey's regiment closed to within seventy-five yards of the dragoons before they were noticed. There they opened a deadly fire that dropped twenty of Tarleton's surprised cavalrymen from their saddles. Lacey's men were then forced back, and Sumter, mounted and dashing back to the center of his line, was struck by a musket ball that pierced his right shoulder and penetrated to his spine. Meanwhile, Colonel Henry Hampton's sharpshooters in the log outbuildings, their rifles protruding between the unchinked logs, delivered such a withering fire on the advancing 63rd that the British counterattack was halted. Fire was also coming into the redcoats' flanks from the woods, where Sumter's riflemen were covered by trees.

Now Tarleton led a nearly suicidal mounted charge into the center of the line in order to extricate his beleaguered infantry. He succeeded, but at a cost, and the fighting came to an end as darkness enveloped the battleground at Blackstock's farm. Both sides withdrew.

Tarleton claimed victory. So did the Americans. Tarleton lost some fifty men killed or wounded out of a total of 270 troops engaged in the combat. Sumter's forces lost three killed and five wounded out of 1,000 troops engaged. Sumter was deflected from his plan to attack the loyalist base on Little River and possibly then to move on the British outpost at Ninety Six. He had also been seriously wounded. But Tarleton and his infamous, dreaded British Legion, veteran professional fighting men, had been stopped cold by dauntless militiamen, America's amateur soldiers.

Cornwallis had reason to be especially unhappy about the news from Blackstock's farm. Young Lieutenant John Money, an aide in whom Cornwallis had taken a fatherly interest, had been badly wounded when the 63rd had come under heavy fire from the rebels and despite Cornwallis's instructions that he receive special care, Lieutenant Money died of his wounds on December 1, plunging Cornwallis into a mood of gloom.

More gloomy news followed. On December 4 Colonel William Washington, a distant relative of the Americans' commander in chief, led his dragoons to Rugeley's Mills, South Carolina (also known as Clermont), in pursuit of a force of loyalists commanded by Colonel Henry Rugeley. Washington found the loyalist soldiers occupying a log barn that had been turned into a strong fortification with loopholes and a raised platform to provide defense by two tiers of riflemen. Surrounded by a ditch, earthworks, and abatis, the structure appeared impregnable without resort to artillery to pound in its walls.

Washington halted his troops before the barn, now a veritable blockhouse, and decided against storming it. Instead, he had his men cut and shape a tree trunk into a cannon, mounted it, moved it into enemy view, within easy artillery range, and pointed it at the barn. He then sent a message to Rugeley demanding he surrender or have his stronghold demolished by cannon fire. Without even firing a shot, Rugeley surrendered in the face of the threat from a fake artillery piece. He emerged from the building with one officer and more than a hundred enlisted men, all of whom became Colonel Washington's prisoners and were marched off to detention behind the American lines. Rugeley, who apparently had been up for promotion to brigadier general, disgraced himself in Cornwallis's eyes, furthering Cornwallis's general disenchantment with militias. Cornwallis wrote to Tarleton and told him that Rugeley would not get the promotion. Rugeley's military career was ended.

Two days before the incident at Rugeley's Mills, on December 2, Major General Nathanael Greene, General Washington's choice to head the American army in the south, had arrived in Charlotte to take over his new command. The army he found was desperately understrength and woefully short of supplies, equipment, and discipline. He quickly set about to correct those deficiencies. On the advice of Thaddeus Kosciuszko, whom Greene sent to reconnoiter and choose a new location for his army to be reformed, Greene shifted his base to Cheraw, South Carolina, near the Pee Dee River, some sixty miles southeast of Charlotte and about seventy-five miles northeast of Cornwallis's base at Winnsboro.

Until his army could gather enough strength to face Cornwallis, Greene determined to do what he could, which was to harry supply and communication lines to and between the British outposts at Augusta, Georgia, and Ninety Six, Camden, and Georgetown in South Carolina. To do so, he decided to divide his force. Before leaving Charlotte, he placed Brigadier General Daniel Morgan in command of a 600-man detachment that would split off from Greene and move some hundred miles to the west. Morgan's command included 320 Continental troops from Maryland and Delaware and 200 militiamen from Virginia, plus the 80 dragoons commanded by the daring Colonel William Washington. To command the troops remaining with him, Morgan named Lieutenant Colonel John Eager Howard of Maryland.

Greene instructed Morgan to march to the west side of the Catawba River and there he would be reinforced by troops from the militias of Sumter and William Davidson. Morgan's mission was to "give protection to that part of the country [the west side of the Catawba] and spirit up the people, to annoy the enemy in that quarter, collect the provisions and forage." Greene also told him that in the event Greene's force was attacked, Morgan was to "move in such direction as will enable you to join me if necessary, or to fall back upon the flank or into the rear of the enemy, as occasion may require."

On December 20, in heavy rain, Greene and the nominal commander of the other half of his army, Brigadier General Isaac Huger of South Carolina, set off from Charlotte for their new post at Cheraw. The next day Morgan moved out of Charlotte with his force and by Christmas had reached the Pacolet River and established a camp at Grindall's Shoals, where he was joined by Major Joseph McDowell, one of the heroes of Kings Mountain, and his 190 North Carolina riflemen.

Wasting no time in carrying out his instructions, Morgan on December 27 sent William Washington and his 80 dragoons plus 200 mounted militiamen to attack a 250-man loyalist party that had been raiding patriot farms. Vigorous in carrying out his orders, Washington struck the loyalist raiders at Hammond's Store, about 30 miles northeast of Ninety Six. He wiped them out, killing or wounding 150 and taking 40 prisoners. He then dispatched a detachment to strike a loyalist post called Fort Williams, just 15 miles from Ninety Six.

On New Year's Day, 1781, reports of the rebel raids reached Cornwallis in Winnsboro. He saw good news amid the bad. He deemed it good news that Greene, against the rules of warfare, had divided his force and the two halves were not only too distant to quickly support each other, but also the main body of Cornwallis's army stood between them. Morgan was vulnerable, Cornwallis concluded.

Banastre Tarleton then offered to his commander a strategy to trap Morgan and his raiders and destroy them. Tarleton wrote to Cornwallis on January 4 to propose that he be sent to seek out and destroy Morgan's army or drive it eastward across Broad River, toward Kings Mountain. Cornwallis would move northward from Winnsboro and trap whatever elements of Morgan's force remained as it fled in retreat from Tarleton. The rebels would be caught between Tarleton's Legion and the main body of Cornwallis's army. With Morgan's force destroyed, Cornwallis could then throw the full weight of his army, including Tarleton's Legion, against the main body of Greene's army in a crucial showdown. It would be the kind of decisive battle that Cornwallis hoped for and was skilled at conducting.

Cornwallis bought the plan. "You have exactly done what I wished you to do, and understood my intentions perfectly," he wrote to Tarleton on January 5.[5] "I propose marching on Sunday." Sunday was January 7; he actually moved out from Winnsboro on Monday, January 8. While Cornwallis moved north toward Charlotte, Tarleton planned to dash through the countryside between Ninety Six and Kings Mountain to run down Morgan and his raiders. Tarleton would take with him his British Legion, consisting of 300 dragoons and 250 infantry, reinforced by the 7th Regiment, a battalion of the 71st Highlanders, 50 cavalrymen of the 17th Light Dragoons, a Royal Artillery detachment that would man two grasshoppers, and a small group of loyalist militia. His command would total about 1,100 men.

The plan got off to a sluggish start. Heavy rains that turned roads into bogs and streams into flooding torrents delayed Tarleton's dash toward Morgan. Cornwallis, too, was hampered by the weather. By January 15, however, Tarleton had crossed the swollen but falling waters of the Enoree and Tyger Rivers and was rushing to find Morgan.

Morgan was aware of Tarleton's presence. In addition to other intelligence, he had received a letter from Greene dated January 13, saying, "It is my wish that you hold your ground if possible, for I foresee the disagreeable consequences that will result from a retreat. . . . Col. Tarleton is said to be on his way to pay you a visit. I doubt not but he will have a decent reception and a proper dismission."[6]

When Morgan's patrols reported that Tarleton had moved up the Pacolet River, Morgan saw the danger of Tarleton's moving behind him and to the east, cutting him off from Greene, 140 miles away. He moved to Old Iron Works on the Pacolet to oppose his crossing. The two enemies were then camped on either side of the river, opposite each other. With typical agility and stealth, in the early morning of January 16, Tarleton stole back downriver and crossed at Easterwood Shoals, six miles below Morgan's position. It was 6 a.m. when Morgan learned of Tarleton's crossing, and he quickly ordered a retreat, so hastily that his troops' breakfast was left cooking on their campfires. Morgan was retreating, but he was also remembering the words sent him by Greene.

Around the middle of the afternoon, a messenger from Colonel Andrew Pickens arrived to tell Morgan that Pickens had crossed the Broad River and was coming to reinforce him with about 150 mounted militiamen. Other militias, he knew, were also on their way to him. Morgan resolved to hold his ground. What he needed now was a site where his troops and those who were hurrying toward him could converge and together make a stand. It had to be suitable for defense. It had to be nearby. It had to be chosen quickly. He asked for suggestions from those who were familiar the area.

Joseph McDowell knew a place. It was called the Cowpens, a site surrounded by pastures and where cattle had been kept in enclosures. McDowell described it. Some of the ground around it was rolling meadowland, good for grazing cattle. The meadowland flattened out in other parts of the site. There were stands of hickory, red oak, and pine. No underbrush. There was a red-clay road, the Green River Road, which passed through the center of it. The site was about five miles from the Broad River and about five miles from where Morgan and McDowell now stood. Morgan promptly made his decision. He sent messages to Pickens and the other militia leaders coming to reinforce him that they would rendezvous at the Cowpens.

Morgan than rode off with his senior officers to reconnoiter the site. They approached it from the south, by way of the Green River Road, the way Tarleton must come. As Morgan's party moved northward up the road and emerged from the woods, Morgan could see that the ground sloped gradually upward from that point, rising to a crest about 400 yards in front of him. A low ridge, its elevation about 70 feet, rose about 300 yards beyond the slope. It was a site ideally suited for the use of Tarleton's cavalry, with no natural obstacles to protect Morgan's flanks. But surveying the lay of the land, Morgan seemed pleased with what he saw and he began planning the deployment of his force to meet Tarleton's imminent assault.

"I would not have had a swamp in view of my militia on any consideration; they would have made for it," Morgan later recounted. "And, as to covering my wings, I knew my adversary, and was perfectly sure I should have nothing but downright fighting. As to retreat, it was the very thing I wished to cut off all hope of. . . ."[7]

The wily combat veteran was turning a minus—the Broad River at his back—into a plus. Confident of his regular soldiers, he was less sure about the staying power of the approximately 300 militiamen who had joined him. The river that would be five miles to his rear would bar the flight of those militiamen. They would have to stand with him and his regulars.

As his troops moved into the site, he positioned them. He placed 150 handpicked militia riflemen as skirmishers to form his first line of defense.

They were Georgians commanded by Major John Cunningham and North Carolinians commanded by Major Charles McDowell. They would be concealed in tall grass and behind trees on both sides of the road. Picked for their marksmanship, they were instructed to hold their fire until the enemy was within fifty paces, then get off two rounds—two telling rounds, aimed at those wearing epaulets—and then quickly withdraw back to the second line, reloading and firing again as they retreated.

Placed in the second line, athwart the road and some 150 yards to the rear of the first line, were some 300 North Carolina and South Carolina militiamen commanded by Pickens. They were instructed to wait for the first line to fall back to their position and reinforce them, then get off at least two effective volleys at fifty paces, aiming for officers and sergeants, and fall back in anticipation of a British bayonet charge. They were cautioned about the tendency to shoot too high on the downward slope. They were told to move off to their left when they withdrew, along with the first line, and dash to the rear of the third line, where they would reassemble.

Morgan positioned the third line 150 yards behind the second line and about 150 yards in front of the slope's crest. The third line would extend across a front 400 yards wide and would be manned by about 450 troops commanded by John Howard. Morgan put his Maryland and Delaware Continentals in the center of the line, his Virginia riflemen on both right and left ends and a company of Georgia militia on the extreme right.

William Washington's eighty dragoons and forty-five mounted Georgia and North Carolina militia infantrymen armed with sabers, commanded by Lieutenant Colonel John McCall, formed Morgan's reserve. It was posted a half mile to the rear of the third line, behind the crest of the slope.

Morgan's idea was to cut Tarleton's force down to size as it advanced on the Americans' position, then attack it. Militia, he knew, had a tendency to run from British bayonets, and Morgan would turn that tendency into an advantage. When his militiamen started withdrawing, Tarleton would assume Morgan's force was being routed and he would press his charge, unknowingly, right into the arms of Morgan's most experienced, most dangerous fighters, the men of the third line.

Morgan took meticulous care to explain his plan to his officers and sergeants and made sure, as sure as he could be, that every private also understood the plan. Aching with sciatica and arthritis, he made his way that evening, January 16, throughout the camp, stopping at campfires to talk with the men, inform them and encourage them, telling jokes and a dirty story now and then, inciting rivalries between his sharpshooting riflemen, fomenting feeling against the redcoats and the hated loyalists, stirring the troops. He made sure every man had rations for breakfast and twenty-four rounds of ammunition.

Thomas Young, a young man who volunteered to serve with William Washington's dragoons, recorded his experiences of that night:

> We were very anxious for battle, and many a hearty curse had been vented against General Morgan during that day's march for retreating, as we thought, to avoid a fight.
>
> Night came upon us, yet much remained to be done. It was all important to strengthen the cavalry. General Morgan well knew the power of Tarleton's Legion, and he was too wily an officer not to prepare himself as well as circumstances would admit. Two companies of volunteers were called for. . . . I attached myself to Major Jolly's company. We drew swords that night and were informed we had authority to press any horse not belonging to a dragoon or an officer into our service for the day.
>
> It was upon this occasion I was more perfectly convinced of General Morgan's qualifications to command militia than I had ever before been. He went among the volunteers, helped them fix their swords, joked with them about their sweethearts, told them to keep in good spirits, and the day would be ours. And long after I laid down, he was going about among the soldiers encouraging them and telling them that the old wagoner [Morgan] would crack his whip over Ben [Tarleton] in the morning, as sure as they lived.
>
> "Just hold up your heads, boys, three fires," he would say, "and you are free, and then when you return to your homes, how the old folks will bless you, and the girls kiss you for your gallant conduct!"
>
> I don't believe he slept a wink that night.[8]

Tarleton roused his troops from slumber with his drummer beating reveille at 2 a.m. Wednesday, January 17. At 3 a.m. he broke camp and set off in the darkness, apparently intending to take Morgan by surprise. He left his supply wagons under guard and gave orders for the wagons to move out at daybreak and follow him.

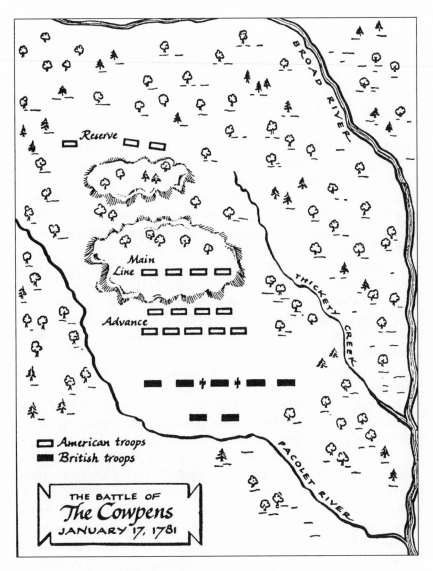

The Battle of Cowpens, January 17, 1781

Tarleton rode near the head of his column, leading three light-infantry companies, behind which marched the infantry of Tarleton's Legion, the 7th Regiment and the 1st Battalion of the 71st Regiment, the Royal Artillery detachment that manned his two grasshopper artillery pieces, 50 troopers of the 17th Light Dragoons and, finally, Tarleton's cavalry. Altogether, the force totaled some 1,100 troops.

The advance guard of the column carefully felt its way up the dark road and reached Thicketty Creek about 5 a.m., an hour before dawn. Believing he was close to Morgan's position, Tarleton ordered a cavalry patrol to move forward and locate it, then crossed the creek and continued the march. The patrol soon ran up against Morgan's forward sentries, a unit of Georgia Rangers under the command of Captain Joshua Inman. Two of the Georgians were captured, but the remainder, including Inman, fled back toward the American lines to warn Morgan.

Questioning the two rebel prisoners, Tarleton learned that Morgan was encamped about five miles up the road, at the Cowpens. Tarleton called in his loyalist guides, who knew the area, and had them describe the place where Morgan had made camp. He also ordered two units of his cavalry, fifty dragoons, commanded by a Captain Ogilvie, to join the probing advance guard and scope out the American position.

About 6:45 a.m. Ogilvie and his troopers emerged from the woods that flanked the Green River Road. In the gray light before sunrise he could dimly see the meadow stretching before him, rising into the distance. Suddenly gunshots cracked in the morning stillness, the scattered sounds coming from both sides of the road and in front of him. He wheeled and galloped with his men back into the protective woods, then quickly dispatched a rider with a message for Tarleton. The rebels, he reported, were deployed for battle.

By now Tarleton knew that the rain-swollen Broad River was at Morgan's back and retreat was virtually impossible. He had him where he wanted him. While his column continued its advance up the road, he galloped ahead to reconnoiter the battle site. As his troops reached the clearing of the meadow, Tarleton ordered them into battle formation, some 400 yards from Morgan's first line. He ordered his dragoons, commanded by Ogilvie, to trot to the front of his formation, spread out, and prepare to ride hard to drive back the rebel skirmishers in Morgan's forward line. On command, fifty saber-brandishing dragoons spurred their mounts and began their charge across the open meadow as the sun rose through the treetops.

Morgan's men were ready for them. They had earlier been rousted from their bedrolls on the frosty ground by Morgan himself. He had mounted his horse and ridden through the camp shouting in his mule-driver's voice, "Boys! Get up! Benny's coming!"

In the grassy meadow and behind trees, Morgan's skirmishers, following their instructions, held their fire as Tarleton's dragoons thundered toward them, their deadly sabers raised, quickly closing the distance to the Americans' first line. When they were within fifty yards, rifle fire suddenly erupted to their front and flanks, and fifteen of Tarleton's fifty hell-for-leather riders dropped from their saddles. The survivors wheeled, turning away from the deadly hail of shot, and sped back to their lines, their comrades' riderless mounts dashing confusedly among them as they recrossed the meadow.

Determined, Tarleton then prepared for a frontal assault on the American position. Arraying his troops, he placed on his left the 7th Regiment; in the center, the British Legion infantry; on the right, the three light-infantry companies. On either flank of the Legion's infantry he placed a grasshopper artillery piece. On the extreme flanks he posted his dragoons and a detachment of the 17th Light Dragoons. He held in reserve 200 cavalrymen of the British Legion and the battalion of kilted Highlanders of the 71st Regiment.

About 7 a.m. Tarleton gave the order to move out, leading the line forward himself, his band striking up a martial tune as the redcoat army, bayonets fixed on their muskets, moved out briskly in the chill January morning air.

As the line of fearful bayonets steadily drew nearer, from the American line spewed a devastating volley of rifle fire. Red-coated infantrymen fell limply to the ground. Then came another volley, and more fell. Still the bayonets advanced. The men of the first line then turned toward their rear and ran, reloading and firing again as they hurried to reinforce the second line, where Pickens's troops stood steadfastly in place, awaiting the steadily approaching redcoats.

Now they were less than a hundred yards away. Pickens's officers commanded "Fire!" and the deadly discharge of the militiamen's rifles tore through the British ranks with terrible effect. The militia's second volley stopped the British advance. Momentarily. Tarleton's officers reformed their tattered ranks and resumed the attack. The men of the second American line, joined by those of the first line, then turned and sprinted off to their left, some disregarding instructions to reform behind the third line and instead making for their horses, which they had left tied in the woods. Morgan's officers managed to retrieve some of those.

Seeing the flight of the Americans and sensing a rout, Tarleton ordered the 17th Dragoons, on the right flank of his line, to charge after them in an attempt to hack them down. As they rushed forward, the dragoons rode into the fire from the third line's Virginia riflemen and were then counterattacked by William Washington's dragoons and James McCall's mounted infantry, who drove them back toward their line, ten empty saddles among them.

The rebel militiamen then reformed to the rear of the third line, reinforcing Morgan's main line of defense to meet the next assault.

About 7:15 a.m. Tarleton redressed the ranks of his weakened attack force and sent them back once more against the Americans' rifles. Confident of victory, the British troops began cheering as they pressed forward. Then the first volley of Morgan's third line smashed into them. The slaughter was on. Morgan's troops poured a steady stream of fire into the red- and green-coated ranks of Tarleton's diminishing army. The British bravely returned the fire, but were taking enormous losses in a prolonged exchange.

Around 7:30 a.m. Tarleton made another move. He ordered Major Archibald McArthur to hit the rebel right flank and turn it with his battalion of Highlanders from the 71st Regiment. To the shrieking skirl of their bagpipes, the 200 kilted Scottish veterans moved smartly out to encircle the American right.

Lieutenant Colonel Howard, commanding the third line, responded by ordering the infantry company that was on his extreme right to shift position and turn to present a new front to the attackers, a tactic known as "refusing a flank." While they shifted, however, the company's movement was mistaken by other companies along Howard's line as being a general withdrawal, and the entire third line began falling back, albeit in good order.

Morgan watched in horror from his command post. He quickly rode to Howard and, given the explanation, told Howard, "I'll choose you a second position. When you reach it, face about and fire!"

Seeing the rebels retreat, the whole British line rushed forward to rout them.

William Washington, standing with his dragoons after turning back the British attack on the American left, sent a message to Morgan: "They're coming on like a mob. Give them one fire and I'll charge them." Morgan sent consenting word back to Washington.

The British infantrymen were now running pell-mell in pursuit of the Americans, down the meadow's far slope. On Morgan's signal, Howard ordered his men to halt, turn, and fire, and with the enemy fifty paces behind them, they wheeled and delivered a withering volley of rifle fire, then charged their stunned and ravaged pursuers with bayonets. The riders of Washington and McCall, at the same time, swept past the dragoons commanded by Ogilvie and crashed into the British infantry's flank and rear, slashing infantrymen down with their sabers.

Weary, bloodied, and beaten, the men of the British 7th, mostly new recruits, threw down their weapons and cried, "Quarter!" On the British right Tarleton's veteran troops attempted to escape by hurrying to their rear. They were cut off and taken prisoner by Morgan's horsemen. On the American right, the Highlanders refused to quit until they were surrounded, pressed into hand-to-hand combat and overwhelmed. Nine of their sixteen officers lay dead or wounded. Their commander, Archibald McArthur, handed over his sword in surrender to Pickens.

Tarleton, meanwhile, too stubborn or too stupid to realize his defeat, tried one last desperate move. He still held in reserve 200 of his British Legion dragoons. He ordered them into the fray in an attempt to avoid complete disaster. They refused his order and, in Tarleton's words, "forsook their leader and left the field of battle." Tarleton did manage to rally fourteen of his officers and forty men of the 17th Dragoons in an effort to rescue his two artillery pieces. It was a futile attempt that came too late. Rebel fighters struck down the blue-uniformed British artillerymen who were fighting to save their guns, and the pieces fell into American hands.

Tarleton and what was left of his dreaded army then beat a hasty retreat. They galloped off and outran their rebel pursuers, reaching the camp of the main body of Cornwallis's army on January 18.

The Battle of Cowpens had lasted but an hour. Of the 1,100 men in Tarleton's force, the British lost 100 killed and 229 wounded, all of whom were taken prisoner. Some 600 other British fighting men were also captured. In addition to their men, the British lost 100 dragoon horses, 800 muskets, 35 wagons, the two grasshopper artillery pieces, the colors of the 7th Regiment, and their musical instruments.

The Americans lost 12 killed and 60 wounded. Morgan's victory over Tarleton was clear and total.

CHAPTER **Twenty-Three**

The Battle of Guilford Courthouse

Cornwallis was encamped with the main body of his army at Turkey Creek, South Carolina, when reports of the disaster at Cowpens reached him on Thursday, January 18, 1781, the day after the battle. Reacting with anger and determination, he wrote on that same day to his commander, Henry Clinton, in New York to tell him that "nothing but the most absolute necessity shall induce me to give up the important object of the Winter's Campaign." The object, of course, was to crush the American army. He swiftly marshaled his army to run down Morgan's force, destroy it, and restore to his army those troops taken prisoner at Cowpens.

Once that was done, he planned to turn the full weight of his army against Nathanael Greene, having apparently reached a state of near obsession in his zeal to destroy the American fighting forces. He resolved to pursue Greene till he caught him, and then to force him to do battle. To do so, he would disregard Clinton's orders to protect Charleston and South Carolina at all costs. After writing his January 18 letter, he broke off communication with Clinton and would not write to him again for three months.

The army that was left to Cornwallis after Cowpens was smaller by about a third, reduced from 3,300 troops to some 2,500. It was not just numbers that Tarleton had cost him at Cowpens. It was Cornwallis's fast-moving, quick-striking light troops. Yet he determined to make do. He knew that the size of his force was the equal of Greene's and he believed the fighting ability of his troops, regular soldiers, was superior to Greene's.

Cornwallis's remaining army included the reinforcements brought up from Charleston by Major General Alexander Leslie, who arrived at Cornwallis's encampment on January 18 at about the same time that Tarleton and his shattered force rode in bearing the ill tidings from Cowpens. Leslie brought a regiment of 256 North Carolina loyalist volunteers, the 347-man von Bose Regiment of Hessians, 103 Hessian Jagers, and 690 men of the British Household Guards, a crack unit commanded by Brigadier General Charles O'Hara.

The other troops of Cornwallis's army were the 33rd Regiment, commanded by Lieutenant Colonel James Webster, the Royal Welsh Fusiliers (23rd Regiment), and the 2nd Battalion of Fraser's Highlanders (71st Regiment), whose comrades in the regiment's 1st Battalion had been lost by Tarleton at Cowpens. Also included were the survivors of Cowpens—200 mounted troopers of the British Legion, 40 men of the 17th Light Dragoons, and 100 infantrymen who had been guarding Tarleton's baggage.

On the morning of January 19, wasting no time, Cornwallis broke camp and led his army on a march to overtake and overpower the victors of Cowpens.

Cornwallis assumed Morgan would consolidate his position on the Broad River, using it as a base for a probable attack on the British outpost at Ninety Six. The assumption, which proved false, cost him two days as he marched his column off in the wrong direction. Realizing that Cornwallis's force outnumbered him and that he was in danger of being cut off from Greene's main body, Morgan had quickly moved out of the area of the Broad River, and some twelve hours before Cornwallis had begun his march of resolute pursuit, Morgan was already twenty miles northwest of Cowpens at Gilbert Town (Rutherfordton), North Carolina. There Morgan had been joined by Lieutenant Colonel William Washington's 3rd Light Dragoons and, careful to prevent the escape or rescue of his British prisoners, Morgan had turned them over to Washington to hurry out of Cornwallis's reach on the far side of the Catawba River. Cornwallis thus was already defeated in one important objective of his mission to overtake Morgan.

On January 21 Cornwallis realized his mistake. Tarleton's cavalrymen had discovered their quarry gone from Cowpens, and while encamped at Cherokee Ford, near the North Carolina line, Cornwallis learned that Morgan had left for Gilbert Town. He would resume the pursuit the next morning. "I shall march tomorrow with 1200 Infantry & the Cavalry to

THE BATTLE OF GUILFORD COURTHOUSE   273

attack or follow him to the banks of the Catawba," he wrote to his former aide Francis Rawdon. He ordered Tarleton's cavalrymen, the 33rd Regiment and the Guards to be prepared to move out at 6:30 the next morning. The remainder of his force would follow those forward units.

On the chill morning of January 22 Cornwallis resumed the chase, leaving behind his camp followers and part of his baggage train in order to speed the pursuit of his foe. On January 25 he reached Ramsour's Mill on the Little Catawba, west of the main course of the Catawba River. Morgan had passed through Ramsour's Mill two days earlier and on the 25th was encamped some twenty miles east of there, on the far side of the Catawba.

Impeded by his baggage train, Cornwallis now more than ever realized what Tarleton had lost at Cowpens, light, highly mobile troops that could launch an assault without the encumbrances that slowed fully equipped infantry accustomed to fighting only in traditional formations. The wagons that bore the equipment and supplies of Cornwallis's troops were making laborious, sluggish progress over crude clay roads transformed into gluey mires by nearly incessant winter rains. He would never catch Morgan at the rate he was going.

In mounting frustration, he decided to rid himself of his cumbersome baggage. "The loss of my light troops could only be remedied by the activity of the whole corps," he later explained to George Germain. To turn his whole corps into light troops, he ordered an enormous bonfire built, and into it went wagons, tents, trunks of clothing, supply chests, all the provisions that could not be carried by individual soldiers. Casks of rum were broken open and their savory contents emptied onto the ground. "Lord Cornwallis sett the example," Brigadier General O'Hara reported, "by burning all his Wagons, and destroying the greatest part of his Bagage, which was followed by every Officer of the Army without a murmur." Fine porcelain, china, silver tea services, silver flatware, bottles of wine, and all the other gentlemanly niceties that British officers customarily carried with them on campaigns went into the flames. The destruction continued for two days. All but several wagons needed to transport medical supplies, the wounded, ammunition, and salt were burned. Then Cornwallis's considerably lightened army resumed the pursuit. "In this situation," O'Hara wrote, "without Bagage, necessaries, or Provisions of any sort for Officer or Soldier, in the most barren inhospitable unhealthy part of North America, opposed to the most savage, inveterate perfidious cruel Enemy, with zeal and with Bayonets only, it was resolved to follow Green's Army to the end of the World."[1]

On January 28 Cornwallis led his army from Ramsour's Mill, headed directly east toward Beattie's Ford on the Catawba River, which he approached the next day. Two days of continuous rain was swelling the river, and by the morning of January 30, when Cornwallis's army stood poised to cross it, its madly rushing floodwaters rendered it impassable.

From the west bank of the Catawba Cornwallis could see Morgan's troops on the far side and he studied their defenses through a spyglass. By then the rain had ceased, the river was soon to start falling, he knew, and so Cornwallis daringly decided to wait twenty-four hours, then force a crossing.

Nathanael Greene had left the main body of his army under the command of Brigadier General Isaac Huger and given orders for him to march to Salisbury, North Carolina, some thirty miles northeast of Beattie's Ford, and there meet up with Morgan's force. Greene then had mounted his horse and in the company of a guide, an aide, and three dragoons had ridden a hundred miles to parley with Morgan on the east bank of the Catawba, in the literal face of his enemy.

In a council of war held sitting on a log, Greene conferred with Morgan, William Washington, and Brigadier General William Lee Davidson and decided to protect as best they could, for as long as they could, the crossing sites that Cornwallis might use. Davidson, commanding 800 militiamen, was given the assignment to guard those fords. He would be expected not to prevent Cornwallis's crossing, but only to delay it while the main body of Greene's army marched hurriedly to rendezvous at Salisbury with Morgan's men and the 280 cavalrymen of Lieutenant Colonel Henry (Light Horse Harry) Lee, summoned from eastern South Carolina by Greene days earlier and now presumably on their way. After their delaying action, Davidson's militiamen were to quickly withdraw and head for Salisbury also. At the conclusion of their twenty-minute war council, Greene and his party galloped off on the main road to Salisbury, to a farmhouse some sixteen miles away, from which he planned to direct the militia's withdrawal. Morgan and Washington left by another route.

Davidson promptly took measures to defend the fords likeliest to be used by Cornwallis. He left part of his force at Beattie's Ford and ordered his cavalry and about 250 infantrymen to march swiftly downriver and take a defensive position at Cowan's Ford, about four miles below Beattie's. There the river was about 500 yards wide, the water up to four feet deep and flowing swiftly. The path that Cornwallis must take through the river led from the west bank to a point about midway in the stream, where it split, one section continuing straight across, the other angling to the right to take advantage of shallower water farther downstream. The bank on either side was thickly wooded and steep.

At 1 a.m. on Thursday, February 1, Cornwallis's troops were rousted from their blankets to rise and prepare for the forced crossing of the Catawba. Cornwallis planned to employ a favorite tactic: He would use part of his force to create a diversion at the expected point of attack and take the remainder of his force around the enemy's flank to sweep in behind the enemy's defenses. He ordered Lieutenant Colonel Webster to take half the army, along with most of the artillery, and demonstrate opposite Morgan's position at Beattie's Ford, as if to cross there. At the same time, Cornwallis himself would take the other half of his army downriver to Cowan's Ford, which he expected to find only lightly defended, and cross there to outflank the rebels.

Leading some 1,200 British and German troops, Cornwallis reached Cowan's Ford around daybreak and through the misty fog that clung to the river he could see rebel campfires on the far side, many more than he had expected. Undaunted, and with characteristic courage and leadership, Cornwallis, astride a spirited mount, entered the water first. Behind him crept his brigade of Guards, their cartouche boxes fastened around their necks to keep their ammunition out of the water, their muskets unloaded but with bayonets fixed; then came his artillerymen with two three-pounders, then the Welsh Fusiliers, all of them easing their way into the rocky, chilling stream, the water soon rising to their chests, the current strong and dangerous.

From the far side then came shouts of alarm followed by sporadic gunfire from the Americans. The Catawba's current became an enemy also. Men and mounts lost their footing in the press of the current and were swept away in the fog, their futile cries shouted into the damp, cold air. The rebel fire was increasing, and there was blood in the water. Cornwallis's horse was hit by gunfire but managed to bear the general to the east bank before collapsing. The loyalist who had been guiding Cornwallis, apparently panicked by the strength of the stream and the hail of musket and rifle fire from the far bank, forsook Cornwallis and vanished, leaving Cornwallis's troops to trudge straight ahead into the deepest part of the ford instead of guiding them into the shallower water.

At last the far bank was reached, and Cornwallis's troops formed up, loaded their muskets and delivered a volley of fire as they advanced on the defenders in the woods. Brigadier General Davidson, seeing the British penetration at the ford's upper exit, sought to reinforce that position with men guarding the lower exit. As he dashed into the fray at the water's edge, he caught a rifle ball in his chest and fell dead. At that, his entire militia force lost heart, turned, and fled.

Upstream, at Beattie's Ford, Webster was able to cross unopposed, and soon Cornwallis's entire force, except for his casualties, was across the Catawba.

Unwilling to admit the true cost of the crossing, Cornwallis reported his losses as four killed and thirty-six wounded, figures at sharp odds with the reports of other eyewitnesses. Robert Henry, who lived in the area around Cowan's Ford and who had volunteered to serve with the militia in protecting the ford, returned to the river with some of his friends the day after the fighting and found fourteen corpses caught in a fish trap, "several of whom," he reported, "appeared to have no wound, but had drowned."[2] Henry reported that others who lived nearby and had visited the scene of combat agreed "that a great number of British dead were found on Thompson's fish-dam, and in his trap, and numbers lodged on brush, and drifted to the banks; that the river stunk with dead carcases; that the British could not have lost less than one hundred men on that occasion."

Once his army was across the Catawba, Cornwallis promptly reformed his column to continue his march. Tarleton, having seen the enemy run, reacted with pack-dog instinct and chased off after them. He caught up with some of them that afternoon at Torrence's Tavern, about ten miles north of Beattie's Ford, on the road to Salisbury. Tarleton reported that his Legion killed "near 50 on the spot, wounded many in pursuit, and dispersed near 500 of the enemy." The number of killed claimed by Tarleton was at wide variance with the report of another British officer, who said he did not see even ten dead.

While Tarleton was conducting his raid on Torrence's Tavern, Greene was but six miles away, at David Carr's farm, awaiting the retreating militia. Late that night a rider came to inform him that Davidson had been killed, that his militia had been scattered and put to flight, that Cornwallis's entire army had crossed the Catawba, and that Tarleton and his Legion were dangerously nearby. Greene promptly mounted his horse and galloped off into the night to the temporary safety of Salisbury, stopping finally at Steele's Tavern to rest a few hours. While there, he dispatched a message to Brigadier General Huger instructing him to march with the main body of the army to Guilford Courthouse instead of Salisbury.

The next day, February 2, with Morgan, Greene began his retreat to the Dan, the river that formed part of the boundary between North Carolina and Virginia. His strategy all along had been to stay ahead of Cornwallis and draw him farther and farther away from his sources of supplies and provisions until he, Greene, was able to turn and confront him at a place and time advantageous to Greene. Now Greene would withdraw all the way to Virginia, where his weary troops could be rested, his supplies and provisions could be replenished, and reinforcements for his army could be collected. Then he would deal with Cornwallis. To reach Virginia, though, he would have to negotiate three rivers, first the Yadkin, then the Haw, and finally the Dan, all of them engorged by nearly incessant rain. He must not be caught by Cornwallis at any of the three.

While hampering rains continued to fall, Cornwallis burned more of his wagons and baggage to provide additional horses to draw the remaining wagons over the miry clay roads. He had reunited the two halves of his army, separated at Beattie's Ford, along the road to Salisbury and now he ordered Brigadier General O'Hara to take a force of cavalry and mounted infantry and speed ahead of the main body and catch Greene and Morgan before they could get across the Yadkin.

When O'Hara's pursuing vanguard pounded up to the bank of the Yadkin at Trading Ford, it made three disappointing discoveries: the river there was too deep to ford; Greene, Morgan, and all of Morgan's troops except a rear guard of militia had already crossed; and the boats needed for O'Hara to make it across were all on the other side. Owing to the efforts of Colonel Thaddeus Kosciuszko, Greene's chief engineer, whom Greene had placed in charge of transportation, the Americans had safely crossed the Yadkin by boat on February 2 and 3 and were, for the time being, beyond the grasp of Cornwallis. Greene's rear guard of militia, some 150 men, when confronted by O'Hara's troops, scattered and retreated downriver, where they crossed the river in canoes left there for that purpose.

Cornwallis himself and the main body of his army reached the Yadkin on February 4, and apparently out of frustration, he ordered his artillery to assault the Americans' position on the opposite bank. His guns began hurling shot across the river, but without effect. On that same day, Greene, having learned that Cornwallis had sent Tarleton to try to find a ford where he could cross upstream of Trading Ford, ordered Morgan to take his Continentals and march to Guilford Courthouse, there to rendezvous with Huger and the other half of Greene's army.

The next day, February 5, Greene, taking note of Cornwallis's persistent eagerness to get at him, wrote to Huger saying that "from Lord Cornwallises pushing disposition, and the contempt he has for our Army, we may precipitate him into some capital misfortune."[3] That was his hope.

Tarleton found an unprotected crossing site upstream, Shallow Ford, about forty miles distant by road, and Cornwallis wheeled his column to the left and started his march over the sticky, wet, clay road to continue his pursuit. Riding in advance of the main army, Tarleton crossed the Yadkin at Shallow Ford on February 6. Cornwallis moved out to follow him on February 7, crossed the Yadkin and reached Salem, North Carolina on February 9.

At Guilford Courthouse, tough Dan Morgan, after weeks of suffering, decided he had had enough. Hindered by crippling arthritis, in agony with intensely painful sciatica and hemorrhoids, he asked for a leave. "I am much indisposed with pains," he wrote in a letter to Greene on February 6, "and to add to my misfortunes, am violently attacked with the piles, so that I can scarcely sit upon my horse. This is the first time that I ever experienced this disorder, and from the idea I had of it, sincerely prayed that I might never know what it was. When I set everything in as good a train as I can respecting provisions, etc., I shall move slowly to some safe retreat, and try to recover."[4] Greene granted him leave until he was able to return to the field. On February 10 Morgan painfully hoisted himself into a carriage and left Guilford Courthouse for his home in Virginia.

Surveying the terrain at Guilford Courthouse, Greene concluded it was a site where he might make a stand against Cornwallis. However, when he floated the idea past his senior officers in a council of war, they turned thumbs down on it. He then decided to resume his retreat to the Dan. He broke camp and with the main body of his army, including the half commanded by Huger, which had rejoined him, left Guilford Courthouse on February 10.

Greene's destination was Irwin's Ferry on the lower Dan, about seventy miles away, the site recommended by Lieutenant Colonel Edward Carrington, to whom Greene had given the job of finding a suitable crossing site and acquiring the boats needed to effect a crossing. At the same time that the main army moved out of Guilford Courthouse, bound for Irwin's Ferry, Colonel Otho Williams, now commanding Morgan's mounted units, also pulled out. His mission was to screen Greene's army from Cornwallis, to fend off Cornwallis's advance units and keep tabs on Cornwallis's movements.

On two or more occasions Cornwallis's advance guard caught up to and clashed with Williams's troops, but each time Williams managed to slip away. On February 14 Williams finally received the message he had been eagerly awaiting. It was from Greene and dated February 13: "All our troops are over and the stage is clear. . . . I am ready to receive you and give you a hearty welcome." According to one report, when Williams passed the message along to his troops, they broke out in cheers, loud enough to be heard by their British pursuers, who probably guessed what the cheering meant.

Williams ordered Henry Lee to form a rear guard and slow Cornwallis's advance unit, commanded by O'Hara, while the rest of Williams's troops dashed for Irwin's Ferry, which they reached at dusk and where they quickly began loading into boats. It was dark before the last of them were ferried over. Lee's mounted rear guard raced up to the crossing around 8 p.m. and were instructed to remove their saddles and have their horses swim across while the troopers boarded boats and were hurriedly carried to the other side.

O'Hara and his troop of pursuers, ranging in advance of Cornwallis's main body, arrived around daybreak the next morning. Too late. By then Greene's entire army had escaped to the far side of the impassable Dan, taking all available boats across with them. They were out of reach. Cornwallis had been thwarted again.

Cornwallis now faced up to his problems. He was unable to cross where the Americans had crossed. If he tried to force a crossing farther upstream, he would undoubtedly be opposed by Greene and suffer substantial losses if not total defeat. Now that he was in Virginia, Greene would be reinforced and his supplies replenished and he would become stronger than ever, while at the same time Cornwallis, his supply line increasingly attenuated, would grow weaker. He had burned his tents and most of his supplies and equipment, all for nought, and his shelterless, wet, cold, hungry troops, their brilliant uniforms now tattered and stained with soil, were weary and suffering from their days of frantic, futile pursuit. He had driven them practically to the breaking point, under severe conditions, and now that he had reached a dead end, he realized that he must, for the time being, give up the chase and do what he could to restore his exhausted army. To Francis Rawdon, Cornwallis admitted that "the fatigue of our troops and the hardships which they suffered were excessive." He decided to march southeast back to Hillsborough, where he hoped to receive welcome and sustenance from the town's loyalist population.

By February 18 Greene had become eager to return to action, his army refreshed and resupplied by the bounty of Fairfax County, Virginia. His first move then was to send Light Horse Harry Lee, with his legion and two companies of Maryland Continentals, back across the Dan to help Andrew Pickens and his militia interrupt Cornwallis's communication lines, harass British foraging parties, and suppress possible loyalist uprisings that might occur when it became common knowledge that the patriot army had left North Carolina. Two days later, on February 20, he sent Otho Williams and his light infantry back across the Dan. At about the same time, Greene himself, escorted by a detail of William Washington's dragoons, recrossed the river to meet with Lee and Pickens and apprise them of his latest plan to move the rest of his army back into North Carolina and take it to Guilford Courthouse. He had not given up on his idea of making a stand there.

On February 23 Greene led the main body of his army back across the Dan River. He was still awaiting additional reinforcements, before taking a position at Guilford Courthouse, but in the meantime he would support the troops of Pickens and Williams, moving toward Hillsborough as he did so.

In Hillsborough, Cornwallis failed to find the sustenance that he had hoped for. He decided he would shift his army to a more promising location and on February 27 he moved to an encampment site south of Alamance Creek, near a junction of roads that led west to Guilford Courthouse, east to Hillsborough and southeast toward Wilmington.

For the next two weeks the two armies maneuvered, sparred, and waited, with no significant action taking place. During that interval, Greene's army increased. Four hundred Continental regulars commanded by Colonel Richard Campbell arrived. Two brigades of Virginia militiamen, one commanded by Brigadier General Edward Stevens, the other by Brigadier General Robert Lawson, arrived, a total of some 1,700 men. Two brigades of North Carolina militia, some 1,060 men, also arrived, led by Brigadier General John Butler and Colonel Pinketham Eaton. Greene's army now totaled 4,400 fighting men.

Greene was certain that if he showed Cornwallis that he was ready to make a stand, Cornwallis would rush to accept the challenge, with more eagerness now than earlier perhaps, following his weeks of frustration. Greene was at last ready to make that stand, and at the spot he had long favored. On Wednesday, March 14, 1781, he marched his troops to Guilford Courthouse and there began to establish the position he would defend against the army of Lord Cornwallis.

The Guilford County courthouse stood starkly in a large clearing on high ground, virtually surrounded by woods, the centerpiece of the community of Guilford Courthouse, where some 100 people lived. Cornwallis would approach it from the south, on the road from New Garden. The road emerged from a defile between heavily wooded hillsides, crossed a stream and entered a clearing, then twisted slightly to the right, then to the left and to the right again, then entered another woods, climbing a gradual slope, and emerged once again in an L-shaped clearing. At the top of the L stood the courthouse.

On his way home to Virginia, Dan Morgan had written to Greene on February 20, giving him the benefit of his experience at Cowpens and suggesting Greene deploy his troops in the same three-tiered defense that had succeeded against Tarleton at Cowpens. He also wrote words of warning about militias. "If they fight, you will beat Cornwallis," Morgan said. "If not, he will beat you, and perhaps cut your regulars to pieces." Morgan's suggestion to his commander was to "put the militia in the centre, with some picked troops in their rear, with orders to shoot down the first man that runs"—a grim indication of the importance Morgan attached to the showdown with Cornwallis.

Greene accepted only some of Morgan's advice (not the grimmest part). He deployed his troops in three parallel lines, as Morgan had. In the front line he placed two North Carolina militia brigades of some 500 men each, one commanded by Brigadier General Butler, on the right side of the line, the other commanded by Colonel Eaton, on the left. The right flank of the first line was protected by William Washington's troops, his cavalry on the extreme right, two companies of infantry between the cavalry and the North Carolina militiamen. On the left side of the front line Greene placed Light Horse Harry Lee's legion, cavalry on the extreme left, infantry between them and the militiamen. Those two flanking wings were angled out, like the handlebars of a bicycle, to allow an enfilading fire on the advancing enemy. In the center of the front line, in the roadway, Greene placed two six-pounder artillery pieces.

In the second line, positioned in the woods, about 300 yards to the rear of the first, Greene posted the two Virginia militia brigades, each with about 600 men, the one commanded by Brigadier General Edward Stevens taking positions on the right side of the road, the one commanded by Brigadier General Robert Lawson on the left side.

The third line, like Morgan's third line at Cowpens, was the main line of defense and was positioned about 550 yards behind and a little to the right of the second line. Greene put it in that right-rear position to take best advantage of high ground on the west side of the courthouse. Manning it were two brigades of Continentals, one composed of 778 Virginia regulars and commanded by Isaac Huger, the other the 630 Maryland regulars commanded by Otho Williams. At the center of the third line Greene placed his other two six-pounders.

Greene's deployment scheme included no reserve force.

As Morgan had done with his militia at Cowpens, Greene told his militiamen to get off two rounds and then fall back. Unlike the situation at Cowpens, however, where Morgan's militia filed off to their left and then reformed, these militiamen would have to withdraw into woods if they moved to their left, and there it could be expected that they would disappear from the field of battle. Anticipating that likelihood, Greene instructed them to withdraw into the second line and instructed the Virginians of the second line to open their ranks to permit the North Carolinians to pass through. Greene also instructed the troops on the flanks of the first line to fall back to the flanks of the second line.

On the clear, cold, cloudless morning of Thursday, March 15, 1781, satisfied that all was in readiness, all troops in position and informed about what they were to do, Major General Nathanael Greene turned his mount and rode to his command post at the rear of his main line of defense, there to await the arrival of his enemy.

His intelligence reports told Cornwallis, falsely, that he was facing an American army numbering between 9,000 and 10,000 men. His army totaled about 2,000. The disparity made no difference to Cornwallis, so certain was he that his troops, all veteran professional soldiers, would outmatch the Americans. Of Greene's 4,400 troops, 1,762 were Continentals, the American army's regular soldiers. The rest were militiamen. Most would be seeing combat for the first time.

At five o'clock on the morning of March 15, Cornwallis's troops broke camp at New Garden, about twelve miles southeast of Guilford Courthouse, and, without taking time for breakfast, began a cold march to where Greene's army lay in wait. In the vanguard was a 450-man force commanded by Banastre Tarleton, both cavalry and infantry.

Around 7:15 a.m., about seven miles up the road, Tarleton's lead element came up against a detachment of Light Horse Harry Lee's legion, posted as a screening force for Greene's main body. The detachment immediately opened fire on Tarleton's dragoons, and its commanding officer, a Lieutenant Heard, raced back to report to Lee on Tarleton's approach. Lee quickly pulled his men back to find a strong defensive position from which to delay the British advance. When Tarleton's troops approached Lee's new position along a lane with fences on either side, Lee ordered a charge that resulted in a fierce skirmish in which Tarleton's entire advance unit was wiped out, some thirty men, either killed or captured, and Tarleton was hit by a gunshot that took away the middle and index fingers on his right hand. Tarleton then turned his main force around and swiftly withdrew. Lee's cavalrymen pursued them until Tarleton's troops rejoined Cornwallis's main body, then gave up the chase and returned to the Americans' position at Guilford Courthouse. Lee's troops suffered no casualties in the skirmish.

About 1:30 p.m. Cornwallis's lead element debouched from the woods that flanked the road from New Garden south of Guilford Courthouse. Now Cornwallis saw for the first time the terrain of the battlefield. The road dipped to a small stream, Little Horsepen Creek, then began to rise. Here were open fields on both sides of the road, but as the road climbed, it passed through woods again, less dense on the right side of the road than on the left. Cornwallis halted and ordered his army to deploy in preparation for assaulting the American positions. He decided to form his ranks to favor the right side of the road, intending to hit hardest at that side of the enemy line, where the woods at the far end of the clearing were less dense and more suited to an attack.

He placed the 33rd Regiment on the left side of his line, and the Royal Welsh Fusiliers (23rd Regiment) next to it, both regiments commanded by Lieutenant Colonel James Webster. To their right he placed the 2nd Battalion of Fraser's Highlanders and the von Bose Hessian regiment, which anchored the right side of his line. Those units were commanded by Major General Alexander Leslie. Behind the left side of the line Cornwallis placed the 2nd Guards Battalion, the grenadier and light-infantry Guards companies, and the Jagers in support of the left side. In support behind the right side of the line he positioned the 1st Guards Battalion. Cornwallis positioned his artillery pieces on the road, between the right and left wings of his army. In reserve were the British Legion dragoons, commanded by Tarleton despite his wounded hand. They were posted in column formation on the roadway.

Seeing the redcoats begin to deploy, Captain Anthony Singleton of the Continental artillery, commanding the artillery pieces at the center of the Americans' front line, opened fire with his two six-pounders. Their rounds were quickly answered by fire from Cornwallis's three-pounders. Neither side effected much damage during a twenty-minute artillery duel.

To the shrill wail of their bagpipes, beneath their faded regimental colors, bayonets fixed, Cornwallis's troops spread out across the muddy, rain-soaked harvested cornfields on either side of the road and began to advance on the rebel line. As the redcoats drew to within 150 yards of the Americans' line, the North Carolina militia manning the first line opened fire with devastating effect. One eyewitness, British Captain Dugald Stuart, reported that "one half of the Highlanders dropt on the spot."

Another British eyewitness, Sergeant Robert Lamb of the Welsh Fusiliers, wrote that the Americans' "whole force had their arms presented and resting on a rail fence [at the far end of the cornfields]. . . . They were taking aim with the nicest precision. . . . At this awful period a general pause took place; both parties surveyed each other for the moment with the most anxious suspence. . . . Colonel Webster rode forward in front of the 23rd Regiment and said with more than even his usual commanding voice (which was well known to his brigade), 'Come on, my brave Fuzileers!' This operated like an inspiring voice; they rushed forward amidst the enemy's fire; dreadful was the havoc on both sides. At last the Americans gave way. . . ."[5]

After getting off three volleys as instructed, though not all did, the North Carolina militiamen quit the field and ran off, not to reinforce the second line, as had been done at Cowpens, but to flee and vanish into the deep woods behind them. Several officers, including Light Horse Harry Lee, tried to stop them, but in vain. Captain Singleton, in charge of the two artillery pieces in the front line, hitched his teams of horses to the pieces and hastened back to the third line with them.

Cornwallis's commanders were delayed in pursuing the routed North Carolinians, for they still faced Captain Robert Kirkwood's Delaware Company and Captain Charles Lynch's Virginia riflemen on their left, and on their right they faced Colonel William Campbell's riflemen and Lee's infantry, all of whom had remained steadfast on the flanks of the first line and who were now delivering a withering, enfilading fire on the attackers.

Webster turned the 33rd Regiment and the Jagers to the left to face the American right flank head-on, while the von Bose regiment turned to attack Lee's infantrymen and the Virginia troops of William Campbell. To prevent a gap created in the center of the British line, Cornwallis ordered his support units to advance into his forward line, thereby throwing his entire reserve, except for Tarleton's cavalry, into the assault.

The battle moved into the woods at the north end of the clearing. On the British left, Webster's units pressed Lynch's Virginia riflemen, Kirkwood's

Delaware regulars and Washington's cavalry and forced them back. On the British right, Lee's and Campbell's units were pushed back, but instead of withdrawing to Greene's second line of defense, they bent their end of the first line into the woods, exacting an enormous cost from the von Bose regiment and the British 1st Guards Battalion and drawing them deeper into the thick woods, separating them and themselves from the main battle, which now was shifting to the second line, also in the woods, far to the right of Lee's and Campbell's units.

Cornwallis, in the forefront of the action with his men, had his horse shot from under him and was brought a new mount, a dragoon's horse that was dragging its saddlebags under its belly, impeding its movement in the thick underbrush of the woods. But the fighting was so intense that Cornwallis took no notice or refused to take time to adjust them.

British Lieutenant Colonel Webster, apparently eager to smash the second line, although its flanks had already been flung back or dispersed, decided to throw his Fusiliers against the center of the defenders' line. There waiting for him was the 1st Maryland Regiment, one of Greene's best units. The Marylanders watched as Webster's troops formed up for the attack some 200 yards in front of them and began their charge. When the redcoats were within 100 feet of them, the Marylanders opened fire, delivering a murderous volley, then sprang from their defensive positions to counterattack with bayonets, forcing Webster and his troops back.

Cornwallis himself now came up to lead a new assault, the regrouped redcoats stepping over and around the bodies of their fallen comrades, the dead and the dying, as they charged once more toward the American line. Taking more losses, Cornwallis's persistent fighters managed to press the defenders back and at last emerged from the woods and into the clearing immediately to the south of the courthouse. As they came out of the woods, they could see, a few hundred yards in front of them, a third line of defenders, uniformed in the blue and buff of American Continentals, waiting for them, watching them advance past all obstacles.

The sight of the scarlet-coated British fighting men steadily advancing, undaunted and unrelenting, muskets and menacing steel bayonets in their hands, threw the green troops of the 5th Maryland Regiment into panic, and they broke and ran without firing a shot. British Lieutenant Colonel James Stuart, who had taken over command for Webster after Webster was wounded, quickly sent his Guards into the gap where the 5th Maryland had been, swiftly sweeping into the defenders and seizing the two six-pounders emplaced in the third line.

Before Stuart could further press his advance, however, his Guards were hit by two counterattacks, the first by William Washington's dragoons, who struck the Guards from their rear, riding through them and slashing them down with sabers, then turning their mounts around and dashing and slashing back through the Guards' broken formation. Lieutenant Colonel Howard, seizing the opportunity for a rout, then led the 1st Maryland Regiment and the Delaware regulars in a bayonet charge against the reeling Guardsmen. In the fierce, hand-to-hand combat that ensued, Lieutenant Colonel Stuart, commanding the Guards, fell under the sword of Marylander Captain John Smith and was killed. Smith was then shot in the back of the head by a Guardsman, but survived.

Cornwallis now emerged from the woods and into the clearing where the center of his line was under a ferocious assault, in a death struggle with a violent enemy, and in danger of being annihilated. In desperation, to break the dominance of the rebels, Cornwallis ordered British Lieutenant John McLeod to load his artillery pieces with grapeshot and fire into the mass of struggling fighting men, British and Americans alike. When McLeod hesitated, Cornwallis repeated the order, over the protestations of wounded Brigadier General O'Hara, and as the cannons blasted the lethal loads of grapeshot into the confused mass of fighters, slaughtering as many redcoats as Americans, those who escaped being hit immediately disengaged and scattered out of the line of fire, hurrying back to the protection of their lines. The field before Cornwallis was thus cleared. He had averted an imminent disaster, another Cowpens.

Cornwallis himself described the final minutes of the battle:

> By the spirited exertions of Brig. Gen'l. O'Hara, though wounded, the 2d battalion of the guards was soon rallied, and, supported by the grenadiers, returned to the charge with the greatest alacrity. The 23d regiment arriving at that instant from our left, and Lt. Colonel Tarleton having advanced with part of the cavalry, the enemy were soon put to flight. . . .
>
> About this time the 33d regiment and light infantry of the guards, after overcoming many difficulties, completely routed the corps which was opposed to them, and put an end to the action in this quarter. The 23d and 71st regiments, with part of the cavalry, were ordered to pursue; the remainder of the cavalry was detached with Lt. Colonel Tarleton to our right, where a heavy fire still contin-

ued, and where his appearance and spirited attack contributed much to a speedy termination of the action.

The militia, with which our right had been engaged, dispersed in the woods; the Continentals went off by the Reedy Fork [Road], beyond which it was not in my power to follow them, as their cavalry had suffered but little. Our troops were excessively fatigued by an action which lasted an hour and a half; and our numerous wounded, dispersed over an extensive space of country, required immediate attention."[6]

At 3:30 p.m. Greene ordered his troops to withdraw from the battlefield. The 4th Virginia Regiment, commanded by Colonel John Green, was ordered to cover the withdrawal, which, according to one account, was "conducted with order and regularity."

In abandoning the field, Greene was conceding defeat. But what he had lost was only the Battle of Guilford Courthouse. He had not lost his army, which had been Cornwallis's prime objective. In that important matter, Greene had defeated Cornwallis.

Greene had lost 79 killed and 184 wounded at Guilford Courthouse. Missing were 1,046, but 885 of those were militiamen who had fled the battlefield and gone home. Greene's army had suffered a casualty rate of 6 percent.

Cornwallis, on the other hand, with a much smaller force, had suffered a casualty rate of 27 percent. The casualties included 93 killed in action and 413 wounded, some 50 of whom died of their wounds during the night. Twenty-six were missing.

Greene marched off to the west, halted temporarily to collect some of his stragglers, then resumed the march, continuing through the night and the cold and the rain until he reached his former encampment site at the Speedwell Iron Works on Troublesome Creek. At Troublesome Creek Greene reported that his men "are in the highest spirits and wishing for another opportunity of engaging the enemy." Cornwallis's victory, he wrote, "was made at so great an expense that I hope it may yet effect their ruin."

Cornwallis encamped on the battlefield he had just paid so dearly to occupy. He remained there with his shattered army till March 18, when he marshaled his hardy survivors, loaded seventeen wagons with his wounded, forsook the bloodied ground he had so recently won, and began a withdrawal to the refuge of Wilmington, North Carolina.

One of Cornwallis's officers, Francis Dundas, wrote home telling what he felt about the battle he and his comrades had just won.

> I wish it had produced one substantial benefit to Great Britain, on the contrary, we feel at the moment the sad and fatal effects our loss on that Day, nearly one half of our best Officers and Soldiers were either killed or wounded, and what remains are so completely worn out by the excessive Fatigues of the campaign, in a march of above a thousand miles, most of them barefoot, naked and for days together living upon Carrion which they had often not time to dress, and three or four ounces of ground Indian corn has totally destroyed this Army—entre nous, the Spirit of our little army has evaporated a good deal. . . .[7]

Cornwallis was undeterred. Soon after arriving in Wilmington on April 7, following a grueling three-week march (during which Lieutenant Colonel Webster died of his wounds), he wrote to Major General William Phillips, newly posted by Clinton to the Chesapeake area, and said:

> Now my dear friend, what is our plan? Without one we cannot succeed, and I assure you that I am quite tired of marching about the country in quest of adventure. If we mean an offensive war in America, we must abandon New York and bring our whole force into Virginia; we then have a stake to fight for, and a successful battle may give us America. If our plan is defensive, mixed with desultory expeditions, let us quit the Carolinas (which cannot be held defensively while Virginia can be so easily armed against us) and stick to our salt pork and New York, sending now and then a detachment to steal tobacco, etc.[8]

He wrote to his commander, Henry Clinton, breaking his long silence, proposing that New York be abandoned for the sake of a different strategy. He also wrote to Lord George Germain in London, urging the same thing. Cornwallis was not going to give up his quest for victory in America.

The Virginia Campaign

When he learned that Cornwallis had left Guilford Courthouse and was withdrawing his battered army to the south, Greene struck camp and gave chase, hoping to lure him into another fight. "We shall follow them immediately," he wrote to Daniel Morgan, "with a determination for another brush."

He ordered Light Horse Harry Lee to speed his legion ahead of the main body of troops and find out Cornwallis's location and condition and harry the flanks of the British column. Lee discovered Cornwallis encamped beside Deep River at Ramsey's Mill, but by the time Greene reached the site, on March 29, Cornwallis had already crossed the river and was on his way to Cross Creek, whence he had pushed on to Wilmington.

The enlistments of many of Greene's men would soon be up, his troops were tired and without adequate provisions, and forage was virtually impossible to find in the wake of Cornwallis's half-starved army, which was plundering the countryside as it withdrew. Faced with those conditions, Greene gave up his pursuit of Cornwallis.

"I am at a loss what is best to be done," he wrote to his commander in chief.[1] But he knew what he wanted to do. "I am determined to carry the war immediately into South Carolina," he told Washington. "The enemy will be obliged to follow us, or give up their posts in that state. If the former takes place, it will draw the war out of this state [North Carolina] and give it an opportunity to raise its proportion of men. If they [the British] leave their posts to fall, they must lose more there than they can gain here. If we continue in this state, the enemy will hold their possessions in both."

With that resolve, Greene made plans to dislodge the invaders from their strongholds in Camden, Ninety Six, and Georgetown and from their fortifications along the Santee and Congaree Rivers—Fort Watson, Fort Motte, and Fort Granby—as well as from their outpost in Augusta, Georgia. Altogether, some 8,000 British troops were garrisoned at those posts. To succeed, Greene would need to augment his army with the partisan forces of Generals Thomas Sumter, Andrew Pickens, and Francis Marion. He promptly sent word to them of his plans, with instructions to take care that none but their fellow generals should know of the plans, lest Cornwallis quickly counter them with moves of his own.

Cornwallis and his wounded army, recovering in Wilmington, were never far from Greene's mind. He had to consider the possibility that Cornwallis would turn his attention anew to Virginia, where the Marquis de Lafayette had recently arrived with a force of Continentals. In the meantime, Greene ordered Brigadier General Jethro Sumner and his North Carolina militiamen to cover his rear against a possible threat from Cornwallis as Greene moved southward into the heartland of South Carolina.

Cornwallis at the same time was busy preparing to do what Greene suspected he would do. He was comfortably headquartered in the home of loyalist Judge Joshua Wright, set imposingly on the corner of Third and Market Streets, near the Wilmington riverfront, where he and his staff were entertained and served tea by Judge and Mrs. Wright's charming daughters. (One of the daughters became smitten with one of Cornwallis's young officers, and the two of them lovingly scratched their initials on a window in the house.) For a while Cornwallis apparently considered marching south to reinforce Rawdon at Camden, who by now, he knew, would soon be facing the threat of Greene's southward-moving army. But his devotion to the idea of a campaign into Virginia overruled direct assistance for Rawdon.

Cornwallis was convinced that Virginia was the key to success in his war against the colonies. It was the vital link between His Majesty's forces in the north and those in the south and control of it would permit free movement and the massing of British armies anywhere along the Atlantic seaboard. It would also bar the movement of Washington's armies between the northeast and the south. Furthermore, Virginia was relatively untouched by despoliation by either army, British or American, and offered a rich supply of food and provisions for His Majesty's forces. At the same time, control of Virginia would choke off supplies of men, food, and matériel to Greene's forces. Conquest and control of Virginia, Cornwallis believed, was a strategic must if Britain was to win the war and regain her colonies.

On April 23 he wrote to George Germain, the British government's secretary of state for the colonies, to rationalize his decision to move into Virginia:

> My Lord, I yesterday received an express . . . [that] . . . brought me the disagreeable accounts that the upper posts of South Carolina were in the most imminent danger from an alarming spirit of revolt among many of the people and by a movement of General Greene's army. . . .
>
> The distance from hence to Camden, the want of forage and subsistence on the greatest part of the road, and the difficulty of passing the Pee Dee, when opposed by an enemy, render it utterly impossible for me to give immediate assistance. And I apprehend a possibility of the utmost hazard to this little corps, without the chance of a benefit, in the attempt. For if we are so unlucky as to suffer a severe blow in South Carolina, the spirit of revolt in that province would become very general, and the numerous rebels in this province [North Carolina] be encouraged to be more than ever active and violent. This might enable General Greene to hem me in among the great rivers and by cutting off our subsistence render our arms useless. And to remain here for transports to carry us off . . . would lose our cavalry and be otherways ruinous and disgraceful to Britain. . . .
>
> I have, therefore, under so many embarrassing circumstances (but looking upon Charleston as safe from any immediate attack from the rebels) resolved to take advantage of General Greene's having left the back part of Virginia open and march immediately into that province to attempt a junction with General Phillips. . . .[2]

Then, anticipating the negative reaction of his commander to his intention to invade Virginia, Cornwallis covered himself by penning a letter to Clinton:

> Sir, I have the honor to inclose . . . copies of all my letters to the Secretary of State. As they contain the most exact account of every transaction of the campaign . . . of my great apprehensions from the movement of General Greene . . . and my resolutions in consequence of it, I have nothing to add to it for your Excellency's satisfaction.

Neither my cavalry or infantry are in readiness to move. The former are in want of everything, the latter of every necessary but shoes, of which we have received an ample supply. I must, however, begin my march tomorrow. It is very disagreeable to me to decide upon measures so very important and of such consequence to the general conduct of the war, without an opportunity of procuring your Excellency's directions or approbation; but the delay and difficulty of conveying letters, and the impossibility of waiting for answers render it indispensably necessary.[3]

Clinton's opinion was that until he could spare additional troops from New York to assist Cornwallis and could be promised more reinforcements by Germain, Cornwallis should hold up on his plans for a major campaign into Virginia. Despite knowing that was his commander's wish and instruction, Cornwallis persisted.

On April 24 he led his refreshed army of 1,435 men out of Wilmington, bound for Virginia.

Available to him in the area of the Chesapeake were some 5,500 troops, approximately 2,000 of whom were under the command of Benedict Arnold, now a brigadier general in the British army, and the remainder commanded by Major General William Phillips. Clinton had first sent Arnold, then Phillips, to the Chesapeake with instructions to harass the rebel troops in the area, thereby creating diversions from Cornwallis's operations in South Carolina. They were also to establish a naval base, preferably at Portsmouth. Both Arnold and Phillips had been active in carrying out their harassment assignments in eastern Virginia.

Cornwallis wrote to Phillips informing him of his plan to march into Virginia and telling him he would join forces with him at Petersburg, Virginia. When he reached Petersburg on May 20, however, he learned that Phillips had died of typhoid fever a week earlier and Arnold had taken over Phillips's command.

On May 24, now commanding an army of some 7,500 men, Cornwallis marched out of Petersburg, crossed the James River at Westover, then proceeded to Hanover Junction, where he arrived on June 1 and promptly began establishing a base of operations.

To contest his taking control of Virginia were 1,200 American Continental troops—three regiments of light infantry—and about 2,000 Virginia militiamen and 40 dragoons from what had been Pulaski's legion, all under the command of Lafayette, sent by Washington to defend Virginia against

Arnold's depradations. Lafayette was expecting to be reinforced by Brigadier General Anthony Wayne's Pennsylvania regulars and by 500 Continentals still undergoing training with Steuben, but for the present he was woefully outmanned. And he was dangerously close to the enemy, a mere twenty-five miles away in Richmond when Cornwallis reached Petersburg.

With his plan well under way, Cornwallis wrote to Clinton to tell him what he now intended to do:

> I shall now proceed to dislodge Lafayette from Richmond and with my light troops to destroy any magazines or stores in the neighborhood. . . . Thence I propose to move to the Neck at Williamsburg, which is represented as healthy and where some subsistence may be procured, and keep myself unengaged from operations which might interfere with your plan for the campaign, until I have the satisfaction of hearing from you.[4]

Aware of Cornwallis's presence and his strength, Lafayette quickly shifted his position to avoid him. "Was I to fight a battle," he wrote to Washington on May 24 (in less than perfect English), "I'll be cut to pieces, the militia dispersed, and the arms lost. Was I to decline fighting, the country would think herself given up. I am therefore determined to scarmish, but not to engage too far and particularly to take care against their immense and excellent body of horse whom the militia fears like so many wild beasts. . . ."[5] He fell back seventy miles to Ely's Ford on the Rapidan River, reaching there on June 4.

Cornwallis marched after him, but only for thirty miles, giving up the pursuit at the North Anna River, where Cornwallis decided to make mischief elsewhere. He ordered Lieutenant Colonel John Graves Simcoe to conduct a cavalry attack on Steuben's trainees and sent Tarleton with 250 mounted troops to conduct a raid on Charlottesville, where the Virginia legislature was meeting with the governor, Thomas Jefferson. Neither raid amounted to much, for Steuben withdrew his troops and avoided a fight, and Jefferson and his legislature, warned of Tarleton's approach, fled to safety, though a few unlucky legislators managed to fall into Tarleton's hands. Unwilling to let the mission go for nought, before rejoining Cornwallis, Tarleton destroyed a trainload of goods, including uniforms, about 1,000 muskets, a supply of gunpowder, and several barrels of tobacco, all meant for Greene's troops.

Lafayette at last was joined by Wayne, which added three regiments of infantry and an artillery unit to his command. Three days after Wayne's arrival, Lafayette was further reinforced by 600 riflemen under the command of Brigadier General William Campbell of the Virginia militia. Also added to his growing army were 425 Virginia Continentals commanded by Colonel Christian Febiger, plus some 2,100 Virginia militiamen. Lafayette now commanded an army totaling more than 5,000 men, including two Continental artillery units with ten artillery pieces, and a 120-man cavalry. The foe Cornwallis faced suddenly became a formidable force.

Cornwallis now turned his columns around and withdrew back to Richmond, arriving there on June 16. He then left Richmond on June 20 to march to Williamsburg, at the upper end of a peninsula that juts into the lower end of Chesapeake Bay, between the James and York Rivers. Lafayette, further reinforced by Steuben's troops, guardedly followed at a distance of up to 20 miles.

At Williamsburg Cornwallis received a message from Clinton saying that captured dispatches showed that the Americans were planning a siege of New York and that Cornwallis should immediately send 3,000 of his troops to aid Clinton in defending the British position there. He further instructed Cornwallis to take a defensive position in either Yorktown or Williamsburg. Although it killed his present hope of conquering Virginia, it was an instruction Cornwallis felt he could not ignore.

To send Clinton the requested troops, Cornwallis on July 4 marched his army to Jamestown Ford, where he could cross the James River and march to Portsmouth, the port of embarkation for the troops bound for New York. In the process of crossing, Cornwallis saw an opportunity to lure Lafayette into a battle on the bank of the James. Lafayette later described the event:

> A warm action took place between the English army and the advance guard [of Lafayette's forces], whom Lafayette had ordered to the attack whilst they [the British] were crossing the river. Lord Cornwallis had stationed the first troops on the other side, to give the appearance as if the greatest number of the troops had already passed over the river. Although every person was unanimous in asserting that this was the case, Lafayette himself suspected the deception and quitted his detachment to make observations upon a tongue of land from whence he could more easily view the passage of the

enemy. A cannon, exposed doubtless intentionally, tempted General Wayne, a brave and enterprising officer.

Lafayette found, on his return, the [American] advance guard engaged in action with a very superior force. He withdrew it, however, (after a short but extremely warm conflict) in good order. . . .[6]

Wayne, with a detachment of 900 troops, had taken Cornwallis's bait and got into trouble when Cornwallis had sprung the trap. Quickly discovering the ruse, Wayne leaped to the offensive and ordered his troops to charge through grapeshot and musket fire, stopping the advancing redcoats long enough to make an orderly withdrawal to Green Spring, where Wayne's reserve was waiting, then during the night the detachment fell back to Chickahominy Church. Wayne lost 28 killed, 99 wounded, and 12 missing. He also lost two artillery pieces. Cornwallis lost 75 killed and wounded.

With his army having crossed the James and on its way to Portsmouth, Cornwallis on July 8 received a letter from Clinton dated June 28 in which he instructed Cornwallis to send a force not to New York but to Philadelphia, where Clinton was planning a raid to destroy rebel supplies. After the raid, Cornwallis's troops were to join Clinton's force and return to New York. Cornwallis immediately replied to Clinton, stating his opposition to the Philadelphia action. He then resumed his march toward Portsmouth to meet the transport ships that were to carry his troops to New York or to Philadelphia.

His approach to Portsmouth was by way of Suffolk, about fifteen miles southwest of Portsmouth, and he arrived there on July 12. In Suffolk he received three more letters from Clinton, dated May 29, June 8, and June 19, all written before the one ordering him to send troops to Philadelphia. In them Clinton emphasized the danger of an American attack on New York. "The enemy will certainly attack this Post," he wrote. If he didn't before, Cornwallis now could see Clinton's instability, yet he was bound to carry out the order of June 28, the last one issued.

On July 20, with preparations for the embarkation completed and the troops starting to board the transports in Portsmouth harbor, Cornwallis at 1 p.m. received a new message from his vacillating commander:

I have received your lordship's letter of the 30th June and the admiral [Marriot Arbuthnot] has dispatched a frigate with his and my opinions in answer to it. I cannot be more explicit by this opportunity than to desire that, if you have not already passed the James

River you will continue on the Williamsburg Neck until he arrives with my dispatches to Capt. Stapleton. If you have passed it and find it expedient to recover that station, you will please to do it and keep possession until you hear further from me. Whatever troops may have been embarked by you for this place [New York] are likewise to remain untill further orders. And if they should have been sailed and within your call you will be pleased to stop them. It is the admiral's and my wish at all events to hold Old Point Comfort which secures Hampton Road.[7]

Under Clinton's new directive, Cornwallis would keep his army intact but would use it to secure a British naval base at the mouth of Chesapeake Bay. On July 21, the day after receiving that order, Cornwallis received another letter from Clinton. This one informed him that Admiral Arbuthnot had been replaced by Admiral Thomas Graves, who, Clinton wrote, agreed with him on the importance of a secure naval base at Old Point Comfort. Clinton told Cornwallis that he could fortify Yorktown if he believed doing so would provide the necessary security for the naval station that was to be established at Old Point Comfort.

In apparent frustration, Cornwallis wrote to Admiral Graves and pointed out the absurdity of Clinton's instructions. "He [Clinton] thought a secure harbour for line of Battle ships of so much importance in the Chesapeake," Cornwallis wrote, "that he wished me to possess one even if it should occupy all the force at present in Virginia."[8]

Meanwhile, the engineer whom Cornwallis had sent to study Old Point Comfort and assess its suitability as a naval base returned to report it unsuitable for defense. To construct necessary earthworks fortifications, soil would have to be transported from distant sites. What was more, there was no bay or inlet in which the British ships could find shelter under the protection of the fortification's guns. To make sure that the engineer was correct in his evaluation, Cornwallis himself, accompanied by the captains of the British ships then anchored in Hampton Road, visited the site. To a man they agreed that Old Point Comfort was not a suitable site.

Cornwallis continued to receive letters from Clinton emphasizing the need for a naval base on the Chesapeake. On July 26 Cornwallis wrote to Clinton and told him there was really no good location for a naval station in the area and that Yorktown, on the south side of the York River, and Gloucester, opposite Yorktown on the north side, were the least problematic sites. They were, he said, the only places where ships requiring deep water could safely anchor. To build the necessary fortifications at either of the sites would require many men, an army in fact.

Cornwallis then committed himself and his army to the erection of the necessary fortifications, to the feeding of his army while it labored, and to its protection from the enemy. He marshaled his forces and loaded them onto the transports originally intended to carry his troops to New York. He then sailed from Portsmouth. On August 2 he disembarked his army at Yorktown and Gloucester and began building fortifications.

Lafayette, nearby and carefully observing Cornwallis's movements, became nearly ecstatic over the developments that had returned Cornwallis's army to Yorktown. In his memoirs he recounted his feelings:

> The English army pursued its route to Portsmouth; it then returned by water to take its station at Yorktown and Gloucester upon the York River. A garrison still remained at Portsmouth. Lafayette made some demonstrations of attack, and that garrison united itself to the body of the army at Yorktown.
>
> Lafayette was extremely desirous that the English army should unite at that very spot. Such had been the aim of all his movements, ever since a slight increase of force had permitted him to think of any other thing than of retiring without being destroyed and of saving the magazines. He knew that a French fleet was to arrive from the islands upon the American coast. His principal object had been to force Lord Cornwallis to withdraw towards the sea-shore, and then entangle him in such a manner in the rivers that there should remain no possibility of a retreat. The English, on the contrary, fancied themselves in a very good position, as they were possessors of a seaport by which they could receive succours from New York and communicate with the different parts of the coast. . . . [9]

Cornwallis had seen the dispatches that the British had intercepted, the ones that revealed Washington's plan to recapture New York and had so alarmed Clinton. Clinton had sent them, or copies of them, to Cornwallis. Like Clinton, Cornwallis apparently believed Washington's primary objective was New York. Therefore the only army he had to worry about was Lafayette's, now encamped on the Pamunkey River. It, he knew, was not strong enough to attack him.

Washington did indeed plan to take New York. His plan called for gathering the 5,000 French troops of the Count de Rochambeau from their base in Newport, Rhode Island, and for raising a substantial militia force to be joined to his army to conduct a massive assault on Clinton's forces occupying New York. The plan had been formed after Admiral de Barras had arrived in May to assume command of the French fleet at Newport and had come with orders that authorized Rochambeau to cooperate with Washington in a major offensive. De Barras had also brought news that French Admiral de Grasse was bringing his warships from the Caribbean to reinforce the French fleet based at Newport and would participate in a joint action against New York or possibly some other important objective. In anticipation of implementing the plan, Washington had moved his headquarters to Dobbs Ferry, New York, to be nearer the scene of the intended action.

Accustomed to plans going awry, however, he had pondered an alternative, a Plan B that would shift his grand offensive to the south. By August 1, he had seen that his plan for a siege of New York was failing and he had abandoned it. He recorded his change of plan—and the reason for it—in his diary:

> By this date [August 1, 1781] all my Boats were ready. . . . My heavy Ordnance and Stores from the Eastward had also come on to the North [Hudson] River and every thing would have been in perfect readiness to commence the operation against New York, if the States had furnished their quotas of men agreeably to my requisitions; but so far have they been from complying with these that of the first not more than half the number asked of them have joined the Army, and of 6200 of the latter pointedly and continuously called for to be with the army by the 15th of last Month, only 176 had arrived from Connecticut, independant of about 300 State Troops under the Command of Gen. Waterbury, which had been on the lines before we took the field, and two Companies of York levies (about 80 Man). . . .
>
> Thus circumstanced, and having little more than general assurances of getting the succours called for . . . I could scarce see a ground upon which to continue my preparations against New York . . . and therefore I turned my views more seriously (than I had before done) to an operation to the Southward. . . .[10]

Washington had been able to secure only about 6,000 of the 10,000 troops he had hoped to get for his assault on New York and when they were combined with Rochambeau's 5,000 men, Washington's army totaled no more than the one it would face, being much smaller than the over-whelming force with which Washington wanted to confront Clinton. Setting aside his hope for taking New York, he turned his attention to Virginia instead.

On August 14, while Lafayette kept a watchful eye on the activities of Cornwallis's army at Yorktown, Washington received a letter that Admiral de Grasse had written to Rochambeau. In it the admiral informed Rochambeau that by the end of the month he would be sailing from Haiti with a fleet of twenty-eight warships, that he would be headed for the Chesapeake, and that he would be bringing 3,000 French troops, plus artillery and 100 cavalrymen.

On August 15 Washington dispatched a message to Lafayette, who already knew that a French fleet was coming to aid the American cause. Washington now urged Lafayette to keep Cornwallis hemmed in at Yorktown and by all means prevent him from slipping away.

Four days later, on August 19, 1781, Washington's army began its march to Yorktown.

CHAPTER Twenty-Five

The Battle of Yorktown

On August 19, 1781, the 9,000 men of Washington's army, approximately half American and half French, began their southward march by loading themselves, their provisions and supplies and equipment, their artillery, their horses, and their wagons onto boats to ferry them across the Hudson River, the Americans crossing at Dobbs Ferry and the French, who had been encamped on the east bank of the river, crossing at Kings Ferry, about twelve miles below West Point. The crossing would take several days to complete.

While Clinton's outposts and informants kept an eye on the rebel army's movements, Washington, assuming that Clinton knew of his plan to recapture New York, carefully moved his army to deceive Clinton into believing the new movements were part of that plan. Once across the Hudson, Washington wheeled his forces toward Manhattan, as if preparing a massive assault. So tight was security concerning the army's actual objective that even Washington's own men were unsure where they were going. One of those marching in Washington's columns was an army doctor, James Thacher, who recorded the uncertainty in his journal:

> [*August*] *20th*— . . . Our destination has been for some time [a] matter of perplexing doubt and uncertainty; bets have run high on one side that we were to occupy the ground marked out on the Jersey shore, to aid in the siege of New York, and on the other, that we are stealing a march on the enemy and are actually destined to Virginia in pursuit of the army under Lord Cornwallis. . . .[1]

With no time left for further deception, Washington on August 21 turned his columns south and marched down into New Jersey, through Paramus, Springfield, Princeton, past sites where his struggling army four years earlier had contested British troops under Cornwallis.

Although made aware of Washington's new direction, Clinton clung to the belief that New York remained the Americans' prime objective and stubbornly resisted warnings by some of his advisors that Washington was moving south to threaten Cornwallis. The more suspicious among his advisors had long doubted the authenticity of the documents captured en route from Washington's headquarters the previous March, including the letter to Lafayette revealing Washington's aim to regain New York. It was that bit of intelligence especially that had been guiding Clinton and Cornwallis.

Some Clinton advisors believed the letter was intended to be captured, to mislead the British while Washington planned a move into the south. Clinton, however, was convinced the letter—and the anticipated attack on New York—represented the true intentions of Washington. Included in the captured packet of dispatches, among other letters, was a letter Washington had written to his wife, Martha, and a letter written to his dentist asking him to provide a pair of pliers that Washington could use to fix his false teeth. That personal correspondence helped persuade Clinton that the Lafayette letter was genuine. And so he kept his troops in New York, behind their fortifications, prepared to defend themselves against the coming American assault.

Washington's American and French troops meanwhile continued their southward march. Washington had much more than deception on his mind now. If this campaign against Cornwallis was to succeed, many interlocking pieces had to fit into place and do so within a limited time. Lafayette had to contain Cornwallis's army. If Cornwallis felt he could no longer tolerate Lafayette's threatening presence, he might successfully attack Lafayette and break free, might even form up his columns and return to the Carolinas to avoid Washington and renew his campaign against Greene, who was now mopping up British outposts there. The fleet of Admiral de Grasse, furthermore, now sailing from the West Indies, must arrive on time, must be able to command the Chesapeake Bay area, must prevent reinforcement or evacuation of Cornwallis's troops, and must stay until the victory was complete. Admiral de Barras must arrive on time from Newport, bringing necessary artillery, ammunition, and provisions. Ships must be in place when needed to transport Washington's army down the Chesapeake to Yorktown. The failure of any one of those parts of the operation could mean failure, even disaster, for Washington.

All the while he constantly faced the danger of Clinton's finally seeing that New York was no longer the objective and sending his garrison, recently increased by new Hessian reinforcements, out of its New York stronghold to attack Washington's columns from the rear. Foreseeing that possibility, Washington had left behind a relatively meager 2,500-man force posted on the Hudson and commanded by Major General William Heath to protect his rear. If Washington's rear were attacked and Heath overcome, the result would doubtless be critical delays that seemed certain to defeat the whole scheme.

Another significant concern nettling Washington was the lack of money to pay his officers and men. Low morale and even desertions became a looming threat, and it was not until promises were made to his troops that they would be paid with gold coins being brought by de Grasse's ships that the danger was passed.

Washington understood the immense importance of what he was about. If he could defeat Cornwallis and capture his army at Yorktown, the victory might prove crucial to the war. Not only would the loss of Cornwallis's more than 7,000 troops be a possibly mortal blow to the British forces in America but a defeat of that magnitude could well become the last straw in weighting British public opinion against continuation of a war that was growing more unpopular in Britain and ever more costly in British lives and fortunes. Britain's obdurate monarch might at last have to bow under the great weight of public opinion and give up the fight, relinquishing his increasingly tenuous hold on his former colonies. Failure by Washington, on the other hand, could have an opposite effect, silencing the British government's critics and prolonging the war.

While the main body of troops continued through New Jersey, Washington and Rochambeau, moving at the head of their columns, sped ahead to Philadelphia and reached the city about 1 p.m. on Thursday, August 30. In his diary, Washington, ever concerned with details, explained why: "I set out myself for Philadelphia to arrange matters there, provide Vessels and hasten the transportation of the Ordnance, Stores, & ca., directing, before I set out, the second York regiment to follow with the Boats, Intrenching Tools & ca. the French River to Trenton."[2]

Washington and Rochambeau were greeted and escorted into the city by the Philadelphia Light Horse Troop and given a spectacular welcome.

The president of Congress entertained them with a dinner, and "In the evening," a Philadelphia newspaper reported, "the city was illuminated, and his Excellency walked through some of the principal streets, attended by a numerous concourse of people, eagerly pressing to see their beloved General."[3]

The warm welcome did little to aid the operation, however. After his arrival in Philadelphia, Washington learned that the ships needed to transport troops, equipment, and supplies to Yorktown were not there waiting for him, as had been promised. A delay was inescapable.

Two days later, on September 1, Washington learned that a British fleet of nineteen warships had sailed from New York, bound for Chesapeake Bay. Now there was the ugly possibility that the British fleet would overtake de Barras's ships on their way from Newport, or that the British would reach the Chesapeake ahead of de Grasse and possibly evacuate Cornwallis's army or prevent de Grasse from supporting Washington's assault on Cornwallis.

On September 2, the American troops began streaming into Philadelphia, receiving the same exuberant welcome as their commander in chief had. Washington, however, was too fretful to join the celebration of their arrival. He wrote to Lafayette that day of his deep concern:

> But my dear Marquis, I am distressed beyond expression, to know what is become of the Count de Grasse, and for fear the English Fleet, by occupying the Chesapeake (towards which my last accounts say they were steering) should frustrate all our flattering prospects in that quarter. I am also not a little solicitous for the Count de Barras, who was to have sailed from Rhode Island on the 23d Ulto. and from whom I have heard nothing since that time. . . .
>
> You See, how critically important the present Moment is: for my own part I am determined still to persist, with unremitting ardour in my present Plan, unless some inevitable and insuperable obstacles are thrown in our way.
>
> Adieu, my Dear Marquis! If you get any thing New from any quarter, send it I pray you on the Spur of Speed, for I am almost all impatience and anxiety.[4]

By September 2 Clinton had finally decided Washington was not going to attack New York after all, that Cornwallis was indeed his objective. On August 27 he had written to Cornwallis and told him:

I cannot well ascertain Mr. Washington's real intentions by this move of the army. But it is possible he means for the present to suspend his offensive operations against this post and to take a defensive stand at the old post of Morristown, from whence he may detach to the southward. . . . This move of the enemy may be only a feint and they may return to their former position, which they certainly will do if de Grasse arrives.[5]

Now Clinton had conclusive information. A British ship had brought him news that de Grasse's fleet had been sighted, making for the Chesapeake, and reports reached him that Washington had arrived in Philadelphia. Clinton was not so dull that he failed now to see the threat: the combined American and French armies would confront Cornwallis by land, the formidable French fleet would confront him by sea. Clinton belatedly wrote to Cornwallis to warn him of the imminent danger:

Mr. Washington is moving an army to the southward with an appearance of haste and gives out that he expects the cooperation of a considerable French armament. Your Lordship, however, may be assured that if this should be the case, I shall endeavour to reinforce your command by all means within the compass of my power; or make every possible diversion in your favour.[6]

The long column of French troops entered Philadelphia a few days behind the Americans, appearing the model soldiers in their bright, multi-hued uniforms that contrasted sharply with the motley clothing of the Americans. The people of Philadelphia joyfully received them into their city.

On Wednesday, September 5, Washington's anxiety at last found relief. To him as he rode from Philadephia came an express rider about three miles south of Chester, Pennsylvania, bringing the long awaited word that de Grasse had arrived in the Chesapeake with 28 ships of war, freighted with 3,000 troops, ammunition, and money with which to pay Washington's soldiers. A French officer who was present when the report came described Washington's reaction: "A child whose every wish had been granted could not have revealed a livelier emotion. I have never seen a man moved by a greater or sincerer joy."[7]

Washington then turned around with his party and trotted back to Chester to await the arrival of Rochambeau, who had decided to travel by ship to Chester. As Rochambeau's ship neared the dock, Washington spotted him on the deck and so eager was he to share the good news about de Grasse's arrival that Washington took off his hat and pulled out a handkerchief and began waving his hat and the handkerchief to capture Rochambeau's attention. When Rochambeau came up to him and heard what Washington was bursting to tell him, Washington, in total elation, gave him an exuberant, impetuous embrace.

De Grasse had arrived and begun disembarking the troops of the Marquis Claude-Anne de Saint-Simon on September 2. Saint-Simon, a major general in the French army, graciously subordinated himself to Lafayette, who was a major general in the American army but who had been only a colonel in the French army. Saint-Simon's three regiments were then joined to Lafayette's force outside Yorktown.

Cornwallis would now have a difficult time breaking through Lafayette's lines to escape his entrapment. In a letter to Nathanael Greene written on September 5, Brigadier General George Weedon, commanding the militia investing Gloucester, opposite Yorktown, exulted over the prospect of an imminent American victory:

> The business with his Lordship [Cornwallis] in this State will very soon be at an end, for suppose you know e'er this that we have got him handsomly in a pudding bag with 5000 land forces and about 60 ships including transports.
>
> Count de Grasse took possession of Chesapeak the 1st instant. Cornwallis with his whole force is in York. Four 32-gunn ships have entered York River, and others have secured James River. Gen. De St. [Simon] with 3000 men are landing to reinforce the Marquis and 3000 more are on their march from the northward. His Excellency Gen. Washington it is supposed will pay this armament a visit. Precautions are taken to prevent his Lordship from sliping over York River to plague you again, and if our stars dont most wonderfully deceive us, we shall shortly do his business. . . .
>
> By the Great God of War, I think we may all hand up our swords by the last of the year in perfect peace and security![8]

The battle for Yorktown and Cornwallis's army was still far from decided, however. There was the powerful British fleet yet to contend with and the persistent possibility that Cornwallis could yet be sprung from his menacing circumstances.

The ships of Rear Admiral Thomas Graves, which had been intended to attack de Barras's French fleet at Newport, had turned back to New York when it was discovered that de Barras had left Newport. At New York, Graves's fleet was joined by the fleet of Rear Admiral Samuel Hood, which had sailed up from the West Indies. Together, the British fleets totaled nineteen warships, far fewer than de Grasse's twenty-eight vessels. Nevertheless, and apparently without knowing the strength of de Grasse's fleet and not expecting to face it, the combined British fleets had set sail from New York on August 31, bound for the Chesapeake.

Three and a half days later, on the morning of September 5, its voyage slowed by damaged vessels in Hood's fleet, the little British armada approached the mouth of the Chesapeake, where Admiral Graves was surprised to find the fleet of de Grasse already anchored, the tall masts of its ships visible from a distance. De Grasse was as surprised as Graves when at practically the last minute he realized the approaching sails were not de Barras's fleet coming to join him, but British warships making straight for him. He quickly ordered anchor lines hastily cut and the fleet to immediately set sail for the open water of the Atlantic, where he formed his ships into a line of battle, determined to bar the British an entrance to the bay.

On his flagship, the *London*, Graves responded to de Grasse's move by ordering the British fleet into battle formation. As de Grasse's vessels spread out in their line of battle, Graves could see just how many ships he was facing. Undaunted by the superior numbers of the French fleet, he maneuvered into a five-mile-long line of battle, gave confusing, contradictory signals to his captains, and with only a few hours of daylight remaining, closed to within about 120 yards of the French line and opened fire. De Grasse's vessels, strung out in a long line paralleling the British fleet, which was to the north of the French fleet, returned fire, beginning a furious exchange, thunderous and deadly, with the advantage in ships and guns—and, apparently, marksmanship—heavily in de Grasse's favor.

By 6:15 p.m., when the fighting broke off and the guns went silent, the damage had been done, much more so to the British than to the French fleet. When reports came in to Graves the next morning, he learned that at least five of his vessels were severely damaged and he had suffered 90 killed and 246 wounded. De Grasse had suffered 209 casualties, counting both killed and wounded.

For three days then, as both fleets wandered farther out into the Atlantic, the battle was stalemated, Graves unable to pursue the fight because of the extensive damage to his vessels, de Grasse observing the crippled British fleet and being content to stand by to see what the British would do. Satisfied the enemy was in no condition to resume the fight, de Grasse on September 9 ordered his fleet back into the Chesapeake, setting sail under cover of darkness. At sunup the next day, Graves discovered he was facing an empty sea.

While the fleets of de Grasse and Graves battled, de Barras with eight ships had arrived from Newport, had seen the battle, avoided it (he later claimed he did so because he couldn't tell the French ships from the British), and slipped around behind the embattled fleets and sailed into the Chesapeake, where de Grasse's fleet joined him on September 10. When Graves finally managed to sail his ships back toward the Chesapeake, he saw that the French fleet had suddenly swelled to daunting numbers. Not knowing that Washington was about to entrap Cornwallis at Yorktown, Graves gathered his crippled vessels and sailed for New York, leaving Cornwallis now with no hope for escape except by breaking through his enemy's lines.

Unchallenged, de Barras took his cargo of siege cannons, ammunition, and provisions for Washington's army up the York River and unloaded it.

General Washington, feeling ever more confident, on September 9 had taken leave and set out for Mount Vernon, arriving there late in the day. It was the first time he had seen home in more than six years. The next day, September 10, he was joined there by his military family, including Rochambeau and his staff. Washington entertained them with a sumptuous dinner, hosted them till September 12, then with his entire entourage rode off to Williamsburg, about ten miles southwest of Yorktown.

Cornwallis by then knew that Washington's army was marching toward him, and by September 17 he learned that the British fleet had been so battered by de Grasse's fleet and so outnumbered that Admiral Graves had turned his ships back toward New York. Cornwallis had also learned that de Barras's ships had arrived in the Chesapeake. Seaborne help now seemed unlikely, and Cornwallis, probably with rising anxiety, pondered the possibility of breaking through Lafayette's lines and escaping before Washington arrived to assemble such an overwhelming force that breaking through it would be plainly impossible.

He turned to his trusted subordinate commander, Lieutenant Colonel Banastre Tarleton, and ordered him to carefully reconnoiter Lafayette's lines and "to use every expedient to obtain exact intelligence of their numbers." With three other officers and six troopers, Tarleton rode off to spy on Lafayette's army, the bulk of it encamped near the campus of the College of William and Mary at Williamsburg. When Tarleton returned to Cornwallis, his information was augmented by the report brought in by a woman who had gained a return of the American and French forces. Her intelligence, Tarleton said, "suggested the feasibility of an attack."

Cornwallis then decided he would attempt a breakout. Conferring with his senior officers, he considered two plans. Plan A called for him to marshal his army and proceed down the road to Williamsburg under cover of darkness and there form up to do battle. Plan B would have him send a 2,500-man force up the York River in small boats to Queen's Creek, which flowed past Williamsburg and into the York River. That force would come ashore behind Lafayette's position and attack it from the rear while the main body of Cornwallis's army hit Lafayette in the front. After some consideration, Cornwallis chose Plan A, apparently feeling that Plan B was too complex.

While he was working out the details of the plan, he received a new dispatch from Clinton, dated September 6. Unaware of de Grasse's repulse of Graves's fleet on September 5, Clinton promised the help of a new British fleet (commanded by Admiral Robert Digby, who been named to relieve Graves) that was sailing from Europe and that would, with the ships of Graves and Hood, brush past the French vessels to rescue Cornwallis. Clinton wrote:

> I think the best way to relieve you is to join you as soon as possible, with all the force that can be spared from hence, which is about 4,000 men. They are already embarked, and will proceed the Instant I receive information from the Admiralty that we may venture, and that from other intelligence the Commodore and I shall judge sufficient to move upon. . . . I beg your Lordship will let me know as soon as possible your ideas how the troops embarked for the Chesapeak may be best employed for your relief, according to the state of circumstances when you receive this letter. I shall not however wait to receive your answer, should I hear, in the mean time, that the passage is open.[9]

Now Cornwallis had another hard decision to make. Should he go ahead with Plan A and attempt to save his army himself? Or should he wait for Digby and the 4,000 troops promised by Clinton? After receiving Clinton's September 6 letter, Cornwallis apparently expected the arrival of Digby's vessels at any hour. Ordinarily a man of energy and aggressiveness, Cornwallis now hesitated. He had already sat passively while Lafayette established his army outside Yorktown, had made no effort to prevent or deter the landing of Saint-Simon's troops, had not bothered to ascertain the strength of Lafayette's and Saint-Simon's forces or to plan a way out until the last minute. With uncharacteristic languor, he now decided to forgo a fight to break out of his entrapment. He wrote to Clinton on September 17 to notify him of his decision:

> If I had no hopes of relief, I would rather risk an action than defend my half-finished works. But as you say Admiral Digby is hourly expected, and promise every exertion to assist me, I do not think myself justifiable in putting the fate of the war on so desperate an attempt.[10]

Cornwallis was betting it all—his reputation, his army, his country's war—on Clinton's promise of imminent relief.

On the same day that Cornwallis committed his army's fate to Clinton's promise, September 17, Washington climbed aboard Admiral de Grasse's flagship, the *Ville de Paris* (whose 110 cannons made it the world's most powerful warship) to confer with the admiral and try to persuade him to stay past October 15, which de Grasse earlier had said was the latest he could remain at the Chesapeake.

That mission was unaccomplished. Though de Grasse greeted Washington warmly, giving him Gallic kisses on both cheeks and charmingly addressing him as "my dear little general" (Washington was taller but not as rotund as de Grasse), the admiral told Washington he still planned to leave by October 15 but he promised to stay at least till the end of September.

Doubtless disappointed, Washington returned to Williamsburg on September 22. By then his army, which had embarked from Head of Elk, was arriving in Williamsburg, streaming off its transport ships. The disembarkation of troops and unloading of equipment were completed on September 26. Wasting no time, Washington on September 27 issued orders for the army to move out the next morning.

At 5 a.m. on Friday, September 28, with the French forces leading the column, the Americans behind them, Washington's army marched out of Williamsburg, headed up the road to Yorktown.

Yorktown had once been a prosperous and growing seaport. It had been founded in 1691 and had grown to a population of some 3,000 people by 1750, when it reached its peak. It then began to suffer in competition with the ports of Norfolk and Baltimore and declined when the center of the tobacco industry shifted away from it. The town was built on a thirty-five-foot-high bluff that overlooked the York River. The community of Gloucester Point sat on the opposite bank of the river, which was about a half mile wide at Yorktown. The river was spanned there by a ferry. Yorktown's main street was attractively lined with handsome brick and wood-frame residences and public buildings. Compactly gathered along the riverfront were wharves, warehouses, and drinking establishments.

Cornwallis had set up a headquarters for himself in the home of Thomas Nelson, sixty-five-year-old uncle of the Virginia governor (the governor, also named Thomas Nelson, a brigadier general in the Virginia militia, was in the army that was now marching on Yorktown). From the windows of the Nelson house, Cornwallis could see much of the town, including the spot where the road from Williamsburg, the route of Washington's march, entered Yorktown from the northwest, through a swamp and across a creek.

Cornwallis had established a main line of defense that extended out perpendicular to the river, then curved around the west side of the town at a distance of about 300 yards from the river, enveloping the town in a roughly shaped rectangle that ran northwest to southeast, paralleling the river and blocking the main roads at the opposite ends of the town. That defensive perimeter stretched about 1,000 yards from one end to the other. Posted along the entrenchments of that line were as many as fourteen batteries of artillery, an estimated sixty-five guns. The line was fortified by ten redoubts. At the upper end, covering the road from Williamsburg, it was anchored by the so-called Fusilier Redoubt, named for the detachment of Royal Welsh Fusiliers (23rd Regiment) that manned it. Anchoring the line at the south end were two redoubts, numbered nine and ten.

In front of his main line of defense, Cornwallis had constructed an outer works to defend against the enemy's approach across a half-mile expanse of flat ground south of the town. It was from that area that Washington's assault was believed most likely to come.

Cornwallis had also prepared to defend Gloucester Point, to prevent Washington from crossing there and attacking his rear, and possibly to protect it as the site for a desperate retreat. He posted there 700 troops, including infantrymen from Tarleton's Legion, commanded by Lieutenant Colonel Thomas Dundas. Gloucester Point's defensive works included four redoubts and a line of entrenchments that mounted three batteries of artillery, nineteen guns.

Washington's army marched in a single column up the narrow, sandy road, which cut through a forest and ran straight toward Yorktown. As the column neared Yorktown, it reached a fork in the road, and the French forces took the left side of the fork, and the Americans angled off to the right. The road on the left, the main road, led to the north end of the town, the road on the right to the south end, toward the flat ground where Cornwallis had constructed his outworks. About a mile from the British line, before nightfall, both French and American forces halted.

By now the French column's leading elements had been seen by Cornwallis's pickets, a light-infantry unit commanded by Lieutenant Colonel Robert Abercromby, which advanced to get a closer look. Two French companies, supported by artillery, were ordered out to engage them, and Abercromby quickly withdrew to report the enemy's arrival. Another British officer, Captain Samuel Graham of the 76th Regiment, recorded the action of that evening:

> On the twenty-eighth September, information was given by a picket
> . . . that the enemy were advancing in force by the Williamsburg road.
> The army immediately took post in the outward position. The French
> and Americans came on in the most cautious and regular order.
> Some shots were fired from our fieldpieces. The French also felt the
> redoubt on our right flank, defended by the Twenty-third and a party
> of marines, but did not persist. The two armies remained some time
> in this position observing each other. In ours there was but one wish,
> that they would advance. . . .[11]

The allied forces deployed in a large semicircle outside the British positions, the French occupying the line at the north end and down the west side of Cornwallis's positions, the Americans posted on the south and toward the east. Washington and Rochambeau set up their command posts to the rear of the spot where the American and French lines met.

Just as Abercromby had withdrawn at the approach of the French on the British right, a unit of Tarleton's mounted troops later fell back at the sight of the Americans advancing on the British left, withdrawing to the farmhouse of Augustine Moore, near the river, southeast of the town.

The situation before him becoming clearly more threatening, Cornwallis made an effort to force de Grasse's ships back and open an escape passage to make a retreat possible. He ordered several British ships, docked at Yorktown, to be loaded with inflammables, set adrift down the York River and set afire as they approached the French warships. The burning ships made a brilliant spectacle, visible in the night some ten miles away, but failed to damage de Grasse's vessels.

If Cornwallis or his officers expected a continued advance and an infantry attack against their lines, they were soon disappointed. Washington had no intention of throwing his men against Cornwallis's fortifications in a hasty, bloody assault. Unwilling to spend the lives of his troops, or Rochambeau's, unnecessarily, he immediately began implementing his plan for a siege that would incessantly bombard Cornwallis's positions with heavy artillery and pound him into submission. On the morning of September 29 Washington and a party of senior officers reconnoitered Cornwallis's defenses, plotting the siege lines. Washington then ordered his siege artillery brought up from Trebell's Landing on the James River, an arduous task to be executed over six miles of sandy road.

The fighting that day was minimal, though deadly for some, as the troops of Washington's army dug into their positions. Lieutenant Colonel St. George Tucker of the Virginia militia described in his diary what he saw:

> *Sat. 29.* This morning about eight o'clock, the enemy fired a few shot from their advanced redoubts, our right wing having now passed over Munford's Bridge. About nine or ten [o'clock], the riflemen and jagers exchanged a few shot across Moore's Mill Pond, at the dam of which the British had a redoubt [in Cornwallis's outer works]. A few shot were fired at different times in the day and about sunset from the enemy's redoubts. We had five or six men wounded, one mortally and two others by the same ball. The execution was much more than might have been expected from the distance, the dispersed situation of our men, and the few shots fired.[12]

On the night of September 29 a fast British ship slipped through de Grasse's blockade and delivered to Cornwallis a new letter from Clinton, raising his hopes and prompting what became a controversial decision. Clinton wrote that the British fleet, bearing 5,000 troops to reinforce Cornwallis, would soon be sailing from New York. "There is every reason," Clinton told Cornwallis, "to hope we start from hence the 5th October." Cornwallis immediately wrote back to his commander:

> I have this evening received your letter of the 24th, which has given me the greatest satisfaction. I shall retire this night within the works, and have no doubt, if relief arrives in any reasonable time, York and Gloucester will be both in possession of his Majesty's troops.[13]

The next morning, Sunday, September 30, Washington awoke to discover that during the night, Cornwallis had abandoned his outer works, those that had guarded the flat ground south of Yorktown. The redoubts, the trenches were empty. Colonel Jonathan Trumbull, Washington's secretary, recorded in his journal the events of that day:

[*Sept.*] *30.* In the morning it is discovered that the enemy have evacuated all their exterior works, and retired to their interior defence near the town. We immediately take possession of Pigeon Quarter and hill, and of the enemies' redoubts, and find ourselves very unexpectedly upon very advantageous ground, commanding their line of works in near approach. Scarce a gun fired this day. At night our troops begin to throw up some works and to take advantage of the enemies' evacuated labours.

Colonel Scammel, being officer of the day, is cruelly wounded and taken prisoner while reconnoitering.[14]

(Colonel Alexander Scammell of Milford, Massachusetts had reportedly been shot in the back and mortally wounded by Tarleton's troopers after he had surrendered.)

Cornwallis, resting his confidence on Clinton's promises, had decided to strengthen his main line of defense to better stave off an assault while desperately awaiting the promised reinforcements and seaborne aid. In doing so, he had yielded a significant piece of ground, a huge tactical advantage, and days of the time necessary for Washington to conduct a successful siege before de Grasse would sail away and allow a British fleet to enter the Chesapeake. Washington now would not have to conduct a time-consuming battle to gain that ground, which he needed to emplace his artillery sufficiently close to Cornwallis's main position.

While 1,200 of Washington's troops were busy in the nearby woods gathering small branches to construct protective gabions and fascines to mount on their works, Cornwallis's artillery poured a steady, harassing bombardment on the allies' positions.

Cornwallis's defense was also active at Gloucester Point. Both forces, Washington's and Cornwallis's, had been reinforced, Tarleton and his dragoons having been shifted there. On the morning of October 3 a British foraging party returning to its lines was encountered by the French forces of General de Choisy as they advanced on the British position outside Gloucester Point. De Choisy's vanguard, a cavalry unit commanded by the dashing Duke de Lauzun, attacked the British troops, whose rear was being guarded by Tarleton and his Legion. De Lauzun recounted the engagement:

> I went forward to learn what I could [after the British troops were sighted]. I saw a very pretty woman . . . [who] told me that Colonel Tarleton had left her house a moment before; that he was very eager to shake hands with the French Duke. I assured her that I had come on purpose to gratify him. She seemed sorry for me, judging from experience, I suppose, that Tarleton was irresistible. . . .
>
> I was not a hundred steps from the house when I heard pistol shots from my advance guard. I hurried forward at full speed to find a piece of ground where I could form a line of battle. As I arrived I saw the English cavalry in force three times my own; I charged it without halting; we met hand to hand. Tarleton saw me and rode towards me with pistol raised. We were about to fight single-handed between the two troops when his horse was thrown by one of his own dragoons pursued by one of my lancers. I rode up to him to capture him [while he was pinned beneath his fallen horse]; a troop of English dragoons rode in between us and covered his retreat; he left his horse with me. He charged me twice without breaking my line; I charged the third time, overthrew a part of his cavalry and drove him within the entrenchment of Gloucester.[15]

Tarleton then joined with an infantry company of the 23rd Regiment in a counterattack. The French fell back until they were reinforced by a battalion of Virginia militia. Tarleton's attempt to break the allies' line failed, despite a fierce assault, and Tarleton retreated to his own lines, which soon came under siege by de Choisy, forestalling any further action by Tarleton. His war exploits in America had come to an end.

By October 5, as the first pieces of heavy artillery arrived, Washington was ready to begin construction of the first parallel, commencing the formal siege of Yorktown. The work was begun at night, hidden from the eyes of the enemy. Sergeant James Sullivan Martin of Connecticut recorded that first night of trench digging:

> One-third part of all the troops were put in requisition to be employed in opening the trenches. A third part of our sappers and miners were ordered out this night to assist the engineers in laying out the works. It was a very dark and rainy night. However, we repaired

to the place and began by following the engineers and laying laths of pine wood end to end upon the line marked out by the officers for the trenches.

We had not proceeded far . . . before the engineers ordered us to desist and remain where we were and be sure not to straggle a foot from the spot while they were absent from us. In a few minutes after their departure, there came a man alone to us . . . and inquired of the engineers. We now began to be a little jealous of our safety, being alone and without arms and within forty rods of the British trenches. The stranger inquired what troops we were, talked familiarly with us a few minutes, when, being informed which way the officers had gone, he went off in the same direction, after strictly charging us, in case we should be taken prisoners, not to discover to the enemy what troops we were. We were obliged to him for his kind advice, but we considered ourselves as standing in no great need of it. . . .

In a short time, the engineers returned and the aforementioned stranger with them. They discoursed together some time, when by the officers often calling him, "Your Excellency," we discovered that it was General Washington. Had we dared, we might have cautioned him for exposing himself so carelessly to danger at such a time, and doubtless he would have taken it in good part if we had. . . .

It coming on to rain hard, we were ordered back to our tents and nothing more was done that night. The next night, which was the sixth of October, the same men were ordered to the lines that had been there the night before. We this night completed laying out the works. . . .[16]

Some 1,500 men had dug into the rain-softened, sandy soil a trench 2,000 yards long, within 600 to 800 yards of Cornwallis's line, and done so in two nights. So stealthily had it been done that Cornwallis didn't notice the trench till the morning of October 7.

On October 9, with the work of those two nights enhanced by the construction of five redoubts and five artillery emplacements, Washington was ready to open fire with his big guns. Ten of the American artillery pieces were ready to fire by noon that day, but Washington waited until Saint-Simon's artillerymen were ready, so that they could be first to fire. The cannonade commenced at 3 p.m. Washington himself fired the first American artillery round. That day, he wrote in his journal:

About 3 o'clock P.M. the French opened a battery on our extreme left of 4 Sixteen pounders, and Six Morters and Howitzers and at 5 o'clock an American battery of Six 18s nd 24s; four Morters and 2 Howitzers began to play from the extremity of our right. Both with good effect as they compelled the Enemy to withdraw from their ambrazures the Pieces which had previously kept up a constant firing.[17]

From inside Yorktown, Cornwallis on that same day reacted to the allies' cannonading with a grim message to Clinton:

Nothing but a direct move to York River—which includes a success-ful naval action—can save me. . . .

On the evening of the 9th the enemy's batteries opened and have since continued firing without intermission. . . . We have lost about seventy men, and many of our works are considerably damaged. With such works on disadvantageous ground, against so powerful an attack we cannot hope to make a long resistance.[18]

With his troops, however, Cornwallis was not so honest. According to a deserter from the British artillery, taken by the Americans on October 9, Cornwallis was telling his men that they should not be afraid of the Americans, that they didn't have any heavy artillery except for a few field pieces, and that the French fleet was inferior and were afraid to attack him. The deserter also reported that Cornwallis's troops had more sense than to believe their general.

Four more batteries, two American and two French, came on line the next morning, October 10. Washington now had at least forty-six artillery pieces trained on Cornwallis's defenses. Their thunderous, devastating fire was continuous. Doctor James Thacher, the army surgeon, described the assault in his journal:

From the 10th to the 15th [of October], a tremendous and incessant firing from the American and French batteries is kept up, and the enemy return the fire, but with little effect. A red-hot shell from the French battery set fire to the *Charon*, a British 44-gun ship, and two or three smaller vessels at anchor in the river, which were consumed in the night. From the bank of the river I had a fine view of this splendid conflagration. The ships were enwrapped in a torrent of fire, which, spreading with vivid brightness among the combustible rigging, and

running with amazing rapidity to the tops of the several masts, while
all around was thunder and lightning from our numerous cannon
and mortars, and in the darkness of the night, presented one of the
most sublime and magnificent spectacles which can be imagined.
Some of our shells, overreaching the town, are seen to fall into the
river and, bursting, throw up columns of water like the spouting of
the monsters of the deep. . . .

The siege is daily becoming more and more formidable and
alarming, and his lordship [Cornwallis] must view his situation as
extremely critical, if not desperate. Being in the trenches every
other night and day, I have a fine opportunity of witnessing the sublime and stupendous scene which is continually exhibiting. The
bombshells from the besiegers and the besieged are incessantly
crossing each others' path in the air. They are clearly visible in the
form of a black ball in the day, but in the night they appear like a
fiery meteor with a blazing tail, most beautifully brilliant, ascending majestically from the mortar to a certain altitude and gradually descending to the spot where they are destined to execute their
work of destruction. . . .[19]

When on October 10 Cornwallis allowed Thomas Nelson, whose home
he had made his headquarters, to pass through the British lines and into
the American lines under a flag of truce, Nelson informed his embattled
countrymen that their bombardment was so devastating that Cornwallis,
with others, had sought safety on the river side of the bluff. Nelson's
house, which Cornwallis had evacuated, had been severely damaged by the
bombardment.

During the night of October 11–12, construction of Washington's second parallel began. When it was completed, the besiegers would be within
300 yards of Cornwallis's line. Some 750 yards of trench, three and a half
feet deep and seven feet wide, were dug that first night, and the digging
continued the next two nights. To complete the trench, however, and
extend it all the way to the river, Washington's troops would have to remove
a major obstacle—Redoubts Nine and Ten on the British left flank.

On the afternoon of October 14, following an intense allied bombardment of the two redoubts, Washington decided to send his infantry to
capture them. A 400-man French force commanded by Colonel Guillaume
de Deux-Ponts would assault Redoubt Nine. A 400-man American force
commanded by Lieutenant Colonel Alexander Hamilton would attack

Redoubt Ten, nearest the river. The attacks would be launched simultaneously, supported by reserves and diversionary action.

At 6:30 p.m. the diversionary demonstrations began, and thirty minutes later signal guns were fired to send the two assault forces out into the
darkness, with fixed bayonets, toward the redoubts, bristling with forbidding abatis. De Deux-Ponts described the attack on Redoubt Nine:

> The six [signal] shells were fired at last, and I advanced in the great-
> est silence. At a hundred and twenty or thirty paces, we were discov-
> ered, and the Hessian soldier . . . on the parapet cried out, "Werda?"
> to which we did not reply but hastened our steps. The enemy opened
> fire the instant after the "Werda?"
>
> We lost not a moment in reaching the abatis, which . . . at about
> twenty-five paces from the redoubt, cost us many men and stopped
> us for some minutes, but was cleared away with brave determination.
> We threw ourselves into the ditch at once, and each one sought to
> break through the fraises and to mount the parapet. We reached
> there at first in small numbers, and I gave the order to fire. The
> enemy kept up a sharp fire and charged us at the point of bayonet,
> but no one was driven back.
>
> The carpenters . . . had made some breaches in the palisades which
> helped the main body of troops in mounting. The parapet was becom-
> ing manned visibly. Our fire was increasing and making terrible havoc
> among the enemy who had placed themselves behind a kind of
> entrenchment of barrels, where they were well massed and where all of
> our shots told. We succeeded at the moment when I wished to give
> the order to leap into the redoubt and charge upon the enemy with the
> bayonet; then they laid down their arms and we leaped with more tran-
> quility and less risk. I shouted . . . "Vive le Roi!" which was repeated by
> all the grenadiers and chasseurs who were in good condition, by all the
> troops in the trenches, and to which the enemy replied by a general
> discharge of artillery and musketry.
>
> I never saw a sight more beautiful or more majestic. I did not
> stop to look at it. I had to give attention to the wounded and direc-
> tions to be observed towards the prisoners. . . .[20]

In the successful assault, de Deux-Ponts had lost fifteen killed and seventy-
seven wounded. Cornwallis's defenders lost eighteen killed and fifty
wounded among those taken prisoner.

The attack on Redoubt Ten was described by Sergeant James Sullivan Martin:

> ... [The] signal was given for us and the French ... the three shells with their fiery trains mounting the air in quick succession. The word, "up up" was then reiterated through the detachment. We ... moved toward the redoubt we were to attack with unloaded muskets.
>
> Just as we arrived at the abatis, the enemy discovered us and ... opened a sharp fire upon us. We were now at a place where many of our large shells had burst in the ground, making holes sufficient to bury an ox in. The men, having their eyes fixed upon what was trans-acting before them, were every now and then falling into these holes.
> ...
>
> As soon as the firing began, our people began to cry, "The fort's our own!" and it was, "Rush on, boys!" The sappers and miners soon cleared a passage for the infantry who entered it rapidly. . . .
>
> I could not pass at the entrance we had made, it was so crowded. I, therefore, forced a passage at a place where I saw our shot had cut away some of the abatis. Several others entered at the same place. While pass-ing, a man at my side received a ball in his head and fell under my feet, crying out bitterly. While crossing the trench, the enemy threw hand grenades ... into it. They were so thick that I at first thought them car-tridge papers on fire, but was soon undeceived by their cracking.
>
> As I mounted the breastwork, I met an old associate hitching himself down into the trench. I knew him by the light of the enemy's musketry, it was so vivid. The fort was taken and all quiet in a very short time.[21]

American casualties at Redoubt Ten were nine killed and thirty-one wounded.

The captured redoubts were quickly turned into fortifications in Washington's second parallel, tightening the noose about Cornwallis, and in despair the next morning, October 15, while de Grasse's vessels still lay blocking his escape, he wrote to Clinton:

> My situation here becomes very critical; we dare not show a gun to their old batteries, and I expect their new ones will open tomorrow morning. Experience has shown that our fresh earthen works do not resist their powerful artillery, so that we shall soon be exposed to an

assault in ruined works, in a bad position, and with weakened numbers. The safety of the place is therefore so precarious, that I cannot recommend that the fleet and army should run great risk in endeavoring to save us.[22]

Although realizing he faced defeat, Cornwallis wasn't ready to give up. He ordered a sneak attack on Washington's second parallel to be launched on the morning of October 16. At about 4 a.m. a handpicked detachment of 350 British troops commanded by Lieutenant Colonel Robert Abercromby stole into the allies' trenches, pretending to be Americans, and spiked four French artillery pieces and two American guns before they were found out and forced back to their own lines, having lost five captured and seven killed or wounded. The spiking had been done with bayonet points, which proved ineffectual, as they were removed by the allies' artillerymen and the guns returned to service.

That night, the night of October 16–17, Cornwallis made another desperate move. He sent orders to Tarleton, now in command across the York River at Gloucester Point, to position his troops for an assault that would burst the allies' lines. The plan was to ferry across the river all of the troops who were fit, hit de Choisy's siege line, break through, and swiftly march to New York to join Clinton. Cornwallis figured it would take three trips by the sixteen ships that were still available to him to move his entire army of effectives to Gloucester Point. The attack was to be launched the next morning, October 17.

Apparently unnoticed, the first third of Cornwallis's troops crossed the river and reached Gloucester Point around midnight. The vessels then turned back for their second load of troops, embarked them, and made once more for Gloucester Point. While they were crossing, a sudden squall swept in, its strong winds making completion of the crossing impossible and scattering the vessels downriver.

About 2 a.m. the storm abated, but Cornwallis saw that his plan had failed. There was not enough time left to complete the crossing and launch the attack. At daybreak, he knew, Washington could observe he had withdrawn troops from his line outside Yorktown and that his army was now divided, his line virtually undefended. The situation was an invitation to disaster. He then ordered the troops who had already crossed to return to Yorktown, and they resumed their positions.

On that same morning, October 17, Washington's artillery, now mounting an estimated 100 guns, commenced the heaviest bombardment of the siege. "The whole peninsula trembles under the incessant thundering of our infernal machines," Doctor James Thacher reported.

Cornwallis now faced up to the futility and risks of further resistance. He described his situation:

> Our works in the mean time were going to ruin, and not having been able to strengthen them by abbatis, nor in any other manner but by a slight fraizing which the enemy's artillery were demolishing wherever they fired, my opinion entirely coincided with that of the engineer and principal officers of the army, and that they were in many places assailable in the forenoon, and that by continuance of the same fire for a few hours longer, they would be in such a state as to render it desperate with our numbers to attempt to maintain them. We at that time could not fire a single gun. Only one eight-inch and little more than a hundred cohorn shells remained.[23]

Facing Cornwallis's redcoats in the American siege works that morning was Ebenezer Denny, awaiting his relief. He related what happened at about 10 a.m.:

> Before relief came [I] had the plesure of seeing a drummer mount the enemy's parapet and beat a parley, and immediately an officer, holding up a white handkerchief, made his appearance outside their works. The drummer accompanied him, beating. Our batteries ceased. An officer from our lines ran and met the other and tied the handkerchief over his eyes. The drummer [was] sent back, and the British officer [was] conducted to a house in rear of our lines. Firing ceased totally.[24]

The blindfolded British officer was taken to Washington, who received from him the note Cornwallis had written to Washington:

> Sir; I propose a cessation of hostilities for twenty-four hours, and that two officers may be appointed by each side, to meet at Mr. Moore's house, to settle terms for the surrender of the posts of York and Gloucester.[25]

Washington read the words with undoubted satisfaction. Their message was clear. Cornwallis was giving up.

CHAPTER Twenty-Six

The Surrender

C ornwallis's offer of surrender had come on the fourth anniversary of Burgoyne's surrender at Saratoga, October 17, sooner than Washington expected. He was no doubt pleased, but was in no mood to be dictated to, to acquiesce, or to be rushed. He kept Cornwallis's envoy standing around till about noon, then sent him back into his lines. Soon after the officer re-entered the British lines, the allies' artillery again opened fire. Washington had no idea of giving Cornwallis a day's reprieve from the assault.

About 3 p.m. the guns again went silent. Now an envoy carried Washington's reply to Cornwallis's message:

> My Lord: I have had the Honor of receiving Your Lordship's Letter of this date [October 17, 1781]. An Ardent Desire to spare the further Effusion of Blood, will readily incline me to listen to such Terms for the Surrender of your Posts and Garrisons of York and Gloucester, as are admissible.
>
> I wish previously to the Meeting of Commissioners, that your Lordship's proposals in writing may be sent to the American Lines: for which Purpose, a suspension of Hostilities during two Hours from the Delivery of this Letter will be granted.[1]

Possibly stalling for time, in dying hopes that Clinton's reinforcements might still arrive, Cornwallis had asked for a twenty-four-hour ceasefire during which commissioners representing the two sides would work out surrender terms. Washington gave him two hours to put his proposals in writing and get back to him.

The response from Cornwallis came about 4:30 p.m. Taking his time, Washington decided to think about Cornwallis's proposals overnight.

That night brought an extraordinary calm. St. George Tucker described it in his diary:

> A solemn stillness prevailed. The night was remarkably clear, and the sky decorated with ten thousand stars. Numberless meteors gleaming through the atmosphere afforded a pleasing resemblance to the bombs which had exhibited a noble firework the night before, but happily divested of all their horror.[2]

Early the next morning, October 18, Washington sent his latest reply to Cornwallis. Foreclosing any possibility of negotiations, Washington spelled out which of Cornwallis's proposals he deemed, as he said, "admissible," and which ones he rejected:

> To avoid unnecessary Discussions and Delays, I shall at Once, in Answer to your Lordship's Letter of Yesterday, declare the general Basis upon which a Definitive Treaty and Capitulation must take place.
>
> The Garrisons of York and Gloucester, including the Seamen, as you propose, will be received Prisoners of War. The Condition annexed, of sending the British and German Troops to the parts of Europe to which they respectively belong, is inadmissible. Instead of this, they will be marched to such parts of the Country as can most conveniently provide for their Subsistence; and the Benevolent Treatment of Prisoners, which is invariably observed by the Americans, will be extended to them. The same honors will be granted to the Surrendering Army as were granted to the Garrison of Charles Town [Charleston].
>
> The Shipping and Boats in the two Harbours, with all their Guns, Stores, Tackling, Furniture and Apparel, shall be delivered in their present State to an Officer of the Navy, appointed to take possession of them.
>
> The Artillery, Arms, Accoutrements, Military Chest and Public Stores of every Denomination, shall be delivered unimpaired to the Heads of Departments, to which they respectively belong.
>
> The Officers shall be indulged in retaining their Side Arms, and the Officers and Soldiers may preserve their Baggage and Effects, with this Reserve, that Property taken in the Country, will reclaimed.

With Regard to the Individuals in civil Capacities, whose Interests Your Lordship wishes may be attended to, until they are more particularly described, nothing definitive can be settled.

I have to add, that I expect the Sick and Wounded will be supplied with their own Hospital Stores, and be attended by British Surgeons, particularly charged with the Care of them.

Your Lordship will be pleased to signify your Determination either to accept or reject the Proposals now offered, in the Course of Two Hours from the Delivery of this Letter, that Commissioners may be appointed to digest the Articles of Capitulation, or a Renewal of Hostilities may take place.[3]

Washington also allowed, on Cornwallis's request, Cornwallis's temporary use of the British sloop *Bonetta* and its crew to carry dispatches and certain troops to New York. Permitting the evacuation of those troops was evidently Washington's way of disposing of American deserters who had joined the British army. He would not treat them as prisoners of war and he apparently didn't want the burden of having to deal with them as deserters.

Left with only the grimmest alternative, Cornwallis accepted Washington's terms. The details, including how the surrender ceremony was to be conducted, were worked out by Lieutenant Colonel John Laurens, Washington's aide, and the Viscount Louis-Marie de Noailles, Lafayette's brother-in-law, appointed by Rochambeau, and, representing Cornwallis, Major Alexander Ross, who was Cornwallis's aide, and Lieutenant Colonel Thomas Dundas. The four officers met in the two-story farmhouse of Augustine Moore, just outside Washington's first parallel. Hampered by more British stalling, their work was not finished till after midnight on the night of October 18–19.

Not one to forget a slight (as when he ordered Major Andre hanged, in the same way the British had executed Nathan Hale), Washington was careful to impose upon Cornwallis and his army the same humiliating conditions that Clinton had imposed on Major General Benjamin Lincoln and his army when the Americans surrendered at Charleston in May 1780. (Lincoln, who had been taken prisoner at Charleston but later exchanged, was now commanding a division at Yorktown and would be observing the satisfying turnabout of the fortunes of war.)

Washington's refusal to grant to Cornwallis's army the usual military honors—which allowed a surrendering army to march from its post with its drums beating, its band playing a tune of the victor, the surrendering troops bearing their weapons, its colors flying—caused Cornwallis's representatives to bristle with offense. But Clinton had demanded that when the Americans came out of their works in Charleston "the drummers are not to beat a British march or colors to be uncased." Now Washington was making the same demand. Major Ross, Cornwallis's aide, voiced an objection, and the subsequent exchange with the allies' representatives was recounted by an American officer who was present:

> That gentleman [Ross] observed, "This is a harsh article."
> "Which article?" said Colonel Laurens.
> "The troops shall march out with colors cased and drums beating a British or German march."
> "Yes, sir," replied Colonel Laurens, "it is a harsh article."
> "Then, Colonel Laurens, if that is your opinion, why is it here?"
> "Your question, Major Ross, compels an observation which I would have gladly suppressed. You seem to forget, sir, that I was a capitulant at Charleston, where General Lincoln after a brave defense of six weeks [in] open trenches by a very inconsiderable garrison against the British army and fleet . . . and when your lines of approach were within pistol shot of our field works, was refused any other terms for his gallant garrison than marching out with colors cased and drums *not* beating a German or a British march."
> "But," rejoined Major Ross, "my Lord Cornwallis did not command at Charleston."
> "There, sir," said Colonel Laurens, "you extort another declaration. It is not the individual that is here considered. It is the nation. This remains an article, or I cease to be a commissioner."[4]

So much for the British objection.

On the day the formal surrender was to take place, Friday, October 19, Washington made this entry in his diary, reporting what his instructions to Cornwallis were: "In the Morning early I had them [the articles of capitulation] copied and sent word to Lord Cornwallis that I expected to have them signed at eleven o'clock and that the Garrison would March out at two o'clock. . . ."[5]

Following Washington's direction, Cornwallis returned to him the signed surrender agreement about 11 a.m. It bore the signatures of Cornwallis and Thomas Symonds, the British senior naval officer at

Yorktown. Washington placed his signature on it—"G. Washington."
Rochambeau, too, signed it, as did de Barras, who signed also for de Grasse.

At 2 p.m., on schedule, Cornwallis's defeated army advanced from its
lines. Doctor Thacher recorded the scene and the feelings:

> This is to us a most glorious day, but to the English, one of bitter cha-
> grin and disappointment. Preparations are now making to receive as
> captives that vindictive, haughty commander [Cornwallis] and that
> victorious army, who, by their robberies and murders, have so long
> been a scourge to our brethren of the Southern states. . . .
>
> At about twelve o'clock, the combined army was arranged and
> drawn up in two lines extending more than a mile in length. The
> Americans were drawn up in a line on the right side of the road, and
> the French occupied the left. At the head of the former, the great
> American commander, mounted on his noble courser, took his sta-
> tion, attended by his aids. At the head of the latter was posted the
> excellent Count Rochambeau and his suite. The French troops, in
> complete uniform, displayed a martial and noble appearance; their
> bands of music, of which the timbrel formed a part, is a delightful
> novelty and produced while marching to the ground a most enchant-
> ing effect. The Americans, though not all in uniform, nor their dress
> so neat, yet exhibited an erect, soldierly air, and every countenance
> beamed with satisfaction and joy. The concourse of spectators from
> the country was prodigious, in point of numbers was probably equal
> to the military, but universal silence and order prevailed.
>
> It was about two o'clock when the captive army advanced
> through the line formed for their reception. Every eye was prepared
> to gaze on Lord Cornwallis, the object of peculiar interest and solici-
> tude; but he disappointed our anxious expectations; pretending
> indisposition, he made General O'Hara his substitute as the leader of
> his army. . . .[6]

Lieutenant General Cornwallis, brave and bold in the face of the
enemy in battle, had refused to show himself in the face of the enemy in
defeat. Doctor Thacher, in his journal, went on to editorialize about the
nonappearance:

> We are not to be surprised that the pride of the British officers is
> humbled on this occasion, as they have always entertained an exalted

opinion of their own military prowess and affected to view the Americans as a contemptible, undisciplined rabble. But there is no display of magnanimity when a great commander shrinks from the inevitable misfortunes of war; and when it is considered that Lord Cornwallis has frequently appeared in splendid triumph at the head of his army, by which he is almost *adored*, we conceive it incumbent on him cheerfully to participate in their misfortunes and degradations, however humiliating; but it is said he gives himself up entirely to vexation and despair.[7]

Cornwallis wasn't the only British general that day who sought to avoid Washington on the field of surrender. Brigadier General O'Hara, Cornwallis's surrogate at the surrender, asked his French escort to show him which officer was Rochambeau and when he did, O'Hara urged his horse forward and attempted to hand over his sword to Rochambeau, scorning Washington. Rochambeau refused it and gestured toward Washington, across the road.

O'Hara then turned toward Washington and apologized for what he represented as a mistake. Outwardly unmoved, Washington, seeing the game being played, refused the sword and indicated it should be surrendered to Benjamin Lincoln, his subordinate, as O'Hara was to Cornwallis.

Following O'Hara's surrender, the British and Hessian troops surrendered their weapons. Doctor Thacher described the British soldiers' behavior:

> . . . when they came to the last act of the drama . . . the spirit and pride of the British soldier was put to the severest test: here their mortification could not be concealed. Some of the platoon officers appeared to be exceedingly chagrined when giving the word "*ground arm*," and I am a witness that they performed this duty in a very unofficer-like manner, and that many of the soldiers manifested a *sullen temper*, throwing their arms on the pile with violence, as if determined to render them useless. This irregularity, however, was checked by the authority of General Lincoln. After having grounded their arms and divested themselves of their accoutrements, the captive troops were conducted back to Yorktown and guarded by our troops till they could be removed to the place of their destination.[8]

Across the river at Gloucester Point the British troops were likewise, and at the same time, surrendering to de Choisy.

The Battle of Yorktown was over, the victor acknowledged, the vanquished disarmed and led away captive. Among the estimated 20,000 American and French troops at Yorktown and Gloucester Point, fewer than 400 casualties had been suffered. Of the estimated 9,750 troops commanded by Cornwallis, some 600 became casualties during the siege; the rest were surrendered.

On the day after the formal surrender, Cornwallis wrote to Clinton:

> I have the mortification to inform your Excellency that I have been forced to give up the posts of York and Gloucester, and to surrender the troops under my command, by capitulation on the 19th inst. as prisoners of war to the combined forces of America and France....[9]

General Washington also wrote to report the news from Yorktown. His letter was addressed to the Congress of the United States of America:

> I have the Honor to inform Congress, that a Reduction of the British Army under the Command of Lord Cornwallis, is most happily effected. The unremitting Ardor which actuated every Officer and Soldier in the combined Army in this Occasion, has principally led to this Important Event, at an earlier period than my most sanguine hopes had induced me to expect....[10]

For Cornwallis, the war was over. He was paroled and permitted to go wherever he desired, including back to England. On November 4 he sailed for New York, thinking no doubt that his future was now in doubt, his career possibly in jeopardy.

Washington, meanwhile, elated with victory, pondered other objectives in the war that was not quite won. Yet.

Epilogue

On the same day that Cornwallis surrendered, Clinton and Graves, with the promised 7,000 reinforcements, finally sailed from New York. They reached the Chesapeake on October 24 and there confronted de Grasse's thirty-five warships, still there, still barring entrance and deployed to do battle. A small boat with three men aboard sailed out to Graves's fleet from shore and delivered the news from Yorktown. After making a vain show of belligerence to de Grasse, on October 27 Graves's fleet turned around and sailed back for New York.

Banastre Tarleton, as he rode through a Yorktown street following the surrender, was forced to dismount and yield his horse by a Mister Day, a civilian who was apparently the horse's rightful owner and who reclaimed it from the powerless Tarleton.

Although the Battle of Yorktown was the last major engagement, the war dragged sluggishly on for nearly two more years. The significance of Cornwallis's Yorktown defeat was immediately recognized by the British government, however. When the news was brought to the prime minister, Lord North, he exclaimed, repeatedly, "Oh, God! It is all over!" It was indeed.

Peace was officially achieved with the signing of the Treaty of Paris on September 3, 1783. In that treaty, Britain at last recognized the independence of the United States of America. Under the terms of the treaty, hostilities were to cease and all British military forces were to be removed from the states "with all convenient speed."

The United States Congress ratified the treaty on January 14, 1784.

Cornwallis, far from suffering disgrace in the wake of the Yorktown defeat, went on to become, in 1786, governor-general in India and gained a reputation as an outstanding civil administrator. In 1897 he was appointed governor-general of Ireland and in 1805 returned to his former post in India. He died there on October 5, 1805.

Henry Clinton was relieved of his duties in May 1782. In 1790 he was elected to Parliament and in October 1793 he was promoted to full general. In July 1794 he was appointed governor of Gibraltar and died there on December 23, 1795.

Banastre Tarleton was paroled to England in 1782 and elected to Parliament several times. He was promoted to colonel in 1790 and to major general in 1794. In 1803 he became commander of the Cork Military District, which included much of southern Ireland, and in 1808 was appointed governor in Berwick and Holy Island. In 1812 he was promoted to full general, made a baronet in 1815, and knighted in 1820. He died on January 25, 1833, leaving a widow but no children.

Nathanael Greene went home to a hero's welcome in Rhode Island in 1783. Because of debt incurred to help finance the war, he had to sell his property and in 1785 moved to Georgia to make his home at an estate that the state of Georgia gave him near Savannah. He died, reportedly of a sunstroke, the next year, at age forty-four.

Daniel Morgan became a large landowner in Virginia, amassing more than 250,000 acres. He was elected to Congress in 1797 and served one term in the House of Representatives. He died on July 6, 1802.

Lafayette sailed home to France in December 1781 and at Washington's invitation returned to the United States, for a time, in 1784. His fortunes as a military and political leader ebbed and flowed. In 1792 he sought refuge in Belgium, ended up in a Prussian prison, and was rescued from it by Napoleon in 1797. He declined President Thomas Jefferson's offer to become governor of Louisiana in 1805, tended his estate near Paris, and revisited the United States in 1824, at the invitation of President James Monroe. He re-entered politics after returning to France in 1825, but proved ineffectual in his hopes of establishing a republic in France. He died on May 20, 1834.

Benedict Arnold, America's most infamous traitor, went to England in December 1781 and became a consultant on American affairs. Refused a military command, he moved to St. John, New Brunswick in 1785 and became a businessman. He moved back to England in 1791, where he died in June 1801.

George Washington, America's greatest hero, became the first president of the United States of America, taking office on April 30, 1789. He served two terms and refused to run for a third. He then retired to his home at Mount Vernon, where he died on December 14, 1799.

Notes

Chapter 1

1. *The Works of John Adams, Second President of the United States*, vol. 2, ed. Charles Francis Adams (Boston: Little, Brown, 1851–1865), 415–16.

2. *The Works of John Adams*, 415–16.

3. *The Works of John Adams*, 415–16.

4. *The Writings of George Washington, from the Original Manuscript Sources, 1745–1799*, vol. 3, ed. John C. Fitzpatrick (Washington, D.C.: U.S. Government Printing Office, 1931–44), 292–93.

5. Douglas Southall Freeman, *Washington* (New York: Touchstone, 1968), 220.

6. Harrison Clark, *All Cloudless Glory* (Washington, D.C.: Regnery, 1995), 214.

7. *The Writings of George Washington*, 293–95.

Chapter 2

1. Letter to Lund Washington, August 20, 1775, in *The Writings of George Washington*, vol. 3, 433.

2. Letter to Mrs. William Emerson, July 17, 1775, in *Correspondence of the American Revolution: Being Letters of Eminent Men to George Washington*, vol. 3, ed. Jared Sparks (Freeport, N.Y.: Books for Libraries Press, 1970), 491.

3. Letter to Mrs. William Emerson, 491.

4. Freeman, *Washington*, 235.

5. Letter to Richard Henry Lee, in *The Writings of George Washington*, vol. 3, 450–54.

6. Letter to Richard Henry Lee, 512.

7. Letter to Joseph Reed, in *The Writings of George Washington*, vol. 4, 124–25.

8. Letter to Joseph Reed, 211.

9. Freeman, *Washington*, 250.

10. Frank Moore, ed., *Diary of the American Revolution*, vol. 1 (New York: New York Times, 1969), 219–22.

11. Clark, *All Cloudless Glory*, 251–52.

Chapter 4

1. George F. Scheer and Hugh F. Rankin, *Rebels and Redcoats* (New York: Da Capo Press, 1987), 158.

2. Scheer and Rankin, *Rebels and Redcoats*, 166.

3. "Extract of a Letter from an Officer in General Frazier's Battalion, Sept. 3, 1776," *American Archives*, 5th serial, vol. 1, 1259–60.

4. Henry Onderdonk, *Revolutionary Incidents* (Port Washington, N.Y.: Kennikat Press, 1970), 147–48.

5. Joseph Plumb Martin, *Narrative* (N.p.: N.p., 1830), 19–21.

Chapter 5

1. *Pennsylvania Archives*, 2nd serial, vol. 10, 308–9.

2. *Memoir of Benjamin Tallmadge*, ed. Henry P. Johnston (New York: Society of the Sons of the Revolution, 1904), 12–14.

3. Scheer and Rankin, *Rebels and Redcoats*, 172.

4. "Extract from the Journals and Original Papers of Sir George Collier," Long Island Historical Society, *Memoirs*, vol. 2, 413–14.

5. "Occupation of New York City by the British, 1776," *Pennsylvania Magazine of History*, 1 (1877): 148.

6. John Haslet's letter to Caesar Rodney, September 4, 1776, in *Letters to and from Caesar Rodney*, ed. George Ryden (New York: Da Capo Press, 1970), 112.

7. Scheer and Rankin, *Rebels and Redcoats*, 175.

8. Scheer and Rankin, *Rebels and Redcoats*, 176.

9. Freeman, *Washington*, 290.

10. *The Writings of George Washington*, vol. 6, 27–32.

11. Clark, *All Cloudless Glory*, 280.

12. Martin, *Narrative*, 25–28.

13. Letter by George Weedon to John Page, September 20, 1776, Weedon Papers, Chicago Historical Society.

NOTES **335**

Chapter 6

1. Letter to Mrs. Joseph Reed, September 17, 1776, Keith Papers, Virginia Historical Society.
2. Letter to father of Tench Tilghman, September 19, 1776, in *Memoir*, 138–39.
3. Clark, *All Cloudless Glory*, 282.
4. Henry Steele Commager and Richard B. Morris, eds., *The Spirit of 'Seventy-Six* (New York: Da Capo Press, 1995), 471.
5. Letter to Lund Washington, September 30, 1776, in *The Writings of George Washington*, vol. 6, 138.
6. Haslet's letter to Caesar Rodney, November 12, 1776, in *Letters*, 142–43.

Chapter 7

1. Clark, *All Cloudless Glory*, 292.
2. Edward J. Lowell, *Hessians and the Other German Auxiliaries of Great Britain in the Revolutionary War* (New York: N.p., 1884), 81–82.
3. Scheer and Rankin, *Rebels and Redcoats*, 200.
4. Franklin and Mary Wickwire, *Cornwallis and the War of Independence* (London: Faber & Faber, 1970), 92.
5. Clark, *All Cloudless Glory*, 300.
6. James Wilkinson, *Memoirs of My Own Times*, vol. 1 (New York: AMS Press, 1973), 105–6.
7. Moncure Daniel Conway, ed., *The Writings of Thomas Paine*, vol. 1 (New York: G. P. Putnam's Sons, 1894–1896), 170–73.

Chapter 8

1. Howard Fast, *The Crossing* (New York: ibooks, 1971), 117.
2. Benjamin Rush, *The Autobiography of Benjamin Rush* (London: Greenwood Publishing, 1970), 124–25.
3. Fast, *The Crossing*, 136.
4. W. J. Wood, *Battles of the Revolutionary War* (New York: Da Capo Press, 1995), 63–64.
5. Clark, *All Cloudless Glory*, 304.
6. Scheer and Rankin, *Rebels and Redcoats*, 212.
7. From memoirs of Elisha Bostwick, quoted in *Spirit of 'Seventy-Six*, 512.
8. Scheer and Rankin, *Rebels and Redcoats*, 212–13.
9. Francis S. Drake, *Life and Correspondence of Henry Knox* (Boston: Samuel G. Drake, 1873), 36–37.

Chapter 9

1. R. Sergeant, "Account of Princeton," *Pennsylvania Magazine of History and Biography* 20 (1896): 515–19.
2. *The Writings of George Washington*, vol. 6, 468.
3. Scheer and Rankin, *Rebels and Redcoats*, 217.
4. Sergeant, "Account of Princeton," 516–18.
5. Sergeant, "Account of Princeton," 516–18.
6. Anonymous, *Brief Narrative of the Ravages of the British and Hessians at Princeton*, ed. Varnum Lansing Collins (New York: New York Times, 1968), 32–39.
7. Clark, *All Cloudless Glory*, 307.

Chapter 10

1. Mrs. E. Stuart Wortley, ed. *Correspondence of Bute and Stuart* (London: John Murray Company, 1923), 105–6.
2. Thomas Jones, *History of New York during the Revolutionary War*, vol. 1 (New York: New York Times, 1968), 170–71.
3. George Athan Billias, ed., *George Washington's Generals and Opponents*, vol. 2 (New York: Da Capo Press, 1994), 156–57.
4. Billias, *George Washington's Generals and Opponents*, 158.
5. Billias, *George Washington's Generals and Opponents*, 161.
6. Billias, *George Washington's Generals and Opponents*, 167.
7. Christopher Hibbert, *Redcoats and Rebels* (New York: Avon, 1991), 178.
8. James Phinney Baxter, *The British Invasion from the North* (New York, Da Capo Press, 1970), 270–74.
9. Hibbert, *Redcoats and Rebels*, 185–86.
10. Baxter, *The British Invasion from the North*, 317–23.

Chapter 11

1. Billias, *George Washington's Generals and Opponents*, 197.
2. *Journal of Nicholas Cresswell* (Port Washington, N.Y.: Kennikat Press, 1968), 251–52.
3. Freeman, *Washington*, 344.
4. *Familiar Letters of John Adams and His Wife Abigail Adams during the Revolution* (Freeport, N.Y.: Books for Libraries Press, 1970), 298.
5. Clark, *All Cloudless Glory*, 330–31.

6. Wood, *Battles of the Revolutionary War*, 99.

7. Freeman, *Washington*, 350.

8. Timothy Pickering, *Life of Timothy Pickering*, vol. 1, (Boston: Little, Brown, and Co., 1867), 154–56.

9. John Andre, *Major Andre's Journal* (New York: New York Times, 1968), 45–47.

10. *The Writings of George Washington*, vol. 9, 207–8.

11. Robert Morton, " Diary," *Pennsylvania Magazine of History and Biography* 1 (1877): 7–8.

12. Mrs. Henry Drinker, "Journal," *Pennsylvania Magazine of History and Biography* 13 (1889): 298–99.

13. Clark, *All Cloudless Glory*, 338–39.

14. Pickering, *Life of Timothy Pickering*, 166–70.

15. Pickering, *Life of Timothy Pickering*, 166–70.

16. Clark, *All Cloudless Glory*, 340.

17. Lamb Papers, New York Historical Society, box 1, no. 217.

Chapter 12

1. Clark, *All Cloudless Glory*, 346.

2. "General Orders, Dec. 17, 1777," in *The Writings of George Washington*, vol. 10, 167–68.

3. Friedrich Kapp, *The Life of John Kalb* (New York: H. Holt and Co., 1884), 137–43.

4. George Washington Papers, Library of Congress.

5. John Brooks, "Letter," *Massachusetts Historical Society Proceedings* 13 (1803): 243–45.

6. Attributed to James Sullivan Martin, *Narrative of a Revolutionary Soldier* (New York: Signet Classics, 2001), 73–76.

7. Albigence Waldo, "Valley Forge, 1777–1778," *Pennsylvania Magazine of History and Biography* 21 (1954): 305–10.

8. Frederick William Baron von Steuben, *Baron von Steuben's Revolutionary War Drill Manual* (New York: Dover, 1985), 87–88.

Chapter 13

1. Clark, *All Cloudless Glory*, 358.

2. Clark, *All Cloudless Glory*, 358.

3. Adams, *Familiar Letters*, 322–23.

4. Samuel Adams Papers, New York Public Library.

5. Clark, *All Cloudless Glory*, 360.

6. *The Writings of George Washington*, vol. 9, 387–89.

7. *The Writings of George Washington*, vol. 10, 29.

8. George Washington Papers, Library of Congress.

9. Gates Papers, box 8, no. 209, New York Historical Society.

10. One of whom, by the by, he was.

11. *The Writings of George Washington*, vol. 10, 263–65.

12. Clark, *All Cloudless Glory*, 365.

13. *The Writings of George Washington*, vol. 10, 249.

14. Clark, *All Cloudless Glory*, 365.

15. Mark M. Boatner III, *Encyclopedia of the American Revolution* (Mechanicsburg, Pa.: Stackpole Books, 1966), 278.

16. Freeman, *Washington*, 381.

17. Freeman, *Washington*, 381.

18. Boatner, *Encyclopedia of the American Revolution*, 277.

19. Freeman, *Washington*, 382–83.

Chapter 14

1. Wickwire, *Cornwallis and the War of Independence*, 105–96.

2. James Hutton, "Account of Hutton's Visit to Franklin," *Pennsylvania Magazine of History and Biography* 32 (1908): 228–30.

3. Wickwire, *Cornwallis and the War of Independence*, 108.

4. Wickwire, *Cornwallis and the War of Independence*, 108.

5. "From a Late Philadelphia Paper," *Continental Journal and Weekly Advertiser* (Boston), July 30, 1778.

6. Marquis de Lafayette, *Memoirs, Correspondence and Manuscripts* (New York: Saunders and Otley, 1837), 50–52.

Chapter 15

1. Clark, *All Cloudless Glory*, 398.

2. Letter from Alexander Hamilton to Elias Boudinot, July 5, 1778, *Pennsylvania Magazine of History and Biography* 2 (1878): 140–42.

3. Clark, *All Cloudless Glory*, 400.

4. Clark, *All Cloudless Glory*, 401.

5. Clark, *All Cloudless Glory*, 401.

6. Alexander Hamilton to Elias Boudinot, July 5, 1778, *Pennsylvania Magazine of History and Biography* 2 (1878): 140–42.

7. Testimony by Richard Harrison, *New York Historical Society Collection*, vol. 6, 71–75.

8. Scheer and Rankin, *Rebels and Redcoats*, 330.

9. Attributed to James Sullivan Martin, *Narrative of a Revolutionary Soldier*, 91–95.

10. Clark, *All Cloudless Glory*, 404–5.

11. Clark, *All Cloudless Glory*, 406.

12. Clark, *All Cloudless Glory*, 405.

13. Clark, *All Cloudless Glory*, 424–25.

14. Freeman, *Washington*, 407.

15. Freeman, *Washington*, 407.

Chapter 16

1. Clark, *All Cloudless Glory*, 411.

2. Freeman, *Washington*, 410.

3. *The Writings of George Washington*, vol. 12, 369.

4. Clark, *All Cloudless Glory*, 413–14.

5. Clark, *All Cloudless Glory*, 414–15.

6. Clark, *All Cloudless Glory*, 413.

7. Clark, *All Cloudless Glory*, 415.

8. Clark, *All Cloudless Glory*, 416.

Chapter 17

1. Billias, *George Washington's Generals and Opponents*, 200.

2. Wickwire, *Cornwallis and the War of Independence*, 114.

3. Billias, *George Washington's Generals and Opponents*, 202.

4. *The Writings of George Washington*, vol. 13, 466–68.

5. *The Writings of George Washington*, vol. 15, 388.

6. Scheer and Rankin, *Rebels and Redcoats*, 359.

7. Clark, *All Cloudless Glory*, 442.

8. Henry P. Johnston, *Storming of Stony Point on the Hudson* (New York: Da Capo Press, 1971), 174–75.

9. Clark, *All Cloudless Glory*, 443.

Chapter 18

1. Billias, *George Washington's Generals and Opponents*, vol. 1, 171–72.
2. Carl van Doren, *Secret History of the Revolution* (Clifton, N.J.: A. M. Kelley, 1973), 439–40.
3. Van Doren, *Secret History of the Revolution*, 464–65.
4. Henry Clinton, *The American Rebellion* (New Haven, Conn.: Yale University Press, 1954), 462–65.
5. Letter by Joshua King, *History Magazine* 1 (October 1857): 294.
6. Clark, *All Cloudless Glory*, 479.
7. Letter by Joshua King, 293–94.
8. Benjamin Tallmadge to Jared Sparks, February 17, 1854, *Magazine of American History* 3 (December 1879): 756.

Chapter 19

1. Wickwire, *Cornwallis and the War of Independence*, page 121.
2. Billias, *George Washington's Generals and Opponents*, vol. 2, 202.
3. Bernard A. Uhlendorf, ed., *Siege of Charleston* (Columbia: University of South Carolina Press, 1970), 117–25.
4. Clinton, *The American Rebellion*, 159.
5. Uhlendorf, *Siege of Charleston*, 179–83.
6. William Moultrie, *Memoirs of the American Revolution*, vol. 2 (New York: New York Times, 1968), 96–97.
7. Moultrie, *Memoirs of the American Revolution*, 96–97.
8. Moultrie, *Memoirs of the American Revolution*, 96–97.
9. Moultrie, *Memoirs of the American Revolution*, 108–11.
10. Billias, *George Washington's Generals and Opponents*, vol. 1, 203.
11. William Dobein James, *A Sketch of the Life of Brig. Gen. Francis Marion and a History of His Brigade* (Hemingway, S.C.: Three Rivers Historical Society, 1996), appendix, 1–7.

Chapter 20

1. Scheer and Rankin, *Rebels and Redcoats*, 405.
2. Scheer and Rankin, *Rebels and Redcoats*, 406–7.
3. Scheer and Rankin, *Rebels and Redcoats*, 406–7.
4. Scheer and Rankin, *Rebels and Redcoats*, 406–7.

5. William Johnson, *Sketches of the Life and Correspondence of Nathanael Greene*, vol. 1, (New York: Da Capo Press, 1973), 494–98.

6. Johnson, *Sketches of the Life and Correspondence of Nathanael Greene*, 494–98.

7. Letter by Charles Magill, *Magazine of American History* 5 (October 1880): 278.

8. Boatner, *Encyclopedia of the American Revolution*, 415.

Chapter 21

1. Clark, *All Cloudless Glory*, 463.

2. Scheer and Rankin, *Rebels and Redcoats,* 414.

3. John Buchanan, *The Road to Guilford Courthouse* (New York: John Wiley & Sons, 1997), 204.

4. Buchanan, *The Road to Guilford Courthouse*, 195.

5. Buchanan, *The Road to Guilford Courthouse*, 195.

6. *North Carolina State Records*, vol. 15, 105–8.

7. Wood, *Battles of the Revolutionary War*, 194–95.

8. Boatner, *Encyclopedia of the American Revolution*, 578.

9. *North Carolina State Records*, vol. 15, 105–8.

10. *North Carolina State Records*, vol. 15, 105–8.

Chapter 22

1. Wickwire, *Cornwallis and the War of Independence*, 221.

2. Wickwire, *Cornwallis and the War of Independence*, 231.

3. Wickwire, *Cornwallis and the War of Independence*, 234.

4. Wickwire, *Cornwallis and the War of Independence*, 234.

5. Wood, *Battles of the Revolutionary War*, 212.

6. Wood, *Battles of the Revolutionary War*, 213.

7. Wood, *Battles of the Revolutionary War*, 217.

8. Thomas Young, "Memoir," *The Orion* 3 (October 1843): 88.

Chapter 23

1. Buchanan, *The Road to Guilford Courthouse*, 341.

2. Buchanan, *The Road to Guilford Courthouse*, 348.

3. Buchanan, *The Road to Guilford Courthouse*, 350.

4. James Graham, *The Life of General Daniel Morgan* (Bloomingburg, N.Y.: Zebrowski Historical Services Pub. Co., 1993), 355.

5. Boatner, *Encyclopedia of the American Revolution*, 464.

6. Boatner, *Encyclopedia of the American Revolution*, 468.

7. Buchanan, *The Road to Guilford Courthouse*, 381–82.

8. *Correspondence of Charles, First Marquis Cornwallis,* vol. 1, ed. Charles Ross (London: J. Murray, 1859), 488.

Chapter 24

1. Letter from Nathanael Greene to Washington, March 29, 1781, in Sparks, *Correspondence of the American Revolution: Being Letters of Eminent Men to George Washington*, vol. 3, 278–79.

2. Letter from Cornwallis to George Germain, *The Campaign in Virginia, 1781,* vol. 1, ed. Benjamin F. Stevens (London, 1888), 420–22.

3. Letter from Cornwallis to Henry Clinton, *The Campaign in Virginia,* 424.

4. Letter from Cornwallis to Henry Clinton, May 26, 1781, *The Campaign in Virginia,* 488.

5. Louis Gottschalk, ed., *Letters of Lafayette to Washington* (Philadelphia: American Philosophical Society, 1976), 197–99.

6. Lafayette, *Memoirs, Correspondence and Manuscripts*, 263–67.

7. Wickwire, *Cornwallis and the War of Independence*, 349.

8. Wickwire, *Cornwallis and the War of Independence*, 351.

9. Lafayette, *Memoirs, Correspondence and Manuscripts*, 263–67.

10. John C. Fitzpatrick, ed., *The Diaries of George Washington*, vol. 2 (Boston: Houghton Mifflin Company, 1925), 248–50.

Chapter 25

1. James Thacher, *A Military Journal during the American Revolutionary War* (New York: New York Times, 1969), 268–71.

2. Clark, *All Cloudless Glory*, 529.

3. Clark, *All Cloudless Glory*, 529.

4. *The Writings of George Washington*, vol. 23, 75–77.

5. Clark, *All Cloudless Glory*, 530.

6. Richard Ferrie, *The World Turned Upside Down* (New York: Holiday House, 1999), 67.

7. Ferrie, *The World Turned Upside Down*, 71.

8. Commager and Morris, *The Spirit of 'Seventy-Six*, 1218–19.

9. Wickwire, *Cornwallis and the War of Independence*, 362.

10. Wickwire, *Cornwallis and the War of Independence*, 364.

11. Samuel Graham, "An English Officer's Account of His Services in America, 1779–1781," *History Magazine* 9 (September 1865): 272.

12. St. George Tucker, "Journal on the Siege of Yorktown, 1781," *William and Mary Quarterly* 5 (July 1948): 380–81.

13. Wickwire, *Cornwallis and the War of Independence*, 370.

14. "Minutes of Occurrences Respecting the Siege and Capture of York in Virginia, extracted from the Journal of Colonel Jonathan Trumbull, Secretary to the General, 1781," *Proceedings of the Massachusetts Historical Society* 4 (1876): 331–38.

15. Boatner, *Encyclopedia of the American Revolution*, 437.

16. Martin, *Narrative of a Revolutionary Soldier*, 166–169.

17. Clark, *All Cloudless Glory*, 543.

18. Clark, *All Cloudless Glory*, 543.

19. Thacher, *A Military Journal during the American Revolutionary War*, 283–86.

20. Count de Deux-Ponts, *My Campaigns in America* (Boston: J. K. Wiggin & W. P. Lunt, 1868), 144–47.

21. Martin, *Narrative of a Revolutionary Soldier*, 169–71.

22. Wickwire, *Cornwallis and the War of Independence*, 382.

23. Benjamin Franklin Stevens, ed., *The Campaigns in Virginia 1781, An Exact Reprint of Six rare pamphlets on the Clinton-Cornwallis Controversy*, vol. 2 (London: N.p., 1888), 205–13.

24. Ebenezer Denny, *Military Journa of MajorEbenezer Dennyl* (New York: New York Times, 1971), 44.

25. Wickwire, *Cornwallis and the War of Independence*, 385.

Chapter 26

1. Freeman, *Washington*, 488.

2. St. George Tucker, "Journal of the Siege of Yorktown, 1781," *William and Mary Quarterly*, 3rd ser., 5 (July 1948): 391.

3. Henry P. Johnston, *The Yorktown Campaign and the Surrender of Cornwallis, 1781* (Freeport, N.Y.: Books for Libraries Press, 1971), 185–87.

4. Scheer and Rankin, *Rebels and Redcoats*, 492.

5. Clark, *All Cloudless Glory*, 545.

6. Thacher, *A Military Journal during the American Revolutionary War*, 288–90.

7. Thacher, *A Military Journal during the American Revolutionary War*, 288–90.

8. Thacher, *A Military Journal during the American Revolutionary War*, 288–90.

9. Stevens, *The Campaigns in Virginia 1781*, 205–13.

10. Freeman, *Washington*, 492.

Index

Page references in *italics* indicate a figure on the designated page.

About the Author

Benton Rain Patterson is a longtime magazine writer and editor, formerly on the staffs of *The Saturday Evening Post*, *The New York Times Magazine*, and *Guideposts*. He is the author of *A Reporter's Interview with Jesus* and *Harold and William: The Battle for England, A.D. 1064–1066*. He is emeritus associate professor of journalism at the University of Florida in Gainesville, where he resides.

OTHER TITLES OF INTEREST

HAROLD AND WILLIAM
The Battle for England, A.D. 1064–1066
Benton Rain Patterson
256 pp., 30 b/w illustrations
0-8154-1165-0
$25.95 cloth

ADAM CLAYTON POWELL, JR.
The Political Biography of an American Dilemma
Charles V. Hamilton
576 pp., 36 b/w photos
0-8154-1184-7
$22.95

AGINCOURT
Christopher Hibbert
176 pp., 33 b/w illustrations, 3 b/w maps
0-8154-1053-0
$16.95

AMERICAN WOMEN ACTIVISTS' WRITINGS
An Anthology, 1637–2002
Edited by Kathryn Cullen-DuPont
656 pp., 17 b/w photos
0-8154-1185-5
$37.95 cloth

AMERICA'S FOUNDING FATHERS
Their Uncommon Wisdom and Wit
Edited by Bill Adler
240 pp., 20 b/w illustrations
0-87833-284-7
$25.95 cloth

A BATTLE FOR THE SOUL OF NEW YORK
Reverend Charles Parkhurst's
Crusade against Police Corruption,
Vice, and Tammany Hall, 1892–1895
Warren Sloat
440 pp., 30 b/w illustrations
0-8154-1237-1
$27.95 cloth

CITY UNDER SIEGE
Richmond in the Civil War
Mike Wright
376 pp., 15 b/w illustrations
0-8154-1220-7
$17.95

THE CIVIL WAR REMINISCENCES OF
GENERAL BASIL W. DUKE, C.S.A.
New Introduction by James Ramage
536 pp., 1 b/w illustration
0-8154-1174-X
$19.95

THE CSS *HUNLEY*
The Greatest Undersea Adventure
of the Civil War
Richard Bak
200 pp., 122 b/w and 10 color illustrations
0-87833-283-9
$18.95

THE DELIGHTS OF DEMOCRACY
The Triumph of American Politics
Christian P. Potholm
200 pp.
0-8154-1216-9
$27.95 cloth

THE KNIGHTS TEMPLARS
God's Warriors, the Devil's Bankers
Frank Sanello
328 pp., 20 b/w photos
0-87833-302-9
$25.95 cloth

MEMOIRS OF MY LIFE AND TIMES
John Charles Frémont
696 pp., 89 b/w illustrations
0-8154-1164-2
$24.95

ON CAMPAIGN WITH THE ARMY OF THE POTOMAC
The Civil War Journal of Theodore Ayrault Dodge
Edited by Stephen W. Sears
372 pp., 11 b/w illustrations
0-8154-1266-5
$16.95

ONCE UPON A TIME IN NEW YORK
Jimmy Walker, Franklin Roosevelt, and the Last Great Battle of the Jazz Age
Herbert Mitgang
288 pp., 35 b/w photos
0-8154-1263-0
$16.95

ROOSEVELT THE EXPLORER
T. R.'s Amazing Adventures as a Naturalist, Conservationist, and Explorer
H. Paul Jeffers
376 pp., 25 b/w photos
0-8154-1256-8
$24.95 cloth

THE SALEM WITCH TRIALS
A Day-to-Day Chronicle of
a Community under Siege
Marilynne K. Roach
656 pp., 11 b/w illustrations
0-8154-1221-5
$35.00 cloth

THE SELECTED LETTERS OF
THEODORE ROOSEVELT
Edited by H. W. Brands
624 pp., 4 b/w photos and illustrations
0-8154-1126-X
$29.95 cloth

THE SILENT AND THE DAMNED
The Murder of Mary Phagan
and the Lynching of Leo Frank
Robert Seitz Frey and Nancy Thompson-Frey
249 pp., 43 b/w illustrations
0-8154-1188-X
$17.95

SO FAR FROM DIXIE
Confederates in Yankee Prisons
Philip Burnham
312 pp., 12 b/w photos
1-58979-016-2
$25.00 cloth

THE SUNSET OF THE CONFEDERACY
Captain Morris Schaff
New introduction by Gary W. Gallagher
320 pp., 2 b/w maps
0-8154-1210-X
$17.95

THE WAR OF 1812
Henry Adams
New introduction by Col. John R. Elting
377 pp., 27 b/w maps and sketches
0-8154-1013-1
$16.95

WOLFE AT QUEBEC
The Man Who Won the French and Indian War
Christopher Hibbert
208 pp., 1 b/w illustration, 4 b/w maps
0-8154-1016-6
$15.95

WRITTEN WITH LEAD
America's Most Famous and Notorious Gunfights
from the Revolutionary War to Today
William Weir
360 pp., 18 b/w line drawings
0-8154-1289-4
$17.95

Available at bookstores; or call 1-800-462-6420

TAYLOR TRADE PUBLISHING
200 Park Avenue South
Suite 1109
New York, NY 10003